The Complete Encyclopedia

of

Homemaking Ideas

BARBARA TAYLOR BRADFORD

HAWTHORN BOOKS, INC.
Publishers
NEW YORK

Prepared with the cooperation of
The National Design Center
New York, N.Y.

An Edward Ernest Book
Design and drawings of period furniture by Laszlo Matulay
Production consultant: Thomas W. Culhane

CONTENTS

PART ONE

The Master Plan

Rich wood paneling soars to great heights in a charming country-style sitting room, designed for TV star Merv Griffin. The paneled walls are a perfect foil for the pieces of Early American furniture and accessories. Autumnal colors in fabrics and flooring reiterate the richness of the wood tones. Designed by John Elmo, A.I.D.

CHAPTER ONE

Home Planning Guidelines

A BEAUTIFUL, WELL-PLANNED home can turn routine living and daily chores into creative living and enjoyment.

The joys of homemaking are manifold. Into the shell of the house go not only your creativeness in decoration, comfort and practicality, but your hopes and dreams for serenity and family happiness. The home is the most personal of all possessions, an extension of you and your family.

Whether you are planning to redecorate or remodel your present home, or are drawing up decorative blueprints for a new one, guidelines are always invaluable. On the following pages of this book you will find a wealth of homemaking ideas to help you in these tasks. Ideas which will inspire you to create a fresh, new atmosphere in your home, and which you can adapt to suit your specific needs.

Finding a first home, or a new home, is an exhilarating experience, and when house or apartment hunting starts there is a wonderful sense of expectation in the air. Just as your home will be born, or reborn in a new location, so will your family with it.

Choosing your home can be fun if you embark on the hunt with an open mind. Naturally you must know your basic space and practical requirements, but after that dismiss preconceived ideas. Otherwise you might turn away from a place that would make a gracious home.

Surprisingly, many houses or apartments that do not seem right on first sight can be transformed into beautiful homes by planning and imagination. Time is one of the most important factors in homemaking. Once you have found the right house or apartment, you will be eager to settle your family and make it attractive as quickly as possible. But Rome wasn't built overnight and neither can a home be furnished in twenty-four hours. Hasty and haphazard planning can spell disaster. Careful planning in the end saves time, tears and money.

When you start house or apartment hunting you need three things: a note pad, a pencil and self-confidence. The latter springs from knowing exactly what you are about, your family needs and the way you want to live.

The following points will guide you. All of them are routine and easy to check. But because they are such routine spot-checks they are often overlooked. Apart from your note pad and pencil, it is a good idea to take along a transistor radio to test the soundproofing of the house or apartment. Simply turn on the radio and leave it in the middle of a room, close the door and go into the next room. In this way you can tell whether walls are soundproof or not.

WHEN LOOKING FOR AN APARTMENT

It is relatively simple to avoid making big errors if you are looking for an apartment rather than a house. You seldom need be concerned about roofs, damp walls, drainage systems and outside maintenance.

Only you yourself can judge the space available and whether it is adequate for your family needs. But here are some routine checks you can make as you view the property.

1. Rooms look larger when they are empty. Carpeting, drapes and wallpapers diminish the size of any area. Furniture takes more space. Visualize an empty room furnished, and if possible chalk furniture measurements on the floor for a better idea.
2. Bear in mind the furniture you own. Will it fit? Remember, if you have antiques they might not look quite right in a contemporary setting, particularly if the rooms are smaller in your intended new home.
3. Consider carpets and drapes from your old home. Will they fit the new place? Or can they be remade or adjusted to do so?
4. Check the central heating and the monthly costs to run it, especially during very cold spells. Is it adequate? Is it effective? Pay close attention to these points, otherwise you may find yourself requiring extra heating equipment later.
5. Check the air conditioning for the same reasons, a point sometimes overlooked when viewing an apartment in winter.
6. Check the plumbing. Is it up-to-date? Try the faucets and flush lavatories to make sure. This is also important for checking the drainage.
7. Pay special attention to walls and floor surfaces. Look for bad plastering, bumpy walls. Check that all floors are evenly laid, and make sure that wooden floors are not rotten or splintery.
8. Make sure all electrical wiring is in good repair and up-to-date. Check the number and location of electrical outlets.
9. Ascertain from the landlord whether you can make structural changes to gain space, if necessary. And most important, who pays for it.

WHEN LOOKING FOR A HOUSE

The same nine points apply to house hunting, whether you are buying or renting. Additional things to remember:

1. Check the basic structure. Is it sound? If necessary call in a professional to assist you with this.
2. Pay special attention to staircases and floors, especially in older homes. Are they sound and safe?
3. Keep an eye open for indoor dampness, often found on ceilings and the inside of exterior walls.
4. Check roof and outside walls to make sure they are in good repair, properly insulated, will withstand bad weather. Also check other areas that need good insulation, such as storm windows and doors.

AVAILABLE SPACE

It often happens that a new home is right in every way, with the exception of a room or two. Don't let this dismay you. The basic structure can be changed by tearing down a wall or with clever decorating tricks.

Let's first look at a few basic problems which often detract from an apartment or house, and which should be remembered when viewing. These might easily be the same problems which disturb you in your present home, and they can easily be overcome through remodeling or redecorating.

SMALL ROOMS

Naturally the placement of the too small room in the apartment or house as a whole is important. Sometimes a small, unattractive room is isolated, and there is no way of expanding it by structural improvements. In this instance, skillful decorating is the only way to overcome the disadvantages.

What can you do with a small, box-like room? You can either give it a feeling of airiness and space, or you can emphasize its smallness by making it cozy and warm with rich jewel colors. If you want to create an illusion of space, the pale shades from the color palette are your best friends. Pastel tones such as primrose, white, sky-blue, apple-green and lilac are a few of the colors which give a feeling of space, as do light-colored carpets, linoleum or vinyls on the floor.

Plan on using the simplest and smallest furniture or, better still, hanging pieces that fix onto brackets on the walls, and save a tremendous amount of floor area. You can further add to this illusion of space by covering one wall with a large, plain mirror or smoked glass. Keep all picture frames flat and modern. Do away with window drapes; keep the windows uncluttered by using simple shades and a decorative valance to give the window(s) importance.

Choice of fabrics in the small room is vital. Velvet, heavy linen, brocades and the thicker materials create a bulky look, can actually diminish the impression of size. Stick to the more delicate materials, such as taffeta, silks, organdy, cotton and nylon for a lighter, airier look.

If you want to play up the feeling of smallness in the box-like room, and give it an intimate atmosphere, you must go in the opposite direction. Choose rich fabrics, jewel colors, antique or frankly rococo furniture; give it character with vibrant pictures, a wall of books or collectors' items. But don't skimp on the room—otherwise you won't achieve the desired effect.

STRUCTURAL CHANGES

Two small rooms adjoining each other can easily be turned into one larger room, by tearing down a wall. Or you can add the small rooms to an existing larger one, for a big area of space. Naturally this is much more costly and complicated, and it is always best to seek the advice of an architect. Often a wall serves as a support, and you don't want to weaken the foundations of your house or apartment. The best way to tackle structural changes is to obtain the original plans of your home, if you can, and go into it in detail with an architect or builder. Not only to find out if it is feasible, but also to ascertain the costs.

You can also save space by tearing out ugly storage cupboards, and re-building them in corridors or rooms that can afford to lose space. If you do not want to rebuild these storage units, you can buy excellent ready-made drawers that fit under beds and divans; units that stack on top of each other; deep chests with dressing table or desk tops.

1.

2.

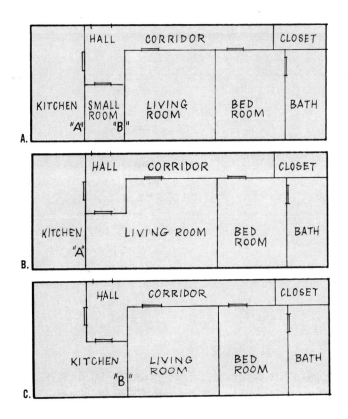

A.

| HALL | CORRIDOR | | CLOSET |
| KITCHEN | SMALL ROOM "A" | "B" LIVING ROOM | BED ROOM | BATH |

B.

| HALL | CORRIDOR | | CLOSET |
| KITCHEN "A" | LIVING ROOM | BED ROOM | BATH |

C.

| HALL | CORRIDOR | | CLOSET |
| KITCHEN "B" | LIVING ROOM | BED ROOM | BATH |

1. TO CREATE A FEELING OF WARMTH IN THE BOX-LIKE ROOM use vibrant colors, rich fabrics. Here you see a too small, extra room which had no real use, cleverly transformed into an intimate study-den. Bright shades from the tartan clan come to life on the floor and set the theme for the entire room. Gordon-green, brown, Stuart-red and black vinyls weave a sparkling base for the mellow tones of the storage wall, and the red and green damask wallpaper. Incidentally, the storage wall seems to be made of fine old paneling, but it really owes its rich patina to a sheathing of vinyl. It adds drama and character to the room, at the same time conserves space and conceals an ugly cupboard. Final flashes of color come in the red and green felt cushions on the late Stuart chairs. Designed by Rhoda Bright, A.I.D.

2. TO CREATE AN ILLUSION OF SPACE IN THE BOX-LIKE ROOM keep furniture to a minimum; walls, floor and ceiling smooth and sleek. Here you see a dining room which plays up these points to the fullest, presenting a feeling of spaciousness in a small area. A canopy of twinkling light bulbs, set across the length of the ceiling, gives adequate lighting and at the same time suggests extra height. Furniture is

A. ORIGINAL FLOOR PLAN. Here you see the original floor plan of an apartment. The very small room between kitchen and living room was too small to be a dining room, in fact was redundant. The owners had a choice of either joining it onto the living room or onto the kitchen. This could be done by tearing down either wall "A" or wall "B," as shown in the two drawings below.

B. FLOOR PLAN WITH WALL "B" ELIMINATED. Knock down wall "B" to join redundant small room onto the living room to make one big room. With extra space, owners created a dining area in corner of enlarged living room.

C. FLOOR PLAN WITH WALL "A" ELIMINATED. Here you see wall "A" knocked down, to join small room onto kitchen, so that kitchen becomes larger, is, in effect, a kitchen-dinette.

light and modern, so sleek it seems to float. Only decorative point is a glass shelf, holding glistening obelisks arranged to intrigue the eye. The plain citron-colored walls sit well against a dramatic black and white vinyl floor, which suggests polished marble pieces set amid chips and shards. The result: a crystal-clear scheme or sparkling dining in the minimum of space. Designed by Al Herbert, A. I. D.

TO TRANSFORM THE SMALL, ODDLY SHAPED ROOM use vivid colors, bold patterns, richly textured fabrics. They help disguise any architectural faults, add character to the off-center room. This dramatic, dual-purpose studio-den was devised to suit the many sided personality of comedian Jonathan Winters. Designer Ving Smith, A.I.D., makes clever use of a small area, both functionally and visually, with bold combinations of vibrant color, pattern-on-pattern. In the studio area (front of picture), sliding frames are covered in a strong red-on-white print and are used as light filters in the window area. The same fabric moves up onto the ceiling and down the other wall for continuity. The studio area is finished with a blue and white tile floor. The lively red, white and blue theme changes character in the den (back of picture), where the mood is intimate and warm. Red painted walls are a foil for the richly covered love seat, brilliant blue rug, and the Jonathan Winters collection of paintings, sculpture and Civil War guns.

Three Rooms in Search of Space

THE BOX-LIKE ROOM need not end up as a junk room or a storage closet. Ingenuity with fabrics, furniture and color will work miracles. The three rooms shown on this page were small, cramped, dark and almost useless to their owners; skillful decorating transformed them and gave them life.

2.

2. Use of one color throughout gives this tiny bedroom a feeling of space as well as an integrated look. The all white scheme is a perfect foil for the splashes of vivid blue and green, picked up on dressing table, stools, painted motifs on furniture and the lamps. A plain, flat window shade dispenses with drapes to ensure the light, airy look of the room.

3. Clever manipulation of furniture made this tiny room service two young boys. At first the room seemed far too cramped to carry two beds; then the space problem was solved by using bunk beds of varying heights. The one with the lowest legs easily pushes underneath the taller of the two, also serves as a seat for reading and homework. Parade-striped blankets on the bunks pick up the gold and blue colors of the wallpaper.

1.

1. This small, narrow room was turned into multiple-purpose quarters through deft use of handsome fabrics and constructive design techniques. The colorful floral fabric was stretched flat against the wall and stapled to wood strips, for quick removal and reuse, should the tenants relocate; the fabric not only brightens and lightens the room, but also covers up ungainly exposures. The plywood box, covered in matching fabric, was chain-hinged and wall-hooked in navy-bunk style, holds the fold-away bed. At right a long closet provides welcome storage without waste of wanted footage; furniture has been kept to a minimum, and the bright red rug ties together the color scheme. The result: a warm, elegant guest-room/study/dressing-room. Designed by Paul Krauss, A.I.D.

3.

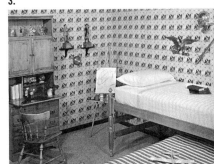

EXTRA-LARGE ROOMS:

The large room which is meant to serve a dual-purpose as both family and dining room, can of course be made into two rooms, by building a dividing wall or an archway.

If you decide to do this, remember you must not diminish the light in either half of the room. Pay special attention to the placement of windows, make sure you are not depriving part of the room of light and air.

The larger room is always easier to cope with. If structural changes are either too costly or not possible, you can cut the room into two by using room dividers. There are many different ways to do it, depending on your budget. You can now buy pieces of ready-made, sectional furniture that start with a basic cabinet and rise into shelves, almost to the ceiling. If these shelves are filled with ornaments, bric-a-brac, modern glass, a flower or plant arrangement and a few books, they can be very successful. This cabinet and shelf fitment successfully splits the room, and can always be moved against a wall to make extra space for the big party.

A small cocktail bar, placed strategically in the middle of one wall and jutting out into the room, is another easy way to create two different atmospheres in one large room. It acts as a divider between the dining room area, and the family or sitting room.

Perhaps the most effective room dividers are screens and gates. They are now available ready-made in wood, metal and various synthetic materials. They are not expensive, and because of their open-work or grille-like effect they do not diminish light at all. Decide where you want to cut the room. Attach a gate to each wall and open them out so that they stretch across the floor area, giving you, in essence, two halves, or two rooms.

They can always be closed back against the walls, for entertaining, when required. If you like indoor plants, planter pots of crawling vines can be arranged at either side of the gates and coaxed upwards for an outdoor look. Many other plants can also be used in this way, to add solidarity to the open-work gates, and they help create a greater illusion of two separate rooms.

Very high ceilings are easily lowered by adding a false ceiling. If you cannot afford to spend money on structural changes, false ceilings or room dividers, skillful use of color lessens the size of a very large room. These darker tones should be used on walls, in carpets, drapes and slipcovers.

For instance, fir-green, cranberry, mustard, rose, coffee and blue pull walls closer in, reduce both height and size. These shades look especially effective if highlighted by white paint on doors and other woodwork. Dark colors on floors also reduce, by illusion, as do heavier fabrics used for drapes and slipcovers.

INTEGRATION:

The most effective and attractive homes are the ones which have continuity throughout. Once you have found your chosen home and start planning its decoration, bear this point in mind.

View it totally empty, and try to visualize it without any walls, as one vast area; two areas if you have a duplex or split-level. By imagining it as one vast area, and decorating it as such, you will avoid many pitfalls. Plan it as a whole, integrating all the rooms, so that your home is harmonious in its entirety. This is particularly important in the smaller apartment or house. Haphazard decorating and furnishing reduces that smooth, fluid look, and, in fact, usually makes the small home look even smaller.

Start with floors and walls, because these are the subtle links between each room.

SEE-THROUGH SERVER SEPARATES COOKING AND DINING in designer Russel Wright's home. Horizontal shafts of birch sheathe electric lighting and lend a "framed" look to interior views. The server does not diminish light in either part of the room, yet brings two different atmospheres to it. Cupboards open on both sides, and the work top can be used in kitchen or dining area. This is an excellent idea if you want to introduce eating into the larger kitchen, and at the same time a real "dining room" feeling is created.

Divide...to Multiply

DIVIDE A LARGE room in two, and its purposes are multiplied because two separate atmospheres are created in the one area of space. *Clever* divisions are not only practical but often add to the character and decor of any room.

1.

2.

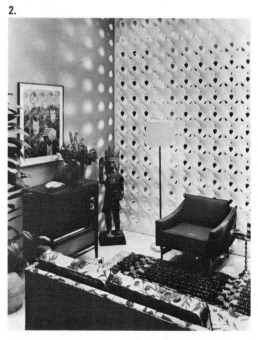

3.

Some apartments are minus an entrance hall or foyer. This problem, also, can be overcome by screens, gates or a dividing wall. This pierced masonry wall was built to cut off the street entrance and doorway from a large living room. At once it created a Mexican mood, and influenced the rest of the decor. Antique chests, a carved bench and lamp were combined with plants and the mellowness of old brick for the hacienda effect. Incidentally, although antiques are genuine, the "old brick" floor is really vinyl.

1. This ingenious divider multiplies fun for the young, and turns one bedroom into two, for a toddler and a teen-age girl. It is an airy "wall" of wood filigree, above chests of drawers in many colors. Two matching chests are placed at the side of the screen (not shown in this photograph). Like many rooms, this one is only medium sized, but a sense of space is derived from the "look-through" quality of the divider. It also gives a feeling of separation and privacy, and can be used successfully in a living room, or kitchen-dining area.

2. A contemporary room needs a divider in keeping with furniture and decor. Eating and living in a New York apartment was separated and defined by this floor to ceiling wall of design, which captures the mood of "pop" and "op" art and modern sculpture. The strong patterns that emerge from the three-dimensional module wall, produce unusual lighting effects; at the same time it defines and demarcates space in a uniquely contemporary manner. Designed by Erwin Hauer.

3. A small cabinet can act as a successful divider in a large room, and is often less aggressive than taller, heavier pieces of furniture. This "two-faced" cabinet is a happy solution for the dividing problem, because it looks good both front and back. It also has a practical, plastic surface at the serving level; storage space behind the latticed Brazilian rosewood doors; front and back locking doors on the taller compartment. It functions as a sideboard, bar server, as well as a divider; can be moved back against a wall when whole area of space is required for entertaining.

Divide and conquer space problems with imaginative use of fabrics. Paul Krauss, A.I.D., created a separate dining area within a living room, by employing this simple yet effective screening device. Three lengths of red, gold and green plaid cloth were fastened to finial-tipped brass rods. The rods were hung from the ceiling, and scored with black tapes and gilt string, spaced to permit see-through separations. Key colors in the screening fabric were repeated in the table runners.

FLOORS:

Use of the same flooring throughout pulls all the rooms together, gives a feeling of true integration, whether you choose wall-to-wall carpeting, vinyls, parquet flooring or other woods. By using the same *color* throughout the *entire* floor area you will achieve even greater continuity. This is not as confining as it sounds. A basic, neutral shade makes a good background for the more vital colors, which you can introduce on the walls, in drapes, slipcovers, pictures, lampshades and other accessories. The best basics to use are cream, off-white, beige, coffee, gold, the gamut of greys, misty greens and blues, as they are all quiet enough to take the more volatile colors which can be used in accents.

Remember, too, that the same flooring everywhere is very practical. For instance, a traffic line in the sitting room may get badly worn. If it does, you can always replace it with a piece of carpet taken from under a bed or piece of furniture that stays put. And it is often cheaper to buy in bulk, when purchasing floor covering.

WALLS:

One basic color used on all walls gives even more fluidity and integration. And it need not be dull. Remember, every color in the palette has its deeper or lighter tones. You can still achieve variety as well as continuity by staying with one color family and its offshoots. For instance, if you use neutral cream as a basis, you can introduce many of its sisters, such as gold, primrose, coffee, beige, white, chocolate-brown, and dark brown into the other rooms, without losing that related feeling. And a good neutral color makes an excellent backdrop for pictures. French toile wallpapers matched to drapes, even slipcovers, bring that integrated look to a room. If you pick out the predominant color in such wallpapers, you can use it as a linker in other rooms. Drapes matched to walls or carpets, in a lighter or darker tone, also give flow to a home. In other words, you can take any color from the palette and vary it in depth and tone from room to room, for a truly related look.

FURNITURE:

Integrating your furniture can be a stumbling block, particularly if you have a mixture of styles and periods. How do you correlate Early American with Traditional, Georgian or Contemporary? Or Regency, Spanish and Traditional? Or whatever mixtures you have?

The best thing to do is to mix and match these styles. Nothing looks more incongruous than an antique style room sitting next door to one furnished with modern pieces, especially in a small apartment or house. If you are blessed with acres of space and plenty of rooms, you can, of course, successfully decorate a couple of rooms with antiques and scatter other styles throughout the home. But basically, it is much better to plan on integrating all the periods, putting a little of each in every room. This makes for proper integration.

Pay special attention to woods. Mahogany next to Danish modern teak does not always blend, for instance; this also applies to other mixtures of varying woods. It is often better to treat and strip woods, so that they blend well. Today there are a variety of quick and easy products on the market for this very purpose.

CHAPTER TWO

Budgets and Major Equipment

❧

THE NEXT QUESTION to ask yourself is: "How much is it going to cost to furnish my new home or remodel my present home?"

The simplest way to arrive at this answer is to start with a notebook and pencil. List all the things which can be used, remodeled or adjusted to suit your new home or remodeling plans. And if you have a budget, mark it down underneath this list.

Now plan each room separately and carefully. Mark a page of the notebook for every room in the home. Start off with the equipment or furniture you already own and, underneath, list your required buys for that particular room. Add up each page as you go along, marking the amounts at the back of the notebook. When you have budgeted every room, you can arrive at the grand total.

It may be that this final amount is far in excess of your original budget, if you had one. If this is the case, go over each room again, crossing off equipment which is not immediately essential. Start another page marked: "Future Buys." For instance, if you are moving in the summer, you can allocate heating equipment to be bought at a later date. And vice versa for air conditioning, if you are moving in winter. But do not dismiss the items you cross off because of lack of funds. They can always be bought later, so leave a space for them in your floor plans.

Incidentally, do not throw your notebook of budgets away after you have moved or remodeled. You will find it invaluable in homemaking. You can use it as a guide as you gradually furnish each room, referring to it continually, and buying the listed items as you can afford them.

By planning each room separately, and costing it, you will be able to assess the real essentials for your new home. For example, you might be able to cut down your bedroom budget to a minimum and use the extra money on kitchen equipment, or economize on floor covering and spend more on furniture for the sitting room. Your budget notebook is a good point of reference, because you can juggle around with the costings to suit your needs, before buying.

It is difficult to generalize about required major equipment for the home, as all families have their different needs. However, here is a list of basic major essentials which should be budgeted for in your overall master plan.

Major Equipment

RANGE—gas or electric. Size and type to suit family needs. REFRIGERATOR—size and type to suit family needs. DEEP FREEZE—if required. DISHWASHER—if required. WASHING MACHINE—if required. DRIER —if required. FURNACE—if required. CENTRAL HEATING. AIR CONDITIONING. MAJOR BATHROOM EQUIPMENT—if new installations are necessary. KITCHEN SINK UNIT—if new installations are necessary. MAJOR GARDEN EQUIPMENT—where applicable. TV—black and white or color. STEREO—if required. RADIO.

*

Before buying your major kitchen equipment, you should know what the market offers you today. Never before has a housewife had such a vast choice of kitchen appliances, and this choice continues to expand as the manufacturers introduce new products on the market.

A personal view of the newest equipment is preferable, and it is worthwhile doing a little leg work around your local kitchen appliances showrooms. In this way you can judge not only what is right for your size and type kitchen, but also for you and your family needs. Use this spot guide as a jumping off point.

RANGES:
Most manufacturers are making easy-to-clean ovens today. On your viewing expeditions look for:

the revolutionary self-cleaning oven.

the easy-to-clean pull-out oven.

oven with replaceable foil linings.

oven with removable panels that can be washed under a faucet.

Incidentally, the surface areas of all these and other major lines are easier to keep clean, because of catch-trays that prevent spill-overs, and tops that lift up and out.

You no longer have to worry about cooking fumes and smells. Many manufacturers now put a built-in fan and venting system in their ranges.

Four manufacturers now make a "second oven" which can be either built-in, wall-hung or placed on a counter top.

Most deluxe ranges have clock controls that automatically start and stop cooking time for programmed cooking. Some models even have a thermostatic control that automatically keeps food at temperatures from 150° F. to 170° F.

All sizes are now available in both electric and gas models. Largest built-in electric oven is 30″ wide, smallest is 23″ wide. Cook-tops start with 2-burners, go up to as many as 7 cooking elements. Largest built-in gas oven-broiler is 30″ wide, smallest is about 23″ wide and made by most companies.

The majority of free-standing ranges have squared-off corners, to fit in line with counters.

If you are looking for a free-standing, high-level oven range that looks built-in, you have 25 manufacturers to choose from who make both gas and electric models.

Also keep an eye open for:

> new electric range designed for cooking indoors or out, with rotisserie, oven for baking, two surface cooking elements and storage compartments.
>
> the combination ventilating hood and warming oven, with thermostatic control.

REFRIGERATORS:

Again the choice is very personalized, depending on your family needs. But remember that today you can buy the combination refrigerator-freezer, updated and designed to do both jobs at once. These king-size combinations have capacities around 26 cu. ft. Other manufacturers are producing a slightly smaller size.

Look for the built-in refrigerator-freezer which converts to all-refrigerator by flipping a switch: the freezer designed as a base, and which holds 175 pounds of frozen foods.

Now on the market is a cooling unit, which is installed under the sink and provides refrigerated drinking water from its own faucet, dispenses 5 gallons per hour.

DISHWASHERS:

If your dishwasher is more than five years old, you can be sure that it is completely outdated.

Manufacturers have now improved washability; increased capacity; many have added cycles for pre-wash, for pots and pans, for delicate china and glass. In other words, today you can put almost everything into the dishwasher without fear of breakages, or of taking out dishes which are still dirty. And better insulation has reduced the noise level. Look for:

the newly quiet dishwasher.

the dishwasher which stores a month's supply of liquid detergent, injecting it as used.

the dishwasher that provides its own hot water for washing and rinsing.

CENTRAL HEATING, FURNACES, AIR CONDITIONING:

Many factors are involved in the choice of heating equipment for your home—the size of the house or apartment, its construction, easy operation of the heaters, local costs of various kinds of fuel, the method of distribution of heat and economy of use. Only a competent heating engineer or heating contractor is qualified to give the best solution to individual heating problems. Before making any decisions, consult him to make sure you are buying the most economical and suitable equipment.

You also need to know a few basic facts about home heating and air conditioning. This is important, whether you are planning a full remodeling job or only upgrading the year-round weather control system in your home.

INSULATION:

The problem of conserving the heat you already have may be solved by simply insulating doors and windows more thoroughly. Check this with a good heating expert, as it could possibly save you a large outlay of dollars. For instance, insulation and storm doors and windows throughout the whole house could mean that you only need new ducts or radiators in some rooms, for an even distribution of heat.

TYPES OF HEATING:

Tremendous steps have been made in the last few years in the field of heating equipment. Gone are the days when furnaces were run on coal, needed constant stoking and attention. Today you can buy warm-air furnaces, others that run on oil, different types of gas; and many of these do double duty, converting to air conditioners and humidifiers in the summer. Incidentally, warm-air and hot-water heat can use gas or oil fuel, and some of the warm-air furnaces are electrically operated.

A large amount of electric heat is being used in homes today. This is because it is easy, clean and, most important, not as expensive as it was. Many electric utility companies offer special, low rates for electric heating. To find out whether this is practical for you, check with friends or neighbors who use it, to ascertain the amount they spend on their fuel bills. Your local electric company will also supply accurate operating cost estimates. The same points apply to gas operated heat.

Heating equipment is also more attractively made. You can find heaters which fit into recessed walls, are concealed in the ceiling, under floor boards, and along baseboards. The choice is extensive, but ask your heating contractor about the following:

The five-in-one furnace which gives total indoor climate control: furnace (for heating), air distribution system, humidifier, central cooling unit and electronic air cleaner. With this furnace you have a choice of fuel—gas, oil, electricity or coal. Three prices are offered, according to the model you want.

The gas furnace which is controlled by indoor and outdoor thermostats. The burner flame is automatically regulated to high or low, depending on outdoor temperatures. In other words, you have precisely measured heat for constant comfort and utmost economy. This furnace is designed for the addition of a cooling system at a later date.

Embedded radiant heating wire, fixed into ceiling plaster or dry wall ceilings, which gives heat from above. Only the thermostat for heat control is visible.

Gas-fired furnaces, that fit into cupboards, closets, kitchens and basements which are 55 or 43 inches high.

The small hot-air blowers, which can stand on tables, counter tops or in drafty corners; moveable to different areas of the home. They convert to cool air in summer.

AIR CONDITIONING:

It is difficult to advise about air conditioning. Like central heating, this problem can be solved only by the individual. However, most homes require about one ton of cooling for about 600 square feet. Exact capacity needed depends on individual conditions. For instance, the more outdoor heat you keep out of the house with insulation and shading, the less air conditioning you will need. Seek expert help with this, as you would for central heating.

If you are putting in central heating *and* air conditioning, your most economical buy would be the furnace which transforms to a cooling system in summer. Or there are the add-on units. These usually sit half in and half out of a window. Some manufacturers make portable air coolers, with their own tables. These are fine if you want to cool only one room. However, if you want to air condition the whole apartment or house, a central system is more efficient and lower in cost in the long run.

This central unit type of conditioning system provides more cooling per dollar, higher efficiency, less maintenance and upkeep as compared with a collection of single room units. Because of continually changing prices, it is impossible to give exact costings of the above appliances. But you can obtain price lists from local dealers and showrooms, so that you can enter them in your budget notebook.

CHAPTER THREE

Floor Plans and Focal Points

❧

FLOOR PLANS ARE invaluable in every stage of homemaking. But many women shy away from them because they look complicated, seem difficult to read and understand.

This is not so. Once you have mastered the floor plan you will soon be making your own. Moving furniture and major equipment on paper is infinitely easier than doing it physically. Just think of the hours of backache it saves! And of course a paper try-out at home, before buying major equipment and furniture, prevents mistakes.

First of all, a few tips on reading and understanding floor plans.

1. Don't read a floor plan as you would a book or newspaper. Place it on top of a table. Imagine you are lying on a ceiling looking down into the room—in other words, imagine you have an aerial view of the room. In this way you will get it into the right perspective.
2. A thick black line or two double lines indicate outer walls.
3. Breaks or half moons in these lines indicate doorways.
4. Breaks in the outer black lines, filled in with fine lines, usually indicate windows.
5. Elevators are generally indicated by diagonal shading.
6. The scale is invariably written in at the bottom of the plan. But the normal way of scaling down a room onto paper is to allow ¼ in. to 1 ft., sometimes ½ in. to 1 ft. to make it more legible.

Your Own Floor Plan

ARRANGING FURNITURE IN a well-shaped, symmetrical room does not require a great deal of expertise. Well-spaced windows, doors and a central fireplace are the perfect arrows in showing you where to put your pieces to their best advantage.

It is the off-center or oddly shaped room which requires a great deal of clever maneuvering with furniture and major equipment.

This is where a detailed floor plan saves time, headaches and wasted money. How do you go about making your own floor plan?

It is much simpler than it sounds. Graph paper and a carpenter's yardstick or good ruler are your points of departure. First measure the given room, and then translate those measurements onto the graph paper. You don't have to be a mathematical genius to do this. Let's say the room is 10 ft. by 18 ft. All you do is measure off a space 10 squares wide by 18 squares long on your paper, and you have the beginning of your floor plan.

Now be sure to indicate positions of windows, doors, entrances, and fireplace (if there is one) and their heights. Also draw in beams, wall jogs and angles. You can also indicate electrical outlets if you wish. When you have completed the detailed plan, measure all your existing furniture, translate these sizes onto graph paper, using the same scale—one square equals

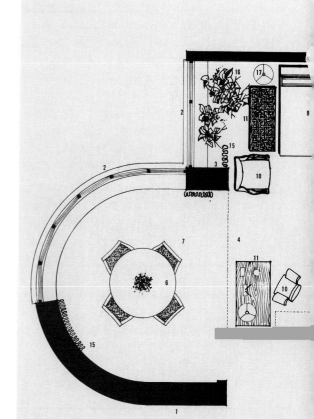

Here you see a floor plan by designer J. Frederic Lohman, A.I.D., for a large living room and curved dining area. Everything in the floor plan has been numbered to make reading the plan easy for beginners. Simply check with the key here, so you can identify every marking on the plan.

one foot. When you have all your furniture indicated on graph paper, cut out and use as miniature models on the floor plan.

You can move these miniatures around until you have the right arrangement in the room. This will also indicate how much space you have left for additional new furniture.

If you want to, you can color your furniture and the carpeted area of the floor plan, to get an idea of color schemes.

OTHER POINTERS ON FLOOR PLAN:

Electrical wiring: before decorating decide where you will put telephones, TV, table lamps and other electrical equipment. By having them installed before actual decorating starts, you will avoid exposed ugly wires, marked walls. Indicate them on the floor plan first, to make sure they are placed in convenient and advantageous parts of the room. It is well to remember, if you are installing color TV, that the set *has* to be 10 inches away from any wall, because of the large color tube. Make sure you pick a really convenient wall for this, so that it does not look off-balance, standing 10 inches away from the wall.

Don't forget to mark traffic lines on your plan. People will be walking around the room, so arrange furniture accordingly, leaving enough space for them to move with ease. Indicate traffic patterns—where your family will enter, leave or cross the room.

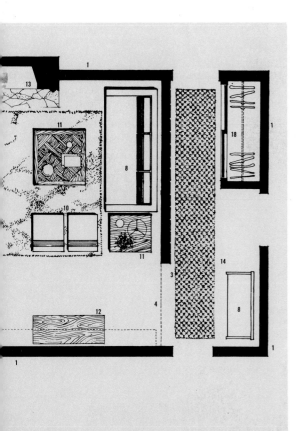

KEY:
1: Outer walls; 2: curved window, straight window; 3: Interior walls; 4: Ceiling beams above open archways; 5: high shelf along length of wall; 6: dining table; 7: four dining chairs; 8: two sofas; 9: chaise lounge; 10: four chairs; 11: four various sized coffee or low tables; 12: bar; 13: fireplace; 14: square carpet in living room, long carpet in hallway; 15: drapes; 16: indoor plants; 17: low standing lamp; 18: hall closet.

Focal Points

A LOVELY, WELL-DECORATED room can fail—if it has no focal point. In the past a fireplace was always the center of gravity in the sitting room. But today many modern apartments and houses are without them. If you are lucky enough to have one, make the most of it. Even if it is a mock fireplace and does not work, give it importance and character with fire irons and a pile of logs in the grate.

Outlook can often be a good focal point. If you have a beautiful country panorama or one of the rare skyline views of a city, arrange your furniture so that the windows become the center of eye interest. If you have neither fireplace nor view, you will have to make your own focal point in the room.

Choose the most suitable and convenient wall, decorate it so that the rest of the room is pulled towards it. For instance, a grand tapestry with antique wall lights at each side immediately draws the eye. A sofa and a group of chairs arranged beneath it indicate this is the central point. The same applies to one large painting, a group of paintings, a wall of books, a massive shelf arrangement filled with collectors' items. A grand piano also makes a good focal point, so does a mirrored wall, a sofa with end tables and two imposing lamps, and a long, narrow chest arrangement containing books, hi-fi and collectors' items.

Arranging Furniture

WHEN GROUPING FURNITURE make sure you can view the groupings from any part of the room, and get as much pleasure from it as you would a picture on the wall. This is particularly important if you have more than one group arrangement. View it from all angles and opposite sides of the room to check that it looks neither muddled nor cluttered. By trying it out on your floor plan first, you will save yourself time and physical exertion.

1. Group chairs and sofa so that traffic goes around and not through the arrangement.
2. Keep chairs reasonably close together for easy conversation and to avoid shouting across the room.
3. If you have lamps away from walls, install floor outlets to prevent tripping over dangerous wires.
4. Choose tables that are about the same height as sofa or chairs to avoid spills and upset lamps.
5. Strike a good balance by separating large pieces of furniture so that the room does not look too heavy at one end.
6. Remember light, slim furniture creates an optical illusion of space, also saves space.
7. Bulky furniture looks better against walls, saves space.

EVERY ROOM NEEDS a center of gravity to pull it together. A fireplace is the most natural one, but wall treatments, windows and furniture arrangements can be just as eye-catching.

1.

1. Hi-fi stereo wall and window treatment in a paneled living room became an attractive yet **practical** focal point. Cabinet arrangement was suspended between two flanking windows, speakers for stereophonic sound system concealed in the side columns. Right cabinet houses a small bar. Well-lighted glass shelves holding collectors' items and a small fireplace were the finishing touches, for a feeling of warmth. Designed by Joseph Freitag, in teak paneling.

2. This dining room was too small for one of the more obvious focal points, so an ingenious rug and furniture arrangement became the center of gravity. A handsome circular rug was the springboard; a round table and round-backed chairs were placed in the middle of the rug, following its circular flow. The result: an eye-catching grouping which gives the room its focal point.

2.

A floor plan can be made of every room in your apartment or house, and as you become more used to working with one, you will find it indispensable—not only before you move, but also after you've settled. Remember your budget? All those items which had to be crossed off because of lack of funds should be allotted space on the floor plan. When you *are* able to buy them, their given corner will be waiting, and you will avoid the necessity of making room for them.

You also might discover that a room arranged with the window as a focal point is ideal in summer, but needs a new center of gravity in winter. Or you may feel the room has grown stale and want to switch the furniture groupings around. Make all your moves on paper first, to make sure the new groupings look attractive, are workable, and that the room keeps its balance.

1.

1. This dramatic window treatment acts as focal point and springboard for the design theme of a one room apartment. Sand and clay beiges, charcoal and terra-cotta-colored fabrics were used along the window wall and picked up throughout the apartment. The charcoal and beige motif of the shades matches the printed linen on the love seat, the beige drapes and chairs, and sets the color theme for the room. At the same time, this shade and curtain treatment breaks the monotony of a long, five-window wall, makes an interesting backdrop to the room. Designed by Augusta Gassner, A.I.D.

2. The skylight window of this "A" frame house was the most natural focal point—but it needed that extra dash of drama. A double-sized sofa, covered in colorful fabric, was set against the window and immediately became the perfect foil. It at once gave shape to the room, and set the grouping theme for the rest of the furniture, which fell into place naturally.

2.

4. This modern fireplace was too small to be a **strong** enough focal point in a large room. A long, floor-level shelf was added to give it more emphasis: fire irons, candle-sticks, ornaments and cushions strike a happy balance, artistically arranged along the shelf. Final decorative point was the modern sunburst clock. The result: a whole new look to the room.

4.

3. A room with a fireplace needs no other focal point. **But clever grouping of furniture is important.** A huddle of chairs around the fire looks cozy—but the rest of the room has an abandoned air. The fireplace in this elegant sitting room serves the whole room because of strategic placing of low glass table, sofa and chairs.

5.

5. A shelf and cabinet arrangement across a long wall can become a versatile and eye-catching focal point if it is assembled with imagination. A collection of shelves and cabinets were used in this modern apart-ment, for both decorative and practical pur-poses. The base cabinets are perfect stor-age units, for records, china, glass and drinks, while the upflowing shelves holding books, plants and other items bring flair and focus to an otherwise dull wall.

This sitting room, designed by John Elmo, A.I.D., has perfect balance, color and furniture coordination, is the essence of good taste in decorating. Pale yellow and beige make a serene shell; accent colors of green and deep blue enliven without detracting from the overall soft scheme. A feeling of symmetry is achieved because chairs and sofa are carefully matched in height, as are the two end tables and lamps on the sofa wall. The result is an elegant but comfortable room, which has both clarity and warmth.

PART TWO

Decorating

CHAPTER FOUR

Decorating and You

DECORATING IS ONE of the most challenging parts of homemaking. It can also be the most exciting.

Creating a beautiful setting for your family is a great adventure, to be embarked upon with enthusiasm and love. It also requires a great deal of thought, skill, and most important—*time*. In this instance, money is truly a secondary consideration. Some of the most charming homes have been decorated on the slimmest of budgets and a *lot of imagination*. Anyone with the right bank balance can fill a home with expensive furniture, but this does not ensure either its beauty or its success. On the contrary, such homes are usually disastrous, and what's even worse—dull.

This is mainly because they lack taste. Which brings us to that old question: What is good taste?

Defining good taste is almost impossible. But in the most general terms it is basically a combination of planning, integration, balance, clarity and skillful use of color. And suitability. Remember a room must be related to the people who are going to live in it; otherwise it will be a complete failure.

Decorating, like everything else of a truly personal nature, is highly individual. Every woman has her own tastes, ideas, and family needs: what delights one woman can be anathema to another. That is why it is difficult to make cut-and-dried decorating rules that are ideal for *every* woman.

One of the most basic things to remember is that the background you create is, to a great extent, a reflection of you. Think of decorating in the same terms as your wardrobe. *The clothes you choose and wear, reveal to the world your taste and, equally as important, your personality. And so do the rooms you furnish, on a much grander, larger scale.* Apply the same rules of good dressing to your home, and you won't go far wrong.

If you are clever, you will use your home as a backdrop for your personality and ideas. It can be an exciting extension of yourself. Remember, too, that decorating is a wonderful, creative way to express some of your interests and tastes, as well as those of your family.

What makes a room successful?

Four things are of equal importance. They are character (or personality), comfort, function and atmosphere.

CHARACTER:

SOME ROOMS ALREADY have a measure of character about them before you even start decorating. These are mainly rooms, in old houses or apartment blocks, that are off-center, oddly shaped or angled. Their construction gives them a certain amount of personality all their own, and because of this they are easier to decorate. It is the square, modern, conforming room that needs much more thought and skill. Many components go into giving a room character: imaginative use of unusual color schemes that are *entirely your own;* strategic placing of furniture; clever use of paintings, sculpture, books, collections, trivia; and the truly individual touches that stamp *your* personality on the room.

For instance, if you are the literary type and enjoy books, don't scatter them in bookshelves throughout the home. Bring them together in one massive library arrangement. They can look both impressive and decorative if carefully arranged so that the bright dust jackets, or leather bindings offset each other. Take the shelves from floor to ceiling, on two walls if possible, leaving space among the books for a piece of sculpture, a photograph, a pretty plant or a picture.

If you have picked up native handicraft or collectors' items on your travels, bring them out of the store cupboard or attic, arrange them on glass shelves on a wall or in a corner and make a feature of them.

Use little treasures, trivia and small photographs in effective clusters on a glass-topped table, or one skirted in a bright fabric.

And if you are an art lover, build a room around a collection of well-grouped paintings, matching your room color scheme to colors in the canvasses, or vice versa.

Most of all, don't be afraid of creating the highly personalized room. Much better that it is compelling rather than colorless. But remember one thing—a room must not dwarf the people in it. You and your family must always be the dominant factors.

If you are strong, vibrant and outgoing, let the rooms in your home be an echo of your personality—in other words, recognizable as *your* creations. Use vivid colors, unusual furniture, highly individual paintings; or create a more tranquil setting as a quiet backdrop for yourself, depending on the mood you want to create.

If you are the more subdued type, you can bring vibrancy and vivacity into your decorating or make your home an extension of your calm, quiet personality. These same basic rules apply to rooms you decorate for the rest of your family.

There is not much point in decorating your husband's den or study in bright colors and dominant furniture if he has conservative tastes and a reserved nature. The room will only overwhelm him, and he will both feel and look out of place in it. In the same vein, a tomboyish girl would only be uncomfortable in a bedroom furnished with dainty furniture and frills; an artistic boy lost in a room which did not cater to his tastes and interests.

Above all, stamp character on your rooms by being an individualist. Strike out, be different, and most decidedly, be yourself.

COMFORT:

It's all very well to have a supremely elegant home, providing your family can live in it and enjoy its elegance. There is nothing worse than rooms which look like museum settings and which are equally as uncomfortable. Consider your family needs, when planning your decorating schemes. Perhaps they prefer a casual way of living; ensure their comfort by consulting with them to make sure that your decorating schemes suit them, too.

Seating and lighting play an important part in your comfort plans, particularly to a home-loving family who enjoy reading, listening to music, watching TV or entertaining friends. If you have only one family/living room, make sure seating arrangements are well-placed for easy conversation; that lights are strategically placed and positioned, are easy on the eyes; that there are "personal" corners where different members of your family can pursue their activities and hobbies. When buying chairs and sofas, test them in the store to make sure they are comfortable and relaxing. Never buy pieces of furniture simply because they look attractive. The same applies to other equipment, particularly lighting.

FUNCTION:

A home must function properly for all members of the family if it is to succeed. WHAT IS YOUR MOST IMPORTANT CONCERN IN RELATION TO THE WAY YOU LIVE?

Do you have to cater to:

1. Teen-agers who want their own room for entertaining their friends?
2. Younger children who need a playroom, where they can be "messy" with finger paints, games and toys?
3. A husband who needs a study-den for paper work, reading; a work-room for his handicrafts and hobbies; a recreation room for pool, card games, where he can entertain his men friends alone?

All these factors are important in the overall *functional* planning of your home and are an integral part of your decorating schemes.

THE EMPHATIC CHARACTER of this exquisite little living room is created by the sloping, oddly-angled walls and the enriching patina of Brazilian rosewood paneling. The rich grain and color of this exotic wood is thrown into focus by the plain cream floor and sofas, makes an ideal background for a collection of Siamese **objets d'art** and a Ralph Humphrey abstract painting on the sun theme. Because of the richness of the classic paneling, very little extra color was needed; just a sprinkling of spring greens and pinks were picked up in the silk cushions and echoed in the bowl of flowers. Final decorative links come in the floor cushions and end tables in Brazilian rosewood. Designed by Evelyn Jablow, A.I.D., for an "A" frame house.

And what about your entertaining? Is it strictly family, built around television, music, books and your children? Or do you give big cocktail parties, buffet suppers? Or are intimate little dinners your specialty? These considerations are just as important as color schemes and all other aspects of homemaking.

Is space your most pressing problem? If it is, be clever and make as many rooms dual-purpose as you can. This is really the only way you will be able to cater to all members of your family and it is not as difficult as it sounds.

For instance, your husband's study, if imaginatively decorated, can easily be transformed into a dining room when you want to entertain guests. Shop for a dining table that fits easily into a small corner of the study which can be extended in size by the addition of two or three leaves. The dining chairs can always be scattered throughout the home when not needed for entertaining.

If you have a basement which is claimed by all members of the family for their *own* recreation room, decorate it in such a way to make it serve all of them. Create a corner for the younger children, which they can use during the day. Put in generous storage units, so that their toys can be cleared away and the room transformed for other members of the family in the evening. If it is large enough, you can always divide a basement room, so that half of it suits your husband, the other half teen-agers.

And should you, yourself, want a quiet corner where you can relax, read and write letters, reserve a small corner in your bedroom and create a study area for yourself. A desk or small writing table plus a comfortable chair and a good lamp are all you need for this.

As soon as you recognize your needs, your decorating plans will clarify themselves, and you will be able to provide for all the activities your family enjoys.

ATMOSPHERE:

The atmosphere in your home is largely created by **you** and your per-sonality—plus the combination of character, comfort and function talked about earlier in this chapter. In other words, atmosphere is the sum total of everything that has gone before in the planning and decorating of your home.

Color is a major ingredient in the creation of atmosphere. For instance, pastels and softer shades always seem to create a feeling of serenity; the more vivid, darker colors when used cleverly can also create a feeling of peace. Color, used indiscriminately and badly, jars on the nerves and gives a room a "noisy" look.

Textures are also important. Fabrics on furniture and used for drapes should blend well with each other and with the rest of the room. For instance, if you are trying to create a luxurious atmosphere, don't use a cheap fabric for slipcovers, or skimp on the length of the drapes. The same applies to floor

SHADES OF THE BOSPHORUS and the perfumed **odalisques** of a seraglio
...this definitely Turkish room with overtones of 18th century exoticism
may be too far out for you. But no one can deny that it does have a
personality all of its own, is the ideal retreat for the pure **INDIVIDUALIST.**
Deep, moody colors have been used, and the combinations of red, yellow
and blue do not clash because of their subdued tones. They make a
perfect backdrop for the highly polished, ornate brass. In keeping with
the Oriental flavor are the deep, overstuffed sofa and chair; the minaret-
shaped, recessed alcoves framing more brass, books and ornaments; the
hanging brass lamp and planter pot. Linking the whole room, in color and
theme, is a paisley-patterned vinyl tile floor which has the luminescence
of stained glass. The key to individualistic decorating is to pick out and
adapt the ideas you like, discard the rest.

COMFORT AND FUNCTION combined with casual elegance are the keynotes of this sparkling family room by Marvin Culbreth, N.S.I.D. Paneling dramatizes the walls, is matched against white wall-to-wall carpeting for the truly integrated look. The basic red-white-and-blue color scheme is picked up in the bright red sofa, splashy blue chairs, and the white accents of table tops, brunch counter, drapes and cushions. The result: a colorful, mellow room that functions for the entire family, is easy to maintain with prefinished paneling, washable cotton and corduroy slip-covers and drapes, wipe-clean finishes.

covering. Deep pile carpets always look lush. If you can't afford good carpeting, don't economize with a cheaper type, or you will lose the luxurious effect. Instead put down a good vinyl tile that simulates marble and which can be as effective as a rich carpet.

LIGHTING is the third vital ingredient in creating a pleasant atmosphere. Keep it subdued, soft and well-placed for tranquility; harsh lighting is like "noisy" color—it jars on the nerves and does not always show off decor and furniture to their best advantage.

Flowers, paintings, books, trivia of all kinds also add to the atmosphere of any room, in any home.

Uniquely different flooring and a wooden horse from a Gay 'Nineties carousel are the decorative focal points of this living room with a carefree personality. The fluid lines in the four-color vinyl floor and the galloping stance of the wooden horse give the room a feeling of movement and gaiety. Other collectors' items, books, a games table and good seating make this a room of comfort as well as character, for the whole family. Search the junk shops for such nostalgic pieces from the past, to set a theme for a decorating scheme.

CHAPTER FIVE

Color Is a Catalyst

COLOR IS THE prime mover, or protagonist if you like, in decorating. It is the multifaceted performer that plays the featured role in your decorating plans. There is no limit to its versatility. It can change the shape and size of a room, disguise its architectural defects, emphasize and dramatize its good points.

Color is the catalyst that brings a room to life. Clever use of color creates the mood and atmosphere in a room—serene, gay or dramatic. Color plays it cool, or turns around and is warm and friendly. You can use any color with any period or style of furnishing and it will be perfectly compatible. Most important, color influences your own mood, evokes a personal, emotional response...it can make your spirits soar or soothe and relax you.

When you enter a room, color makes the first impression, and so it should be one of the first considerations in your decorating plans. Creating your own color scheme is not as difficult as it sounds. An analysis of your wardrobe might provide a clue to the colors you are happiest with, your favorite color in fact. If you favor neutral shades and spark your ensembles with more vivid-hued accessories, then a subdued background with bright accents is your best bet in the home. If your wardrobe reveals more pungent-hued clothes with a repetition of one color, select this color and work around it. Wherever you go—a friend's home, a hotel, a restaurant, a store's model rooms—be on the alert for color combinations that suit your fancy. Then again, you may own an original painting, which you treasure. Display it against a neutral background and key your color scheme to the painter's palette. In fact, let any colorful, prized possession inspire your color scheme.

Designer Erica Lemle, N. S. I. D., used **shocking pink and purple,** a combination once thought too **hot** for each other, and created an unusual and striking effect in a one-room beach apartment. She succeeds with this daring scheme because she used plenty of cooling white and other subtle color links. She worked on the principle of two basic colors (pink and white) repeated throughout the room, plus one "stationary" color (purple) used in a solid mass. Shocking pink carpet links pink painted bookcase, cyclamen tablecloth, pink and white patterned fabric used for wall jog, chair cushions and lampshade. White is repeated on walls, doors, chairs, marble tabletop and other accents. Purple is used along one wall only, massed together for divan covers, wall-hung cushions and painted chests, is successful in the room because it is a "stationary" color.

Remember that a small swatch of color looks totally different than when it covers a whole wall. In fact, always bear in mind that color *changes color* when used in a large area. It becomes stronger, brighter and more intense. For this reason we do not use the usual color charts here—because a small square of color cannot be correctly judged. Instead we show you a series of beautiful color schemes, rooms where skillful use of color plays a major role.

IMAGINATIVE USE OF UNUSUAL COLORS MIXED TOGETHER sets the mood for any room, but placement of color must be deft and sure. A combination of dark, earthy tones were cleverly used by Paul Krauss, A. I. D., to create a masculine effect in a New York bachelor apartment. He added a sprinkling of spicy shades, which sit well against the muted background, and give the room a lift at the same time. Basic theme was set by the wall unit of sparkling rosewood, autumn-gold walls, and the deeper, autumn-gold carpet. The olive-green sofa keeps to the earthy theme, while the bright yellow chairs echo the gold walls. Red chair and scatter cushions add vivid splashes of color, are keyed to the books and flowers. A white painting and lampshade were used to highlight the gleaming rosewood, also match the narrow slat window blinds.

We show you use of one color in varying shades, repeated to give a room unity and an integrated look; a clutch of schemes built around fabrics; color underfoot; monochromatic schemes with a vivid splash of color intensified in one area; unusual color schemes that work. In all, we show you how color can transform and beautify any room in the home.

Create the Mood with One Color Repeated

Varying shades of one basic color used throughout a room give it a feeling of integration, serenity—need never be dull. Here are eight rooms illustrating this point. Each one is highly different in concept and style, with one thing in common...a repeated color creating the individual atmosphere.

JADE AND PALE GREENS perpetuate a spring-like freshness in the study-bedroom of a country home. The imperial jade-green of the carpet is the color anchor, is matched to the taffeta drapes and is picked up again as a decorative motif on wall baseboards and ceiling molding. Pale green moves across walls, doors and up onto ceiling, is echoed in the filmy nylon curtains, tiebacks and edging of jade taffeta drapes. The white painted fireplace and desk add to the fresh look, help to bring out and emphasize the greenness of the room; only other splash of color is the red chair cushion and floral bedspread.

VARIOUS SHADES OF YELLOW were used in this romantic bedroom, designed by Ving Smith, A.I.D., and Charlotte Smith. To achieve a warm, sunny feeling, and yet not overwhelm, bright yellow was used on the floor instead of on the walls. By keeping the yellow underfoot, the designers avoided the glare that **too much** yellow can create: at the same time the room reflects a sunny feeling. The daffodil floor tiles offset the paler, primrose carpets, and both blend well with the buttercup and white floral bed fabric. Walls are covered with a softening, butter-colored vinyl in keeping with the yellow theme.

VIVID CRIMSON was used boldly to create a dramatic look in a small, city apartment. The room revolves around the bed, the key to the whole color scheme. Quilted headboard and tailored quilted spread are made of identical material. They match the full-length drapes and the walls, which were painted crimson for unity. The white background of the Roman shades is repeated on the tiled floor, in the fluffy bedside rug and other accents, such as the lamp, scatter cushion and flowers. The dash of white acts as a "cooler" and throws the vivid crimson into relief.

FIVE DIFFERENT SHADES OF BLUE create harmony and tranquility in a Williamsburg-style bedroom of a country home. The room succeeds because varying depths of blue were blended and spiced with white, plus pattern on some fabrics. Color anchor is the pale blue carpet matched to three of the walls; bed canopy in plain fabric is keyed to background of patterned drapes, while ice-blue and white spread creates a pool of light in the middle of the room. The blue and white striped wallpaper behind bed makes a light backdrop for bed canopy of darker blue, creates extra interest in the room.

HOT ORANGE was used by designer William Pahlman, N.S.I.D., to create a warm, vital mood in a small sitting room. Color theme of the room revolves around the handsome screen: flower colors are picked up in the carpet, silk pleated drapes and embroidery on the deep sofa. Black chairs, table and plant-stand match the background of the screen; other accents are orange box, bowl and flowers on black table.

1.

2.

1. A BLENDING OF AUTUMN GOLDS bring a mellow atmosphere to this modern apartment. Long sectional sofas upholstered in a plain gold fabric sit well against the squared wallpaper; two upright chairs (foreground) repeat muted shades from the autumnal rug. Finishing touches, in keeping with the color theme, are the marble-topped tables matched to creamy tiled floor, and the simple lamp color toned to wallpaper. Designed by Everett Brown, A.I.D.

2. WHITE AND CREAM bring an understated elegance to this weekend ski lodge and also create a feeling of peace. White and cream are repeated and repeated, on floor, fireplace, woodwork, even furniture. Only additional color comes in the coffee and chocolate tufted rug, and even these shades belong to the same color family. This scheme is equally as effective when used in a city apartment or house.

3. A MIXTURE OF GREENS, from the palest to the darkest in the spectrum, were daringly used by designer Gary Pizzarelli, A.I.A., in a penthouse apartment high above New York. Pale green floor reflects the ceiling and ties in with the nylon window drapes; fir-green splashes on all the walls, carries through onto bookcase and tufted area carpet. A handsome kelly green sofa sits well between two turquoise green chairs; this same color is picked out in the bookcase shelves, and in other parts of the room (not shown here). The designer kept to this "forest" theme and used an abundance of indoor plants, strategically placed around the apartment.

3.

Pick a Posy of Colors from a Patterned Fabric

Let a multicolored fabric be your color inspiration. Use it cleverly in one part of the room, for window shades, drapes, slipcovers or a bedspread. Then key your overall color scheme to its predominant shades, or if you prefer, to the more subdued shades in the pattern. Either way, you will have an integrated color scheme.

LIME-GREEN, AVOCADO AND GOLD, with a surprise dash of pink, were used to create a restful bedroom by Pete Cano, A.I.D. Color key to the room is the lime-green and white patterned bedspread with its matching headboard and petticoat. The designer used the same fabric for the full-length drapes, adding a sculptured valance of avocado velveteen for contrast. Avocado is repeated in a table cover, while chaise and bench are upholstered in deep gold velveteen. These colors are used for the lazy-back pillows, with lush pink as the surprise accent. Tying the color theme together are walls and carpet of lime-green.

RED, PINK, TANGERINE AND OLIVE-GREEN on a cool white background are the color ingredients in this gay family room. Springboard for the room was a vibrant floral print of acetate and rayon, used for the long draperies and also laminated onto the venetian blinds. Colors from the print are picked up in other fabrics throughout the room, on the cupboard doors and on the floor. Tangerine antique satin appears in the chair and stool covers; red pillows and white bolsters are a perfect foil for the olive-green quilted throw on the day bed, which becomes an island of color coordinated with the scheme of the room. Balancing these bright colors are the white walls, furniture, and the white vinyl floor which features a red and pink floral motif. Incidentally, this unique little room is not only pretty and cheerful to be in, but immensely practical too. It has its own efficiency kitchen, and when not being used as a family room, transforms into a guest room with ease.

A GREEN, BLUE AND SCARLET paisley-patterned print sets the color theme of this charming living room designed by Paul Krauss, A.I.D. He uses the Early American inspired fabric to false-front a marred wall, freshen upholstered sofa and for the drapes, picking up the three basic colors of the print throughout the rest of the room. Subtle green is used on the western pine walls; blue on the two fireside chairs and as a backing for the drapes; red for cushions, trimmings and rug.

57

A RED AND WHITE French-inspired fabric sets the color theme, as well as the mood, of a city apartment bedroom. The fabric is used throughout the room for bedspread, drapes, chair cushion and is repeated on the wall behind the bed. Vivid red is picked up on a wall and as a lining for drapes for that extra dash of color, is balanced by off-white carpet. Red and pink plus white is an effective color combination if used cleverly and with deft touches. Incidentally, a fabric can not only be used to set the color scheme, but to create an atmosphere: this elegant city bedroom might easily be in a 17th century French chateau.

AN EXCITING, SPLASHY FABRIC used on a handsome sofa calls the color tune in a modern apartment. Orange, red and yellow predominate in the fabric, and are repeated throughout the room: orange silk wallpaper on the wall, red fabric on the deep chair, orange and gold pattern on the squared-off rug. Even the painting behind sofa picks up these colors. The white lampshade, white mount on painting and white floor have a cooling effect, as do the other white walls in room, not shown here. Splashes of green in plants and bench and the black table add additional contrast, throw the hot shades into relief.

Make a Splash
With Color Concentrated in a Small Area

LET COLOR SING out . . . on a wall, a door, a chair, a dining table, a bedspread or drapes. It gives a lift to tired rooms, emphasizes paler shades, revitalizes dark, dull corners.

THIN RED LINE in flooring splashes up onto refrigerator doors, wall mural and woodwork to liven a roomy family kitchen; bright red helps to emphasize stark white walls, dark woodwork. Kitchen designed by Bette Lebow.

LILAC CHAIR, SKY-BLUE DRAPES create a pool of light in the study corner of a paneled sitting room; more important, these almost iridescent colors contrast well with Brazilian rosewood paneling, bring out its rich patina. Finishing touch of color is the lilac and blue tufted rug.

1. BRILLIANT SEA-BLUE bedspread is the color focal point of this charming bedroom; it focuses attention on the antique Spanish headboard, seems to reflect light. Varying shades of blue are picked up in the drapes and accessories.

1.

4.

2.

3.

A TABLE SETTING CAN BE AN ISLAND OF COLOR, THE ATTENTION-GETTER, IF
ARRANGED CLEVERLY AND WITH IMAGINATION. A COLORFUL TABLE ENHANCES
ANY DINING ROOM, AS ILLUSTRATED IN THE TWO PICTURES ON THIS PAGE.

2. SCARLET WALL in a bathroom throws the white washbasin and dressing table fixture into relief, is a dramatic accent against the black marbleized floor and black grille work. Chair cushion and rug are color coordinated for the finishing touch. Too much red in this small bathroom would have been overpowering: painting only one wall created the desired effect.

3. TOMATO-RED doors in the hall of this elegant New York sitting room enhance rather than detract from the glowing gold silk walls, tea-paper ceiling and rich ebonized parquet floor. Splash of matching red in the cushion is the subtle color link in a serene, Chinese-influenced room of muted colors and antiques, designed by J. Frederic Lohman, A.I.D.

4. An arrangement of California poppies in a gold basket was the springboard for this colorful luncheon table. Raspberry-pink linen tablecloth is the anchor; paler peony-pink napkins blend with the floral arrangement and the pink and white dinnerware. The gold artificial fruit scattered on the table matches the gold grapes' basket and flatware. Centerpiece designed by table setting stylist Janice B. Gordon.

5. A BLUE PAISLEY-PATTERNED tablecloth, blue candlesticks, blue tinted, platinum-banded crystal are the ingredients which bring sparkle to a casual buffet setting. Even the wine cozy is carefully color matched, with a napkin knotted around the neck of the carafe.

PEACH AND BLUE paint were effectively combined to bring a positive yet soft splash of color to this kitchen, and create a demarcation line between work area and raised, open-end dining room. Orange upholstery on chairs blends easily with the peach-painted cabinets, adds lively interest to white floor and drapes. Designed by Ving Smith, A.I.D.

BRIGHT YELLOW coverlet gave this old fourposter bed a new lease on life. The owner painted the bedback and the four posts an identical yellow, added tangerine and yellow cushions for a finishing touch. The result: a flash of sunshine in a small attic room.

Come Alive! with Color in the Kitchen

LET COLOR BURST forth in your kitchen. Dispense with that antiseptic look which modern equipment, combined with sterile white, often creates. Match walls to the new colored refrigerators, ovens, washing machines, dishwashers; make floors, ceilings, cupboards sparkle with bright, gay shades to cheer your working hours. But remember, a daring color combination must be used adroitly: color changes the shape and size of any room, gives it totally new dimensions. Here you see how highly individual kitchens were given atmosphere and new life, by the expert use of color.

PALE GREEN, BLUE, GOLD AND WHITE are the four essential color ingredients in this charming kitchen with a country air. The unusual blue and white squared floor reflects the blue walls around the work area, the blue chair cushions and the white cupboards; gold table skirt is toned to the golden-blond wood paneling used above the white cupboards of the work area and on the dining area walls; yellow of the work tops is repeated on the window ledge and in the softer yellow stripe of the sofa; dashes of pale green come in the refrigerator and other kitchen equipment. Designed by Ving Smith, A.I.D.

MILK CHOCOLATE AND RED is the unusual yet effective color combination used by Ving Smith, A.I.D., for a luxury look in a compact city kitchen. The rich chocolate and red go well together when spiced with gleaming white, on floor, ceiling, work tops and chairs.

YELLOW PLUS WHITE AND SHINING STAINLESS STEEL brings an air of elegance to this streamlined kitchen with its own dining area. Yellow doors, white paneling picked out in yellow help to dispel antiseptic look some modern kitchens have.

Color Underfoot Provokes a Theme

VIVID COLOR ON THE FLOOR in vinyl, mosaic, terrazzo, tile or carpet makes a good jumping-off point for a color scheme. Certain vivid colors which can look too harsh on walls, are doubly effective underfoot. They look more subdued while still remaining lively, make successful backgrounds for white rugs, painted furniture, antique as well as modern pieces. Pale-colored floors reflect light, help to enlarge a small room. Either way, a bright floor can be the color anchor of your decorating scheme.

BLUE TILES went down on the floor of this small study to set the color scheme. A darker shade of blue is picked up in the wing chair, echoed in the wooden window frames and the blue and green beads which form a novel curtain. A white rug, backed with red, ties in with the white walls and the red accents of the wastebasket, enameled coffee pot, cushion and displayed plates.

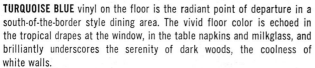

TURQUOISE BLUE vinyl on the floor is the radiant point of departure in a south-of-the-border style dining area. The vivid floor color is echoed in the tropical drapes at the window, in the table napkins and milkglass, and brilliantly underscores the serenity of dark woods, the coolness of white walls.

GOLD AND RED CARPETING is the color base of an easy-to-care-for apartment designed for a bachelor. Designers Seldon H. Curry, A.I.D., and Paul B. Rogers, A.I.D., used the two rich colors of the nylon carpet throughout the apartment, for a truly integrated look. Yellow sofa, chairs and drapes reiterate the golden carpet in the sitting room; red nylon velvet with a gold stripe used on cane-sided chairs and ottoman echoes the red carpet in the adjacent kitchen, but keeps to the golden theme with its stripe. White brick walls and dark wood throw the rich colors into relief.

A STRIPED AREA RUG BECAME THE COLOR KEY in this cool-looking, one-room apartment. Olive-green sofa, tapestry, lamp and a blue chair all blend well together, as do these same shades in the rug. A striking lime-green wall sits well between stark white floor and white brick wall, and emphasizes the darker greens. White and blue ornaments add the finishing touches on the room divider and white marble table.

Wallpaper Inspires a Color Scheme

MAKE WALLPAPER WORK well for you. Build a room's color scheme around one of the pretty or unusual wallpapers now available. Silk, embossed, velvet-flocked and handpainted papers give a handsome look to the walls of any room, and often spark off color ideas.

GREEN AND GOLD shiki silk-textured wallpaper sets the color scheme in this elegant sitting room. Lustrous gold silk draperies and the skirted tablecloth pick up the gold in the wallpaper; greenish-blue upholstery echoes the green of the wallpaper's base. Gold antique lamp and blue glass ornaments help to accentuate the green-gold-blue theme.

A PINK, GREEN, TURQUOISE & GOLD plaid wallpaper is the color springboard in this living room. It is perfectly matched to the fabric used on sofa. Pink and turquoise upholstery on chairs pick up two of the colors from the plaid. Carpet is an understated pale gold, matched to the inset panel of gold paper.

Bamboo panels on the walls of this restful bedroom designed by Mark Nelson, A.I.D., establish both its Oriental mood and its color theme. The handsome bamboo patterned paper, in brown, a subtle green and pale yellow on a textured gold ground, is one of the new scenics. Fringed bedspread mingles orange, gold, white: rug is gold, striped in orange, cobalt and brown. White lamps, tabletops and headboard are all cool white.

Six Rooms where Color Triumphs

Formula — Bright colors used boldly, with flair and a sure hand

Don't let the brighter colors of the palette intimidate you. When deftly used they bring distinction and personality to any room, make a rich background for furniture and accessories.

1.

1. COLOR FORMULA: Bright red and blue, softened by brown and thrown into relief by black and white floor. Designer Paul Krauss, A.I.D., uses rich colors and fabric to create an affluent look in this elegant, old world dining room decorated with non-pedigreed furnishings. The brown paisley fabric used on walls, for drapes and tablecloth echoes the red and blue painted woodwork and chairs, simulates authentic tapestry or needlepoint.

2. COLOR FORMULA: Yellow, red and orange cooled by stark white. Why not build a color scheme around a rich painting? A picture of tropical fruits became the springboard for this contemporary bedroom flashing with vivid colors. The shell of the room—walls, ceiling and floor—are in shades of pale yellow, white and cream; all are bland and soft enough to take the hot orange bedspreads, yellow and red painted furniture. The throw rug picks up these same colors, with a dash of green to tie in with the painting. Softer tones of orange, yellow and red in the drapes echo the basic color scheme, while pristine white lamps and window frames reflect the cool white ceiling .

2.

COLOR FORMULA: Green and white massed together on bright blue. Clever use of color created a feeling of space, coordination and tranquility in this too small sitting room. Designer Ving Smith, A.I.D. used sleek, understated furniture to avoid a cluttered look, made color the prime factor in the room. Green and white stripes at the windows reflect the olive-green sofas and white coffee tables, while bright blue carpet brings color contrast to the room, throws the mixture of green and white into relief. The result: a cool, restful room.

COLOR FORMULA: Red, yellow, orange and olive-green mixed and matched against white. This lively color scheme works because the hot shades are carefully blended with each other. The yellow window frames echo the baseboard color and the paler yellow floor; red and gold fabric on the chair blends with red striped fabric on sofa and in window shutters, is in keeping with the red-yellow theme used throughout the room. Olive-green area rug is carefully matched to olive painted lamp table, white brick walls for the cooling effect in the room. Designed by Paul Krauss, A.I.D.

COLOR FORMULA: Yellow-on-yellow, softened by cream, spiced with gold. Yellow always creates an illusion of sunshine in a dark room as shown in this elegant bedroom designed by Gary Pizzarelli, A.I.D. He used a combination of yellow-on-yellow and off-white, concealed lighting and mirrors for the desired sunny effect. Yellow patterned drapes reflect the yellow carpet and yellow plaid spreads, with cream chairs echoing walls and furniture. Concealed lighting under window valances and behind bookshelves enhance the room without being too harsh; mirror frames and wall panels are picked out in gold to match gold decorated furniture.

COLOR FORMULA: Emerald, kelly and lime greens repeated. A combination of greens were used to bring an airy, cool look to this too dark back room, cleverly transformed into a summery dining room. Lime-green walls match the alumaloy furniture, while panels on cupboard are picked out in emerald to match the carpet and chair cushions. A kelly green lampshade on hanging lamp echoes the tableware. Only other color used in the room, is the blue in the bead curtains, picked up in the blue milk glass water set.

CHAPTER SIX

Kitchens: A New Concept

❧

Top-notch planning, streamlined, labor-saving appliances, glamorous new materials and accessories, and 20th century know-how all combine to give today's kitchens an updated new life

KITCHENS HAVE UNDERGONE a vast change in recent years. The final result today is a totally new concept in kitchen planning, and most important, decor. The majority of them have lost that sterile, laboratory look so prevalent in the 'Fifties, have become "decorated" rooms that have more than one life. In this chapter are many new ideas . . . kitchens that are not only functional but fun; kitchens which are also family rooms, offices, dining rooms, in fact many rooms in one. All of them have been planned for the ultimate in efficiency and beauty, designed to please the woman who wants not only labor-saving equipment, but comfort and luxury as well, in her working hours. Even the most super-stream-lined kitchen filled with every new scientific and electrical gadget does not have to resemble a launching pad at Cape Kennedy. New materials for walls and floors, colored or decorated refrigerators, ovens and washing machines, plus handsome furniture and the use of vivid color schemes transform the average kitchen into a room of true beauty.

Function and elegance are combined in this up-to-the-minute kitchen designed by David Barrett, A.I.D., N.S.I.D. Clever use of color and accessories dispenses with that antiseptic feeling sometimes prevalent in the modern kitchen; apothecary jars, paintings, plants and the designed floor give the room a decorated look and a feeling of warmth. Easy on the eye, but strictly functional, are the floor to ceiling custom-built cabinets and the two-tone wood blocks on the work top areas. Ideas worth noting: pegboard walls, spotlighting over work tops, eye-level oven, raised cabinets for easy cleaning. The dining area is integrated into the kitchen through its matching floor and color scheme, at the same time it is clearly defined and demarcated by its raised level and wrought-iron railing.

Planning

TOP-NOTCH KITCHEN planning makes good use of all available space. To be a success, every kitchen must be well planned, down to the last detail. Convenience is just as important as appearance in kitchens that are large, small, new or remodeled. Work out your plans on paper first. This not only saves time and headaches later, but money and disappointments as well.

There is no point in learning too late that the ultra-large family refrigerator you want won't fit into the space between oven and work counters. If you are arranging cabinets and other appliances, work on graph paper to exact scale. And remember that you can utilize walls from floor to ceiling for storage units, that will save floor space. Do this preliminary planning before you go to your architect, builder or designer, so that you know what you want.

Versatile Peninsulas and Islands

PENINSULAS AND ISLANDS have manifold merits, have come into their own in the last few years, are in fact an essential in the well-planned modern kitchen. One of the secrets of good kitchen design is to avoid wasted energy. The less walking you have to do between oven, sink, range and refrigerator, the better. Islands and peninsulas help to bring work areas closer together, and in doing so alleviate this traffic problem. An *island* is any free-standing base cabinet, with counter top, set out in the middle of the kitchen floor. In many ways it is the modern version of the old kitchen table. Certainly it serves the same purpose, with a difference. And the difference is that it combines a sink or cooking top, or both, in its work counter, carries cabinet or drawer storage in the base. A *peninsula* is any counter extending from a wall, so that it is accessible from three sides. Peninsulas can also accommodate range tops, sink and base storage, although this is not essential. Peninsulas and islands also solve other kitchen traffic problems, especially when more than one person is working in the kitchen. By isolating various areas of activity, two, even three, people can work happily at different chores, without crossing paths.

Floors

KITCHEN FLOORINGS come in all prices, are designed to flourish with any decorating scheme, and are more glamorous than ever before. Careful thought should be given to several basics, before buying flooring material. These are: traffic expected; amount of exposure to sunlight, moisture; durability wanted; amount of quietness desired.

Many different types of *vinyl flooring* are available, and continue to be popular because they are versatile, practical and not too expensive. You have a choice of *vinyl tiles, vinyl asbestos, solid vinyl and sheet vinyl.* All wear well, look good, are grease and alkali resistant. Your dealer will give you more detailed specifics, depending on the type of floor on which the vinyl will be laid. Many of these vinyls simulate brick, tile, wood, and marble and can create a luxury look in any kitchen. *Ceramic tiles* are hard wearing, easy to keep fresh, come in lovely colors. *Linoleums* are less expensive than vinyls and ceramic tiles, they wear fairly well, but have to be installed above grade only. However, they are easy to maintain and are grease resistant. *Cork* is good acoustically, and when treated with a new resin combination may be used at any grade. It resists stains, burns and indentation. *Asphalt tile* is another low-cost favorite. It resists alkalis well, is generally fairly durable and can be installed above or below grade. Because it's hard it's not so quiet underfoot. *Vinyl carpet* and other *fiber carpets* that resist moisture, spots, and are easy to maintain can also be used successfully in kitchens.

Walls

KITCHEN WALLS CAN sing with color and beauty today. The choice of wall coverings is wide. Washable wallpaper, plastic-coated fabrics, plastic-finished hardboard paneling, laminated plastic wall surfaces, wood paneling, ceramic tiles, metal and copper tiles or stainless steel sheets all give walls a new impact. When color and texture are matched to floors, they give the kitchen an integrated, truly "decorated" look.

Remember also to plan your lighting and ventilation carefully. Lights should be well placed, so that you work in shadowless comfort and avoid eyestrain. Ventilation equipment keeps kitchens clean and fresh. Ventilating fans and hoods remove food odors, grease, smoke, heat and moisture before they do any damage to walls and furniture. Your dealer will advise you of all the new products now on the market that help to achieve kitchen comfort.

This colorful kitchen epitomizes the best in modern planning, while clever use of beams painted bright red and mahogany-colored plastic laminate add both character and dash. Ample storage cupboards are arranged above and below sink, range and work top areas, are easy to reach, aligned for a feeling of coordination and symmetry. Ceiling beams continue down walls, and clever placement of beams at open-end of kitchen creates a useful serving hatch and look-through effect into dining room. Peninsula cupboard turns corner from dining room into kitchen, does double duty in both areas. The red and white color scheme, combined with mahogany, is repeated in telephone-writing corner and dining room for color integration; red chair at desk also serves in dining room.

Gone are the days of the sterile white refrigerator; colored and decorated doors come to the fore and set the scene for ingenious kitchen decor. This modern kitchen with an old world air owes its charming **provencal** atmosphere to skillful decorating and furnishing, the theme inspired by the Dutch tiles on the refrigerator door. Matching tiles are used on the walls, set the color scheme of blue and white. The beams and the leaded window are in keeping with the general theme of the room, match oak table, chair, pewter, willow pattern plates and other timely accessories for the real farmhouse look. The modern work tops and cupboards are strictly functional, are understated to blend with decor of the kitchen.

Extensive use of quarry tile is one of the main features
of this ultramodern kitchen designed by Edward Durrell
Stone. Three different types of quarry tile are used on
work tops, island counter and floor. They are perfect
for use in kitchens because they are unaffected by
wear, weather, are easy to keep clean, need no waxing,
polishing or other special care. Other talking points:
compact wall unit, with long work top above cupboards
and dishwasher, and triple sink; ample storage in floor
to ceiling cupboards flanking wall unit; island cooking
counter in center of room, which can be used from all
angles.

CAREFUL PLANNING IS important, whatever the size of your kitchen. Strategic placing of cupboards, work tops, oven, range, sink and dishwasher is vital, is the determining factor in efficiency and convenience.

All the space in this roomy kitchen has been utilized for maximum efficiency. Range and oven are at opposite ends, with sink and dishwasher centralized for convenience. Island for preparing food is directly across from sink, other work tops run from sink beyond cooking range, and round the entire wall area of kitchen. Ample storage cabinets also follow this pattern, above and below work tops. Beams, tiles, polished wood and decorative accessories help to create a country look in a kitchen planned for modern living.

An oddly placed corner or wall jog need not sabotage your kitchen planning. Here you see an efficient and compact work counter which turns the corner to utilize all the space in an irregularly shaped room. Separation of oven and range means two can easily work together in a small kitchen normally reserved for one. Storage cupboards are massed together in one unit for extra utilization of space.

81

The working area of this kitchen was centralized by combining all equipment in the U-shaped section of cabinets and work tops. Refrigerator, range and double sink make a strategic triangle, minimize movement which makes for greater efficiency. The peninsula counter top containing double sink also separates breakfast-dining area, creates two atmospheres in one room. The wall oven is next to small desk, which also does double duty as a counter top, when needed. Other talking points: refrigerator and oven doors color matched; additional single sink near refrigerator; indirect spotlighting; use of pretty patterned wallpaper for a decorated look.

Streamlined kitchen designed for actress-executive Joan Crawford presents a dramatic new concept in shape, color, kitchen equipment and efficiency. Elegance comes in striking blocks of pure black and white and silvery stainless steel finishes for surfaces such as storage cabinets, counter tops, floor and ceiling tiles, and the highly individual "Carriage Lamp" appliances. Designed by Marvin Culbreth, A.I.D.

A window corner, cut on the diagonal, was utilized to create an efficient wash-up-and-work area in this small but carefully planned kitchen. Deep drawers under the sink provide ample storage space, while circular cupboard suspended over sink is handy for china and glass. Unwanted space at tip of triangle near windows was filled with plants for a garden look. Other appliances and work areas revolve round this corner sink unit, which is the focal point of the kitchen. Finishing touch is the cleverly laid floor. One of the advantages of sheet or roll type flooring materials is the flexibility. These materials can be flashed or coved-up baseboards and wall, as shown here, to form an almost seamless continuation of flooring. The flash-cove method of installation not only eliminates many dirt catching corners, but also gives the room a streamlined appearance.

83

If your kitchen is small, don't be dismayed. It can still hold all the things you need and be a **happy** room, with careful thought. Here you see a tiny kitchen that really works well. Cabinets, sink, range and oven are ranged along two walls, are compact and streamlined, yet still ample enough for any woman's needs. Clever color cueing of ceiling, striped wallpaper, oven and range hood helps avoid a crowded look; hand towels and matching red jars add a splash of color, while plants on shelves break monotony of lined-up cupboards. White breakfast table and yellow chair also double as desk area or sewing corner when needed.

Kitchens that Work Well

PUT YOUR KITCHEN to work; in fact make it work for *you*. Small or large, it should be planned, furnished and decorated so that it undercuts most of the hard work, and at the same time makes you feel cheerful and relaxed throughout the day. Main contributing factors in kitchens that work well are: strategic placing of equipment, labor saving appliances. Carpet underfoot, a desk and chair, telephones, plants and decorative accessories, gay walls, also figure prominently in the relaxed kitchen.

Large kitchens can be just as difficult to decorate as smaller ones. In fact careful planning is vital in the larger room; equipment should be closely linked to minimize wasted energy, if the kitchen is to work well. This elegant kitchen was designed for the woman with a big family. Large capacity appliances, roomy cabinets

and shelves were essential; clever manipulation of appliances with shelf-counter units incorporated them all into the room for a streamlined look. Spacemaker refrigerator has an 18.8 cubic feet capacity, yet is only 67 inches wide, saves time because it never needs defrosting. Automatic wall oven with picture window makes for easy see-through cooking; surface unit with exhaust hood provides the ultimate in flameless cooking, and hood dispenses with cooking smells. Under counter dishwasher holds up to 15 place settings, relieves busy housewife of hand-washing china. A communications center with a radio-intercom system linked to the rest of the house also relays music. The snack counter sees double duty as a desk and planning center, with books and other items on hand in the shelves.

The charm of grandmother's kitchen combines with mid-twentieth century efficiency to make this room the comfortable hub of the home. It is full of good ideas, if you want to make your kitchen work well. Butter-yellow cabinets, with old-fashioned drawer pulls, file and store every cooking need. Decorative black hood removes cooking odors, acts as a plate warmer too. Eye-level, see-through oven doors eliminate bending, lessen chances of scorched cooking failures. Natural wood chopping block is incorporated in counter top; built in spice rack above has extra-large capacity. And finally, the ultimate in kitchen luxury, wall-to-wall carpeting underfoot. Made of olefin fiber in a blue and green tweed, to complement wipe-clean wall tiles and window shades, this carpet is a practical as well as colorful addition to any kitchen. It is dirt and moisture resistant: spots and spills can be sponged away, daily vacuuming removes surface crumbs and dust.

This pace-setter kitchen is not only beautiful but practical too. Versatility is the keynote, and a variety of factors combine to make it work well. Extensive use of ceramic tile makes for continuity, is easy to clean and care for; use of one color repeated creates a feeling of integration; plenty of space and easy-to-move furniture ensures flexibility; well-planned wall unit incorporates refrigerators, range, oven, and work counters for efficiency; double-faced sink unit in island counter (hidden by flowers) is multi-purpose with work tops reached from any angle. Clever plant arrangements and use of other decorative accessories add final touches for an open-air, carefree feeling. Designed by John deKoven Hill, in association with architects John W. Geiger and Paul L. Soderburg. Thomas H. Landise, Jr., Supervising Architect.

Versatile Peninsulas and Islands

PENINSULAS AND ISLANDS solve many problems in the modern kitchen. They consolidate work and cooking areas, control traffic routes, create isolated areas for special chores, introduce two atmospheres in one room and offer additional storage space.

This immense cooking peninsula is a 20th century version of the big, old-fashioned kitchen hearth. It offers ample cooking facilities with range top and grill, and work tops on all sides. Large terra-cotta-colored tiles match the scale of the peninsula, as does the huge wooden hood. Concealed lighting in the hood provides perfect illumination for the cook.

This lively kitchen revolves around a split-level peninsula, half for working, half for eating. The result is an efficient, self-contained inner kitchen that is visually united with neighboring areas, but doesn't cross paths. Old beams are a good decor excuse for use of picturesque detail —old hooks, hanging pots, painted hinges and copper. Peninsula tops and walls are covered in olive-colored plastic laminate for easy maintenance and long life.

Two peninsulas at each end of this kitchen appear to create a maze-like effect at first glance; are in fact the height of convenience. Area above peninsula in foreground is utilized for cabinet space, while angled, double sink combines with cutting board (inserted in counter top) to make a food preparation area. Far peninsula affords a handy work top next to stove, can also be used as a snack counter. Both peninsulas provide additional storage cupboards in their bases.

Island in the middle of this well-planned kitchen serves many purposes. Charcoal broiling as well as other cooking can be conducted efficiently, while end of island provides an adequate work top. One side of island provides storage space, the other an eating counter. Incidentally, the gas-fired broiler works on ceramic coals. These are permanent, self-cleaning, replace charcoal, eliminate inconvenience and expense yet give charcoal flavor to all foods. This type of unit is completely insulated and can be installed in wood, metal or plastic counter tops, is operated by a turn of the gas control switch.

EVEN IF YOU have a separate dining room, an eating place in the kitchen fits the tempo of today's living. Dining in the kitchen can be elegant and lots of fun. Don't restrict it to family only; guests will enjoy it too. Certainly *you* will. As the hostess you can stay in the mainstream of the conversation while tending to your bubbling pots and pans.

1.

1. Unused floor space, in front of the cook-and-serve island, became the dining area in this streamlined kitchen. The owner chose light-as-air, easy-to-move metal furniture, which can be switched to another part of the room when necessary. Table and chairs, convenient to the cooking island, and an extra glass serving table, make an elegant ensemble for beautiful meals.

2. All equipment is massed together along two walls of this small kitchen, leaving adequate space for the drop-leaf dining table and gay fabric covered chairs. Strategic placing of hanging lamp provides spotlighting over the dining table; table and chairs can always be moved back against a wall when extra space is required.

2.

4. If you have a large kitchen with plenty of unused floor space, adapt this semi-circular bar. It makes a perfect "island" for dining, yet has manifold uses as an extra work counter, a desk, or a place for children to read and play when mother is busy cooking. Built on the peninsula principle, it flows from the work top next to stove and is joined to the two storage columns. It is also highly functional as a storage unit, with cupboards and drawers underneath the counter at the work side of the kitchen. Plastic-finished paneling with a wood grain effect was used on the storage columns and the base of the bar, creating a look of character and warmth. Other plastic paneling was used on the walls and for the ceiling tiles. It is practical as well as attractive; food stains, smoke discoloration, cooking splatters and fingerprints all wash off with a damp sponge, as the paneling is impervious to dirt, grease, grime and moisture. For these reasons it greatly reduces kitchen chores, and is perfect for covering the shell of the room.

3.

3. This small dining area in the corner of a kitchen has all the elegance of a separate dining room, yet cooking and serving facilities are within easy reach. This was achieved by clever decorating and planning. To camouflage functional aspects of the kitchen at dining end, an open-plan peninsula was built to accommodate major equipment such as sink, range, work tops; at the same time, the peninsula creates a demarcation line between eating and working area, is also within arm's reach of table service. Its wood-grained sides give it "furniture" character, and even the oven hood has lights in the manner of a chandelier. The decorated look of the dining corner was created by use of wallpaper, elegant furniture and a distinctive window treatment. Shades are matched to walls, with full-length drapes and a lavish plant arrangement adding further importance. Louvered doors, vinyl floor simulating marble, handsome French provincial breakfront and other accessories complete the setting. Designed by Fred Shrallow.

5.

5. Clever decorating can transform any kitchen into a lively, comfortable place to eat, as illustrated in this family kitchen. It has a distinct dining room air, is an inviting place for meals — even for guests. The luxury look was achieved by use of wall-to-wall carpeting, color-cued to the gay paisley wallpaper and matching window shades. Extensive use of antiqued wood adds to the dining room flavor, as does the clever use of accessories such as the colorful painting, plants and other trivia. At the same time kitchen efficiency is not diminished. The peninsula table extends from a compact work counter which contains all basic equipment; table doubles as a food preparation counter or desk when not in use for dining. And the carpet is not as impractical as it looks. Made of one of the new hard-wearing fibers, it resists splashes and spills, does not soil or stain.

The Kitchen is a Family Room

THE KITCHEN IS no longer a room apart where a woman must isolate herself to "hot-stove" slavery. It has become a family room, through efficient planning and design. Peninsulas and islands demarcate work and relaxing areas; use of living room furniture, TV, books, pictures, wallpaper and carpeting make it a comfortable place for all members of the family. Most important, it keeps a busy woman in the mainstream of family activity during working hours, takes the drudgery out of domestic chores.

Exceptional allocation of space and a long window wall made this kitchen of a modern home ideal for transformation into a family room. Functional equipment such as oven, dishwasher, sink, cook top were centerized in a compact peninsula, while the giant-sized refrigerator was placed next to long work counter. This compact work center leaves the rest of the room free for dining and relaxing. While each area is separate, the room has a flowing continuity. This coordinated look was achieved by using one flooring material throughout; the generous window wall; wood paneling in kitchen and living room; matching wicker furniture. The result: an elegant yet comfortable room which meets all the requirements of modern living.

A kitchen buried in the center of the house, surrounded on all sides by rooms and without one real window to call its own. Yet because of clever ceiling and skylight arrangement and excellent artificial lighting, it becomes as airy as any other "windowed" room. It is also the center of gravity in the home, designed for cooking, dining, socializing—or all three at once. Major equipment is situated in far corner behind dining bar, is handy for table service. Remaining floor space is used for comfortable chairs, TV set, coffee table. A Japanese effect is created by unusual beamed ceiling, wooden hanging lamps, and pull-down blind which hides TV set. The handsome wood paneling blends with the autumn color scheme, brings furniture character to the room.

THE KITCHEN, LIKE any other room in the house, is what **you** make it. Gone is the sterile look which dominated kitchens of the 'Forties and the 'Fifties. In its place, a whole new decorated look which brings both charm and comfort to the room at the hub of the household. Don't be afraid of making your kitchen over; give it color, comfort and flair by using pretty fabrics, vivid schemes and furniture.

A big kitchen has room for everything, and can be many rooms in one. This kitchen with a country flavor has its own compact laundry corner; cooking and work area built next to the double refrigerators; a table and chairs ensemble for dining, sewing or even a game of cards with friends. Ving Smith, A.I.D., used colorful accessories and bric-a-brac, plaid fabric matched to staircase wall, and antique brick vinyl for the decorated look.

What could be more relaxing than this fireplace corner in a modern kitchen. It is inviting enough to entertain friends, while still keeping an eye on laundry and cooking chores. The kitchen was originally the living room of an old house which was remodeled; the fireplace became the natural focal point for the restful corner at the end of the busy work area. But even without a fireplace, you can create a similar setting with a rug, pretty curtains, chairs and a coffee table.

A greenhouse built onto the end of this colorful kitchen caters to the woman with a green thumb, who wants to bring the garden indoors. Clever use of furnishings, such as chair, dining ensemble and wall-to-wall carpeting give the kitchen all the mannerisms of a dining-living room, do not detract from efficiency. Major equipment is lined along one wall: range work-counter fitted into wall jog and wall oven save space, leave room for dining table and chairs, while chair corner makes a peaceful area for reading or sewing. Warm red, lemon yellow and wood tones accented with white add to the room's country atmosphere; yellow and red carpet echoes the color scheme. Kitchen designed by Ving Smith, A.I.D., and Charlotte Smith.

Traditional elegance is the keynote of this striking dining room decorated by Erica Lemle, A.I.D., N.S.I.D. She used a two-color theme of electric-blue and white to create a tranquil feeling. Blue walls above the white dado match the blue area rug, and blue piping on the white leather chairs and linen drapes repeat the theme. As the room was small, the designer let the dining table dominate the room; other furniture is kept to a minimum, is placed against the walls. An unusual crystal chandelier with candle branches adds drama and importance, while dispensing with table candelabra to avoid a cluttered look. Traditional crystal goblets, silver, blue and white china add the finishing touches.

CHAPTER SEVEN

Dining Rooms and Table Settings

⚜

IN GRANDMOTHER'S DAY there was never any question about the dining room. It was there. It was the room where the entire family met, at least twice a day, not only to take their meals in comfort and elegance but to enjoy good food and exchange gossip in a family atmosphere.

Today, to *have* a dining room or *not* is the burning question.

In some instances, necessity dictates the dining corner or alcove, particularly when space is at a premium. There are also many people who prefer to live and eat in the same area. On the other hand, there are those who like a separate dining room away from the general living area for its manifold advantages—not the least of which is the benefit a dining room is to children. *Manners in general* are learned at the table, and there is a big swing away from snacks and dinners in front of TV sets. Food can only be properly enjoyed and digested in a genial atmosphere away from distractions. Consequently, the dining room is coming back with a boom. Space is really a secondary consideration, for even the smallest of rooms can be made appealing and comfortable. Your basic ingredients for creating a successful dining room are ample table surface, comfortable chairs, adequate serving tables and good lighting.

You can easily take the backache out of maintenance by flooring the room with materials that are easy to clean. Vinyls, tiles and other hard surface floor coverings are ideally suited to the dining room, as spills and accidents with food and drink can be wiped up. However, if you prefer a soft floor covering, investigate the newest fiber and nylon carpeting which also resists staining and can be sponged or washed. The majority of these are also colorfast and are not harmed by a little home laundering.

If you want to make the total shell of the room practical, look at the new wall coverings which are treated against staining and discoloration, and which are truly hard wearing. Wallpapers and wood paneling, as well as plastic laminates and vinyl fabrics, all come into this category today. They are easily adaptable to any decorating theme, whether you prefer traditional, contemporary or antique furniture.

Remember that it is the table which is the focal point in the dining room, and table settings are also included at the end of this chapter. Setting a good table is the hallmark of a good hostess. The accessories surrounding food add to the pleasure of eating, and this applies to family meals as well as entertaining. Again a variety of settings are illustrated to appeal to the widest of tastes and the lowest of budgets.

The Garden Look

IF YOU LIKE elegant dining, yet want to avoid the stiffness that often accompanies a formal setting, the *garden look* in dining rooms is ideal. It is a "look" with a casual kind of elegance that makes for graceful dining without too much pomp, is carefree without being sloppy. Also, it ideally suits the tempo of today's living, wears well the year round. In summer it is cool and fresh; in winter it is a happy escape from the drab weather. The shell of the room is of primary importance when you are creating a garden look in a dining room. Floors must be carpetless, laid with vinyl, tiles, terrazzo or marble for the terrace effect; walls should follow the outdoor theme covered with paper or murals patterned with flowers, vegetation, animals or birds. Plants and flowers should be plentiful; mirrors and glass can be used for an added airy look. Furniture need not necessarily be "outdoors" in feeling, but to be effective it should be of wicker, rattan, bamboo or metal. The pictures on these pages show you four superb little dining rooms with the garden theme. Adopt some of the ideas if you like this look.

An unusual, three-sided banquette arrangement creates an "enclosed" **garden look,** in this highly individual little dining room. Designed for casual living, but with touches of true elegance, it is both practical as well as gay. The open-air feeling comes from the extensive use of pebbled and marbled vinyl, the see-through wall of beads, plants, an exotic bird tapestry and the individual tables. The pebbled vinyl on the floor is repeated on the banquette tops, the marble vinyl on the banquette moves up onto two walls. All these areas and the white plastic cushions are easy to keep clean by simply sponging with a damp cloth; top of the banquette acts as a serving table at kitchen end of dining room; individual tray tables simply fold away when not in use. The kitchen, obscured when bead curtains are fully drawn, is handy for service; its mock cane walls and vinyl-covered cabinets add to the garden effect. Touches of elegance come in the individual flower vases, silver pepper mills, and other accessories. This banquette is easy to adapt. A carpenter can build the banquette with wood, sheathing the structure with vinyl or plastic laminate for the finished effect. Designed by Ellen Lehman McCluskey, A.I.D., N.S.I.D.

SHELL OF THE ROOM: Dark green vinyl floor tiles; Grecian garden murals of white and green on walls; matching green ceiling decorated with painted cloud formations. To add to the **outdoor** feeling in this elegant little dining room, decorator Leona Kahn, A.I.D., built a trellis archway and recessed alcoves along the window wall. She added a white Austrian blind, and mirrors in the recessed alcoves to create an illusion of daylight. Hanging plants in the alcoves, a stone garden column holding more plants and the Pan garden statue, bamboo and wicker furniture complete the garden effect. The dining table and chairs were marbled for a more formal look. The beautiful crystal chandelier and lemon pottery lamp also add a touch of formal elegance to the room.

The **garden look** can be formal without losing any of its charm. Rich wall, window and floor treatments act as the springboard for the mood here—as do fine crystal, tableware and candelabra. If you want to achieve a garden feeling, yet keep to traditional elegance, adopt some of the ideas shown above in this graceful room by David Barrett, A.I.D., N.S.I.D. It is almost Florentine in flavor, with an exciting wall treatment of mirrored archways surrounded by exotic garden murals and a marble vinyl floor. Silk curtains make a muted backdrop for the long glass table, which dominates the room with its crystal candelabra, goblets, antique silverware and flowers.

Flowers on the ceiling and all around the walls set the **garden theme** here—also create a feeling of continuity and an illusion of 3-D height and depth. Designer Arthur Elrod, A.I.D., used one of the new scenic wall coverings, handprinted on woven saran for this effect. A smart, squared-off vinyl on the floor offers contrast, while streamlined furniture blends well, is "outdoors" in feeling yet elegant. An unusual antique mirror frame flows into and follows the floral theme of the walls, looks effective over the antique marble-topped console. Wrought-iron base of the glass table is another antique. Finishing touch in this pristine dining room is the handsome chandelier, hung low over dining table.

Dining in a Small Space

YOU CAN MAKE an effective dining room in any small space. A dining table and chairs are the only *real* essentials; other furniture can be dismissed entirely or minimized. Walls, windows and floors thus become vital elements in a small room, and should be used cleverly. Here are some ideas which could inspire you.

Wall and window treatments come to the fore in a small contemporary dining room. Room looks like the inside of a sleek wooden box, achieved by paneling. This adds richness to the room, counteracts minimum of furniture and lack of space. An unusual window-shade treatment above a collection of plants, adds both color and depth to the room, and shades are color-cued to carpet. Modern furniture is clean-lined without being austere. Decorator, William Pahlmann, A.I.D.

The close-up of the raised level dining-foyer shows how space problems were conquered by designer Andrew Delfino. A minimum of furniture was used — a see-through glass dining table and airy cane chairs. The furnished effect comes from the spectacular floor and door treatments which add drama and interest. The black and white floor is echoed in the doors which are covered in russet and white vinyl and outlined in black.

Small **foyer** with a domed ceiling became the eating area in an apartment without an actual dining room. Demarcation line between the foyer-dining area and sitting room was created by two narrow wooden columns, running floor to ceiling. Far wall of foyer was covered with mirror to give an illusion of space and to reflect the sitting room, not shown here. Designer Miriam Whelan, A.I.D., took the two basic colors of cream and orange used in the sitting room, and repeated them on table and chairs for continuity. Simplicity is the keynote with the crystal chandelier adding just the right touch of opulence.

This is a full view of the same room which is shown on preceding page. Note how paneled walls add richness, counteract space problems.

Many modern homes have one large room which must serve as sitting room, study **and dining room.** This kind of open floor plan makes for an exciting feeling of space—but presents problems when it comes to defining each separate area. And usually the dining area suffers because only a small space is allocated. The problem was solved in this elegant town house by building a raised level entrance hall which doubles as a dining room, and certainly demarcates it from the rest of the room. Here you see a long view of the dining-foyer from the study area. The idea is easy to adopt by building a wooden base, raised on blocks and covered with vinyl, carpet or tiles. Designed by Andrew Delfino, A.I.D.

This **extra-narrow** room was simply too confined to take the usual dining table, chairs and serving tables. The solution: a handsome peninsula which combines dining and serving, alleviates space and traffic problems. Made of walnut and white plastic laminate to match paneled walls and white vinyl floor, the peninsula houses cupboards in its base for dishes, glass and other tableware.

In the Country Manner

NOTHING SURPASSES THE RICH, yet unpretentious, comfort of a dining room in the *country manner*. It's easy to achieve even if you can't afford genuine antiques. Today there are excellent reproductions on sale which should inspire you to recreate this look with ease. You need: Early American, French provincial, or other period furniture; fabrics with a Colonial motif or a French toile; wallpaper with the same theme; and decorative objects such as pewter, copper, Bristol glass, pottery and old prints. The latter are also reproduced and often look as good as the genuine thing. If this is your style in comfort and decorating, don't be afraid to adopt it, even if you are a city dweller. The rural look sits well anywhere.

Early American flavor in this modern house was achieved through coordinated decorating. The shell of the room: simple white wallpaper patterned with a greenish-gold American Eagle, color-cued to window shade; stained wooden floor left bare except for green-blue plaid carpet which might easily be one of great grandmother's hooked rugs. Reproduction Early American furniture blends well; old clock and Delft plates on dresser add authentic touches.

French provincial atmosphere in this opulent-looking dining room is achieved through clever blending of furniture, fabrics, accessories and color scheme. Handsome French country furniture is reproduction, carved with a shell-leaf motif on table apron and repeated on china cabinet doors. Chicken-wire grille and lighted glass shelves of cabinet help to show off decorative objects; the buffet has a high, antiqued brass gallery. The black and white checked chairs complement the striped drapes and French grey walls. Wine-red of the carpet is repeated in table napkins, goblets, wall prints and other accents.

Brilliant blue and white wallpaper sets the background for a charming dining room in a fresh, **provincial manner.** Crisp organdy curtains and tile flooring create the light, airy look of the room, with soft wood tones of maple furniture adding a touch of warmth. Perfect for a small dining room is the decorative chest, used as a serving piece and as extra storage for linens and china. Reminiscent of Early American styling, the panels of chest are delicately decorated in folk art in green, yellow and red. Bright blue accents are repeated at window with painted molding and braided tape on bamboo blinds. Blue goblets and wall-hung lavabo carry out the color theme for a young-looking room with a French farmhouse atmosphere.

Country look in the modern manner: a combination of contemporary furniture and antique accessories gives this room its elegant yet rural flavor. The austere lines of the wall-hung cabinet are softened by the old china and painting. Chairs around the sleek dining table are painted bright red to match rug, and upholstered in the same fabric as the drapes. Finishing touches are the antique chandelier and wall lights. Wall-hung cabinet acts as a serving table, also contains hi-fi speakers plus ample storage space for china and other table accessories. Decorator is Paul Krauss, A.I.D.

This elegant dining room with a **seascape feeling** is the essence of good **contemporary** decorating. Color and textures have been carefully coordinated for a truly integrated look. Blue tiles on floor move up onto walls, while ceiling beams flow through from the sitting room. The highly practical yet attractive 20 foot wall-to-wall buffet in blue plastic laminate repeats color scheme, offers spacious storage and serving facilities, also has a topside panel which opens up on electric burners. Linen, china, candlesticks and sea shells follow the oceanic theme, as do the gold metal filigree fish dangling overhead. Designed by Camille Lehman, A.I.D.

This modern dining room owes its effective **ranch house look** to the rich brick and tile treatments on the walls and floors. The handsome mahogany furniture echoes the warm overtones of the room, while the modern tapestry, drapes and glass-fronted wall cupboard soften the plain brick walls. The floor and wall treatments are not only practical, but also offer endless possibilities for making changes with decorative accessories. In winter, the addition of white area rugs, candelabra and other artifacts dispenses with the cool, bare look of the room.

In the Contemporary Mood

CLEAN-CUT LINES, pure clear colors and an overall simplicity are your key ingredients in a *contemporary dining room*. This mood fits the pace of today's living, because it is both flexible and practical with its easy-to-move double-duty furniture, durable fabrics, stain-protected woods and synthetic materials covering many surfaces. To create this mood, walls and floors should have a smooth look, achieved by using vinyls, plastic laminates, wood, marble or tile; furniture should be sleek and simple. And remember, the contemporary look need not be cold and austere. Bright colors, gay accessories, books and pictures easily counteract this feeling.

Minimum of furniture was used in this dining room for an airy look. Comfortable cane-backed chairs follow the circular movement of the dining table which extends to suit dining needs. Unusual sideboard blends into wood-paneled walls for the smooth look. Touch of luxury comes in thick wall-to-wall carpeting, color-cued to chair upholstery. Plants, antique pottery vases and brass items bring added interest to paneled wall.

Simplicity reigns supreme in this small contemporary dining room. Furniture is sleek and light, yet has clearly defined lines. Sideboard and wall-hung cupboard do not obtrude, yet offer ample storage space; dining table is easy to move around on its castered legs, has hidden extension leaves to suit large family needs. Grasscloth walls, cane-backed chairs and unusual treatment of doors add decorative interest, also blend well together.

Traditional furniture and accessories have been combined with modern floor and wall coverings, for a practical, updated look here. Because both floors and walls echo the traditional feeling of the room in texture and design, none of the serenity of this gracious setting has been lost. The mood of the room, designed by Janet Reisner Traeger, N.S.I.D., is elegant and cool. Soft green and gold solid sheet vinyl wall covering in a Pompeii pattern sets the tone of the room. Coolness is continued in the green-on-white vinyl floor tile, and the handsome marble-topped server. The fine table and chairs and patterned area rug provide the warm tones of brown, bringing finishing touches to the room.

Antique dining table and handsome French armchairs create a **traditional mood** in this dining room. A modern vinyl floor looks like marble, adds to the traditional feeling yet remains immensely practical. The clean sweep of the floor helps throw the furniture into focus, while antique candelabra, shelves of prize china and old prints follow the traditional theme.

This opulent dining room personifies **traditional elegance.** The main design feature is the glazing of the walls, giving a marble look to the room, and th architectural detailing of the pilasters and cornice molding. A scheme of blue and gold brings continuity, adds to the rich feeling of the setting. Gold drapes and upholstery echo the golden hues of the carpet, while the pale blue silk tablecloth reflects the varying shades of light and dark blue walls. Darker blue tassels, edging drapes and swags, pick up the color of the pilasters. A crystal chandelier, candelabra and other fie accessories nhance the traditional mood of th room. Designed by Ellen Lehman McCluskey, F.A.I.D.

Three Dining Rooms that are Different

ANYTHING MIGHT INSPIRE you to create a dining room that is individually yours. An unusual color combination, a clever juxtaposition of fabrics and woods, a special piece of furniture, a collection of paintings or sculpture. If you feel like being different, don't be afraid of taking the plunge. A room that does not conform has many rewards, and makes for personalized dining and entertaining. The three unusual dining rooms illustrated here might give you incentive and inspiration.

Circular marble inset in the center of a wall-to-wall carpet is a novel innovation. It is both decorative and practical. Teak paneling on ceiling is repeated on walls and lined with black to echo black Oriental chest. Recessed alcoves on opposite wall are also lined with black and decorated with brass motifs for the same Far East feeling. Alcoves house antique blue and white china vases, while other similar pots are used for flowers and plants. Unusual window looks out onto a Japanese garden, which completes the Oriental feeling of this dining room, designed by Joseph Freitag, A.I.D.

You don't necessarily need genuine Oriental antiques for a **Far Eastern** look in a dining room. Ving Smith, A.I.D., created the look here in a highly individual dining room, with clever use of color, fabrics, wood, plants and a minimum of Oriental accessories. Paneled walls are covered in washable vinyl which looks like grasscloth. Travertine floor, sliding screen doors and low seat running under fireplace add to the Oriental flavor, as do plants, bird cage and Chinese wall scroll. Hanging lamp, hibachi in recessed fireplace and an old Chinese chest holding plants add authentic touches.

Vast expanses of marble and white stone create a pristine dining room in the home of architect Benjamin Gold, Jr. The raised marble platform looks out onto the sitting room, serves as a floor for dining table and chairs, and as a hearth for the Moorish effect fireplace and chimney. Concealed lighting in ceiling and a table candelabra offer adequate illumination. The beauty of this highly different room is its tranquil feeling of space and the play of the marble against white stone.

Table Settings

that enhance food, delight the eye

THE TABLE IS the focal point of your dining room. It holds the eyes of your family and guests throughout a meal. And so the disposition of silver, china, glass, linen, plus choice of colors, candelabra and floral arrangements are as vital as the choice of food you serve. A beautiful table flatters food and drink. The simplest meal can appear like a banquet if every detail is right. An ingenious or carefully set table, that has been thoroughly thought out, not only enhances your menu, but brings visual pleasure to your guests. Traditional and modern, formal, casual and buffet table settings are shown here. They illustrate clever use of colors, china, glass, linen, centerpieces, and floral arrangements, which all bring flair to your dining and entertaining.

A round table always brings a feeling of cozy intimacy to the most formal dining. This traditional setting of crystal and silver shows thoughtful planning—the hallmark of a good hostess. Each place setting has its individual pepper and salt, cigarettes, ashtray, matches and nut dish. Adapt this idea by using china or pottery accessories, if you prefer. The four tall candles surrounding the arrangement of fir cones, artificial fruit and flowers make an unusual centerpiece, and conserve space on the small table. The pretty organdy tablecloth makes an ideal backdrop for the sparkling silver and crystal.

Quality crystal, china and flatware are of primary importance in a **traditional** table setting. This elegant table, arranged for a formal dinner party, shows some fine old pieces combined with modern linen for an updated look. Bowl of roses and leaves sets the two-color theme of red and green. Moss-green linen tablecloth makes a solid yet muted background for the flowers, rose linen napkins, red candles and red-gold Fleur-de-Lys-patterned china. Gold-plated flatware and the crystal add sparkling finishing touches.

Clever color-cuing of glass, linen and flowers bring gaiety and a rustic charm to this table with a **Mexican flavor**. Flame-orange-pink striped ribosas (woven stoles) with ball fringe serve as table runners, replacing place mats. Napkins are matching red cotton squares with ball fringe. The rich red glassware echoes the linen, as do the fake flowers arranged in a brass bowl. A little license is taken with the inexpensive Japanese flatware, with the bamboo handles painted green to match the authentic Mexican chairs.

A modern table can be arranged with as much formal elegance as one of the more traditional settings. This long, narrow contemporary dining table has an austere beauty, is just as visually impressive as a more ornate arrangement. Black linen place mats and brown napkins blend well with the finely grained table top, teak place plates and teak flower bowl. China is white and brown, carrying on the two-tone color scheme. It is contemporary in shape and style, as is the silver. Arrangement of apples, magnolia leaves and white daisies is both different and decorative. It was placed at the far end of the slender table for effect and to save space, a good idea for long modern dining tables.

Simplicity is the keynote of this **traditional setting**, with the accent on the clean lines of the silver and glass, and the classic English china. A fine linen cloth, appliqued with a scroll design in the center, shows off these pieces to their best advantage. Silver bowl of flowers is in keeping with the understated theme of the table and was kept low to make for easy viewing across the table. Remember, a centerpiece should never obscure your guests from each other.

The Buffet

settings which inspire sparkling entertaining

BUFFET ENTERTAINING HAS become increasingly popular, and certainly it fits the tempo of today's pace. Many more people can be catered for at a buffet than at a "sit-down" meal; it is convenient and less restricting to the hostess; and it makes for a relaxed atmosphere and congeniality among guests. Use a buffet setting for both formal and casual parties, let some of these inspired table arrangements guide you in your buffet decor.

There is no mistaking the festive spirit of this Christmas party buffet. It has all the seasonal ingredients which have been arranged with considerable flair. Three broad pieces of red felt have been laid across the white felt tablecloth, to sectionalize the table into four quarters. Multi-colored glass candle holders are lined along red felt strips, add a "fairy light" effect and further demarcate section for coffee, drinks, plates and flatware, and after-dinner drinks. Fir tree twigs tied to Christmas tree baubles are the final decorative touches. Variations on this theme can be used effectively for children's parties, and throughout the year with different table linen and accessories.

This handsome round buffet table relies on its dramatic color scheme and beautiful silver for effect, is strictly winter season in feeling. A large, circular piece of red felt was used to cover the table, is floor length for the skirted look. The solid texture and coloring of the cloth makes a wonderful backdrop for the gleaming silver, white china and napkins. Red candles and red carnations, arranged in a garland around base of punch bowl, were color matched to the felt cloth for an integrated look.

Violets patterned on white and blue dinnerware set the color and decorative theme of this simple yet effective luncheon buffet. Bunches of real violets, echoing the dinnerware pattern, are used to decorate the table's centerpiece. This is an oval breadboard holding an antique butter churn and an assortment of appetizing cheeses. More violets peep out from behind an old wooden butter mold, used as a dish for walnuts, while a deep violet linen cloth and hyacinth napkins lend color harmony, along with the amethyst-tinted goblets.

Creative Centerpieces

A HIGHLY INDIVIDUAL centerpiece can be the talking point of your dinner table. Use imagination and flair to create a decorative theme that is different, whether it's with flowers, fruit, vegetables, candles or ornaments.

An antique **wooden bird cage** is the key to the flowers-and-birds theme of this formal table setting. The cage, used as a centerpiece, holds a beautiful china bird, has a butterfly perched on its roof. Two china ornaments, combining apple blossom branches and birds, flank each side of the cage. These ornaments in turn are flanked by two crystal candlesticks holding tall white candles. These were purposely kept simple and clean in line so as not to conflict with the ornate china pieces. China dinner plates, place mats and napkins are floral patterned, in keeping with the theme.

Strawberries and cream is the appetizing theme of this terrace table setting. Inspiration for the centerpiece and decorative theme of the luncheon table came from the linen cloth patterned with clusters of strawberries and daisies. An antique three-tier glass stand was lavishly filled with bunches of imitation strawberries and artificial daisies, repeating the pattern of the cloth. An extra white daisy was placed on each red napkin for final decorative touch.

Large chunks of **glossy black coal and multi-colored blown glass balls** in jewel tones are combined with sprigs of rhododendron and tall, slender tapers to make a centerpiece of rare beauty. Turquoise linen napkins, blue painted wood tabletop and blue and white plates echo the colors of the centerpiece balls and the tapers. Setting by Janice B. Gerton.

This elegant table with an autumn theme was laid buffet style for a **sit-down meal.** But the table arrangement works well either way. The rich setting, color keyed in autumn tones of orange, brown, yellow and red, features a raffia turkey surrounded by a display of bright-hued fall vegetables—all artificial here although real ones could be used. This imaginative centerpiece replaces the usual floral arrangement, gives the table a talking point. Contemporary dinner plates and dishes made of lightweight, long-lasting melamine were effectively combined with traditional silver, crystal and antique brass candlesticks. The result: a highly individual table with a traditional theme and an updated feeling. Designed by Janice B. Gerton.

Offbeat combinations can create a distinctive effect, when handled with flair. Here you see a **most unlikely mixture of vegetables and hothouse flowers** mingled together to make an elegant centerpiece for a round buffet table. A high mound of onions was built around five amber candle holders of varying lengths, and lavishly decorated with sprays of white and colored orchids. Sprays of white orchids were wound around the tall, center candle holder for the finishing touch.

CHAPTER EIGHT

The Living Room

✣

THIS ROOM IS usually the hub of the house, not only for family activities but for your entertaining. Whether your tastes run to traditional, modern or antique furniture, arranged in a formal or casual style, comfort is of primary importance. Along with furniture, wall and floor coverings and lighting are integral components in your comfort plans. Even if you are decorating your living room on a budget, you can still achieve the maximum of comfort through careful choice of the above ingredients.

Investigate all the newest products, such as vinyl or fiber carpets that wear well, resist staining and soiling; wallpapers and wall coverings that have been specially treated or plastic coated for long life and easy maintenance; the laminated plastics and hardboards that also wear well and long on all walls. Look at the latest in lighting products; pick out those items which will give you the best in convenience and comfort. Other ingredients that create both mood and comfort in your living room are fresh color schemes and clever furniture arrangements.

Certainly this central room of the home deserves to be outstanding in both appearance and livability, and some of the rooms illustrated in this chapter might inspire you in your decorating plans.

This colorful living room has a traditional colonial character plus sleek, modern practicality . . . achieved through the combination of 20th century materials with Americana accessories and reproduction colonial furniture. Wall panels are covered in forest green, wipe-clean vinyl, studded with brass tacks; same material, in red, is used to cover chest decorated with brass lock and hinges, which is used as coffee table and storage unit. Ceiling beams add architectural interest, help to give room an old-world air. Matching posts follow this theme, also separate living room from dining area, with their pull-down blinds. Shining brass accessories and Americana add finishing touches to this charming room where old and new easily blend. Designer: Edmund Motyka, A.I.D.

Handsome living room and lanai designed for a house in the Hawaiian Islands has the kind of traditional elegance plus comfort that easily transplants to any home, anywhere. Far East furniture and antiques have been combined with Western comforts—lush, shaggy carpeting, softly cushioned sofa and chairs. Subtle colors and texture contrasts are important elements in this room. The color scheme of the living room and **lanai** is an interplay of beige, white and off-white, with rich lacquer red accents in accessories, and the green of tropical plants. The shaggy texture of the carpet contrasts with the rough sandstone floor of the **lanai.** Texture is apparent, too, in the upholstery fabrics, in the large scale ceramic lamps, and in the hand-carved native art objects. Sliding Koa wood doors shut off the **lanai.** At the window, sheer white casements of dacron polyester fiber filter sunlight without being harmed by it. The quiet colors and restraint of this lovely room make it a perfect background for art and handcrafts, as well as a pleasant setting for relaxed living and entertaining. It also has long-lasting wearability. The beige and white carpet is made of hard-wearing nylon, with a deep, resilient pile; the low, black-lacquered sofa and chairs are upholstered in textured off-white fabrics styled with nylon for long wear and cleanability. Designers, Phyllis Spalding, A.I.D., and Jack Shea, A.I.D.

The best elements of contemporary decorating—style, comfort, practicality—are featured in this elegant living room, designed for modern living. The color scheme of gold, blue and white makes a cool, yet soft backdrop for the sleek black furniture and eclectic mixture of art, sculpture and accessories. The three black leather chairs on steel frames blend in line and color with the steel-frame sofa upholstered in smooth black tweed, and with the round coffee table. All are designed for comfort, long wear and easy care. The suspended feeling in the room is derived from the unusual, light-as-air staircase that seems to float upwards, furniture that scarcely touches the floor, hanging glass wall shelves and the high ceiling. Paneled wall, pottery, cushions, and other accents repeat the gold wall-to-wall nylon carpeting for an integrated look.

Open fireplace with a generous hearth and hood, set in a stone wall, inspired the country manor look here. Ceiling was beamed, floor tiled to echo this mood. Splashy upholstery fabric, zebra rug and antique chandelier add to the country atmosphere in this handsome living room designed by Janet Langerman, N.S.I.D.

The fireplace in a modern home is sometimes too small and dull. Here you see a living room which underwent a character change when the fireplace was remodeled. Rough-hewn stone was used to surround the fireplace for added importance and a traditional look. The stone dado effect at once dispensed with the flat, sterile feeling of the contemporary living room, and inspired the owners to decorate in a more traditional style. However, furniture was chosen with care so as not to conflict with the modern architecture. Pieces with clean lines, wall-to-wall carpeting and understated accessories were used to this effect. The result: a modern home with the traditional comfort and elegance the owners wanted.

Although a fireplace always remains the most natural focal point of any room, furniture does not necessarily have to be arranged in a cluster around the hearth—particularly in a very large room which can look abandoned in parts if furniture is concentrated around fireplace. Space was cleverly utilized in this sumptuous living room, by spreading out pieces in a calculated pattern. The large circular rug helped to create the pattern. Two king-size sofas and three chairs are ranged around the edge, while an antique glass table under a low-hanging lamp introduce themselves as the focal point of the conversation area. Because of its size and prominence, the huge fireplace still remains the dominant factor in the room, even though furniture was arranged away from its immediate vicinity. When a change of feeling is needed, chairs can be swiveled round and sofas moved closer in towards the fireplace. Designed by Erica Lemle, A.I.D.

A Fireplace Creates a Mood

IF YOU ARE lucky enough to have a fireplace in your living room, many of your decorating problems are simplified. The fireplace is the focal point, or point of departure if you like, in your furnishing scheme. It pulls a room together, and at once suggests a flow and pattern for your floor plans and furniture arrangements. Its shape and size could inspire your style of decorating, choice of fabrics and flooring, even color scheme. Since time immemorial, the fireplace has been the hub of the house, offering a feeling of welcoming warmth. It also creates a mood of luxury and comfort. Whether your fireplace is traditional or modern, take advantage of its assets. Here are four rooms where the fireplace has inspired both mood and decor.

ch teak paneling and a fire-ace create warmth in a high-linged, contemporary living om, which otherwise might ve looked cold and uninviting. ite splines balance low fire-ace, and wall was kept starkly nple and undecorated to give tra emphasis to fireplace. Lotion of soaring window and all jog created a natural conrsation area around fireplace. ight red sofas, Persian rug, ustrian blinds and antique chest end well with contemporary eling of room, bring just the ght extra touches of elegance.

Contemporary Living Rooms

where the accent is on color

DON'T MAKE THE mistake of putting contemporary rooms into the "colorless" pigeonhole. Certainly a room furnished on contemporary lines relies on uncluttered, often stark, simplicity, but this does not mean it has to be drab and monotone. Vivid color is just as important in the modern room as it is in the traditional room. Here are vastly different contemporary living rooms where color was combined with sleek furniture for a highly individual look. You might adapt some ideas shown on these two pages if contemporary decorating is your favorite and, particularly, if your living room is small.

This tiny living room was given new, airy dimensions with delicately mixed pastel shades and tailored furniture. Basic color scheme is apple-green and white with flashes of gold repeated throughout as the accent color. The pastel tones give the room a feeling of space, light and integration, while the close-to-the-floor sofa, chairs and coffee table add an illusion of height to walls and ceiling. Storage wall gives the room an interesting focal point, contains stereo set, bar, books and objects of art.

A small room can take the maximum of furniture, provided pieces are well matched in design, scale and color. Accessories must also blend for the unified look. Here sofa and chairs are strictly tailored with clean, contemporary lines; upholstery fabrics are color toned in varying shades of greens. Coffee and lamp tables, bench and chair frames are all of matching oil-finished walnut. Orange, green and brown patterned drapes echo the basic autumnal color plan, as do lamps, pictures and area rug.

Masses of white and two walls of solid orange create the rich sunny feeling in this Los Angeles apartment. Catherine Armstrong, A.I.D., designed the living room to suit the tempo and weather of California. White looks good in the sun, but too much creates a glare. The orange walls deaden this effect, at the same time throw the white into focus. An unusual grille at the window helps filter the strong sun, adds decorative interest. White wall-to-wall carpet and long white sofas give the room continuity and flow, make it seem larger than it is. The handsome living room has its practical side; custom-made couches are covered in easy-to-clean vinyl. Coffee tables have laminated plastic tops.

Rich Contemporary

*a designer revamped the shell of a modern
living room, created two major focal points
and a feeling of glowing warmth*

Designer Leif Pedersen, N.S.I.D., created a rich look in a contemporary living room by cleverly manipulating such diverse materials as plain red brick, ebonized wood, sailcloth and velvet. Because the room was squared-off and dull, with no true focal point, the designer built a brick fireplace and chimney piece, covered the two flanking walls with bricks for continuity. Window wall was also brought into focus and defined by the addition of sturdy timbers. These were carried along the ceiling as beams to continue the flow and as a base for the concealed lighting. Stained ebony to match the floor, the timbers give the drapes an unusual framed look. The same sailcloth fabric used for the drapes was mounted on the adjoining wall, sets the room's color scheme of olive-green, orange and black. These three colors are repeated in the black leather chair, olive velvet sofa, and orange and black patterned Afghanistan carpet. Flashes of yellow in the velvet chair, red lamp and matching cushions add the finishing touches.

Uncluttered Contemporary

two rooms which emphasize this look

Space and airiness are personified in this contemporary home, which has an open floor plan. A minimum of understated furniture was used in the living room to give extra emphasis to the height and light created by the high ceiling and huge window expanse. Sofa and chairs are the best in modern design, sleek and softly rounded without any sharp, hard angles; ·coffee and lamp tables follow this same pattern, are left uncluttered for the look now synonymous with contemporary design. The result: a room of simplicity and elegance with the maximum comfort and tranquility.

Walls and floor seem to flow into each other, here. Both have been left bare to show off their individual patterns of polished tile and wood grains and to help create an illusion of space. The two long couches and coffee table have clean, tailored lines in keeping with the uncluttered concept of the living room. Designed by Erica Lemle, A.I.D.

Mixing and Matching
Old and New, Real and Fake

for updated, formal elegance

HERE ARE TWO living rooms where genuine and reproduction antiques have
been mingled with contemporary pieces and the newest synthetic wall and
floor coverings. The result is a look of formal elegance with the accent on
comfort, visual beauty and updated practicality. Floors, walls and upholstery
materials simulate the opulent textures usually associated with period furnishings—marble, silk, leather. Yet all are man-made 20th century wonders, easy
to clean, hard wearing and long lasting. This blending of the old and the new,
the real and the fake only works well if furniture lines, woods, furnishing materials, accessories and color schemes are truly related to each other and mixed
and matched with skill.

This charming living room is a perfect example of clever mixing and matching. Walls owe their silky texture to white vinyl fabric wall covering, while opulent marble floor is really made of veined vinyl floor covering squared-off with turquoise strips for a decorative effect. All furniture is French reproduction, except for clean-cut contemporary sofa in foreground. This blends easily with the French sofa because their basic lines do not clash, and because both have been upholstered in white matching vinyl. Reproduction chair and bench are covered in a mustard shade of the same material for texture integration. Lamp bases are traditional in feeling, topped with contemporary shades. Pottery pineapples and crystal cigarette boxes and lighters are traditional, paintings contemporary. In the background, an antique blackamoor holds a potted plant, and a handsome crystal chandelier glitters in the dining alcove. Designer Robert Hanley, A.I.D.

Close-up of foyer and dining alcove of the Los Angeles apartment designed by Robert Hanley, A.I.D. Hanging plants, and a trellis screen covering a mirrored wall, create a fresh garden look. So do wooden chairs, painted turquoise to match floor motif, and upholstered in lime–yellow vinyl to match skirted tablecloth of vinyl. Beautiful chandelier, suspended low over table, adds just the right touch of elegance, while the two antique blackamoors carrying plants enhance the bower-like effect of foyer and dining alcove.

133

This living room designed by Miriam Whelan, A.I.D., shows the clever blending of antique and modern furniture and the newest wall, floor and upholstery materials. The antique sofa mixes easily with the buttoned, contemporary couch and rounded chairs because all are covered in vinyl upholstery fabrics; sofas in cream, two chairs in orange. Walls are lined with the same cream material, floor looks like marble, is really streaked vinyl. The high Oriental screen is a perfect foil for the straight lines of the modern couch, while rounded chairs seem to follow the curvacious movement of the antique sofa. The result is a truly integrated room of balance and clarity.

This long-range view of the living room designed by Miriam Whelan, A.I.D., was taken further back, from the chess corner. It shows coordination of color, textures and furniture styles for harmony and a tranquil look.

Elegance Plus Comfort

THESE THREE LIVING rooms, all decorated by designer J. Frederic Lohman, A.I.D., N.S.I.D., emphasize cool elegance combined with comfort. They are supremely livable. Each one shows clever use of fabrics, wall and floor coverings, blended with carefully chosen pieces which were selected to harmonize with the setting. His overall color schemes are subtle and subdued, with the accent colors adding warmth. He is ingenious with mirrors, accessories and art, uses them with flair.

Blue-tinted mirror runs the whole length of the fireplace wall right into the window. The clever juxtapositioning of glass and mirror brings a feeling of light and space to this small living room, creates an illusion of infinite depth. Ebony-stained floor makes an effective backdrop for white carpet, orange **art nouveau** print used for upholstery, and the antique furniture from the William and Mary period.

Shell of this living room is dramatic gold and black, specifically designed to show off the beautiful Chinese antiques and paintings. Floor is stained ebony, walls covered in gold silk paper, ceiling in gold tea-paper. Sofa and chairs are upholstered in muted gold fabrics, with bright splashes of orange acting as the accent color.

Dark, antiqued mirror runs the length of one wall, makes an unusual background for three beautiful, old Chinese paintings. These appear to have been set in the center of the mirrored wall itself, have actually been suspended on fine wire from the ceiling. Overall color scheme of orange, beige and taupe sits well against a white vinyl floor.

Conversation Corners and Furniture Arrangements

SKILLFUL ARRANGEMENT OF furniture is vital in all rooms—particularly in the living room where a family relaxes, and spends the most time. Chairs, sofas, tables and lamps need to be strategically placed for comfort, easy conversation, entertaining, and traffic. These different living rooms show conversation corners and other furniture groupings. Remember your floor plans when grouping and arranging furniture. It is much easier to do it on paper first, which saves time and energy.

This loose group of furniture has plenty of traffic lanes, yet is skillfully arranged so that conversation is easy. Sleek modern sofa sits well under window, doesn't obstruct comings and goings, yet remains part of the setting. Small antique cupboard next to sofa serves as an occasional table for an ashtray or drink. Second sofa and two chairs face each other in a companionable arrangement with two coffee tables within easy reach. **Other traffic paths** skirt edge of white area rug, while wall shelves were cleverly lined up to accommodate piano. Designer Elsie May Gross, A.I.D., has a contemporary way with color and decor that gives this living room a warm elegance in the modern manner. Unusual window shades contribute textural interest in a novel "up-and-down" installation, beige draw-curtains frame the whole.

Window wall with its colorful shades becomes a gay backdrop for this well-planned conversation area in a large living room. Long sofa covered in a muted fabric is flanked by two side tables with ample surfaces and two comfortable chairs. These are upholstered in same material as shades for texture and color integration. Traffic lanes are flexible, as chairs can easily be moved around on tiled floor. Decorator Erica Lemle, N.S.I.D.

Sofa and matching chairs are graciously arranged around a fireplace, in this country living room, for a traditional conversation corner. Table heights are matched for balance, and lamp is strategically placed for reading or sewing. Although this is a cozy grouping, plenty of room has been left between all pieces of furniture for traffic. A moss-green carpet underlines the striking black and white furniture upholstery, while rich brown drapes match wood tones in the room.

This unusual wood-paneled room with a novel, curved ceiling easily lends itself to an ingenious furniture arrangement. Identical sofas sit end-to-end on a raised platform, are flanked by two tables of butternut plywood matched to wall and ceiling paneling. Modern glass table on a stainless steel base services both sofas, is small enough to leave plenty of space for movement between the two. Because this living room is small, other furniture was kept to a minimum. Wall-hung shelves are decorative, also leave floor area free. Final touches are the pieces of modern art and the diffused overhead lighting. Designer Evelyn Jablow, A.I.D.

137

You can create two different areas of interest in one room without losing the look of formal elegance and integration. In this huge country living room you can see how a study-work corner has been effectively coordinated with the conversation-entertaining area. This was achieved by carefully matching styles of furniture and fabrics. Legs on the desk follow the lines of the legs on the two side tables and armchairs; needlepoint cushion on the bench echoes the pattern of the sofa upholstery. The two areas are linked by the rich wall-to-wall carpeting, and the blending of woods. The end result is a traditional room which has comfort, elegance and is also practical.

This Early Georgian living room styled in the fashion of an Irish country manor proves that antiques can be elegantly blended with modern man-made materials. Mahogany furniture is reproduction Chippendale set in a shell of emerald-green vinyl on the walls, nylon carpeting on the floor. Even the linen upholstery fabric on sofa and chairs is really vinyl, custom-embroidered with white field daisies for a handmade look. Designer Richard Himmel, A.I.D.

Piano, fireplace, lavish crystal chandelier and rich colors create a truly graceful effect in this country living room, designed by Ving Smith, A.I.D., and Charlotte Smith. The designers used an Oriental rug, an old painting, books and other antique accessories to echo the 18th century mood of elegance and refinement. But they added a dash of 20th century practicality by covering walls with beige vinyl wall fabric, chair and chest in red vinyl upholstery fabric. Walls have the texture of slubbed silk, are infinitely more serviceable because they are hard wearing and clean with a damp sponge. Club chair and chest are equally as hard wearing, upholstered in rich red. The result: a room with all the mannerisms of traditional elegance and a streak of updated practicality.

In this living room by Bill Leonard, N.S.I.D., emphasis is on balance and integration, with furniture matched and arranged for a strictly formal look. Yet the austerity of the traditional grouping has been softened by the two sofas which add a feeling of comfort and intimacy. Wall of tailored drapes, antique chairs and pedestal occasional table offset the bulk of the double sofas, while a wall of mirrors creates a two-dimensional effect in the room.

A bedroom in a modern home can be furnished in period style and look just as effective as it would in a Colonial mansion. And often a room of average dimensions can acquire new proportions through skillful choice of furniture, fabrics, wallpaper and accessories. Here, a beautiful French imported wallpaper has been used to create an air of formality in a Southern style period bedroom of a modern house. The wallpaper lends architectural interest and height to the average-sized room; it also sets the delicate spring color scheme of leaf-green, magnolia-white and daffodil-yellow, repeated in carpet, bedspread, drapes over bed, chaise and bench. Traditional furniture, in styles of many periods and in a variety of painted and wood finishes, has been successfully used together. The key is their similarity in scale, mood and finish; the result is a striking room which offers both tranquility and comfort, essentials in any bedroom. Designers Lucille Morgan, A.I.D., and Clyde Pruitt, A.I.D. Incidentally, all fabrics and carpet are made from modern fibers, are easy to clean and care for, can be used and enjoyed without kid-glove treatment.

CHAPTER NINE

Beautiful Bedrooms

that work night and day

To be successful a bedroom should please you twenty-four hours a day. It should not only be a restful place to sleep but an inner sanctum where you can escape during the day for an hour of quiet and solitude—to read, write letters or simply relax. It should also be the kind of room where the door *can* be left open during waking hours—in other words, an integral part of the total decor of your home.

Colors, lighting and materials used on floor, walls, for drapes, bedspread and upholstery are vital ingredients in the bedroom decorating scheme. All help to create a mood of tranquility, comfort and relaxation.

The bedrooms illustrated in this chapter range from contemporary and clean-cut to traditional and dramatic, but always the emphasis is on comfort through the day to sleeping hours. Planning is just as important here as in any other room of the house. Work out your ideas on graph paper first, before buying furniture. The bed is the essential piece of furniture followed by night tables, chests of drawers, a dressing table, storage units if closet space is limited.

If you are lucky enough to have ample storage cupboards in other parts of the home, you can dispense with them in the bedroom and leave more space for a small sofa or chaise. The same applies to a vanity or dressing table which can sometimes be fitted into the bathroom. Creating a comfortable *sitting-room-corner* in your bedroom is simple: you need a comfortable chair or chaise, a writing table or a desk, a lamp and pretty accessories like a bowl of flowers, a painting, *objets d'art* and family photographs.

Carpeting on the floor is the most obvious way to create a feeling of luxury and comfort, but some of the new vinyls, cork or plain varnished wood can be just as effective. Rich fabrics, brilliantly colored or pastel pretty, underscore the mood of indolent harmony as does lighting. Subdued, concealed lights and small lamps are the most effective in a bedroom. They should never be harsh, and should always be strategically placed for reading in bed or in a chair, or for working at the writing desk.

Distinctive Bedrooms

Antique bedroom in the Spanish manner where brilliant use of high voltage colors creates the dramatic effect. **Don't** be afraid to use strong colors in a bedroom; **do** make sure they are cleverly keyed to each other. Boldly patterned bedspread is custom-made, has matching drapes. Bolster and window valance are of a textured fabric in solid red; table cover is a bright gold felt; wall behind cathedral headboard (a Spanish import) is covered in burlap, color and texture matched to casement curtains. The red painted chairs echo the key color, while lazyback pillows in red and citron repeat the red-gold theme of the room. Linking the whole scheme is the shaggy textured dull gold carpet.

This bedroom has an easy elegance and a feeling of the Victorian era. It is full of good ideas to adapt such as many sided mirrored screen, old sofa used as a novel bedback, high standing bookcase holding TV and glass objects. The essentially sunny, airy feeling in the room is achieved through use of gold fabrics on walls and bed, gleaming vinyl floor, organdy curtains at window. Free-standing mirrored screen also adds to the illusion of space and light, with its many sided reflections.

Contemporary bedroom has an Early American look. Brass fourposter bed is strictly modern, yet has an old-fashioned air with its fresh white drapes, and blue and white "Dutch tile" fabric used for spread, bolster and bedback. Breakfast china and old pottery jars on bedside table echo the fabric. Dark blue walls and red felt table cover add splashes of color, while mirror behind bed makes room seem larger than it is.

Simplicity is the keynote here, with Oriental overtones adding interest. Because bedroom was very small, a minimum of furniture was used—just bed, side table and a chair not shown in picture. Everything was kept low and decorative objects were carefully placed, Japanese fashion, to show them off to their best advantage. Color scheme is a subtle variation of the earth family with pristine white acting as the accent color. Play of textures is important, too, in a room with little furniture. Ribbed spread, rattan headboard and carpet sit well against rough plaster wall.

Headboards and Bedbacks

are important in your bedroom decor;
they can be decorative, functional or both

HEADBOARDS AND BEDBACKS give the simplest rooms a more furnished look. They can be useful storage units and shelves, simply decorative or both. Style, materials used and scale are of prime importance. Your bedback *must* be in keeping with the general look of the room, the material used *must* blend with the total decor and the size and scale of the bedback *must* be perfectly balanced with the bed. If it is too small or too large it will look out of place.

This bed is framed by an ingenious birch-wood structure that combines twin night tables, bookshelf and hidden lights. Laminated plastic sheathes the night tables, is practical and easy to clean. Posts go through tabletops to make a shelf notched below for an alarm clock, tiny radio or night creams. The construction is simple, the look modern. Designed by Russel Wright.

Twin beds are united by a giant headboard which keeps radio, phone and intercom within easy reach. Night tables with matching lamps balance the headboard; small window, plants and pictures **add** to the decorative effect. The tailored spreads and chairs give the room a sleek look, **add** to its sitting room air. Incidentally, this is a basement room converted: attractive asphalt tile went down on the floor because it wears well over concrete subfloors.

A gay little canopy that's just for fun is made from material that matches the quilted spread. It creates a dramatic effect in this small bedroom with practically no effort. The canopy slips over a metal frame supported by brackets that screw into wall.

The entire wall behind this bed has been treated in an unusual and decorative way. Strongly grained wood planks cover the basic wall area. The metal grille controls light from the window it conceals; the gay Austrian shade above the plants masks another awkwardly placed window. The long narrow shelf unites all the visual elements and has a multitude of uses, while the hanging lamps do their job without taking any space at all.

If you can't afford an elaborate bedback or headboard, a pretty curtain hung from ceiling and falling behind the bed is the answer. Try to integrate it into the room, as shown here; printed sheer ninon was used for the sill-length curtains across the window wall, repeated for ceiling to floor panel behind bed to substitute for headboard, and taken down onto floor as dust ruffle round bed base. Panel behind bed is hung on a curtain rod which rests on small wall hooks. Bedroom designed by John and Earline Brice.

148

Bedrooms to Relax In

*create a quiet corner in your bedroom, where you can relax in solitude,
read, dash off a note to a friend or simply daydream.
Today a bedroom seems incomplete if it can't double as a sitting room*

A fireplace is the most natural focal point, even in a bedroom. One can always be built and, even if it is only mock, it will bring a sense of luxury to the room. In this bedroom designed by Ving Smith, A.I.D., it is real, of course, and adds an air of both comfort and elegance. At the same time, the soft glow from the logs makes the pale pink walls look like slubbed silk, and not the practical vinyl wall covering which they are. Among the room's additional features: arched wall panels repeating the window motif, comfortable chaise and other seating arrangements, decorative accessories. The room's "split personality" is created by the two steps which make a natural break, divide it into bedroom and sitting room.

This bedroom is a study, too, and its two functions blend as beautifully as the modern wall furniture combines with heavy antique pieces. Pale yellow and off-white walls and floor are a cool background for multicolored books, decorative objects, brightly patterned fabrics and darkly gleaming wood.

This generous room has space for everything—a sunny reading corner, a separate desk area, as well as the king-size bed. Decorating materials are rich but handled with simplicity. Glowing cherry plywood paneling, deep blue carpeting and a strong, color-keyed print are used abundantly. Almost nothing else appears, aside from personal accessories. The total effect is a bed-sitting room of comfort, informality and spaciousness. French country furniture is in mellow fruitwoods; paneling in adjoining bath and dressing room is finished with a clear plastic which protects against steam and splash. Room designed by Marvin Culbreth, A.I.D., N.S.I.D.

Bring a Touch of Flair to Your Bedroom

combine unusual colors, brilliant fabrics, diverse textures for a striking effect

The art of combining unusual things is strikingly exemplified in this handsome bedroom. The mood created by the sharply intersecting rectangular shapes and the scarcity of clutter is distinctly modern, yet the printed fabric that hides built-in closets is from an 18th century design; the bed is covered in antique satin; chair, lamp and clock are antiques and bed table is an old campaign chest. Behind the bed, a wall of dark brown cork travertine is contrasted with a melon-colored rug which continues from floor to wall to supply an exciting color accent and texture contrast. Designed by Daren Pierce, A.I.D.

This cool, sophisticated color scheme is built around a luxurious quilted spread. Sharp lime walls, amethyst carpet, dark green headboard, drapes and tablecloth, and a pale blue chair repeat the colors in the spread; throw pillows in a hot medley of related shades also echo the theme. The result: a bedroom with texture and color coordination and a best-dressed look.

This sophisticated bedroom borrows much from the Far East for its striking look. The raised platform, shiki silk spread and drapes and grasscloth wallpaper all combine for a Western version of the Oriental boudoir. Panel painting, bamboo plant, antique gold lamp and floor cushions add other authentic Eastern touches.

Exotic shades of melon and avocado are boldly
used to create a luxurious bedroom. Tufted
headboard, quilted spread, well-stuffed pillows
and chaise incite reclining; heavy drapes and
pleated shade further emphasize the suppleness
of the silky fabrics used throughout this room.

**Blue roses bloom, in tight profusion on a quilted
spread** and, in airy abundance on coordinated
drapes in this bedroom furnished in a traditional manner. More blue appears on boudoir
chairs and in the peacock-and-olive carpet,
and white walls and accessories make for a
well-balanced whole. Clever placement of mirrors behind lamps makes room appear larger.

Spring-green is the springboard for this fresh-looking room. Mixed with a little yellow, lots of white and a dash of tangerine, the effect is lighthearted. The trellis headboard, dappled green rug and wallpaper enhance the bower-like feeling. Practical note: window-housed air conditioners are camouflaged and current-controlled by three layers of cafe curtains, staggered so that the screening panel can be opened or closed at will. Further checking flow of air are braid trimmed shutters which can be angled towards bed for screened-off privacy. Designer Paul Krauss, A.I.D.

All the key elements of modern planning are emphasized in this luxury bathroom that serves as a dressing room. Harmony prevails. Not only in the unusual and restful color scheme of blue, beige, brown and lilac, but in the ingenious placement of fixtures and lighting. The well separated washbasins serve two people, and the ample storage unit runs length of one wall, holds his and her toiletries, linen, towels and turns into a seating arrangement near tub. Use of textures comes to the fore here—shaggy carpeting, mottled tile, and smooth grained wood. The change of levels is dramatic, an architectural element not often found in bathrooms. But it can be adopted if you are making two rooms into one, or modernizing a large, old-fashioned bathroom. Other bright ideas to note: wide striped wallpaper over tub, wooden slatted window shades, camp stools, floor cushions, use of plants, decorative accessories and linens. Finishing touch is the subdued, partly concealed lighting used in ceiling and in strips flanking mirror.

CHAPTER TEN

The Updated Bathroom

*looks to the past for inspiration—
yet its primary elements are clever planning,
luxury materials, coordinated color schemes,
slick storage, decorative hardware, stunning accessories*

THE REVOLUTION IN this most functional room of the home started when women decided they wanted a bathroom they could enjoy and not simply use. Mindful of this, manufacturers of bathroom equipment introduced a selection of products which help turn this hygienic room into a place of comfort and beauty. Today's updated bathroom has not only taken a step forward and become the ultimate in planning and streamlined efficiency, but also a step backward to the days of the Romans and true bathing luxury. Uniquely shaped tubs, sunken baths, decorated washbasins, decorative faucets and hardware, as well as ceramics, terrazzo, marble, tiles all combine for the lush look in bathing. In this chapter almost every kind of bathroom is illustrated, many of them inspired by the past, all of them full of good ideas. There are bathrooms which two can comfortably share, boudoir bathrooms, dressing room bathrooms, or simply bathrooms to relax in and enjoy.

Planning

LIKE THE KITCHEN, the bathroom must be cleverly planned. An architect, designer or plumber will of course guide you on the correct arrangement of tub, shower, basins and lavatory. But nevertheless, it's a good idea to work out your own ideas on paper first. Consider that each bathroom unit must not obstruct traffic lanes, particularly if the bathroom is shared by two. Hard-fact storage planning is important, and cupboards should have plenty of room for towels and linen, and clothes if bath doubles as a dressing room. Surfaces are important, and plenty of top space should be left for cosmetics, brushes and other toiletries. Lighting is an essential part of planning here: lights should be bright enough for shaving and make-up, pinpointed over mirrors if possible. Yet the overall bathroom lighting must not be harsh, but should suffuse the room in a soft glow that adds to the comfort.

Floors and Walls

NEVER BEFORE HAVE we had so many products to line the shell of the bathroom. Marble, ceramic tile, terrazzo tile, or quarry tile can easily go onto both floors and walls for that integrated, lavish feeling. Excellent vinyl products, often simulating marble or tiling, are equally as effective, hard wearing, resistant to water and moisture, and of course less expensive than tile or marble to install on floors. Vinyl can hit the walls too, for a zingy look, while many wallpapers are specially coated to withstand steam and damp. If you prefer carpeted luxury in your bathroom, then look to some of the new vinyl or fiber carpets that won't spoil with spills and splashes. Nylon carpet is another ideal flooring, and is very practical, easy to care for and wash. Some of the plastic-finished or laminated hardboards, suggested for kitchen walls, look good in bathrooms, and, again, are hard wearing and easy to maintain.

If your bathroom is small, and opens off the master bedroom, tie in the decorating and color scheme with the bedroom for an integrated feeling. Mirrors help to push out walls in the smaller room, can be used to line walls and doors for real effectiveness. Bathrooms with glass doors opening onto a garden or small patio also have the luxury look.

This pretty bathroom is not only the height of feminine luxury but the essence of skillful planning. Tub and shower are carefully placed at opposite sides of room, separated by double basins, and specifically designed to make this room work for two people. Uncluttered floor and walls, hinged three-way mirror and lighted glass shelves over basins add to the feeling of roominess. Design details are the tent-like ceiling canopy, the period furniture and cabinets in the same mood. Deft control of scale is important here: delicate flower print of fabric balances differing floor, wall and counter tiles. Designed by Ellen Lehman McCluskey, F.A.I.D.

This bathroom has all the elements of a dressing room, combines both comfort and practicality. All surfaces are easy to keep clean, including carpet, while washbasin unit acts as a dressing table, also offer plenty of storage space. Bamboo furniture, exotic colors, lush plants, shells, wall mural and starfish bath hardware combine to create a gay South Sea Island atmosphere. Chaise and carpet add touches of luxury. Designer Ving Smith, A.I.D.

Bathrooms to Relax in, With the Emphasis on Comfort

This **HIS AND HERS** bath-dressing room is spacious, convenient and ingeniously planned. **SHE** gets her own basin, set in a roomy dressing table, theater-style make-up lights and a full-length mirror. **HE** gets his own sink, just the right height for shaving, his own individual mirror, and a cabinet for his toiletries and linen. **BOTH** get the benefit of closet space where it's most useful, a sun couch, ample and well-planned storage cabinets. Cork floor and all other surfaces are waterproof and easy to clean. Sunny color scheme of orange and yellow, unusual wall covering and decorative accessories make this a happy room to relax in.

Brilliant color and bold Oriental motifs give this bathroom drama and importance. Chinese window design is repeated on couch (fabric) which also holds storage drawers underneath. Black and white offset the strong red, while gold hardware and plumbing fixtures and wallpaper add to the sumptuous feeling. Bath is white to match basins and other fixtures.

The Shape's the Thing

unusual baths for the individualist

The **height** of luxury — a **sunken** bath made of richly-grained marble. Cool, understated blues are played against each other here, on walls, floor and at window, with effective results. Silver bath accessories complete the sense of casual elegance, white overall tiling is both pretty and practical.

A corner tub creates a refreshingly different bathroom. Here it leaves enough extra space to tuck in a statue, on its own glassed-in ledge, for decorative purposes. Matching wood paneled cabinets and walls and carpeting are other short cuts to elegance in the bath.

This unique bathroom is built around a custom-designed shower-bath which boasts its own comfortable seats right in the bath, a skylight and lush vegetation. Every bit as gracious as the bedroom it adjoins, the room is lavishly faced with marble on floor, counters and walls. Sea shells, seahorses and deepwater plants appear in bas-relief on the far wall and the fixtures are fanciful sea monsters.

Boudoir Bathrooms

*planning, skillful decorating and attention to detail make
these rooms dual-purpose. They are practical and good-looking,
and provide both bathing and dressing facilities
without detracting from the luxury look*

This "best dressed" bathroom was planned as carefully as a living room. It serves a variety of needs, and its visual effect is flawless and stunning—golden in spirit as well as color scheme. Design details are: classic pillars flanking the bath; marble-like floor with a custom-designed look; white painted motifs on cabinets following the floor pattern; unusual gilded wallpaper; crystal lighting fixtures; gilt cherubs and other "golden" decorative accessories. The sunny color combination of mustard, primrose and ochre is emphasized by the touches of gold and the contrasting soft grey used on cabinets and bathroom wall. The room itself was skillfully divided by the wooden half partition covered in gilded wallpaper; it creates two distinct atmospheres in the room yet does not detract from spaciousness. Wall cabinets flanking dressing table offer ample storage. Close-up on next page shows dressing area in detail.

Crisp colors and smooth surfaces create a trim, tailored bathroom, here. The rich autumn shades and wood tones are brightened by gleaming white fixtures in this small but well-planned room. Sliding doors can close off toilet. Down-lights illuminating a little counter, half partition and a bamboo chair help to transform a corner into a dressing room. The rattan shade adds texture interest. Designer Ving Smith, A.I.D.

Gilded wallpaper is carried over from partition to highlight dressing table wall, flanked by neutral toned cabinets. A distinctive mirror, wired for modern make-up lights, and a handsome old phone complete the corner. Designed by Betty Cavallon, A.I.D.

*Clever wall and floor treatments, plus gay accessories, create a
decorated look*

A variety of colors and patterns are united by their common material—TILE. Here a large and comfortable bathroom is kept functional and easy to clean, yet has great visual interest. Glazed ceramic tile used is also long wearing and highly durable, ideal for large family bathrooms such as this. Designed by Robert M. Schroyer, A.I.D., S.I.

Modern wallpapers are specially treated to withstand steam and damp and can be used successfully in bath-rooms. They help to give a decorated look to the room, add both color and charm. Here wallpaper and shower curtain are matched for coordination. Their hot-pink and white shades are completed by the deep sea-blue floor and streaked marble counter top, with pinks again echoed in the towels. Using the same pattern throughout gives an illusion of height and depth.

Close-up on Detail

*the newest decorated plumbing,
elegant hardware, vivid towels and accessories
bring a touch of gaiety to the bathroom*

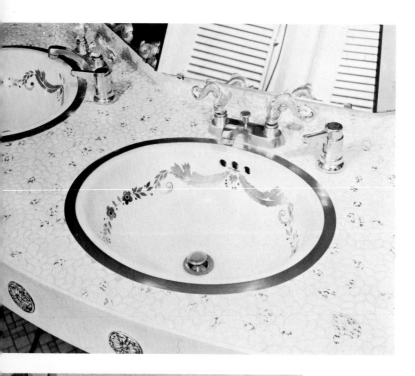

Gilded sea creatures transform mere faucets into objects to be admired. Here they are paired with a gold decorated washbasin set in a pebble-textured counter; they bring real elegance to any bathroom.

The delicate colors in this fresh-as-violets ensemble are restful and feminine. Porcelain fixtures have been cleverly matched to washbasin. Wallpaper and towels follow the same violet theme for true coordination; counter top is of soft green.

If towels help to bring out a color scheme, display them effectively on a decorative towel rack. Here, a three-tiered brass fitment, built in style of a hatstand, adds an air of luxury to a small bathroom, as do the other brass accessories.

This opulent bathroom is not as unattainable as it seems since it is the product of 20th century planning. It is cleverly built into a recess in the wall and an adjoining recess holds washbasin and mirror. The intricately laid "marble" covering walls, closet doors and floor, is actually vinyl, easy to care for yet splendid in effect. Use of fine furniture, lamps, drapes and other lavish accessories helps to echo the room's grand manner. Closets behind chaise and along flanking wall hold clothes and linen.

Plants, floral towels and other pretty accessories are used decoratively here. They help dispel cold look in large room. Unusual cabinet not only solves storage problem, but breaks up wall expanse. It holds towels and accessories as well as a super-sized medicine cabinet.

169

Alice in Wonderland nursery for two little girls personifies the best in juvenile decor. Any little girl would be entranced to have such a pretty room—which grows as the child grows. Window alcove creates a compact sleeping area, leaves rest of room open for play and "girlish entertaining." Twin beds on the bunk theme save space during waking hours; bottom bed simply pulls out for daytime seating and play, for sleep at night. Pink and white color scheme is repeated throughout, from floral wallpaper to tufted bedspreads and painted furniture. Floor is a pretty pebbled vinyl, hard wearing and stain-proof, easy to keep looking good.

CHAPTER ELEVEN

Nurseries and Children's Rooms

Make them grow with the child

How FAST DOES your baby grow? Any parent will answer "too fast," and this applies to the practical side as well as the emotional, for too soon has baby outgrown those frilly dresses and the crib. Clothes can always be handed down to a younger brother or sister, but a room must *grow with the child*— and it often becomes a room shared by two. Decorating a child's room can be great fun and, with a little imagination and some of the newest products, tiny tots can have rooms that are not only pretty but very practical.

If planned with care, a room can be transformed from nursery to toddler's room right up to a teen-age hideout with a minimum of work and expense. Other than the crib, most of the furniture from your youngster's first room can be retained. A few extra pieces of furniture, a new color on the walls, a pretty area rug and some fresh, imaginative accessories and the room grows with the child. When planning your baby's room, it is important to concentrate on keeping it simple and easy to clean for hygienic reasons as well as your own work schedule. Choose chests with washable vinyl or plastic coated tops. Paint the walls in a bright color that will appeal to baby, and from which his tiny finger marks can be whisked away with a damp sponge. Most important of all, put down a hard-wearing, easy-to-clean vinyl floor. Curtains should be light and airy with a simple shade to dim the room when baby takes a nap. Select a few bright and colorful cutouts from fabric or wallpaper to decorate the main wall of the nursery. These or handy decals can also be used to decorate furniture, lamps or window shades. Overall, the room must be accident proof. Avoid chests, tables, chairs or bookshelves which can easily be tipped or pushed over; remove area rugs, when baby starts to walk, to avoid falls; place lamps out of reach.

In this chapter are some practical, yet inviting, nurseries and children's rooms, most of them designed to look ahead during the child's growing years. There are also nurseries full of good ideas to adapt, rooms that double up or split in two, rooms for little girls and little boys of all ages.

Nurseries that Look Ahead

A NURSERY SHOULD be decorated so that it grows with the child. You should be able to make overnight changes as the baby grows day by day. Furniture should be carefully chosen, with an eye to the future. Chests, cupboards, floor and wall coverings should be designed to wear through infancy to school age; the crib should be the only piece needing replacement. Floor and wall coverings should be chosen with wearability in mind. They should be child-proof and able to take plenty of wear and tear.

Brick and wood-paneled walls and vinyl floor are not only "child-proof" and hard wearing, but specifically designed to age with baby. Handsome chests match the crib, but will go equally as well with a bed when crib is defunct. In fact, manufacturers of this Nantucket reproduction furniture make a bed which identically matches chest. Walls, shutters and door are easily freshened or changed with a coat of different colored paint, should they become finger marked or scratched. Small area rug is folded away to curtail accidents as child grows to play-age.

Here the shell of the room is decorated to "grow." Wallpaper is not too babyish, yet is juvenile in spirit. Rug is gay, will take any furniture in any age group. Chests, wall shelves, small table and stools all do double-duty through infancy up; only piece that needs changing is the crib, as baby outgrows it.

The nursery can be sophisticated, clean-lined, modern, if that is the look you like. This child's furniture ensemble is adult in styling; except for the crib it need never become obsolete. Crisp floor stripes, echoed in the window shades, and modern lighting, further emphasize the room's uncluttered good taste. Designed by Paul McCobb.

This nursery is not only pretty but practical too. Gay hearts-and-flowers wall covering is of a wipe-clean vinyl; wicker crib and chair are washable; floor is simply repainted when scuff marks appear; area rug is of washable nylon. Easy to handle, inexpensive felt covers shelves, crib canopy and chair cushions, is more practical for a growing child than some of the sheerer fabrics. Coral and pale pink wall covering sets the color scheme of the room; shocking pink felt blends happily with the paler shades, is accented by white furniture and rug, and royal blue floor. With the addition of a bed, in place of crib, nursery services a growing girl. Designer John Elmo, A.I.D.

Bright surroundings keep baby cheerful. In this simply furnished nursery imaginative accessories come to the fore—smiling rug, wall cutouts and mobile hanging near window. Vinyl floor, washable furniture and sponge-clean, painted wall are practical and hygienic. Window chest and other furniture (not seen in picture) is all designed to service child through the growing years.

Nurseries Full of Good Ideas

This sleekly modern nursery is full of bright ideas you can adapt for yourself. Sleep area is lushly carpeted, while rest of floor is covered in practical vinyl for playtimes. Wall shelves above chest are ideal for books, toys and other decorative objects, some low enough for child to reach, higher ones to store more fragile possessions. Painted furniture is washable, also sets room's color scheme of pastel shades. Pint-sized table easily adapts to larger chairs as child grows, only obsolete pieces are crib and baby chairs.

This room for a happy child is a colorful answer for mothers who want easy cleaning without an antiseptic look, and some "do-it-yourself" projects. Designed by Lawrence Peabody, A.I.D., the room is in deep gold, soft yellow and orange, sparked by bright blue. Neither wax crayons nor fingerpaints can damage the walls of scrubbable satinesque vinyl wall covering. Panels in stipple satinesque at the back of the room are gradations of the color scheme. The vinyl wall covering is repeated on small wastepaper baskets turned upside down for play stools, which are topped by "do-it-yourself" vinyl cushions. Large floor cushions are also made of this washable, easy to sew upholstery vinyl. **Because** wall covering is so **long-lived**, a subtle color scheme was used, so that it can be artfully changed as child grows. By removing washable orange cotton fabric on screen, which shields the crib from drafts, an entirely new color scheme can be evolved. Walnut furniture has a grown-up look, and serves child many years; crib is simply replaced by a junior bed. Even the warm gold rug, put down in modular strips, sees long service, and can be tossed into washing machine for cleaning. For the man of the family, the practical play table, which doubles as a toy chest, can be a simple workshop project. Made of lightweight wood, covered in oilcloth which can be wiped for cleanliness, the box is on casters, is easy for child to push around. Graduated wall shelves store toys and objects, while five hanging lamps add a decorative look to far wall and have special controls which dim or brighten lights. **Final decor idea: the bright paper flowers pinned to wall covering.**

little and big

A room like this makes a little lady feel important. The scheme begins with the deep coral-colored vinyl used in shades, chair and cushion covering. Same color appears in round, decorative rug. A distinctive print fabric in coordinated colors has been used with ingenuity. It forms a shirred valance all around top of walls, and is extended out over bed as a canopy (upper right corner). The same material is used for curtains, bed cushions and also trims base of spread. A creamy, white shell makes a good backdrop for the bright splashes of color. Furniture is grown-up but also child-proof. Storage unit acts as dressing table, desk and bed table, while chest under window holds toys. Designer Liane Zimbler, A.I.D.

Bookcases and a ceiling valance create a frame for twin beds on the window wall of this dainty bedroom for two little girls. Scheme for room is planned around this frame and the perennial color favorites of pink and blue. The frilly, feminine spreads are covered with pom-poms; the same fabric is used along homemade ceiling cornice and for lampshades and cushions. Each girl has her own storage chest topped with toy shelves. These and the other furniture were all inexpensive, unpainted pieces. Books are covered with vinyl jackets for color coordination and easy cleaning. The gay patterned pull-down shade repeats the color scheme, adds sparkle. Pink rugs at foot of each bed complete the picture.

Rooms for Boys

little and big

This handsome room for a little boy combines fine furniture with practical materials. Walls are covered with washable vinyl, emphasized by nail tacks. Two elegant little armchairs pull up to a modern, **bang-and-scratch-proof** table. The plush carpet is nyon. Well-chosen accessories and the warm color scheme help create the rich yet masculine effect.

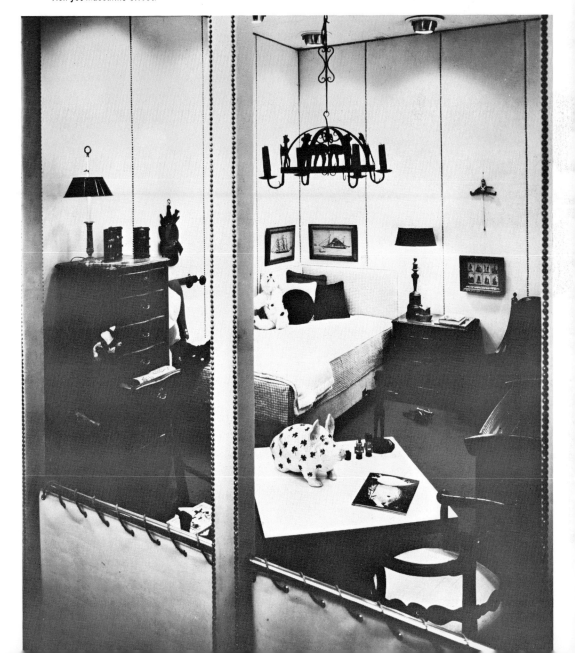

Wall-to-wall carpeting and storage units that are easy to handle are the talking points here. Because little children spend most of their waking hours on the floor, a carpet that is easy to clean (nylon), cushions bumps, protects against drafts, is gaily patterned to hide spots and delight the childish eye, is unbeatable. This rich nylon carpeting serves these purposes, makes a vivid splash in a room of natural wood and blue painted walls. Toys displayed on open shelves provide the only decoration needed, while plants behind pull-down shades create a garden look. Other storage is provided in sliding drawer beneath the bed and in painted boxes under bookcase. Designed by Tom Woods, A.I.D.

Doubling Up

*make one room serve two children, conquer space problems with
built-in furniture, dividers, hidden storage units*

Small room was made to service two boys through clever planning. Bunk beds solve part of space problem. These two are strictly tailored and masculine, can be unstacked and used as two separate beds when necessary. The built-in wall cubbyhole keeps model boats and other breakables safe. Bulky toys and blankets are stored in pull-out drawers under bottom bed; even desk has its storage corner. Richly textured wall covering keeps to the tailored feeling of the room, is both distinctive and easy to clean; color scheme of gold and white, with a splash of red adds to feeling of total integration and illusion of space.

Here double bunk beds solve both sleeping and space problems in a bedroom-den designed for two young boys to share. Ladder makes access to upper bunk easy; hinged shelf attached to bedback serves as a desk, also conserves space. Olefin fiber carpet on the floor can stand up to any game of "rough house." When decorating a boy's room, it's wise to remember a carpeted room is a safe room. Besides being so durable, fiber carpet is highly dirt resistant and most messy spills can be sponged away in a flash. The menagerie on the wall was created from pieces of carpeting left over after installation—a fun project for a rainy day.

Split A Room

*two highly individual atmospheres were created
in a medium-sized room, divided ingeniously for a boy and girl.
Skillful decorating and attention to detail
gave each area its own personality as well as privacy*

One room, divided into two highly personalized "looks," makes for happy coexistence between brother and sister. The dividing wall, entirely covered with easy-care laminated plastic, begins with a bank of chests which open in alternate directions. Chests turn into tables along back wall. Louvered panel above chests in dividing wall can be opened or left closed. The same efficient layout is used on both sides but individualized decorating and color schemes have achieved entirely different results.

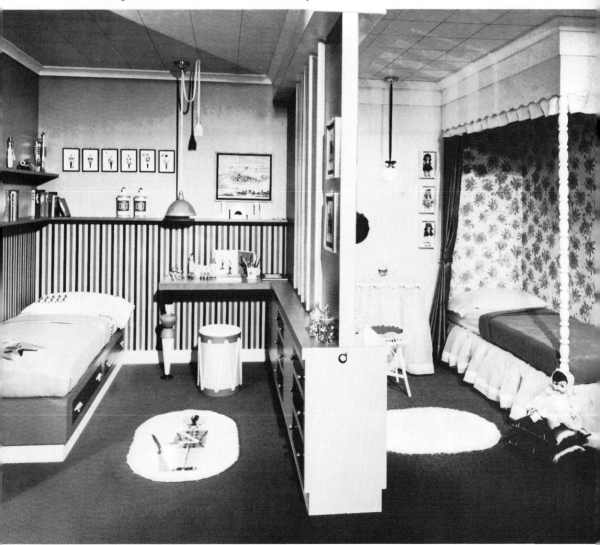

Rigid adherence to the red, blue and gold theme spiced with white, and dedicated use of a military theme, create a room that is well-unified, orderly, in minimum of space. Chests in dividing wall, drawers under bed, wall shelves and hanging lamps are all space savers, and bright red wall-to-wall carpeting seems to stretch floor area. Drum stool, novel table leg, area rug and bed linen add to the room's special military flavor.

The little girl's side of the divided room is completely different in style and concept. A fresh color scheme of green, yellow and white has been cleverly coordinated to control space problems. A built-in bed canopy is the perfect excuse for adding romantic curtains, ruffles, pom-poms and a frilled cover on bed base. The floral wall covering has been wisely restricted to bed alcove; pale, solid colors do a better job of unifying and enlarging area. Hanging lamps, mirror and curtain on shelf help create a feminine dressing table corner. Storage cabinets are concealed behind base frill on bed and dressing table curtains. Collection of dolls, dainty accessories, and use of delicate fabrics contribute to the feminine look.

CHAPTER TWELVE

Teen-Age Rooms

*built-in furniture, resilient materials, hard-wearing
fabrics, lively color schemes and ingenious planning
come to the fore in rooms for the younger set.*

TEEN-AGE LIVING in the middle of a family can pose many problems, particularly if overall space in the home is small. Yet all teen-agers want some au-
tonomy and a room of their own in which to pursue their activities, study and
entertain friends in a genial atmosphere. The solution to this is to furnish a
teen-ager's bedroom as a studio, bed-sitting room or den-bedroom that works
during the day and serves these purposes. Planning is just as important here
as in other rooms, particularly if the space available is limited. Built-in
units, and double-duty furniture particularly, come to the fore in teen-age
rooms. For instance, a studio bed works as a sofa during the day, looks even
better if it is fitted into an alcove; wall-hung shelves and cabinets hold books,
accessories, hi-fi and TV, also supply base storage. Some of these units even
have a drop-leaf desk top which serves as a counter top for snacks. Walls can
easily be utilized, either hung with the units described above, or lined with
cork which acts as a marvelous giant-sized bulletin board for teen-age para-

A teen-ager's sprawling, colorful possessions enliven any room, but sensible planning should come first to
ensure good looks and comfort. To save space this bed was placed in an alcove, paneled in rich wood for
a handsome French Provincial look. Shelves hold plants and pottery, while back wall makes a perfect backdrop for other decorative accessories. Because room was small, delicately scaled print was picked to cover
walls and the armchair. Its muted shades do not compete with the bright blue bedspread or the lesser
color bursts of decorative paraphernalia. Rolled blankets, fastened with belts, make novel bolsters. Carpet
and all the fabrics are durable, easy to clean and care for.

phernalia. The shell of the room needs special attention, and both walls and floors should be lined with materials that are extremely hard wearing. If carpeting is preferred, there are the latest nylon, fiber and vinyl carpets that take all the scuffs, spills, and traffic of teen-age living. Vinyl tiles and wood also make ideal floors; leather tiles, plastic-finished hardboard, wood paneling, laminated plastic, vinyl-coated fabrics and specially finished wallpapers make hardy wall coverings. Decorating a teen-age room can be fun for all concerned. Once the shell of the room and the basic furniture have been planned, let the teen-age occupant of the room add the finishing touches. Imaginative teen-agers often have specific notions of what they want and ingenious ways of displaying their possessions.

This charming room is ideal for a studious youngster who is every bit a female. Versatile wall-hung furniture system provides bookshelves, bureau, ample storage and a drop-leaf table that doubles as desk, or dining table should she want to entertain friends in private. Imaginative use of a colorful print fabric transforms bed wall into a cozy alcove, with curtains and valance. Window shutters and rich carpet further enhance the aura of grown-up planning. A small space handled wisely yields delightful results, as illustrated here. Designer Paul Krauss, A.I.D.

Two brothers can coexist happily in this colorful and eminently practical room. There is plenty of room for books, sporting equipment and other prized possessions. They can be stored away in the deep drawers beneath the built-in bunk beds, kept in easy reach on the wide shelves, or displayed on the cork wall. Contemporary window shades made from a yellow and orange abstract print eliminate the need for fussy curtains, set the room's color scheme. Same fabric is used for bed cushions. Desks and chests are also built-in to save floor space, while large cubes act as stools, open up for storage purposes. Practical vinyl floor in black and white spatter pattern echoes the cork wall.

This clever scheme lets two young ladies lead "private lives" within the confines of one room, of average size. The room was designed by Paul Krauss, A.I.D., who fastens a hinged screen to the back wall, to divide the area into separate quarters. Illuminating the setting with gay fabrics, he makes the room divider by filling wooden frames with back-to-back layers of textured cloth, creating reverse color schemes for each section. In one half, bright geranium is used for the facing fabric panels, upholstered headboard and scatter rug; in the other, vivid tangerine dominates the key elements. Color inspiration for the room is drawn from the gay print fabric covering the entire back wall and drawers of a white painted chest, which also lend a look of unity to the room when folding screen is pushed back. White wall, floor, spreads and paintwork cool the hot shades; painting and contemporary accessories repeat the key colors in the room.

Here are some more good decorating ideas with girlish ways, which are easy to do yourself. This soft and sweet teen-ager's room takes its cues from a delicate gingham checked wallpaper, over-patterned with flower-seed packets. Matching plain gingham paper covers easy-to-build lambrequin, which dispenses with need for heavy drapes. Collection of old chests and a Victorian swing mirror were revitalized with Prussian blue paint, stacked along one wall to form a practical storage-desk-dressing-table unit. Stain-free counter tops match creamy white bed, table and kitchen chair which were also freshened and unified with new paint. Olive-green carpet and throw cushion add color contrast, in this room with a country air. Unrelated pieces of discarded furniture can be used successfully together, if painted one color, as shown here.

This handsome room with a nautical flavor was designed for a teen-age boy who wanted his own "bed-den" to entertain friends, follow his many hobbies. Cleverly built-in furniture offers plenty of storage, hi-fi, and spot for TV set, and studio couch works as a bed at night. By centralizing shelves and cupboards along one wall, floor area is left free and spacious; desk becomes a counter for snacks. Most important, the handsome wall paneling, cabinets and desk can be constructed by the young man himself. Pre-finished plywood paneling makes it easier than it looks. Plastic laminated counter tops are easy to keep shipshape, make a pristine contrast against rich wood grain. Sea-green rug and bookshelves, plus naval accessories complete the nautical look, in room any young man would be proud to occupy.

Teen-Age Bed-Sitting Rooms

most people like a place to call their own,
where they can entertain friends, read and relax in peace.
These two rooms are full of good ideas,
solve some of the problems of teen-age living in the midst of a household

Masculinity is the keynote of this simple room, decorated for a studious boy who also wants to entertain on his own. Room is compact and well planned. The bed, filled with corner cushions, doubles as a couch. Storage cabinet utilizes space often wasted above bureau; desk and chair (foreground) can be moved at will, should a group of friends gather. Louvered doors, rugged fabrics, vinyl tiled floor assure hard wear, while autumnal tones of wallpaper, bedspread and other furniture contribute to the male look of the room.

Simple lines and bright, gay colors set the mood for a happy combination of bed-sitting room for an active teen-age girl. Space-saving day bed and neat arrangement of furniture allow for entertaining friends in an uncluttered atmosphere. Walnut sweetheart chest serves dual purpose, doubling as window seat, as well as storage space. Bright accents of red, orange and yellow sit well with the warm, walnut tones of furniture and black corduroy bedspread and draperies. Wicker chairs and tile flooring create a crisp, clean-cut look with sparkling notes of color added in red and fuschia checkerboard rug, gay toss pillows and whimsical accessories. Roomy storage shelves, strategically hung contemporary lamps complete the picture.

Tailored for the Sports Addict

THESE TWO BEDROOMS are slanted towards the tastes of teen-age boys, active in sporting pursuits. Bold colors, strong fabrics, strict lines all blend well, denote the masculine look young men like. Sporting equipment has been successfully incorporated into the overall decor, for a feeling of identity and ownership.

A corner arrangement of beds is a great space saver in a rather small room shared by two brothers. Table under window and between beds holds two-sided lamp, takes up little room, services both boys. Because of space problems, furniture was kept to a minimum, walls utilized to display and "store" sporting equipment. The bulletin boards hold underwater mask and flippers, baseball glove and ball; other items are securely held by screw-in wall hooks. (Boards are easy to adapt by simply thumbtacking felt or thick paper onto any ordinary bulletin board for this effect.) Curtain and spreads in man-sized plaid of blue and green on white looks good against apple-green walls; orange pillows add a "hot" spark to this "cool" room, and the hide rug on polished floor reiterates the sporting theme.

Blues and greens are good colors to use in vigorous, boyish rooms. And striped and plaid fabrics add lively interest, are agreeably unfussy for young men. Here this combination has been used cleverly, to create an integrated look and an illusion of space in a small attic room. Handsome fabric used for bedspread and drapes suggested the colors for both walls, carpet and painted chair. Warm wood tones of the other strictly masculine furniture compliment the coolness of the scheme. The small "schoolboy" desk fits into a compact corner, holds a surprising amount; contemporary wall lamp adjusts to any position, takes up no desk space; straw basket makes the perfect container for oar, fishing rod, other sporting things. Gay wall prints blend well with eagle bedside lamp and the reproduction Early American furniture.

Femininity Plus

SHEER FABRICS, DELICATE colors, pretty accessories, frills and flounces delight every teen-age girl. These bedrooms are pretty and practical, designed to delight the eye and for easy maintenance.

Pink roses bloom all over the bed, and even hang from the walls in this bower-like room. White painted furniture, delicately decorated with gold, is a further touch of femininity; and the bed boasts a miniscule canopy in the fashion of a fourposter. Chair seat and window sill are covered in matching pink fabric. Spring green walls, sheer curtains, pearly tinted vinyl floor complete the fresh, romantic picture in a room designed for **easy maintenance.**

Nothing is more romantic than an old-fashioned fourposter bed—here covered with a pretty print that matches the bedspread and drapes. The frilled dust ruffle sits well under the quilted spread, is color-fabric toned to the cafe curtains. Window treatment is carried down to the floor, to enhance the Colonial look created by Early American reproduction furniture. Canopy takes off easily, for quick laundering with drapes and spread, while carpeting is of hard-wearing, easy-clean nylon fiber.

CHAPTER THIRTEEN

Dens and Studies

A DEN OR study used to be a rare luxury, particularly in the small apartment or house. Today, with modern materials and skillful planning, anyone can have a study—even if it's only a tranquil corner in the living room. In this chapter is a selection of dens and studies that illustrate this point, all of them decorated by well-known designers. Each one is different, slanted towards the particular needs of the individual. What are your needs? Do you want a full-fledged "office" in the home, a highly contemporary writing room, a cozy den or a study corner? You will find plenty of ideas to help you on the following pages. And remember an attic, a store-room, an alcove, a bay window, or a space between wall jogs can all be successfully transformed into a personal retreat, through inspired decorating.

Even the smallest space can be turned into a library-study, when that space is used imaginatively. Here the window corner of a room was successfully transformed into a den area by designer Ving Smith, A.I.D. An alcove was given shelves and a handsome curtain, becomes the focal point of activity in the corner. Shelves hold not only books, but art objects, a small television and a dictating machine. Because wall space was at a minimum, the designer placed one picture on the bookshelves, another on a window stand that catches the afternoon light. Everything is within easy reach, for the occupant of the armchair, who also has the benefit of excellent reading light coming in at the window. The elegant brassbound desk is lit by an antique lamp, ceiling-hung to give more surface space to the owner's bibelots. The study's rich, comfortable look is derived from the intricate interplay of textures and materials: leopard-patterned rug, parquet floor, smooth, brilliant colored chair, deeply pleated drapes, gold-wrought book bindings and picture frame. The pale "wood" paneling is actually a vinyl wall covering.

An Office in the Home

An office at home can have the efficiency of the one, plus the comfort of the other. Here, a small spare room was converted into comfortable office-retreat. An unusual fireplace, fine furniture, plants and other cheerful accessories make this room pleasant to be in; the big desk, ample bookshelves and almost invisible wall cupboards ensure its convenience. Wall-to-wall carpeting of a red-green-gold tweed adds luxury, is a colorful foil for the natural wood desk, beige walls and tweed furniture. The built-in storage shelves were painted red to repeat the carpet's accent color. Designer Tom Woods, A.I.D.

When space is valuable, a wall system that combines files, cabinets, drawers, bookshelves and room for gay accessories, is the perfect solution. Here you see how a tiny room, previously used for storage, was cleverly transformed into an office within the home, by using such a piece. The wall system centralizes and compartments office "clutter," has two adequate desk tops attached. Modern chairs, and an additional desk are slim and sleek, fit easily into the small area. The result is a room where three members of the family can work or study in their individual corners. Wall system is not a permanent fixture, simply dismantles should tenants relocate.

The most unlikely space can be transformed into an office. This attractive, light work corner in a country home was once an ugly porch. By adding windows and an extra wall, the porch became a new room attached to the house. All of the architectural features, even to the balustrade, were retained to create its unique atmosphere. Thick, white wall-to-wall carpeting gives a feeling of warm luxury set against the brick wall and windows, makes an effective backdrop for the well-chosen pieces of reproduction furniture. A Hatfield hunt table, once the gentleman's social table that graced the fireside in English country manors, performs beautifully as an unusual desk. It has drop-leaves, a removable half-round center, and an additional leaf. The Farthingale wing chair and straight chair, both with ladder-backs, match the mood of the office, as does the Hudson washbasin stand, used here to hold a dictionary and hide clutter. Rough wooden shelves, antique accessories and an assortment of plants add to the atmosphere of the room.

Study Corners

A DESK, CHAIR and a few bookshelves are all you need to create a study within a living room. The addition of these pieces not only gives you a quiet corner to work in, but often adds to the decorative appeal of the room. Choose pieces of furniture carefully, so that they blend with the total look of the room. If you are a book lover or collector, find a small space to display your pretty possessions. They too will add character to the room, give it a personal touch that is strictly your own.

A country French feeling was achieved in the corner of this room. Desk, lamp, chairs, picture and handsome fabrics blend well togther for an old world feeling. The Louis XV painted and distressed desk is nicely proportioned, is in the same antique green as the lamp shade. Color contrast is provided by the cheerful red cane-back chair, and the bold red and white antique print used for upholstered chair. Handsome lamp dominating the desk, is Directoire Period inspired, has graceful golden trumpet arms which support white candlesticks.

Style is apparent everywhere in this elegant study corner. The fine old furniture is not only elegant but convenient; the cabinet desk is extremely roomy, and the bookcase is the perfect place for displaying art objects as well as storing books. The distinctive carpet is in keeping with the understated feeling of the decor, as are the crystal desk accessories, painting and sculpture.

In this compact study corner old and new are combined boldly, with fresh results. An old antiqued table makes a good-sized desk, modern leather chair ensures comfort. Wall-hung, contemporary shelves are within easy reach of the desk, also save space, blend easily with old accessories. Hanging lamps are strategically placed, also save desk space.

Furniture chosen for the study corner can easily set the decorative theme of the total room. This close-up shot of the tranquil study area in a spacious living room, shows how antiques, modern flooring and unusual accessories were cleverly combined for a French Provincial look. This look was repeated throughout the rest of the room, with elegant results. The unique, crescent-shaped desk is the talking point, and actually inspired the rest of the decor. Its slender, airy lines give emphasis to the ornately carved antique chair, as well as to the twin footstools. The wall shelves are strictly modern, yet they blend easily with the mood of the room. They hold all manner of both useful and decorative things, have been imaginatively planned to frame and emphasize works of art. Finishing touch is the onyx vinyl floor, which simulates its marble counterpart. The flooring of white, amber and green sets the room's color scheme: amber-toned walls repeat the amber bands of the squared vinyl for a golden glow, with red cushions and green plants adding a fillip of color. Designer Rhoda Bright, A.I.D.

Celebrity Dens

The dens on the following pages were designed for two well-known men—former New York Giant football star Andy Robustelli, and writer-broadcaster Walter Cronkite. Although the rooms are totally different in style and concept, each reflects the personality and special interests of the man himself. The rooms illustrated offer lots of ideas, if you are decorating a den for the man in your life. Remember to stick to strong, masculine fabrics, colors he likes; give him plenty of space for trophies, trinkets and the memorabilia he cherishes. In fact make it his own, very special room.

In this colorful, well-planned den, Mary Davis Gillies proves that catering to the male ego can be an exciting excursion into a world of bold color, rugged texture, and strictly masculine interests. The "trophy room" she designed for Andy Robustelli, former New York Giant football star, combines imagination and originality with solid he-man comfort and practicality. Most important, there is a special place for all the assorted miscellanea and memorabilia men hold dear—the kind that too often winds up in a mess of messy clutter. For Mr. Robustelli's den, Mrs. Gillies has created a striking storage wall with provision for books, stereo, trophies, award plaques, footballs, vintage sporting prints, and newspaper clippings. An adjacent fabric-covered wall becomes an attractive showcase for an asymmetrical arrangement of autographed photos, a lucky horseshoe, and the initial "R."

The lively colors and rugged textures that bespeak a masculine presence in this versatile den-study-guest room are contributed by nubby, woven upholstery fabrics that cover the hide-a-bed and sofa wall, and also fashion a series of window shades on opposite wall. Made of nylon, these fabrics possess gridiron strength, easy maintenance virtues, the look and feel of fine hopsacking. The bright, earthy tones, reminiscent of football in the Fall, create excitement in the room. A rich, tomato-red fabric with a wide, black-flecked stripe covers the sofa bed; same fabric in a solid tone is used on the wall, punctuated by floor-to-ceiling battens painted to match the deep charcoal-brown of the built-in storage wall. The fabric is repeated a third time, on the window wall in the series of shades, with floor-to-ceiling divider strips echoing the paneled effect of the sofa wall.

Underfoot, a looped-pile nylon carpet provides additional texture interest, in a tweedy mixture of brown, gray and white tones that does not show soil. The furniture is simple, strong and well-designed, with warm wood tones that mesh perfectly with the brown-orange-red color scheme. Braid trimmed sofa pillows restate these colors, plus a bright green accent note. The latter is repeated in foliage plants and small table accessories.

A man's study, if elegantly decorated, can be a room PLUS. Not only a place to work and relax in, surrounded by very personal things, but a comfortable den in which to entertain friends. This charming room, designed for newsman Walter Cronkite by Virginia Conner Moseley, A.I.D., illustrates this concept beautifully. It is a mellow blending of contemporary fabrics and traditional furniture. All the 18th century reproduction pieces are upholstered in a modern vinyl fabric, hard wearing and highly practical, yet with the appearance of the rich leather men favor around them. The same vinyl fabric, silk-screened in a porphyry pattern, is repeated on the ceiling and echoes the rich coral chair in the foreground. The bookcases and walls offer an unusual combination of texture and print. Chocolate-brown leather on bookcases is really vinyl, and walls are covered with a coral vinyl printed with black and gold for a marbled look. The rich color scheme of coral, brown and mocha is livened by the luxurious cream tufted carpet and white brick fireplace wall. The bookcases flanking fireplace hold precious pottery ornaments, leather-bound books, and are illuminated by two brass lamps with pristine white shades; vinyl-covered panels along sofa wall create a frame for caricatures, photographs and other memorabilia, plus shelf for other objects. Total effect is masculine yet intimate.

Another angle on Walter Cronkite's study-den, this time the working end of it. Long wall of louvered shutters meets a mirror-covered wall; the resulting corner has an intricate interplay of light and repeated patterns, strong but restrained in effect. Large plants provide an interesting cluster of other random shapes in this austere but far from forbidding work corner. Eighteenth century desk is flanked by two straight chairs, upholstered in dark green vinyl to match lamp shade and leather inlay on desk top. Polished wood floor is really rosewood vinyl. Finishing touches are the antique globe, subdued overhead contemporary lights in ceiling.

This ultramodern writing room is the contemporary version of the study-den, and illustrates a new concept in modern living. Twentieth century man-made materials are used throughout, for a lavish and coordinated look, as well as wearability. The big writing table for instance, is covered in mustard vinyl that has a fine writing surface and cannot be scratched or dented. The unusual shaped niches in the rosewood paneled wall are lined in brilliantly colored vinyl too, make a striking showplace for a collection of exotic artifacts. The woven screens at the far end of the room are color coordinated to the niches. Travertine fireplace and handcrafted floor tiles are additional touches of luxury. The gentle curves of the antique French chairs blend well with the clean-cut, modern shell of the room. Vinyl wall covering is combined with rosewood paneling on walls and ceiling, while spotlights in niches and ceiling add finishing touches. Designed by C. A. Korkowski, A.I.D., and Gene Adcock, A.I.D.

This second writing room has a definitely feminine air, is incorporated into a split-level room with an unusual circular dining area on a raised dais. The writing room was designed by Milton Glaser, F.A.I.D., to fit into a traditionally styled home. The silk-screened vinyl print which appears on the lounge chair, ottoman and wall panels is taken from an original old design. It blends beautifully with the graceful furniture in Louis XIV style. Other furniture pieces of this same period are done in fruitwood, upholstered in mauve and green-gold vinyl; vinyl floor is laid in hexagonal tiles, again with a white background echoing the walls. The dramatic raised dining area is outlined with an antiqued wrought-iron railing and side draperies of mauve silk. The mirrored walls in this area give an optical illusion of a full-size room. Writing area of the split-level doubles as a small sitting room for after-dinner drinks.

A Den He Can Relax In

THESE TWO DENS were designed for **his** comfort and ease. Wood paneled walls, textured floors, skin rugs, smooth surfaces, bold colors and fabrics all have a masculine quality, make a man feel at home. You can easily create a luxurious little den in a small space, by using fine materials, a few exotic accessories, lots of imagination. But remember, decorate **his** den to suit his tastes and personality, otherwise he will feel ill at ease in it.

The conversation pit works well in a den, where casual comfort is the thing that matters most. This very masculine room makes use of some bold new ideas. The fire-engine-red, see-through fireplace hanging in mid-air is surely an attention getter. So is the blatantly fake zebra-patterned chair resting on a real zebra skin rug. The picture gallery seen through the hanging fireplace wall lends color and interest to a room which could either be a **bachelor's paradise** or a **pampered husband's personal retreat**. Sleek white sofa covered in vinyl echoes raised white floors, makes a perfect background for multicolored cushions. The parquet floor in the conversation pit blends with wall panels of wood patterned vinyl for a handsome effect, while chandelier, plants and other accessories contribute to the richness of the room. Designer Ving Smith, A.I.D., and Charlotte Smith.

Just plain relaxing is one important activity that should not be ignored when planning a den. This den is simple in concept, but fine materials give it a solid feeling of quality. Rich, dark wood paneling and a rough, natural brick floor form an ideal "den-like" shell here, give the room overtones of masculinity. The heavy linen covering the sofa is in a bold, green-blue plaid that introduces color against the dark walls. The built-in wall cabinet is covered with hard-wearing, stain-free vinyl, offers plenty of storage. An animal fur rug and nautical accessories add flair.

CHAPTER FOURTEEN

A Miscellany of Optional Rooms

ANY ROOM THAT is not needed for functional, everyday living can be turned into a leisure room that all members of the family can enjoy. All that is needed is skillful planning, imaginative decorating, and a theme that pleases everyone in the home. This miscellany of optional rooms includes an attic that became a luxurious family room and which doubles as a guest room; a dark basement that got a rainbow treatment and was turned into a rumpus room; a deep storage closet that was done up as an elegant bar. Libraries, guest rooms, recreation, hobby and family rooms as well as a specially designed music-conversation pit are also illustrated, and might inspire you to take advantage of that neglected space in your home. You might even think of making the optional "leisure" room a do-it-yourself project for the whole family. The newest floor and wall products are usually easy to install at low cost, and most are hard wearing, heat and moisture resistant as well as decorative. They go down into the basement or up into the attic with ease, ensure warmth and comfort. Once the basic shell is up, furniture can be added gradually. Hi-fi, TV, recording equipment, artists' materials, pottery wheels, weaving frames and musical instruments all find a place in the home of today, and can often set the theme of a room, as is shown on the following pages.

This family room at the top of the house is many rooms in one. Unique plastic skylights invite stargazing, but other less exotic types of recreation go on here as well. Counter areas at opposite ends are a good place to study or pursue a hobby; cork insulation wall above makes a magnificent bulletin board. Tucked in under the eaves are couches which invite lounging, also comfortably sleep two. Concealed drawers beneath the built-in beds provide ample storage space. A soda pop color scheme reverses lemon with lime and lime with lemon to make mirror image rooms in the one area. This unusual and gay room could be a bedroom for two boys, family recreation room or a hideaway for guests.

Multi-Purpose Family Room

with the accent on art

Clever designing and wormy chestnut paneling converts a narrow, lower level area (basement) into a spacious family room. Recessed storage, cabinet wall, with concealed lighting and plate glass mirrors at ceiling line, create an illusion of space and at the same time mask heating ducts and electric wires. Wood-covered posts and vertical grooves in plywood paneling lend a sense of height to room, while horizontal strips in vinyl flooring add a feeling of width. Color scheme of orange, yellow and red is picked up in window shades, studio couch and chess table. Wall above bank of cabinets makes an ideal "art gallery" for paintings.

Close-up of the TV storage area, in the cabinet arrangement that spans an entire wall, sharply outlines the design elements of the wormy chestnut paneled unit. Shelves within the cabinets are adjustable to accommodate odd-sized toys and sports equipment. Note the sweep of white cabinet tops of laminated plastic, which require only damp-sponge care.

Different view of the paneled family room shows the double, wall-length sofas and under-stair storage area. This has a two-door touch-latch arrangement to permit easy access to wagons and bicycles.

Family Room with a Music Theme

Music and conversation can both go on, in this well planned "pit," part of a large family room. The music wall contains, besides organ and color television, complete hi-fi equipment, tape recorder, speakers, storage for sheet music, records and tapes. Facing it is a built-in bench running on three sides, for lounging, TV viewing or for seating guests at an informal concert. You could even give large concerts here, by utilizing the upper level. Seating on the brink of the "pit" is kept low in oriental fashion, to make conversation easy between both levels. Vinyl wall covering and wood paneling are used on the music wall, for good acoustics, as is wall-to-wall nylon carpeting on floor. Benches and cushions are covered in matching vinyl upholstery material for hard wear and easy maintenance. A white wall spotted with black enlivens the large blocks of intense color.

Rumpus Room

Here's a family room with the emphasis on the junior members of the family. Hot colors were used abundantly and in jazzy ways for a gay look, are a frank invitation to fun. Good ideas here include the built-in bookshelves and cabinets, painted inside and out and decorated with whimsical birds; the cheery, yellow pegboard wall which supports phonograph and other accessories; easy-care, hard surface floor, with furniture kept light for easy moving. This room illustrates how easy it is to transform a dark, dull basement into a room all members of the family can enjoy, at little cost.

This colorful bedroom was designed specially for the ham radio enthusiast. Built-in bed and corner for radio equipment, give the room a compact air, and under-bed drawers are ideal for storage. The intense blue nylon carpet and bright green bed alcove lend a contemporary feeling to the old brick fireplace wall and barn lumber surrounding bed. Black leather swivel chairs flank a matching contemporary breakfast table, while a director's chair in blue and white completes the radio corner.

A room for serious hobbyists is built around the activities it serves, which in themselves provide striking decoration. Foreground half holds pottery wheel, sink, and accompanying accessories; far end of room is a weaving studio, contains a loom and weaving materials. Separating the two areas is a relaxation center dominated by a compact column which contains TV and hi-fi, plus comfortable swivel chairs and a small table. Golden walls and neutral-toned carpeting create a simple shell against which the crafts themselves stand out. Carved wooden door, hanging lamps, pots of sea-grass are effective accents. Because of the double life the room leads, everything was chosen for function, durability, easy maintenance as well as beauty. Nylon carpeting is easy to spot clean, a basic requirement in a crafts room, while casements are washable and drip-dry. Room can also serve as a guest room, has a sofa bed, not shown. Designers Mark Nelson, A.I.D., and Zita Zech, F.A.I.D.

Libraries

A custom-built wall fixture can turn any room into a library, as shown here. Potato-colored grasscloth and natural toned oak were combined to create the library wall of this luxurious den. Ample shelves house books, while top of cabinets make buffet surfaces for snacks; alternatively magazines, art objects or flowers. The cabinets themselves provide ample storage for liquor, games, records, as well as hi-fi equipment. Lift-up panels conceal record player. Artful arrangement of wall units leaves space for a painting, lit by concealed lighting contained in ceiling soffit. Same soffit also houses hi-fi speakers. Designer George Cohen.

Hideaway library designed by J. Frederic Lohman, A.I.D., has an unusual carpeted entryway that leads from a raised doorway at left over mantle area, and down cantilevered steps to raised deck at right which doubles as casual seating area. To counteract lack of space, the designer made extensive use of carpeting, wood paneling and a window wall of curtains. Texture contrasts plus the subtle, monochromatic color scheme give the small room a feeling of both luxury and space. Book jackets, brass accessories and gilded foliage add bright splashes; furniture was kept to a minimum to avoid a cluttered look.

This library wall unit is not only attractive but practical, too. Sleek-lined, contemporary fitment holds books, artifacts, has base storage cupboards; while a slender table attached to the wall arrangement serves as a desk, with a light on one of the supporting vertical poles. Beauty of this library fitment is that it is free-standing, can be moved against any wall, or new home should owners relocate.

Put a wall to work for you, and at the same time give a room the library look. A shelf and cupboard unit such as this, spanning the length of one wall and floor to ceiling in height, solves a multitude of storage problems. And books and accessories arranged cleverly can become an effective part of the decor. This library wall unit has a drop-leaf desk top, and even the extension lamp, TV and record player fit back into the shelves. Other furniture in the library is kept to a minimum, so that the book wall becomes the focal point of the room.

The Bar

YOU CAN CREATE a bar almost anywhere in the house. An unused cupboard, a corner behind a wall jog, an entrance hall or a basement can be transformed into a cozy "social" spot, with clever decorating.

A Toulouse-Lautrec mural within, and garden scenes without, adorn this charming Parisian style bar, which is ingeniously built into a tiny closet. White-with-pink antiqued cupboard holds a bartender's every need, while top makes a perfect mixing counter. Excellent lighting, rows of glasses on glass shelves add to the sparkle. Strip of vinyl flooring below is stain free, folding doors permit easy access, don't get in the way. This bar is so pretty it became a decorative asset in the sitting room. Designed by Leona Kahn, A.I.D. Idea of a built-in bar in a roomy closet is worthwhile adapting.

A once bland entrance hall has been transformed into this exciting bar, which exudes atmosphere. Hot-red chairs, wall chest, bar stools, corridor walls and door establish a gay, party mood. Strikingly grained dark wood paneling is made even more dramatic by the brass medallion hinges and handles. The intricate, gold-wrought screen, hanging lamps of Eastern inspiration and gold metal legs of the bar stools echo this theme. Custom-designed floor of hard-wearing vinyl, again with an Eastern motif, has a rich look. Bamboo soffit around ceiling tops off the exotic look.

This intimate-sized bar adds yet another touch of luxury to this elegant sitting room designed by Louis Malamud, N.S.I.D. The bar is designed down to the last detail, from its plump, buttoned leather front and brass footrail, to its full complement of bar accessories and antique telephone. Access is through the glittering, folded screen at back. Wicker-backed bar chairs are pleasingly light when seen against the heavy leather and rich velvet, are also extremely comfortable. Photograph by Robert. L. Beckhard.

Here you see a lovely hall cabinet which has been utilized as a bar in a small sitting room. This type of cupboard solves many problems if you are short of space, and don't have room to make an actual bar. This one is just the right height for serving purposes, has plenty of room for bottles and glasses inside. It is made of pecan Barcelona fruitwood with pewter hinges, is antique Spanish in style. The hammered metal candelabra attached to the wall above the cabinet is an inspired touch.

THE ROOM YOU decorate and reserve for guests need not go unused when there are no visitors. Design it so that it can be utilized by other members of the family, as a den or study, a sewing room, or a spare sitting room for relaxing.

This guest room is also a restful place for the hostess to listen to music, or simply sew or read, when guests are absent. It is done in a golden mixture of mustard, lime, beige and white, tones which make it seem larger than it really is. The inspiration for the color scheme came from the painting hanging on the handsome wall paneled in laminated plastic. Dark wood bookcase and other furnishing accents provide contrast. The oversized end table, topped with lime laminated plastic is an ideal place for a snack, or a "sprawl out" project. The occasional table in front of the sofa bed is actually a large brass urn, filled with a prized shell collection and topped with a round pane of plate glass. Oyster-white carpet of acrylic fiber not only adds an elegant note, but is hard wearing and practical, as are other upholstery fabrics.

This guest bedroom was designed to double as a study for the man of the house, has a strong masculine quality as well as rich warmth. Designer Edmund Motyka, A.I.D., has used a beautiful collection of fabrics and furniture (inspired by designs from the archives of the famous maker of fine chinaware, Josiah Wedgwood) to create the rich provincial look. The red and black floral jacquard is used consistently throughout the room, is underlined by a solid red rug. Built-in closets and bookshelves provide a cozy niche for the sofa-lounge-bed. French wing chairs have backs and sides covered in a black textured fabric. Stark white walls temper the glowing red of the room.

CHAPTER FIFTEEN

Difficult Rooms

*A collection of good basic ideas which solve a variety of problems
in the awkward room, plus treatments for Alcoves,
Bays, Corners, Dividers, Halls and Staircases*

THERE ARE ALL manner of difficult rooms. Some are too large, others too small.
Many have architectural defects such as alcoves, corners and wall jogs. Ceilings are often too high or too low for the size and shape of the room, and
exposed pipes and radiators also create awkward problems. Halls and staircases
are often difficult to decorate, and careful attention to detail is needed if they
are to succeed and be an integrated part of the home's decor. The one room
apartment poses its own special problems, whether it's small or large. Planning,
clever decorating, use of new materials and fabrics all contribute much in the

A one room apartment can be gracious and comfortable, as illustrated here. This room has the personal, at ease feeling of a bedroom, yet the use of smooth, efficient surfaces, vivid colors and strictly tailored lines have kept it from becoming too intimate to serve as a living room. Walls are covered with an unusual cane-patterned plastic, with laminated plastic covering chests and sofa enclosure. An interesting interplay of textures gives the room its special character: nubby woven fabric on chair and sofa, deeply carved carpet design, and flowers—real, in paintings and blooming on curtain and cushion fabric—all contribute individual patterns. Accessories such as clock, candles, shelves of plates and plants add to the living room atmosphere. Designer Barbara Healy, A.I.D.

difficult room, help to disguise its faults. And surprisingly, the ugly duckling room often turns into a real swan through the skillful use of ingenious ideas. In this chapter are a variety of difficult rooms . . . one room apartments; bed-sitting rooms; attics; rooms with architectural defects such as alcoves, bay windows, odd corners; rooms that need to be divided; staircases and entrance halls. All of them have been cleverly decorated to hide their basic defects, and these well-proven treatments may help to solve some of your problems with the difficult room.

A touch of drama turns this tiny, multi-purpose room into a charming apartment. Bold pineapple-patterned wallpaper, exotic rug and lavish use of brilliant turquoise are effective guarantees against dullness. Dramatic, too, is the swathed and tasseled drapery, with a coordinated window shade. Deep-set window allows room for a decorative bird cage, while window-seat-table is actually a storage chest. Smartly designed cabinets along left-hand wall conceal kitchen needs. Fine antique furniture lends added importance to the room, and corner divan transforms into a bed. Clever decorating turned a cramped bedroom into a dining-sitting room any bachelor girl would be happy to occupy. Designer Bette Sanford Roby.

One Room Living

THE ONE ROOM apartment may seem difficult to furnish and decorate graciously, at first. But with a great deal of thought and ingenuity its obvious problems can be solved, even when space is at a minimum. Planning is the vital element here, more than in any other kind of home. For unless the multi-purpose room is skillfully planned, it will look messy and cluttered at all times. Work out furniture needs and arrangements first, preferably on graph paper to scale, before attempting to furnish. Pay strict attention to storage, consider all those things which make the wheels go round in daily life, but which cannot be on view. Where will they be hidden? You may be lucky enough to have ample closet space. If you do not, plan for wall-hung units with storage cabinets, and which also hold books and bric-a-brac. Drawers under the bed and a couple of deep chests also provide plenty of storage. A folding bed, one that pulls out of the wall or a studio couch are the obvious answers to sleeping and living in one room; so is the compact kitchen, or cooking elements hidden by screens or a louvered door.

If the one room apartment is small, it is much better to choose two or three large pieces of furniture and leave it at that, rather than clutter the room with too many scaled down pieces. Selection of fabrics and color scheme is of prime importance. Different patterns will only make the room seem smaller, and even messy. Make sure all textures, patterns and colors blend. This also applies to the overall color scheme: it should be of one or two colors that are carefully balanced and blended. On the following pages are a number of one room apartments, illustrating some brilliant planning and decorating ideas.

One Room Elegance

HERE IS A ONE ROOM BACHELOR apartment, designed to suit the needs of a busy man, yet with an eye on elegance and comfort. From the two photographs you will see how one room can look like a living room by day, transforms into a more than adequate bedroom at night...without losing its character or charm.

This versatile one room apartment has a gracious country look, is utterly deceiving on the surface. It reflects the owner's very individual taste for decoration and old world comfort, is also planned carefully to serve numerous functions. Because the room is small, furniture is kept on the light side. Writing table serves as a desk, is of pale, grained wood: sofa is two-person size: other pieces are kept small: area rug defines the central space without smothering the entire room. The Chinese-red bookshelves are chock-full of treasured objects, yet take no floor space: tiny table has a "split-level," also holds a lot for its size. White walls and dark floor add to the feeling of space, while accessories and other pieces are either flush to wall, or wall-hung. Designed by David Barrett, A.I.D., N.S.I.D.

Its secrets revealed, the elegant living room becomes a comfortable bedroom, with a character all its own. The beauty of this room is that clever planning means very little rearranging of furniture—in fact none at all. Sofa simply opens up to make a bed, and well-placed lamps on desk and far table provide bedside reading light without being moved. The dark, unobtrusive cabinet conceals an entire kitchenette—sink, range and refrigerator, while "split-level" table holds morning coffee. Even the area rug projects just enough to serve desk side of bed, for cold mornings. Bathroom is hidden behind curtained, glass doors: clothes closets are at far end of room, not shown in picture. This one room apartment illustrates some of the ingenious ideas which can be used to bring character and convenience to the bed-sitting room. Designed by David Barrett, A.I.D., N.S.I.D.

A small apartment has been handled with great sophistication. Although room has a luxury look, materials used are inexpensive. The framework around the window, designed to hide architectural defects, holds up-down shades. Plants peeping out behind them suggests that a garden lies beyond. Colors and fabrics throughout the room have been carefully coordinated; even the ceiling is included in the scheme of apricot and gold. Cork tile floor is a subtle background for the bolder squares of the area rug. Upholstered stools make comfortable, extra seats. Coordinated colors and fabrics, a minimum of furniture cleverly arranged, and window wall make room seem larger than it is.

This is the second view of the sophisticated small apartment shown above. It shows the wall facing the sofa area. The wall treatment does a multitude of things. It provides storage and work space handsomely; in addition, the long table swings out from the wall to seat six for dining. The teak-like shelves and table, as well as window frame in first picture, are actually built of inexpensive lumber and covered with a self-adhesive vinyl. Soffits conceal lighting on ceiling, and also again at desk level. Movie directors' chairs are simple, lightweight, yet comfortable; also fold away to save space.

This elegant, clean-lined sitting room is triple purpose, serves for dining and sleeping too, is the perfect one room apartment for a young married couple. Furniture was carefully chosen to meet immediate needs, yet transport to larger quarters later. Imaginative treatment of an entire window wall is responsible for the room's air of spaciousness. The wall is actually punctuated by nondescript, old-fashioned windows. To conceal them and create an impression of greater width, translucent corrugated vinyl was hung along lower half of wall; upper half was united by a huge window shade, trimmed with white wool fringe. Window treatment sets the room's color scheme of beige and white, which is echoed in white fabric-covered walls, beige-yellow textured carpet, and beige sleep-sofa. Accents of red and blue add verve, come in the red chair and ottoman, and red-white-and-blue painted hutch bookcase, on top of chest. A long, slim table runs the length of the window wall, is topped with practical floor tiles, can be used for working, writing, dining. It echoes the strong horizontal lines of the room. Above the window shade, a flat wood cornice is covered with matching shade cloth, hides extra light. Above that, so unobtrusive as to be almost invisible, a strip of mirror reflects back the design of the beige and white striped acoustical ceiling. This enlarges the horizons of the room in an entirely new way. Color scheme is subtle enough to live well; furniture arrangement clever enough to function in many roles; all surfaces, from window shades to walls and carpet, are easy to upkeep. Designer John Van Koert, A.I.D.

This efficient compact kitchen serves the dining area of a small two room apartment, has been streamlined to sit well with the room's total decor. Elegant louvered doors and a soffit conceal the compact kitchen when it is not in use; vinyl tiled floor is color matched to carpet in living area, while end wall is papered in same handsome fabric as the rest of the room. Compact kitchen has range top, oven, base storage cupboard and refrigerator, ample work surface with additional cupboards above.

THE ONCE UNUSED room at the top of the house can easily be turned into a den, family room or unique bedroom. It need not be the place to store junk, suitcases and trunks. With careful planning and clever decorating it can become an integrated part of the house, a gay "extra" room to entertain friends, pursue hobbies or even accommodate a guest.

An attic's hidden assets are all exploited to the fullest to create a family room par excellence here. **Asset no. 1:** Top-of-the-house slanting roof is the perfect place for a skylight. Here triangular openings, scissor-snipped into the roof, are filled with weatherproof plastic domes. **Asset no. 2:** Since there is bound to be a chimney in the attic, a fireplace can be added with relative ease. This gleaming copper one is prefabricated. **Asset no. 3:** An attic's rough-sawn paneling and exposed beams are adaptable to a relaxed country look, attainable with a minimum of do-it-yourself work. Here barn-red and white paint covers most of the wood, though some of the rafters have been left exposed. Armchairs were made from old barrels upholstered in plaid. Final fillip: A clutch of Buck's County Americana antiques, and a sofa strappingly buckled like a horse blanket. The result is a colorful sky lodge for teens or parents who'd like a second sitting room, with a study-hobby area behind chimney.

High Fashion for the Lowly Attic

TIME WAS WHEN an unfinished attic was used for storage space, or perhaps a playroom for the younger set. Too many problems were involved with slanting walls, unfinished floors and walls for the average homemaker to attempt to add that "spare" room without stripping the family budget. But with the wealth of new products on the market today, (made available through extensive research to meet the needs of the modern budget) an unfinished attic can be turned into a room of beauty. Colorful tiles in vivid shades, a variety of paneling from inexpensive hardboard to elegant finishes, and exciting wallpapers that are easy to apply are but a few of the aids designed to make your decorating problems easy. Add to this stain resistant and water repellent fabrics, carpets and wall coverings. Perhaps your attic is not large enough for traditional furniture, and also requires decorative touches to give the illusion of spaciousness. Try placing a simple narrow bed against the wall and frame with a fabric valance and side draperies to create the feeling of a sleeping alcove. Choose light, pastel shades for walls, add a spark of color with gay, imaginative accessories. If you are planning a room for children, pegboard is a marvelous catch-all for all that important paraphernalia that adds clutter to the room; hanging shelves provide extra space for books and games. And don't throw away old furniture. It can be refinished, painted or camouflaged with left over lengths of fabric. An old chest can be transformed into a pretty window bench with just a new coat of paint and a fabric covered seat. A discarded round table can add an intimate touch to the room when covered with a floor length table cover. With a little imagination and a minimum of expense, an unattractive attic room can come to life and be a pretty place to live in, or house guests.

An attic's defects can be turned into advantages. A sloping ceiling and window alcove add charm to this high-in-the-sky bedroom. Traditional furniture has been wisely chosen to carry out the Early American theme suggested by "attic architecture"; the rush-seated wooden-backed bench settee is well-placed under the eaves, while poster bed and other pieces add importance to the room. Floral wallpaper, in orange tones, echoes the plain orange wall behind bed, while antique gold-colored bedspread sits well on the rich brown carpet. Oil painting, lamp, and other accessories were carefully chosen to fit color scheme and feeling of this attic guest room.

Alcoves, Bays, Corners, Dividers

Ideas to solve some of the problems created by odd nooks and architectural defects in rooms

ALCOVE: It's better to dramatize an alcove, rather than try to ignore it. If you have an alcove big enough to take a bed, you're in luck. You can save space, create an inviting lounging place, and no one will think of calling the alcove an architectural defect. In this alcove, carpeting was boldly used, brought up the walls from the floor to emphasize its coziness. Sea-blue antique chest, chair and other accessories make a sophisticated color contrast to the glowing apricot wall and carpeted areas.

BAYS: Here you see how an old-fashioned bay window takes on new, decorative values. The bay has been drawn into the room, with wallpaper-covered valances and ceiling which continue the floral design of the

walls. Sheer, shantung textured shades filter glare, yet let in maximum light. Wide borders have been painted on these translucent shades in two tones of cerulean-blue, to pick up the colors in the wallpaper. The deeper color, which outlines the border, gives a subtle three-dimensional effect. Delicately shirred miniature cafe curtains of net add softness and interest to the floor-length windows. A blue vinyl floor and washable white area rug echo the color and practicality points made by the window treatment. Chest and chairs in a yellow patina finish are other flashes of sunny color. The result is a charming dining alcove created in a formerly ugly bay. Designed by Paul Krauss, A.I.D.

233

Dramatize a cramped corner. This awkwardly placed window is made interesting by painting the woodwork a fresh distinctive color, carefully keyed to an elegant shade plus valance treatment. Plants and decorative stone pot give it further importance. The narrow space between sofa arm and wall is made handsome and useful by the wall unit. The cabinet keeps magazines within easy reach, doubles as an end table, creates a spot for lamp and flowers.

This corner changed from "nothing" to "something" when wall paneling of rare wormy chestnut was installed and furnishings with outspoken character introduced. The painted chair is Mexican Colonial in design. A simple strip of red cloth unites the hanging storage components. Wrought-iron accessories are another Spanish style touch. Study designed by Bernard S. Vinick, A.I.D.

Get an angle on corners, if your kitchen storage space is vital. Corner space, so often lost, is used down to the last inch here. The simple device is a built-in storage unit, with counter top, that cuts the corner; wall-hung cupboards and range hood have also been cleverly worked **around** the corner to capture space. The unusual, bold-striped flooring in red, white and yellow brings a strictly tailored look to the moderately sized kitchen.

Glamorize a corner with an arrangement of plants, statues and a painting. This high standing cherub is an excellent foil for the sleek, ultramodern chair and bold picture. Cool white wall meeting unadorned, light-filtering drapes, is a restful background. Finishing touch is the smooth, fringe bordered rug and the modern marble table.

235

DIVIDERS: This intriguing room dividing screen suggests a real wall in its solidity; but it has a novel see-through quality, the more so since its own contours appear to change as the occupant of the room moves around and sees it from different angles. It lends an exciting quality of depth and dimension to any area, also creates light diffusing effects. Dividing screen is available in three versatile sizes for interior and exterior use, with complete scale adaptability to most rooms. Designed by Erwin Hauer.

DIVIDERS: This beautiful, free-standing room divider not only creates two atmospheres in one area, but serves a multitude of purposes. It holds books, magazines, art objects, offers ample storage and has a drop-leaf bar. What's more, because of its see-through shelves, it does not obscure light in either half of the room it is dividing. It can be moved against a wall, when whole area of room is needed for entertaining.

Room Dividers with a Difference

DIVIDING A ROOM is not so difficult as it once was. Today you can use beautiful screens, three-dimensional see-through walls, free-standing units and many other devices to separate one area into two.

In this elegant room, a divider was needed that would make a barrier as substantial as any wall, yet would not look awkward when it stopped short at the dining area. The strategy was to find an unusual material, and designer J. Frederic Lohman chose the perfect one for his divider. He used slabs of dark brown cork to cover the actual "wall" which splits the room. Their variations in tone create a pattern of modulated rectangles, which blend beautifully with the herringbone parquet floor of similar color. The curves of the antique furniture show up well in these subtly textured surroundings. Shelves were added to the cork divider, to hold books and other accessories, for the finishing touch.

THE FORMAL HALL: Elegance par excellence finds statement through **understatement** in this spacious and formal hall. The sumptuous floor is of custom vinyl cork tiles, laid on the diagonal and brightened by pristine white, star-shaped inlays. Smooth melon-colored walls, painted to tone with the floor, serve to emphasize the white door and other woodwork. Real show of luxury is to be able to leave so large a hall impressively empty, except for the few fine pieces and antique crystal chandelier. Yet every object that **is** used in the hall is just the right piece in style and mood.

THE FORMAL HALL: This huge, rather grand entrance hall relies on its unusual floor for effect. Black and white vinyl tiles were laid in slightly off key lines to create this eye-catching three-dimensional look. Furniture was kept to a minimum to show off floor to its best advantage. Decorative panels above doors and dados lend formality, as does buttoned sofa, candelabra and crystal chandelier. Any additional pieces here would have been superfluous.

THE ELEGANT HALL: This small foyer was given just the right touches of elegance through clever and careful planning. The soft green carpet, with its novel central section of bright rugtiles, is the talking point of the hall. It has been carefully color balanced to the olive and white striped fabric wall covering, also used to upholster the slender gilt chair. Because of small space, furniture was kept down to a minimum. Yet black wood console, mirror and stands, boldly decorated with gold, add character and a decorative look. The result is a tiny entrance which is colorful and elegant, yet uncluttered for traffic lines. A rugtile is easy to put down, is a 12" square of carpet bonded to a tile base the same size, made of high impact polystyrene plastic, with edges designed for interlocking with adjacent tiles. It is an easy, do-it-yourself task, can be used in any room in the house.

THE ELEGANT HALL: Medium sized, squared-off hall was given character by its white vinyl floor edged and patterned with black, and its wall length mural above dado. Console table and matching chairs unobtrusively blend into background, while artificial orange tree adds a decorative touch.

The Long Narrow Hall

1.

1. This narrow entrance and corridor was dark and forbidding. Clever decorating gave it a whole new look. Sparkling white vinyl tiles, with lines of diamond-shaped inlays, were carried through from the living room. It at once created an illusion of light. Exotic garden wall murals above a marbled dado add an illusion of width, while spotlights above provide ample lighting. Decorative archway leading into living room blends well with murals.

2. **Marbled walls and floors** brought light airiness and a luxury look to this narrow entrance hall and corridor. Marble-effect vinyl wall tiles were used above wood dado, texture matched to the wide banded vinyl tiled floor. This is custom-designed, laid in broad stripes of black against mottled white for a novel effect. False ceiling along corridor conceals diffused lighting; mirror on end wall acts as light reflector.

2.

3.

3. **This narrow and oddly proportioned** hall was given continuity through its custom-designed flooring and wall of smoked glass. The two combine to create a feeling of space and balance, while designed floor adds a feeling of true proportion. Furniture was kept discreet and understated, so as not to detract from mirrored wall and floor.

Gracefully decorated hall, full of country dignity, serves as an extra sitting room in the summer months. Its striking, squared-off floor is played against the delicate floral print used for drapes and upholstery. Unusual canopy chair is a talking point, and velvet trimmed window valance and tiebacks add sparkle.

241

When a hall has to serve many purposes, it must be carefully planned so that traffic lanes don't interfere with other activities. This hall, besides providing access to stairway, and to other rooms, is a television and conversation area. Since adjacent rooms are always visible through archways, total area was decorated as a coordinated unit. Striped wallpaper, dark stained beams and doorways continue from room to room; colors in the matching, fringed rugs are picked up in the staircase carpeting and chair. The result is a hallway with a double life, integrated into the whole. Designed by Leif Pedersen. N.S.I.D.

This double hall was cleverly decorated to work as a small study. The narrow entryway is lined with bookcases, for the library look; larger part of hall holds a table which can double as a writing desk and a small stool. A deeply tufted rug with an unusual fringe is the focal point of the entrance, and helps create a luxury look, as do marbled walls.

A doorway that is not used is unexpectedly dramatized rather than concealed in this hall that doubles as a conversation-sewing corner. The sizzling colors of the drapes pick up those of the rug, woodwork echoes the yellow floor. A bench placed in front of the draped door is a useful catch-all. White walls set off the antique Spanish chair, and the Granada iron convex mirror, hinge plaques and decorative rosettes. Decorator Paul Krauss, A.I.D.

This large hall doubles as a second sitting room and game room, but retains its necessary walk-through space. A large area rug, over polished plank floors, defines its central, open quality. Exotic furnishings sit well in the spacious setting, combine with the rich rug to create a manor house look.

Spiral staircase in the grand manner has dark, polished wood stairs and an antique wrought-iron railing reminiscent of a Spanish castle. The right accessories were needed to restate and emphasize the medieval character of the stairway. A 12th century Spanish table of dark walnut, two Ming vases and an antique tapestry were carefully selected to reiterate this mood, while 20th century nylon carpeting of bright delphinium-blue lends dramatic unity to the circular foyer and the two-story staircase. The carpeting also echoes the blue in the Ming vases, was chosen for its long lasting durability as well as for its vibrancy of color. The rich tapestry, hung in the curve between the two windows, adds warmth to the natural stucco walls.

This top-of-the-stairs shot shows how brilliant blue carpet sweeps round circular foyer and up spiral staircase for a feeling of color and texture unity. Ming vase in wall niche matches vase on old Spanish table in stairwell.

Staircase Treatments that Cater to a Variety of Tastes

1.

1. Curved, traditional stair gains from the addition of a decorative railing. Black border of custom-designed marble floor serves to emphasize beginning of carpeted stairs. Silk wallpaper is taken throughout hallway and up stairs for smooth look, while antique furniture and picture in stairwell add finishing touches. Designer David Barrett, A.I.D., N.S.I.D.

2. Modern cantilevered staircase features steps of two-tone wood raised up and out on plain wood blocks painted white. Stainless steel railing gives staircase a light as air look, helps emphasize unusual steps. Collection of plants in stairwell lends a decorative look to hall, which is covered in smart squared-off vinyl.

2.

3. Wide staircase, with curved wooden banisters and decorative wrought-iron railings, swiftly descends into large entrance hall. Area rug was color and texture matched to staircase carpeting for integrated look, and to diminish feeling of isolation stair would have had in large foyer.

3.

MODERN STAIR RISING FROM A LARGE LIVING ROOM is unobtrusive because stair treads and railings of dark wood blend easily with dark woods of furniture. Staircase also acts as an effective see-through divider, creates two separate areas in the one room.

SWIFTLY RISING, MODERN STAIRCASE, in actor Glenn Ford's Beverly Hills home, features stair treads made of unusually shaped quarry tile. Same Provence-red tiles, with brushed surface, were also used in entrance hall for coordination. Decorative wrought-iron railing continues from staircase round landing. Profusion of exotic plants were grouped together to form an indoor garden next to stairs.

STAIR DESCENDING RIGHT INTO A LIVING ROOM needs special handling. Here this two flight modern staircase has been cleverly integrated into room. Polished wooden treads and handrail are matched to furniture, while tread-base and railings are painted white to blend with walls and custom-designed vinyl floor. Plants on turn of stair break up corner effectively.

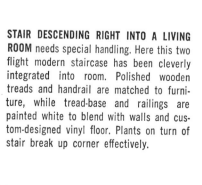

SMALL, CRAMPED STAIRWAY WAS OUT OF PLACE in this spacious entrance hall of a duplex apartment. It was given touches of elegance to reiterate grand manner of foyer. Dark stair carpet gives stairs a solid look, also throws decorative railing into relief. Unusual wall mural round curve of stairway creates a feeling of space as does wall of mirror, which faces onto hall. Antique chairs and custom-designed floor echo colors used on stairway.

LONG, DOUBLE-FLIGHT STAIRCASE had a huge expanse of wall and ceiling, that needed some decorative touches. Easy-to-maintain, plastic-finished hardboard paneling with a marble look was used to cover these areas. Handrail was added to break up monotony of far wall, and as a safety measure. Crystal chandelier, plants and a small, wrought-iron railing over stairwell add finishing touches. Marble-like paneling is not only rich looking, but is unaffected by dirt, grease, grime or moisture. It is perfect material for a busy stairway in frequent use.

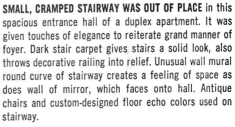

Even the most unique and sumptuous settings are considerably enhanced by skillful lighting. Here, an entrance leading from darkness into light is cleverly illuminated to point up the intricate patterns of the filigree screening and foliage, and the smooth ceramic tile floor. High gate lights at either side emphasize the doorway's symmetry.

CHAPTER SIXTEEN

Lighting

Skillfully placed fixtures, clever techniques add new dimensions to any room, create mood and atmosphere

LIGHTING YOUR HOME today is much more than choosing useful fixtures and lamps for practical purposes. This is an essential of course, but just as important is the mood and atmosphere you create through skillful lighting. Illumination in the home has gone far beyond the single ceiling bulb, or a few lamps scattered around the room. Dramatic effects have been achieved on theater stages through brilliant manipulation of lights, and whereas you may not consider your home a *stage,* many theatrical lighting ideas can be adapted for home use. Manufacturers of lighting fixtures are producing more and more exciting equipment, which brings glamor as well as practicality to the home. Today you can have almost any kind of lighting, in the most unusual places. **Incandescent, concealed lighting** can glow on the ceiling or walls; **pin-spot lights** can be used to focus attention on sculpture, plants, artifacts and paintings; **strip lighting** can be concealed under window valances, along the top of bookshelves, under soffits and in alcoves to throw direct light onto objects and accessories; some wall fitments and even furniture come equipped with lights. And of course lighting has gone outdoors, to create a magical, fairyland effect in gardens, around swimming pools, and on terraces. Lighting in your home needs as much careful thought and planning as all other aspects of decorating. Two of the main factors in lighting are mood desired and comfort of vision; in other words what will be going on in the area, and what will the light be

A WELL-CHOSEN LIGHTING FIXTURE CAN BE A DEFINITE DECORATIVE ASSET. The crystal and gold chandelier helps create a sense of lavishness in this simple dining foyer, designed by Miriam Whelan, A.I.D.

used for specifically? To achieve desired results, you should control the following:

INTENSITY:
Intensity of light should depend on brightness of objects to be looked at, and color scheme of room. For instance, darker objects need more light, as does a darker color scheme. Therefore a room with white walls needs the least light.

DISTRIBUTION:
Distribution of light of course depends on the size of the room. Naturally, a larger room needs more lights equally distributed to avoid too many contrasts in light and shadow. Some contrast is desirable, but increased illumination may make sharp contrasts uncomfortable. When there is little contrast in colors, surfaces and objects *more* light is needed.

DIRECTION:
Direction of light is vital, to avoid either all shadow or all glare. Location, size and source of light are important here. Remember that the direction of lighting can correct awkward shapes, can create illusions of either space or coziness in any room. For instance: *indirect* light reflected down from ceiling raises the ceiling height, while all light coming *directly* down from ceiling can have a gruesome effect, so try to avoid it; *all indirect* lighting in a room gives off very little shadow, therefore little contrast, and puts you to sleep. Ceiling bands of direct light, slightly diffused, plus special wall panels are pleasant. Good, functional lighting consists of indirect lighting plus lamps, so that the whole room is softly lit, with brighter areas from lamps where specific activity goes on. Down lights, plus special wall panels and lamps produce high contrasts, are stimulating, give a real cocktail party effect. Remember to watch out for reflecting surfaces which bounce light back, such as glass, mirror or highly polished wood. If you want to show off a glass wall or picture window, spotlight plants and paving *outside,* to lead the eye outdoors at night, and so that the glass does not become a black mirror.

There are three basic elements of lighting to work with in planning effective lighting in your home. Each one provides its own distinct type of light, and each can be used separately or they can be skillfully combined for a truly glamorous effect. They are: *focal glow,* such as the pool of light a lamp casts around your favorite chair; *general luminescence,* an overall light (such as you would see in a theater before the show) which seems to emanate from nowhere. You can identify this type of light as light reflected off pale surfaces, such as brilliant sun on snow when the reflector appears more brilliant than the actual source. *Pin-point brilliance* is the last type of light, and is recognizable as the spotlight directed on an actor on a darkened stage, or lighting up a specific object in a cabinet or on display on a shelf or table.

Four Chandeliers
that Create a Decorative Theme

1. CLASSIC CHANDELIER with a hint of formality has a cascade of crystal prisms that reflect light in sparkling rainbow hues. Traditional Greek key motif is underscored by the black arms and contrasting brass accents.

1.

2.

4.

2. A CHANDELIER MAY BE SAFELY HUNG LOW over a dining table, for a decorative look. This one hides its candle-like lamps in cylinders of rippling, smokey-toned glass, also gives the room a luxury look.

3. DESIGNER EMILY MALINO, A.I.D., selected a cluster of unusual pendants to highlight this dining area, and create an intimate mood. The cluster of lights is arranged at random heights, like a centerpiece of flowers, and provides a luminous glow. Light source is totally concealed within the ebony cylinders. The lights are particularly versatile, can be hung singly or arranged in a constellation to suit the size, scale and ceiling height of any room.

3.

252

4. THIS THREE-IN-A-ROW light fixture is ideal for hanging above a desk, where evenly distributed illumination is particularly important. It also saves the space that would otherwise be occupied by a desk lamp, gives this home-office a sophisticated look.

5.

5. CREATIVE LIGHTING HELPS MAKE THIS COLORFUL BEACH HOUSE A FUN PLACE TO BE. The rows of bulbs across the ceiling are unusual and gay, have a theater atmosphere; they also provide excellent lighting and are economical. No fixtures are required; wiring and spaces for bulbs were put in with the ceiling. Since there are so many bulbs, each can be of low wattage, again inexpensive, and not too bright to look at exposed. Two hanging lamps, smooth and white and almost like enormous light bulbs themselves, hang above table and desk areas.

6. THIS SECOND VIEW OF THE BEACH HOUSE shows the desk-cooking unit. Small standing lamp offers extra illumination on counter near sofa-bed, while flat wall fixture lights up bunk bed. Designer Jim Adler.

6.

253

This contemporary standing lamp
is part of the room's
distinctive decor.
It is easy to move around,
offers subdued lighting,
has the appearance of a slender
stemmed goblet.

Unusual table lamp is designed
to simulate a giant white candle,
inside a glass case.
This type of light looks attractive
on dinner and buffet tables,
has the appearance of
candlelight without the inconvenience.

The contemporary hanging light fixture
has many advantages.
It offers immediate, direct lighting
over a given area without glare.
Three identical metal lights are
decorative and effective over this bar.
Simple lines make them easy to clean,
and flex can be adjusted to any length.

Second version of the ultramodern
hanging light fixture.
This time fixtures are graduated in size,
are of gold metal
with black bands, cylindrical in shape.
Hung over dining table
for diffused spot lighting during meals,
or for study, and table projects later.

The new compact lamps
are neat and appealing.
They can fit in
with any decor and the
light they supply is excellent.
This one is lightweight,
easy to move around,
has a jointed arm
for adjusting,
comes in colors
keyed to match
the telephones.

Single version of the hanging lamp.
This one has three
black shades, graduated in size
and inserted in each other,
topped by a shining metal dome.

Concealed Lighting

A panel of lighting integrated in the soffit of this bookcase sheds soft light on painting beneath, also illuminates the room. A small lamp, in the foreground, stands ready to swivel round towards dictionary; by the comfortable reading chair, a slender standing lamp. General room lighting is rarely sufficient for lengthy reading. Here lamps have been strategically placed to solve this problem.

Both a bookshelf and a light, this ingenious fixture is the perfect companion to a desk. Illumination is evenly distributed over desk surface, it's also a wonderful space saver on desk top.

Two Ways to Light a Kitchen

The major work tops in this kitchen are not near windows. Concealed lighting fixtures underneath wall-hung cabinets give adequate light just where it is needed.

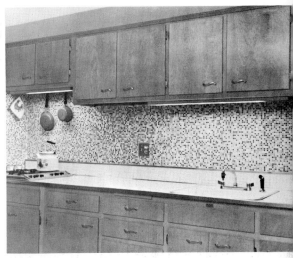

A small compact kitchen can be well lit by one large, bright ceiling fixture. In this kitchen, the work tops are just below a bank of windows, which furnish additional light much of the time. Ceiling light is strong enough to cover this small area.

Dressing Room Lights
Utilized in the Bathroom

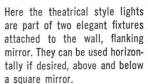

Here the theatrical style lights are part of two elegant fixtures attached to the wall, flanking mirror. They can be used horizontally if desired, above and below a square mirror.

Good lighting is important near a make-up mirror. Both of these lighting fixtures draw their inspiration from theatrical dressing room lights—suggesting the glamor of the theater and supplying perfect illumination for making up, or for shaving. In this picture the lights are actually part of the mirror frame.

Imaginative Bedroom Lights

The lighting in this snug, ski hideaway might do well in any bedroom where a headboard is not used above the bed. Shelf over the bed has strip lighting underneath, provides an ample surface for clutter, and supplements a night table. Spotlights set in the ceiling illuminate the entire room, highlighting touches of bright yellow and sleek pecan paneling on walls. Ski lodge bedroom designed by Vladimir Kagan, A.I.D.

Round lamps hang above round night tables, which flank a double-arched headboard behind a large bed. They give an added feeling of symmetry to this good-looking bedroom. Lamps are available in every conceivable design—the bold stripes of these provide a strong counter-rhythm that balances the profusion of flowers on fabrics. They also offer ample light for reading.

Don't let an unusual, seemingly difficult bed arrangement prevent you from making sure adequate reading light is available. This is especially important where children are concerned. Here compact wall fixtures, with tiny louvered shades, light both top and bottom levels of this double-decker bunk arrangement. Easy-to-reach chains operate lights from beds.

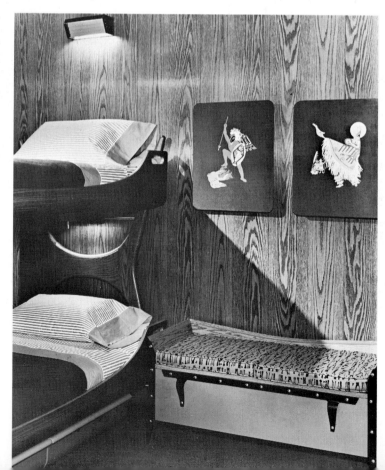

The Magic of Outdoor Lighting

Skillful lighting dramatizes this setting, both indoors and out. The bright lantern hanging above the table dominates the attractive sitting room, glowing like an indoor moon. From the terrace, the interior is a striking view as shown here. This is partly because the well-placed spot washes the white sitting room wall with light. The terrace is efficiently and romantically lit by spot fixtures set into the narrow roof overhang.

Magical things happen to your garden when you light it in unusual ways. Two innocent-looking lily leaves, floating on this pond, are actually pads concealing underwater lamps which radiate a soft glow on pond surface and upwards into night air. The decorative lily pads clip over bulbs in watertight sockets, cord plugs into permanent outlet beside pool which is concealed in shrubbery. Other tiny spotlights accent tree trunks and foliage.

An attractive entrance looks its very best when lit to full advantage. In this case, the wide, white frame and unusual door molding are best illuminated by an even strip of light, rather than a single spot. The fixture fits smoothly into overhang.

Safety lights are necessary on dark paths and entrances leading up to house. Here, these dark steps were extremely hazardous until lit by this charming little garden lantern. The glow from its bulb ensures safety, also sets off the pattern of the flagstones, highlights nearby shrubs and greenery.

A long hallway must be carefully lit to avoid a barren, institutional feeling. Here this attractive covered entranceway has indirect lighting, which shines up to illuminate the ceiling areas. This reflects against the white painted domes and bounces back, softly diffused. Small perforations in the metal shades allow for a little direct light as well. White painted brick walls (set above unusually tiled floor) also reflect light.

Show off your house at night. A handsome, well-placed house looks especially attractive when imaginatively lit against a night sky. The appealing textures of rough brick and clapboard are emphasized by light directed up the wall at a sharp angle. Other lights flood the doorway and illuminate the steps, two engaging ways to say "welcome," and also shed light on the driveway, left of house. Trees and shrubs are beautifully shown off at night, when illuminated by hidden spotlights.

This small hall was transformed into a sparkling shell, with an Oriental flavor, through clever unification of materials, colors and accessories. In this picture you can see how **window, door, floor and walls were all treated as one complete unit,** for this look of total integration. Door and adjacent wall were covered in a pretty white and green, grass-patterned paper; same material was laminated onto window shade and used to cover tiny valance. Textured green paper, with a grasscloth look was used on other wall, matched to wood-work painted olive green. A red tiled floor completes the "shell," while brass-hinged Chinese antique chest, grass plant and other accessories underscore the Far East feeling. Adapt this idea of using wallpaper on doors and windows, for the coordinated look. Today many are specially treated to withstand hard wear, can even be sponged clean for the pristine look.

CHAPTER SEVENTEEN

The Shell of the Room

windows, doors, walls, floors and fabrics

THE SHELL OF the room is the cocoon into which you fit your furniture. By necessity then, it is an integral part of your decorating scheme. The treatment of windows, doors, walls and floors is as important as the choice of furniture and accessories. All should blend, in texture and color, to create a harmonious whole. And the use of fabrics within this shell is just as vital. The material used for drapes does not necessarily have to match that used for upholstery, but each should coexist happily with the other. Both should coordinate with wall covering and flooring. In this chapter are a galaxy of sparkling ideas for ingenious window treatments, dramatic doors, exciting walls, beauty underfoot and flattery with fabrics. All these treatments have been used in actual rooms, to illustrate the importance of the basic shell, and also to prove that they really work.

Windows

WINDOWS SHOULD GET as much attention in your decorating plans as the choice of a color scheme or a piece of furniture. Apart from being the "eyes of the house" for light, windows are an integral part of the formation and balance of a room, and should be treated as such in the early planning stages of decoration. In other words, a treatment for a window should not be *an afterthought,* but should be truly coordinated into your decorative theme right at the beginning. For instance, if you are furnishing with antiques, your window treatment should be highly stylized, and if possible of the same period as the furniture. Certainly the treatment should blend with and complement the total decor of the room. The same rule applies to a modern room; the window treatment should be strictly tailored and simple, in keeping with the lines of the furniture. An ornate swag and drapes would just look out of place, in this more austere type of room. The essential thing to remember, when planning your window treatment, is that a badly dressed window can spoil the total effect of a room, and also throw it off balance.

Once you have settled on the type and style of window treatment, study the window itself. Unfortunately, not all windows are perfect architecturally. Some are too small, too large, oddly shaped, set in a bay, or built above heating equipment. The ugly and oddly-placed window can always be disguised by clever window treatments, whether you use shades, shutters, drapes, lambrequins, or even a built-in unit to disguise radiators. The problem window need no longer be a problem, in fact. In particular, the manufacturers of shade fixtures have done an excellent job of keeping pace with the great array of window designs that are to be found in homes and apartments throughout the country. More than a dozen different types of brackets and shade mountings insure proper fit and, in most cases, there is a choice of installation method for every window style. Techniques may be varied, or combined, to satisfy individual tastes, and help overcome many decorating problems. It remains only for you to determine your particular needs for privacy, light control and the special decorative effects you wish to achieve. Shutters also come in all sizes, shapes and designs, and can be extremely decorative. Even cafe curtains and other types of drapes and swags come ready-made today, while most drapery fabrics are now hard wearing, color fast and machine washable. There is no window, be it casement, skylight, picture, bow, bay or jalousie that cannot be dressed to perfection.

Create a Bay Window

Formerly a long window recessed against a wall, this attractive backdrop for a study or sewing corner was created by Paul Krauss, A.I.D. He utilized colorful fabrics and fresh decorating ideas, rather than costly design changes. Using textiles throughout, the designer draped lengths of floral print cloth from angled frames, which reproduce the look of a bay window, then screened off the three sections with sheer white casements. The result is an intimate bay, with a touch of formality, which becomes the focal point of the room.

An ingenious way to dress up that plain window, and dispense with dust-catching full-length drapes, is with a composition board lambrequin, with an unusual design such as this Eastern inspired keyhole shape. Lambrequin is attached to window, then hung with the same pattern of wallpaper used on the walls for an integrated look. Edges of lambrequin are finished with an important looking braid, to emphasize unusual shape. Window is completed with sheer, full-length casements.

Shades of Elegance

Today's window shades are colorful, decorative and elegant. They can be used as the color springboard for an entire room, as shown here. A handsome combination of Bristol-blue, beige and cocoa-brown used for the shades, is repeated in accessories and furnishings throughout the room. The blue predominates in this unusual window treatment that combines laminated shades in a daisy pattern and a striking wood frame. A wide, valance-like wood strip, painted blue, spans the three windows, dividing the shades into three large and three small separate areas of gay pattern. The matching sill is cut out to accommodate long, wire-and-wood shade pulls. Frame continues down wall under window. Beige and brown walls and floor, blue table accessories, repeat the shade colors, with a dash of green in the sofa and chair to add spice. Designed by John Van Koert, A.I.D.

Here you see how a long wall of windows was unified by a striking shade and valance treatment that also acts as a backdrop for furniture and as a focal point in the room. The three empire-green shades are headed by one encompassing valance made of matching shade cloth. Shades and valance are all decoratively outlined with white carpet tape, and finished with white tassels in two sizes. Underscoring the dramatic window treatment is a long, walnut sill-bench that runs the length of the windows. Bench is broken in the center by a loveseat made from two foam rubber cushions, upholstered in a Scottish plaid. This ingenious idea not only breaks long line of window seat, but adds extra seating in the conversation group. Designed by James Childs Morse, N.S.I.D.

Window shades need no longer simply pull down. They can be cleverly installed to work both ways, and create a fresh, new look at any plain window. Here you see how two pairs of shades were used to this effect. One pair of shades pulls up and the other pulls down, to meet at any point desired to control the amount of light, air, and view one wishes. Both sets are hung reverse-roll for a scroll-like effect, and are architecturally perfect for contemporary decor. Designer Paul Krauss, A.I.D., combined shades in equal color portions of shocking and pale pink, nasturtium and Bristol-blue. How much of each color shows depends on one's mood and needs at the time. This flexibility adds fresh flavor and interest to a room that accents the clean lines of Danish modern design. White walls and a large branch of budding cherry make striking background contrasts.

Transform a Window with Shutters and Shades

make it a focal point of the room

before

after

Framing this old-fashioned window, with a radiator below it, are banks of fruitwood shutters with fabric, cane and metal mesh inserts concealing storage units. A window shade laminated with a glamorous fabric, in a melon and lemon floral pattern, has a scalloped, fringed trim and a matching cornice above. Designer Richard Himmel, A.I.D., brought his talent to solve this usual window problem, making it a music center and focal point, with the fruitwood shutter panels and smart new inserts. Here are ideas galore to intrigue the owner of an old-fashioned apartment or house, with former wasted space around an ugly radiator under a stock window. By flanking the window in fruitwood shutters with contrasting inserts of yellow linen, and by using cane inserts across lower part of window, with metal mesh inserts in front of radiator to permit heat to circulate, the window becomes decorative and useful. Storage units were carefully planned, with upper cabinets for television on right and record storage on left. Below the open bookshelves are spaces for record player on left and stereo on right. In the large cabinets below are twin stereo speakers. Window shade fabric is repeated on the stool, while lemon-yellow of the shade and of the linen inserts is echoed in yellow textured carpeting.

Shutters Dramatize Library Windows

A double bank of shutters, finished in bronze-olive glaze with bright floral print inserts in lower tier, is a center of interest in this library. The folding, double tier of shutters provides sun and light control when needed, as well as a decorative focal point in the room used by all the family. Walls are painted in matching bronze-olive, which continues the color glaze of the folding shutters. In the lower bank, the colors of the floral inserts include turquoise, bronze-olive and gold, highlighting the color theme of the room. Carpet is gold-twist, square coffee tables are finished in Spanish gold color glaze, while built-in bookshelves continue the bronze-olive of the walls.

Shades and Shutters do Double Duty

Shades and shutters make an ideal window treatment for a nursery—one that is both decorative and functional. Room-darkening window shades can be drawn for nap time, and on sunny days folding shutters provide extra light protection. Note that the shutters are in two tiers, with upper bank painted dark green to match the wide borders surrounding the whimsical jungle wallpaper. Lower tier is painted white to match wall, and is closed when complete privacy is needed, for day or night sleeping. Whole treatment is easy to care for and keep clean. Designer Richard Himmel, A.I.D.

SIMPLE, FLOOR-LENGTH DRAPES, GRACEFULLY HUNG AND TIED BACK, always lend an air of elegant formality to any room. They can also give a new dimension to the plainest of windows. Fabric is of prime importance in the simple drape. Here you see rich document-inspired linen and cotton draperies, copied from an original French court fabric design. They are trimmed with a red-green fringe, also used on tiebacks. Brass pole and matching handsome rings dispense with a valance, follow the room's general uncluttered theme. Brass window accessories, so popular in the last century, are making a comeback today. Here they underscore the wall light fixtures, and gilt-colored lampshade. Designer Daggett and Enright.

Formal Valance and Formal Swag

A VALANCE HELPS to give any window and its drapes a finished look. Here you see a sculptured valance made of asparagus-green velveteen, topping generously full drapes in lime-green and grey floral fabric. Valances can be covered with the same fabric used for drapes; contrast material was used for this one to give a feeling of height to the window. French voile casement curtains add extra dimensions to the window, and also hide an unsightly radiator beneath the window. Avocado velveteen is used for table cover, citron velvet for the chaise, following the green theme set by the valance.

A SWAG LENDS elegance to a high window, and when used with floor-length, full, sheer casement curtains it dispenses with the necessity for drapes. Idea is illustrated here. These misty white sheers in a "daisies" pattern are imported from France, can be finished to any width and any length, to fit any window. Graceful swags are made to order in any fabric, and installed by merely hanging over post-type drapery holdbacks. This is an excellent way to bring importance to a summer window, when heavy drapes are not needed. The swag also fits easily over winter drapes, adds a lush look to the most ordinary window.

Cleverly Draped Windows that Echo a Room's Theme

WINDOWS ARE AN integral part of a room's total decor. The style of a window treatment should echo the theme set by the walls and carpet or flooring; it must also be in keeping with the style and period of furniture used. For instance, you would not put a lavish swag and brocade drapes in a contemporary room, or strictly tailored, French pleated curtains in a stylized period

HERE YOU SEE THE ROOM DECORATED IN MODERN STYLE. Sheer, floor-length curtains are tailored and simple, blend easily with plain white brick walls and the Danish teak furniture. Because wall-to-wall carpeting is in a colorful floral pattern, curtains were made of an unpatterned fabric, so as not to clash.

room. Both treatments would look out of place, and spoil the final effect. All rooms must have balance and integration, and your windows are an important factor in your overall planning. If you are decorating in Danish modern, stick to simple, tailored drapes that underscore the uncluttered lines of the furniture; if antiques are your choice, let your windows echo the spirit of the period you adopt. These two photographs illustrate this point. The architecture and carpet in both rooms are the same, but the rooms look totally different because two styles of furniture and drapes have been cleverly blended.

THE TRADITIONAL VERSION OF THE SAME ROOM LOOKS TOTALLY DIFFERENT, because of window treatment and antique furniture. Formal, emerald striped silk draperies gracefully tied back, and topped by a matching tailored valance. They sit well against soft yellow walls, give extra emphasis to the antique feeling of the room created by the mahogany Newport furniture. Again plain fabric was used for the draperies, to underscore the multi-colored patterned carpet. Both rooms designed by Tom Woods, A.I.D.

Unusual Window Treatments

A CLEVER WINDOW treatment can become the dominant focal point in a room without a fireplace or a center of interest.

Cafe Curtains

Apart from being gay and fresh looking, **cafe curtains do much** to break up a wide expanse of window, or a long window. Here they are used in three tiers, made of fabric matched to the checked bedspread. The cafe curtains are excellent for controlling light, and are easy to make, can even be bought ready-made today. These are generously full, add a feminine feeling to the room. Note the low hanging light over bed, which easily zooms up to ceiling when not needed for reading. This pulldown type of fixture is ideal for saving space, also offers up or down light.

These novel cafe curtains with matching valance are the focal point in a gay kitchen. They are made of the new unbreakable beads which can be bought by the strand, slipped into a hollow rod to make any color arrangement, and just snipped off to fit any size window or create a scalloped valance. Here they are of orange, red and yellow to echo the color scheme of the kitchen. Apart from being pretty, they are practical. They can easily be wiped clean, also filter light, are easy to do yourself. Kitchen setting by Rebecca Petrikin, A.I.D.

THIS DRAMATIC WINDOW TREATMENT FEATURES bronze-green window shades, installed in a unique way to roll from the bottom up, for extra privacy. Black wood filigree panels, backed with white fiberglass, replace draperies in this exciting room, give it an air of spaciousness. Strong, cheerful colors and simplicity of design are the outstanding features in a suburban living room designed by Erica Lemle, A.I.D., with the window wall acting as backdrop for the contemporary furniture.

DESIGNER PAUL KRAUSS, A.I.D., USES NEW, BLACK AND WHITE SCREEN-PRINTED WINDOW SHADES AS A FOIL for bright red walls, to imbue a traditional room with daring contemporary color. The highly original window treatment is set off by a white wood, ceiling-to-floor lambrequin used as architectural camouflage for a pair of ordinary, double-hung windows. The tall, slender line is accentuated by hanging the shades reverse-roll within the frame, and by finishing the lambrequin with a wide band of black and white braid, keyed to the Adam-like motif of the shade. To further the illusion of height, the shades are long enough to pull all the way down to the floor. Queen Anne chairs, lacquered red, are silhouetted gracefully against the black and white background of the shades.

SHARP COLOR CONTRASTS AND A CLEVER WINDOW TREATMENT create decorating excitement in a dining room designed by Erica Lemle, A.I.D. Black and white striped window shades are pitted against elegant, white linen tieback curtains set off, in turn, by vivid red burlap-covered walls. Black hemp scroll-work braid outlines the tiebacks, coordinating shades, black cafes and long curtains into a stunning unity. The cafes, hung below the sill from a white rod, also serve to conceal an ungainly radiator. The strong red of the walls is repeated in the frames of the white leather-covered dining chairs and on the brilliantly striped bench. The result: a once ugly window transformed into a splendid focal point.

Dramatic Doors

IN THE PAST a door was often the ugly duckling in a room. Painted dark brown or muddy beige, it stuck out like a sore thumb, totally unrelated to the rest of the room's decor. Today a clever decorator knows that all doors in all rooms should blend with the style and color scheme and be an integral part of the decorating motif. Paint, fabric, wallpaper, plastic upholstery fabric and vinyl can all be used on doors, with dramatic effects. Ready-made, contemporary doors can be used to replace the standard types, and they give a room a whole new look. The unusual doors illustrated might offer some inspiration, if you are planning to discard ordinary doors in your apartment or house.

THIS LARGE, DOUBLE-SIDED DOOR was given a beauty treatment, and at the same time integrated into the color theme and mood of this modern study. White paint was used on the door frame, to link it to ceiling and floor. Russet-colored vinyl covers the door, with panel inserts of white vinyl, outlined with black paint. Doors on the bookcase-storage unit behind desk are lined with creamy-butter vinyl to match walls. Designer Andrew Delfino, A.I.D.

Contemporary Doors

with the "OP ART" look

THE THREE DOORS illustrated here are the newest in modern design and durability. They not only add a touch of elegance to a room, but are easy to install and maintain. These bi-folding doors are available as packaged pre-hung units, with frames, trim and hardware in place and can be hung in less than ten minutes. Frames are made of thick, kiln-dried wood, with a honeycomb core, and a surface material of pressure-bonded plastic. This surface material makes the doors tougher than steel, aluminum, fiberglass or plywood: surface will not stain, mar or scuff, and is specially treated to resist dust. Soap and water or common kitchen cleansers quickly restore built-in beauty. Raised, patterned surface of the doors gives them a highly individual look that blends with contemporary or traditional decor.

These double, bi-folding doors add a luxury look to wood paneled walls in a cozy den. Doors are patterned in an unusual oval design with an embossed effect. They can be left white, as shown here, or painted for an individual look.

Handsome doors have a stylized louvered design that easily fits into the traditional decor of this hall. Here they are used to screen off coat closets, but can also be used in other rooms to hide laundry and utility areas, or as room dividers. Raised, undulating sections in door panels could be painted a different color for a novel effect.

A cheerful composition of circles, raised above the surface of this durable bi-folding door adds an OP art look to a den. Doors also work well in bedrooms and bathrooms.

The dining area of this elegant living room is screened off by floor-to-ceiling folding doors. Apart from being decorative, doors act as the perfect room divider. Panels have been covered with the same wallpaper used on walls, for an integrated look, edges picked out in black paint.

Interior designer George Bockman, N.S.I.D., created a set of attractive folding doors to divide this large living room. See-through metal panels in top half of doors make dining area visible, yet wooden frame and lower panels create a solid division. Doors can be pulled right across to totally separate two areas, or pushed back against wall when large area is needed for entertaining.

The Walls Around You

*a selection of ideas which will embellish
the intrinsic shell of a room,
designed for varying tastes and moods*

WALLS ARE THE obvious shell of any room. Inside them you create the comfort and atmosphere you and your family desire. For this reason they should not be left to chance or haphazard planning. They should not only be beautiful, but an integral part of your decorating schemes. Today there are enough new wall products on the market to make walls anything from daring and dramatic, to distinguished or delicately pretty—and certainly different. You can use wallpaper, silk, grasscloth, wood, fabric, vinyl, plastic laminates, marble, tiles, leather, stainless steel or painted murals to create a beautiful shell for your furniture and accessories.

These three carefully matched panels might be hung with old world tapestries. In fact they have been filled in with a contemporary wallpaper, based on an original old design. Rich gold, patterned with muted pinks and browns, creates the look of bygone splendor, sets the theme of the decor. Wood beading framing wallpaper was painted antique pink to match chest and tone with chairs. Soft cream paper lines the rest of the walls, with panels repeated at other side of the room. The framed panels of paper dispense with the need for paintings or other wall accessories.

1.

1. The back, columned wall of this dining room looks as if it has been painstakingly lined with genuine gold leaf. It is actually covered with an elegant wallpaper. This has a pattern of birds, butterflies and delicate grasses, adapted from old Chinese panels, and makes the perfect background for traditionally styled furnishings. The paper is in warm beiges and dull golds, with bright apricot against a metallic gold. It blends beautifully with the rich woods, crystal and marble, used in the room designed by Dorothy Paul, A.I.D. This particular paper was chosen because it suits the opulent mood of the dining room.

2. A boldly patterned, brilliantly colored wallpaper can be used in a small room to create a jewel-box effect. Here you see a large country plaid paper used to illustrate this point: it seems to draw the walls together for an intimate, cozy feeling. Reminiscent of a Scottish tartan in feeling, the paper sits well with the genuine antique furniture. It is patterned in subtle colors—pistachio, maple, bronze-green, and blue mist— and makes a soft, subdued background for the furniture and accessories.

3. The Spanish mien of this sitting room has been reemphasized by the fireplace wall, which appears to have a tiled or brick surface at first glance. It is really covered with vinyl, in alabaster-beige with a white grille pattern. The wall covering repeats the mood of the Spanish inspired furniture, grille work and genuine Spanish accessories. The vinyl is mildew and flame resistant and easy to upkeep. It is available in medium and heavy weights; it is easy to install with a special adhesive, but in most cases a wall covering mechanic is recommended. Other colors range from pastels to the more vivid shades, and there are a variety of textures which simulate terrazzo tile, grasscloth, wood, damask, slubbed silk, marble or leather. Here the vinyl has been silk-screened and flocked. It makes the perfect backdrop for the brilliant pink, orange and red upholstery and accessories. Room designed by Ving Smith, A.I.D., and Charlotte Smith.

2.

3.

4. Marble look of these walls is achieved through a new **marbled wallpaper,** which sits well in a living room as illustrated here, or in other rooms such as a bathroom or kitchen. This pale blue paper, veined with dull brick-red, is color toned to nylon carpeting. Both walls and flooring are specifically designed for hard wear. Nylon carpet's inherent strength and non-absorbent nature permit maximum wear and ease of upkeep, while wallpaper has sponge-clean qualities.

5. Chantilly lace lining these walls is really **plastic-finished hardboard paneling**—although you would never guess it. The satin-finished panels have been used in this sitting room to underscore a collection of beautiful antiques, and to contrast with the plain wood paneling. Hardboard-with-the-lace-look can also be used in a tub-shower area, because it is highly resistant to heat, moisture and is hard wearing. It can be damp-wiped clean and never needs refinishing. The Chantilly lace-patterned paneling illustrated here is also available in green, gold, rose and beige, with harmonizing moldings. It is easy to install yourself, comes in large four foot wide panels which are simply attached to any solid backing with wallboard adhesive. Incidentally, the paneling is perfect for covering up marred or scarred walls, and it brings a touch of old world elegance to any room. Designer Ving Smith, A.I.D.

4.

6. Leather tiles are used on the walls of this hallway for a rich, modern look. Smooth texture of the leather contrasts with the rough grasscloth vinyl wall covering on the other walls, adds a feeling of space and height. The warp-proof tiles, made of top grade leather with beautiful natural markings, are easy to install, can be sponge-wiped clean, and come in many colors. Apart from their decorative uses, the tiles add much in acoustical value to all walls.

5.

6.

Scenics and Murals

*are highly decorative on any wall,
add a feeling of depth and dimension in any size room*

Subtle earth tones predominate in the unusual Mediterranean mural, ceramic tile floor and other furnishings of this conversation corner designed by Arthur Elrod, A.I.D. The collage-like, five-panel-scenic wallpaper is the talking point of the corner, and creates an in-depth dimensional feeling along the back wall. Colors are clay-beige, pale bronze-green, sky-blue and terra-cotta; the woven saran wall covering lining the fireplace niche picks up the terra-cotta of the mural; same shade is repeated in the accent pillows. Combination of the Mediterranean mural, ceramic tile floor and open fireplace creates a French Provincial look.

A tropical landscape scenic wallpaper brings an air of distinction to this small entrance hall, makes the narrow space seem larger than it really is. The handprinted scenic comes in four panels, in four different colors. It can be used in any small room to create a feeling of depth and space.

A handsome, contemporary mural with a subtle Oriental flavor is used along the back wall of this sitting room, for a highly decorative effect. The handprinted mural, on a soft textured background, dispenses with the need for pictures or other wall decoration. This same mural makes a perfect backdrop behind a bed, or looks equally effective in a hall.

Wood Works Wonders on Any Wall

*rich wood paneling, bookshelves and built-in furniture
add drama to a wall.
Make a wall work for you.
Some of the ideas on this page might inspire you*

Make a wall work well, with a floor-to-ceiling built-in unit. Here you see a handsome full-length fixture which adds drama to a study—and serves a multitude of purposes. Shelves hold books, plants and other decorative ornaments, plus TV, hi-fi set, sound units and ample storage space. Unusual ceiling beams conceal diffused lighting, carry out the theme set by the wall treatment.

This free-standing wall unit is decorative in itself, with its unusually shaped sections, decorative doors, stained glass panel and plant box. A few books, prize pieces of sculpture and a painting above greenery add finishing touches. Fixture sits well against a wall, also offers ample storage.

Beautifully grained wood surrounds the walls of this unique study-guest-room. Bed fits into alcove, is closed off by folding doors during the day, so that room has a totally paneled look. Here you see the bed pulled down to reveal inside of alcove, papered in a mottled gold paper to match insides of folding doors, and color toned to floor covering. Wood paneling adds an aura of luxury to any room, looks equally well in bedrooms, sitting rooms and dining rooms.

Make Floors and Walls Work as a Team

carry carpet, fabric, tile, vinyl, onto
both areas for an integrated scheme

This traditional dining room is given excitement and a luxury look by bringing the rich acrylic fiber carpet up to the chair rail in an unbroken sweep. The vivid blue carpet sits well against olive and white walls, also throws the orange upholstery into relief. This is a good idea to use in any room with a chair rail or dado; it also works well in a room with an alcove which can be covered with the carpet for an upholstered look.

The black and white checks on this floor are repeated, in a diminishing scale, on the walls in a smart entrance hall. Floor is covered in plush black and white 12 inch square rug tiles, easy to install yourself with their interlocking edges. Walls are covered in black and white double-check fabric, for an integrated look.

The 17th century country charm of this kitchen evolves through the extensive use of Delft tiles on both floor and walls. The Delft tiles, made of hard wearing vinyl, first appear on the floor, set in rows amidst more vinyl tiles with the grained look of parquet. They jump up onto the wall, and blossom in clusters to form a wall-long backsplash above the work counter. Antique furniture adds to the country air, while the pristine wall cabinets and easy up-keep surfaces make for 20th century efficiency.

Vinyl brick flooring extends up the wall, to form a panel behind the stove and frame these gay scenics, set on a companion paper with a tiny floral pattern. Clever use of the vinyl tiling on both floor and walls gives this family room a smooth, flowing feeling, also makes an ideal background for the Provincial chairs, antique ceramic stove and other furniture. The country-style murals reflect the blue, brown and ivory shades in the floral companion paper; these colors are repeated throughout the room, with yellow upholstery fabric adding a touch of sunny warmth. Designer Dorothy Paul, A.I.D.

In this ultra-small dining room two handcrafted carpets were combined as a team on floor and wall, for a rich effect. The black bordered carpet with the look of a fine old tapestry went up onto the wall. The floral-patterned carpet underfoot blends easily with the hanging rug, because it is similar in color strain and texture. Carpets are Polish imports, available in New York, as are table, chairs and other accessories shown in picture.

Floors

*some up-to-the-minute suggestions which beautify
your floors and offer the latest in comfort and luxury*

TODAY'S FLOOR PRODUCTS offer the latest in 20th century ingenuity. They are less expensive, harder wearing and more attractive than ever before. Carpets are stain and moth proof, color fast, resilient and lush; vinyl is easy to install and maintain, hard wearing and as beautiful as some of the materials it simulates . . . marble, terrazzo, tile, brick and parquet. The newest ceramic tiles are now specially processed to resist splintering or cracking; cork with a resin finish is perfect acoustically and wears well; even fabric with a plastic coating sprayed over it can go down on your floor today. Wood, stone, slate and brick can also be used for true beauty underfoot—as shown on the following pages.

Stark white room with modern white furniture relies on the multicolored brilliance of the harlequin floor, for decorative drama. Red, orange, lilac, olive, yellow, blue and black vinyl squares are laid haphazardly and spiced with white for an offbeat look. Sometimes two squares of the same color are placed next to each other, to avoid a stereotyped effect. The result is a colorful melange that underscores the pristine white of the room.

Vinyl tiles have been custom designed and laid to look like a carpet in this magnificent hall. Mulberry colored, paisley-patterned tiles in the center of the hall are surrounded by a wide border of pale pink plain tiles, which are in turn edged with a white border. The mulberry paisley tiles are repeated on the rest of the floor. The result is an area carpet look, color toned to the overall decorative scheme.

The glowing beauty of parquet flooring is hard to top, as illustrated here. The rich floor of this study is accented by the creatively designed area rug, in shades of pale yellow and blue which help to highlight the mahogany tones of the floor. The carpet adds not only a touch of luxury, comfort and color, but is hard wearing, has a non-skid backing.

1.

2.

1. **Ceramic tile has a three-fold purpose** in this comfortable living room. It **echoes** the blues in the color scheme, **highlights** the luxury of the carpeting, **defines** the two separate, split-level areas of the room. For a total integrated look, the same tile is carried beyond the picture windows and used for the terrace and swimming pool. The tile has hard-wearing, easy-clean qualities. Here the three steps double as extra seating facilities when lined with cushions.

2. **This novel flooring treatment defines** the dining area in a living room. It is not only unusual but practical too—as spills and stains are easy to clean off the circular, vinyl tiled floor. The vinyl part of the floor was laid first, and the carpet cut to fit around it. Good idea to adopt for a nursery or children's room.

3. **This charming closed in patio** is covered in one of the new vinyl carpets, with a white tweed texture. It brings a luxury look to the area, is also hard wearing, flame resistant and self-extinguishing. Its non-slip surface is practical for any area where spilled water presents a hazard—in kitchens, bathrooms, playrooms, or outside at poolside or on the patio. It can even be used on boats and at boat docks. This vinyl carpet has also proved to be unaffected by sunlight, salt or water, and is mothproof, verminproof and mildewproof. Simple cleaning by vacuuming, scrubbing, shampooing or hosing is all the maintenance needed, which makes it perfect for the above mentioned floor areas. It comes in a variety of tweed combinations, and bright colors, is easy to install, either laid loose as a runner or area rug, seamed with special tape for room sized rugs, or installed wall-to-wall.

3.

4.

5.

6.

4. The dining room of this open-plan house has been covered with unusual-shaped quarry tiles, for an antique look which blends with brick fireplace and furniture. Tiles are of hard-burned shale, fireflashed red in color, with a smooth surface. They are non-fading stain-resistant, and require little care—which makes them ideal for a dining room. They can also be used in kitchens and bathrooms, as well as outdoors. Here they are given extra prominence by the adjacent, smooth white vinyl floor; they also underscore and counterbalance the rough brick walls. Interior by Glenn Craft A.I.A., and John G. Murphy A.I.D.

5. Tailored stripes cut across the floor of this living room, to create a crisp look. The floor offsets the patterned wallpaper and antiques, also acts as unifier between traditional furniture and modern built-in cabinet. Custom designed, it is made of hard wearing, long-lasting vinyl tiles. Photograph by Dennis Purse.

6. Gleaming black vinyl tiles are used to bring a touch of drama to this traditionally shaped hall. Borders of white and gold add an "area carpet" look to the custom-designed floor. This idea can also be used in living and dining rooms.

7. This lavish-looking marble floor is really high-gloss vinyl. It echoes the simplicity of the window treatment, makes a clean background for the furniture and marble-topped dining table. Floor has a neutral background, with darker flecks and veins which simulate marble and give it a genuine look.

7.

Flattery with Fabrics

MATCHING FABRICS, used for drapes, upholstery and to cover walls, bring a fashionable, coordinated look to any room. What's more, a fabric treatment can be used to hide many architectural defects, disguise ugly windows, integrate wall jogs, and dress up old furniture. And the results are often breathtaking. Lavish use of a fabric throughout a room is not as impractical as it sounds. Today most of them are specially hard wearing, and many can be sprayed with a colorless plastic finish that makes them oblivious to stains, finger marks and dirt. Some materials treated this way can even go down on the floor.

Candy striped bed sheets of pink and blue on white set the theme of this dainty bedroom. They were used to make the quilted spread, the miniature cafe curtain, and to cover one wall. Finishing touch is the elegant window shade, chosen because it coordinates beautifully with the multi-stripe fabric. White walls, blue paint and blue bed frill echo the blue stripe of the fabric, while cyclamen-colored rug adds a bright splash of color.

A beautiful, silk-textured fabric sets the mood and color theme of this room. It is used to upholster antique sofa and for drapes, and its two colors of red and gold are repeated in straight-backed chairs upholstered in a muted brocade, and in dark red carpet. Wooden frame of the sofa is painted with antiqued-red paint picked out in gold, to echo the two-color theme of the room set by the fabric.

Fabric is used extensively here—on walls, storage cupboards and at windows, to create a beautiful shell for dining. The blue, green and white rayon and cotton fabric has been stapled onto walls, shirred into curtains on doors of storage unit, and used for drapes at windows, and for cushions. The look is one of total integration. The setting focuses on a storage unit built of plywood around a high-placed window above a radiator. The latter is topped with a rigid shelf, doubling as a serving table. Folding double doors of white-painted lumber are filled in with the printed fabric, and shirred, plain white fabric in lower half. This idea can be adapted in any room that has architectural defects and storage units that need glamorizing. The rayon and cotton fabrics used throughout this dining area are strong, hard wearing and shrink-resistant. Designed by Paul Krauss, A.I.D.

295

Frills and flowers make just the kind of bedroom any young teenage girl would love, and here fabrics come to the fore to set this mood. A pretty floral print is used as a wall covering, and repeated at windows for gathered drapes. Pristine white broderie anglaise makes a fresh-looking, fitted bedspread and deep base frill; while a nylon yarn carpet underscores the feminine mood of the room. Incidentally, fabric has been used on cupboard doors under bookcase and on bedroom door (not shown in photograph) to reiterate the integrated feeling of the room.

Fabrics can set the decorative theme of a room. Here you see an intimate little sitting room with a Moroccan flavor, inspired by the North African styled fabric used on the long comfortable sofa. This is a linen and cotton cloth, randomly striped in a dozen different color combinations and texture patterns. The repetition of pattern-on-pattern so predominant in North African fabrics has been adapted here in the fabric used for upholstery and cushions. Moroccan table and other accessories echo the mood initiated by the fabric.

Fabric with an Early American tapestry look was inspired by the hand-painted motif on a 1784 bride's dower chest in the Henry Ford Museum—shown here in picture. Made of screen-printed cotton in vibrant colors, the fabric comes with a matching wallpaper. Both are perfect for use with Early American furniture and accessories. This dower chest pattern is just one of the many new American legacy fabrics now available. They range from casement cloth to upholstery materials, come in quilt and coverlet weaves, doubleweaves, plaids, a cut velvet and several new weaves simulating textiles representative of 18th & 19th century America. The wallpapers which match, all screen-printed, are notable for a new printing technique which captures the feeling of the old papers that inspired them. Colors throughout the collection are warm and mellow. Like the designs, they were chosen primarily for creating serene rooms that are comfortable rather than ostentatious. Certainly they are ideal backdrops for antiques and Early Americana.

Massive grilled doors, antiques from Mexico, keep to the spirit of this South-of-the-Border entrance hall, are a decorative asset. At the same time, they hide a wall full of dull storage closets and shelves, which otherwise would have looked unseemly and out of character. Doors were simply hinged together, and then to the wall, open outwards for easy access to closets. This is a good idea to adapt, using any unusual or antique doors and gates to hide modern storage units.

CHAPTER EIGHTEEN

Be Clever with Storage

*bright ways to solve storage problems
and make space multiply*

GOOD STORAGE IS of vital importance in every home. There are a thousand and one things which make the wheels of a well-run house go round, but which cannot be on view. Yet most of them have to be within easy reach, and so placement of storage cupboards, closets and shelf fitments is important, if they are to work. There is no point in having a broom closet in the basement, for instance. A household cleaning cupboard is best located on the main floor, let's say at the intersection between two wings of the house, or at midpoint between living and sleeping areas. Records should be alongside the hi-fi set, games handy to a seating group, watering can and vases on the plant shelf, coat closets in the entrance hall. In the kitchen, cupboards for glass, china, mixing bowls and serving dishes should be aligned above the dishwasher; canned goods are best stored in the highest cupboards if they are not in constant use; basic cooking ingredients and spices should go on shelves above a preparing counter, set next to the range.

The storage wall is an excellent solution to storage problems, particularly if space is at a premium. In addition to its primary duties, the storage wall unit has other uses in many rooms. It can create an alcove, or act as a room divider. Storage can also be built in places unheard of in the past, such as under a bed, in its footboard or headboard, along one wall cleverly disguised with draped fabrics or unusual doors. Children's outdoor toys, a heavy stock of canned goods, sporting equipment and terrace furniture are only headaches unless you plan where you will stow them before you get them. About ten per cent of the average home interior should be given over to storage, at the least six per cent. With a little ingenuity you can make every inch of storage earn its keep.

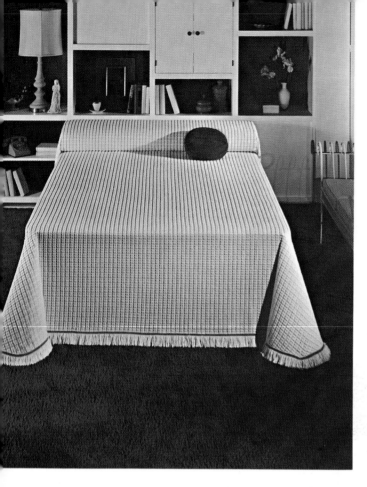

Floor to ceiling storage wall, specially built-in, makes the ideal headboard in a modern bedroom. It also serves a multitude of purposes with its storage cupboards and roomy shelves. Basic wooden structure is painted white, with alcove walls painted a rich mulberry to match the carpet. Juxtapositioning of cupboards and shelves, and varied sized alcoves gives the unit its interesting look. Telephone, address books, reading lamp, books and other accessories such as the vase of flowers and the painting all find a home in this ingenious arrangement. Actual cupboards can be used to store anything from linen to nightclothes. This idea works in any size bedroom, is also ideal in a teen-age or junior bedroom. To follow the clean lines of the unit, the bed itself is strictly tailored, with its handsome bedspread picking up the room's color scheme of white and mulberry.

TV, books and spare drinking glasses are cleverly hidden in this unique built-in cupboard. An attractive framed painting has been hung on the door of the cupboard, to blend with the mural behind it. Cupboard below holds beverages and bar equipment. When the cupboard door is closed this storage corner looks like a gaily decorated wall. Designed by Leona Kahn, N.S.I.D.

A Wall Can Solve Your Storage Problems

whether you use a built-in unit, pegboard lining, or pull-down shades

1. This multi-faceted shelf, cupboard and drawer unit solves almost every storage problem in your sitting room. At the same time it is a handsome addition to any room. This unit contains a bar with a drop-down shelf for a serving top, books, ornaments, records, stereo set and speakers, as well as a set of miniature drawers for games, cards, stationery and other small things Final touch is the container for the collection of plants. The unit is floor to ceiling, completely free-standing and self-contained, can also be used to divide a room, and moves with you if you relocate to a new home.

2. These two wall fixtures flank each side of a nursery door, are united by the long shelf which runs between the two and above the door. Shelf easily dismantles, so that the two pieces can be used in any part of the room. Here you see how this kind of storage unit really works in a child's room. Shelves are filled with books and toys; more precious things go on higher shelves to avoid breakages; drawers hold clothes, linen, extra toys, while drop-leaf desk is a perfect spot for drawing, or homework as the child grows.

3. Space and storage problems were ingeniously met in this small room for a scientific-minded teen-ager. Sliding screens, designed like blinds, are made of hard wearing nylon yarns, hide the ample storage shelves. The shelves flank a desk-shelf, built-in unit. Storage drawers hide underneath the daybeds which run along the other two walls, and hold linen, blankets and sporting equipment. All materials used in the room are easy to clean and hard wearing right down to wall-to-wall carpet, circular rug and daybed covers. Designer Lois P. Munroe, A.I.D.

4. A two-panel entertainment center is the bright spot in this recreation room. Taking minimum room because the prefinished pegboard holds table tennis paddles, a portable TV set and other leisure-time articles, the wall can be put up for less than $30 by the do-it-yourselfer. The walnut-grained hardboard panels are attractive in themselves, besides being functional, and can be used in children's rooms, laundries, garages, kitchens and in storage closets. Here the pegboard panels are flanked by matching walnut-grained hardboard panels, without the perforations.

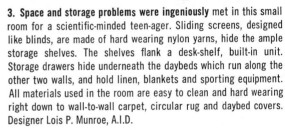

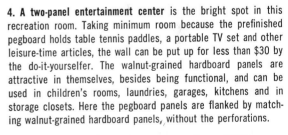

How to cut corners in creating storage space, without costly furniture additions, is illustrated here by Paul Krauss, A.I.D., in a dining room utilizing color-cued rayon fabrics. From a wooden frame across the joint of two walls, the designer hangs a length of cloth which has been fashioned into a braid-trimmed Roman shade, to permit quick access to shelves or cabinets holding table appointments. The same upholstery fabric is used for the chair cushions, in a bright orange which complements the pumpkin tone of the pull-up shade. This clever storage corner is truly integrated into the room, through clever color cuing. This is an idea which can be used in any corner, in any room of the house, to hide unsightly storage units. It also works well in an entrance hall, creates a coat closet at little cost.

In this hall, window shades are used as "doors" to give handsome color and design interest to a closet wall. They transform a purely utilitarian area into a dramatic, decorating high point, are much less costly to install than storage closets with wooden doors. The laminated shades are set behind a narrow molding, so that they pull up and down inside the frame. The bottom hems of the shades have been squared out so that the slats can be used as shade pulls. For accent they are painted the same bitter-green as one of the major color accents in the crewel-like cotton print. White walls and vinyl covered floor, deeper green area rug and chair seat pick up the major colors of the shades—as does the beautifully painted chest. Other laminated shades on the windows opposite (not shown in picture) repeat the high point once more. Designed by Paul Kraus, A.I.D.

An attractive chest in a corridor or entrance hall can solve a variety of storage problems. And if it is ingeniously combined with another piece of furniture or accessories it can have great decorative value. Here you see how an Early American sweetheart chest becomes the real decorative accent in this hall, when used beneath recessed bookshelves. The chest has a deep storage area for linens, blankets and other household items, while its lustrous maple finish adds a soft glow to a bright color combination of blue walls and red carpeting. This same chest fits well into a bedroom, with its top surface acting as a catch-all for possessions.

This study-guest-room has ultra-practical, built-in units in the window area to counteract storage problems. Comfortable, upholstered sofa doubles as a bed, has deep drawers underneath for bedding. Side table between sofa and bookcase has a roomy surface, with double drawers underneath for other hide-away items; ceiling-high shelves are cleverly fitted in between table and wall for a truly compact look. The same paneling is used on storage pieces, bookcase and walls for an integrated look, while embossed inlaid linoleum has a parquet floor appearance echoing the paneling.

Specially designed for a man, this large walk-in closet solves all clothes storage problems. It features mirrored inside doors, and a smart vinyl floor in a brick pattern. Shirts are stacked in built-in shelves above deep chests for underwear, suits are arranged in a double rod arrangement. Spaciousness and practical floor make cleaning easy, ceiling lights ensure perfect illumination. Designed by Leona Kahn, A.I.D., N.S.I.D.

Twin armoires (one not shown) are painted antique white and connected by a space-saving dressing table in this elegant bedroom. The armoires are outfitted to hold linens, shirts and suits, solve the basic storage problem for clothes and bedroom necessities. Six pull-out drawers line one side, with hanging space at the other. Shelves above drawers are roomy for sheets, towels, while drawers in base of armoires hold blankets or woolens. Connecting dressing table surface has two spacious drawers and ample surface for accessories. Bedroom designed by Kass Seigal, N.S.I.D.

PART THREE

Flair
and the Personal Touch

A very deft hand created this striking arrangement in the corner of a sitting room. The intricate design and subtle coloring of the wonderful old carved door and grilles on the wall have been masterfully picked up in a brown and black print fabric, used to upholster the sofa. Although other accessories and furnishings are of several different styles and periods, all are bound together by subdued black-brown-gold coloring and elegant design. Underscoring the room is a custom-designed floor of green, three-dimensional vinyl tile accented by solid opaque vinyl inlays. The antique clock flanked by the two carriage lamps, old books on the table, the checked lamp shade and placement of the china cat near the sofa bring a finishing touch of flair to the room.

CHAPTER NINETEEN

Flair with Accessories

❧

FLAIR IS ONE of those overworked and often misused words whose true meaning is sometimes hard to define. In the literal sense it is derived from the Latin word for smell or scent. The dictionary defines it as *a discriminating sense, a keen perception, an instinctive discernment,* and so it can be summed up as a combination of talent, taste and unerring instinct.

Flair in decorating is the brilliant, the individual and often unexpected touch that lifts a room out of the regions of conformity and gives it a flashing, unique look all its own. Flair, in fact, is the stamp of the individualist.

A color scheme, an arrangement of accessories, a grouping of paintings and sculpture, collectors' items, use of mirrors, fabrics, wallpapers can all contribute that special touch of flair to a room.

Mirror Magic

*Make mirrors work for you in rooms that are
too small, too dark, too confined. Or simply use
them decoratively to enhance a setting*

A MIRROR IS more than a looking glass, even though this is one of its prime assets. Skillfully used, mirrors perform magic . . . space, light, focal and decorative magic. Think of a mirror in many ways and view its visual effects from many angles. Remember that mirrors build in windows of light in tired, drab walls, giving them a touch of sunlight, and used as architectural tools they strengthen weak room dimensions. They will expand walls outward, take ceilings upward, bring visual depth and the exciting dimension of space to rooms which need a new point of perspective.

Mirrors are functional. They can introduce a fool-the-eye element to distract attention from structural defects. As a sparkling decorative prop, a mirror can be used to transform a plain table into a decorator's piece, give coordinated beauty to a haphazard furniture grouping, or decorative unity to problem areas in any room. Mirrors can serve a definite purpose in your decorating scheme. Don't make them afterthoughts in the room plan. Whenever possible, mirrors should reflect beauty, whether it's a natural or staged reflection. A mirror that reflects a blank wall is missing out on all its potential.

Mirrors have been making history for over four thousand years. On the following pages we show you *new* ways with mirrors. Decorators have found some ingenious ways to use mirrors, to make homes brighter and more spacious. Ways with mirrors can be featured in every room in the home. They are old ideas, with a new twist. Mirrors can look like windows, shuttered or draped for authenticity, and placed where they were never visualized before. They can be used to create corners of interest; or corners of practical use where, without the mirror, the setting couldn't survive. They can be used behind doors and on doors; in one instance they might serve as a hidden check-up beauty spot, in another they dress up a room and line a wardrobe area. They add sparkle behind shelves, giving art objects and colorful book-bindings rich dimensional appeal. Or they can simulate a pass-through window in a game room or at a snack corner. These are some of the new ways with mirrors. Adapted to your home, whether the objective is functional or decorative, they can add beauty and elegance.

A few pieces of furniture and a collection of unusual accessories easily bring flair to a corner. Here you see how a bookcase, chair and ottoman were skillfully surrounded by plants, pictures and leather cushions to create a unique and restful corner in a room. The russet toned pouffs and the graceful 17th century wood statue suggested the harmonious color scheme that was extended throughout the corner with complete success. The tall French bibliothèque and cream upholstered seat with ottoman were painted in coordinated colors: handstitched blanket and gilt-framed pictures contribute to the well-organized color scheme, also picked up in the Roman shades made from a lovely flowered fabric designed after a French museum piece original. Small study corner designed by Yale R. Burge, A.I.D., N.S.I.D.

Mirrors elaborately framed and grouped provide a gallery of "pictures" that change with a nod of the head, and a different image. They mix well with real pictures and wall ornaments, make an excellent background for a display of other bric-a-brac. A feeling of balance is achieved through clever placement of smaller mirrors against large modern one, and an otherwise dull wall has been given a glittering "lift."

Mirrors make an interior sparkle. Hanging on a modern, raised fireplace, this one plays fascinating optical tricks, suggests a transparency that contradicts the solidity of the stone. Cleverly placed statue, glass jars, ash tray and chess board ranged along fireplace add that little touch of flair to the strictly modern structure.

Mirror paneling covering one wall of a small dining room from floor to ceiling doubles interest of furniture and accessories. It also creates the illusion of a long and lavish dining hall, with twice as much elegance of furnishings as actually exists. Note the pleasing double image of handsome objects close to mirror. This same idea can be used in any room of the house to give a feeling of extra space and light.

In this elegant New York apartment, specially created for a top fashion model, mirror and glass are the talk-points. An unusual set of double-sided mirrored screens divides the foyer and living room. Rising from floor to ceiling, the unique screens reflect the beautiful antiques and other furnishings, while a large glass coffee table echoes the sparkling theme and throws off more light, additional reflections. Color scheme of the room is basically white—white silk walls, white velvet sofa, white-on-white chairs and white lamb rug. Only accent color comes in the red cushions on the Louis XVI armchairs. This white-on-white scheme, plus the extensive use of mirrors was purposely chosen to show off the model's beautiful clothes, as well as the antique accessories, flowers and plants. Double-sided mirrored screens such as these also work well in a bedroom. Living room designed by Harry Mark Schule, N.S.I.D.

Mirrors can glamorize an awkward corner,
give it dimensions of space and extra light

Adjoining mirrors reflect colorful beauty from many angles in this small dressing room. More importantly they bring space and light to an otherwise dull corner, and make it work efficiently as a dressing table and washbasin corner for several members of the family. This same idea of adjoining mirrors can be used above a dressing table in a bedroom, or in any room that is small and cramped looking.

310

In this corner you see how mirror and glass are used effectively together to provide an optical illusion of double window area and double space. In this small bathroom a structural mirror runs flush to the window, reflects back the outdoor scene. At the same time the wall-length mirror above washbasins and counter top offers maximum efficiency for shaving, make-up and dressing.

Mirrors can be used in a variety of decorative ways. Here an ordinary wall mirror, shuttered to simulate an authentic window, provides unusual decorative and dimensional effects in this teen-ager's attic bedroom. A second shuttered mirror (not shown in picture) above the second bed duplicates the effect. The shutters really work, and can be closed when desired. This idea works well in a dining room or a dark, narrow hallway or entrance

Structural wall mirror adds a feeling of depth and dimension to this small dining area. Placed above the built-in cupboard and counter top, it runs flush to the ceiling, thus adds height to the area, as well. Candlestick, fruit and other accessories are reflected in the mirror, create an additional decorative effect at night. This type of mirror can be used at the end of a long corridor for the same space and dimensional reasons.

Accessories...the Personal Touch

ACCESSORIES ALWAYS ADD just the right finishing touch to a room . . . in fact, the very *personal* touch that puts your individual stamp on it.

Any setting, however beautifully decorated, somehow looks cold and unlived in without those intimate objects that add warmth, whether they are family photographs, memorabilia, collections, sculpture, paintings or books. Something specially your own, whether treasured or new, adds the necessary spark of life to the decor of a room. A collection of old snuff boxes, glass paperweights, pieces of Early Americana, native handicraft, in fact any colorful or unusual accessories perk up a dull corner, add interest to a bookcase. They should be arranged deftly, with symmetry and balance, and combined with other varied objects for true flair.

Antique collectibles are now **seen,** not hidden away as they used to be, on shelves behind glass. A popular way to display one's treasures is on a table or desk, where they can be picked up and handled, as well as admired. The collection of late 19th century crystal paperweights shown here belongs to New York antiques dealer Michael Bertolini, and portions of two of his other collections are also pictured. The pink opaline plate at left is one of numerous pink and green opaline objects—plates, tumblers, decorative little boxes and bottles—scattered around the apartment. Portraits above the table are from Mr. Bertolini's collection of 18th century English and Continental miniatures, displayed on walls and in open cabinets. If you collect miniatures, adopt this idea of hanging several within a large frame for a composite look.

Soft green wallpaper with an Oriental design sets the mood here, and accessories gathered from around the world echo the theme. Bamboo plant and ocelot cushion on chair blend beautifully with high-standing piece of native sculpture, Chinese lacquered red pot, and other objects on white topped table. Colorful coffee cups, old brass coffee pot add extra spark. The result is a corner with talking points, which otherwise might have been dull.

A mixture of colorful accessories adds flair to this modern bedroom wall. Black and white grille work panel is flanked by a piece of native art and a gay modern painting; hanging brass light fixture contributes sparkle as well as efficient illumination. Plants underneath the multi-patterned Roman shade, wicker hanging lamp, other pieces of native sculpture on brick wall add finishing touches. Sleek mustard-colored bedspread, deep blue carpet pick up the basic color scheme of the room, with red chair bringing just the right splash of brightness in the corner.

The right accessories make a room sing. This dramatic curtain of sparkling beads catches the mood of the blue-green jewel-like colors used in an airy dining nook. It also repeats the feeling of the other glass used here. The hanging lamp is an ideal match to the curtain; even the painting and the glass on the table echo the color mood. Pots of ivy are massed to form a virtual hill of greenery around statue. Placement and arrangement of pieces give the area a feeling of true balance. Designed by Rebecca Petrikin, A.I.D.

New idea to replace an ordinary headboard are these swag-and-pendant plaques forming a shapely frame for the bed. The pieces, carefully arranged for a rich, old world look, are complemented by the cherub plaques on the side wall. These accessories can be used in any room for decorative wall effects.

A collection of antique three-dimensional paintings and carvings are combined with pieces of hanging sculpture and plants in this studio bedroom. They give the room its focal point, also reiterate the Spanish theme set by furniture and arches along far wall. The carvings, as well as plants and candelabra, are hung on a wall of pegboard to make new arrangements easy. This is a good idea to use in any room where a collection is to be displayed.

Treasured prints, sculpture and ceramics as well as handsome books are all displayed with studied casualness in this good-looking hallway. Dark, sleek finished shelves match the table top and the vinyl floor. Shelves and table are purposely severe in line to emphasize the objects on them. Similar distressed gilt frames unite all the pictures, which are hung in seemingly random arrangements for a truly casual effect.

Any collection can be seen at its best in a cabinet like this, made to order for the purpose. Its six sides are alternately glass and rosewood. The adjustable glass shelves allow the shielded down-light at the top to illuminate the entire interior, and show off precious objects, glassware or china.

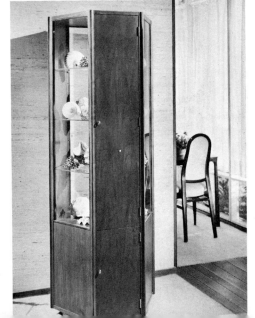

Use Books as Decorative Accessories

A LIBRARY WALL or a small set of bookshelves can easily become the decorative focal point in a room. Handsome leather-bound books and vivid paper jackets bring a sea of color to a dull wall or dark corner. Books can be used with a mixture of other objects, sculpture, ceramics, a painting or family photographs. Arranged with flair they have a truly individual look.

Here is an example of books carefully combined with favorite objects, in a room designed by Ving Smith, A.I.D. Shelves of generous height insure visibility of objects scattered among books. The large painting hanging over fireplace has books ranged behind it. Room incorporates a good decorating idea. The air conditioner is covered with a panel of fabric that matches drapes.

Here is a way to house an abundance of books and antique accessories: mingle them on your bookshelves. English and American collectibles such as pitchers, teapots and Staffordshire figures provide interesting contrasts of shape, color and texture to rows of books. Wing chair and table are American. Included among accessories are several Chinese porcelains, such as the lamp.

Books are mixed with ornaments for a decorative effect on these bookshelves lining one wall of a dining room. Imaginative arrangement is achieved through utilizing shelves of varying heights and effective placement of books among other objects. Library wall becomes the focal point. Warm glow in the room is created through use of orange nylon fabric used on ceiling and walls and repeated for chair, upholstery and tablecloth. Designed by John Elmo, A.I.D.

Books and other decorative objects come into play in this large L-shaped living room with a dining area.
In front of picture, in the conversation area, a white wall is a subtle backdrop for distinctive shelves, decorative in themselves. They in turn display a few selected art works and ornamental objects, grouped with just a handful of the most luxuriously bound books. Handsome clock on right balances the shelves.

Here you see a close-up of the dining area of L-shaped living room. Wall-length shelves above a serving counter hold a wealth of books and records simply arranged. Use of books here gives the dining area more of a living room look, with other objects and paintings adding a warm touch. Designer Renee Lind, N.S.I.D.

Built-in under an unusual curved ceiling, these simply constructed shelves flank a whole wall, hold a complete library. The desk and cabinets beneath add a feeling of solidarity, hide hi-fi speaker and heating panels. The pale grey finish of the wood paneling is perfect for reflecting light, also makes a soft background for the brightly-bound books, plants, flowers and artifacts arranged among the books. Two-toned blue carpet also seems to reflect light, and underscores the pale shades in the room.

ART CREATES A DRAMATIC EFFECT. Drama and surprise characterize this fresh, bold handling of art work in the home. One entire wall of this living room has been transformed into a gigantic shadow box. Lights range along the top of the alcove to focus on vivid modern paintings, while the wall itself is black, a striking background for the white framed paintings—a reversal of the usual procedure. The immense black and white blow-up of the Boticelli head is in itself an unusual approach to the business of viewing art. Many people scorn reproductions. But this one, focusing as it does on **one** detail, (here much larger than the original, and devoid of its color so that shape and value are more apparent) has in effect been transformed into a **new** work of art. The blow-up is imaginatively hung. Its modern framelessness is boldly contrasted with elaborate candelabra on either side, and the entire wall receives a rich texturing from a facing of blocks of end-grain wood. The room's furnishings are planned to hold their own against the unusual art treatments, without detracting from them. Pieces are few and simple in line, but brilliant color makes them visually interesting on their own, and unites the room and its art into a pleasing whole.

CHAPTER TWENTY

Art in the Home

ART CAN PLAY an important role in your decorating plans. Paintings not only add life to a room, they also emphatically underscore the style already created by furniture. A modern room seems to have more character when the mood is echoed by the paintings and sculpture used. The same applies to a period room, when the paintings are of the same era as the furniture.

But there are no set rules, and part of the fun in collecting art is to mix and match a variety of different paintings. The main thing to remember is that the final effect should be pleasing to the eye.

Collecting art is not necessarily a pastime for the rich. If your taste runs to Picasso and Chagall but your bank balance doesn't, you can still acquire your favorite paintings. Almost all of the pictures painted by the great French painters are now available in reproductions. They are excellent and cost very little. If you scorn reproductions, start collecting good paintings by young unknowns—if you are lucky you might discover a budding genius. Watercolors, lithographs, old prints and charcoal drawings can be just as effective as oils, and you can occasionally pick up something genuine by a well-known artist for very little.

Wall Groupings Make a Room Sing with Color and Interest

IT'S ALL IN THE GROUPING. The owners of this Los Angeles apartment wanted to display a large number of paintings and drawings. The solution was to create a pale, neutral shell to act as background. The sofa and other furnishings have also been kept pale. Across the walls, diversely framed pictures have been grouped without specific order, but with a careful eye to distribution of large and small. Occasional non-rectangular hangings help create extra visual interest, and the result is a selection of pictures presented with flair. Dark area rug is an important low-level counterweight for all the high-up activity. Interior by Lulu Ross, A.I.D. Den of the Micky Katz apartment, Los Angeles. All paintings by Mrs. Grace Katz.

ART IN THE KITCHEN—AND WHY NOT? A handsome, even sumptuous kitchen like this one, deserves brilliant treatment. Paintings and prints of fruit and vegetables ranged along one wall provide a feast for the eyes, and are perfect "mood" pieces for a kitchen. They also set the rich color scheme of gold tones and black. A mirror in the corner near the yellow curtain makes the picture wall seem larger than it is. Entire wall is covered with pegboard, from which pictures hang. Black and gold built-in cupboards echo the theme of the black and gold carriage-lamp-style refrigerator. The result is a kitchen as glamorous as any other room in the house.

Reproduction and genuine, oils and water colors, prints and lithographs can all be successfully mingled together. Grouping together a varied mixture of art offers you a chance to use your inventiveness and your sense of composition. For instance, a bank of mixed paintings grouped closely together on a single wall can provide a dramatic focal point. The easiest way to lay out such a grouping is on the floor, so you can visualize how it will look on the wall. Keep in mind balance of the small and the large, points of eye interest composition of color, relationship of neighboring forms. Frames need not all match each other.

However, framing and mounting *is* important. Modern paintings usually look best in simple frames, while the more intricate, baroque frames sit well with period paintings, although there is no set rule. It is the mount, which surrounds the painting and runs to the edge of the frame, which offers you a chance to be creative. Instead of the usual hard paper or board, use velvet, silk, linen, burlap or taffeta. Pick a color that not only blends with the painting but echoes the color scheme of the room; in fact, often a painting and its mount will inspire a color scheme. You can give a room a truly integrated look by using picture mounts made of the same fabric which is used for upholstery and drapes. Plain fabrics look best and patterns should be avoided. A colorful mount can give life and importance to a black and white sketch or monochromatic print which would otherwise be dull.

Restoring and maintenance of good paintings, framing and mounting should be done by a professional. The cost is relatively small, in view of the finished results. You might ruin a good picture by trying to clean and restore it yourself; and even the most trivial little picture gains in character with the addition of a good mount and frame.

Ideas on how to use art effectively in the home are shown in this chapter. Pinpointed are picture groupings, colorful combinations, paintings and sculpture mixed. They illustrate a fresh approach to the use of art in the home, and most importantly show its value in decorating.

A WALL OF OLD, BLACK AND WHITE PRINTS is treated with all the respect of a gallery—special ceiling spotlights and a decorative railing which suggests "be careful." Picture-covered wall is especially effective since other walls are left bare. Spicy red, black and white color scheme and intricate patterns of sofa and antique chair complement the delicate artwork. Designed by Kass Seigal, N.S.I.D.

Combine Paintings and Sculpture for that Individual Look

A LARGE WOOD CARVING IS WELL-PLACED on a low table, as illustrated here, so that it can be displayed to its best effect. Painting and other wall objects behind add interest, yet are subtle enough not to detract from the sculpture's three-dimensional quality. A piece like this often looks even more effective when softly illuminated by a small spotlight focusing on it from the other side of the room.

SCULPTURE AND PAINTINGS ARE NATURAL COMPANIONS. Here you see how they have been cleverly combined for a truly artistic look, in this small sitting room. Smooth white walls show off the highly different pictures, while veined marble top of buffet cabinet makes an effective background for the pieces of sculpture. Even the plants in this room have been skillfully placed, for an almost sculptured look themselves. Concealed lighting above focuses on both paintings and sculpture.

BY CHANGING JUST ONE PIECE IN A GROUP-ING, the entire character of the whole may be altered, as shown in the two pictures here. In the first picture you see how the gentle-toned painting, its colors similar to those of the background drapes, unites the composition by visually tying together the two statues with the background. It also helps to create a mood of softness which in turn heightens the feminine aspect of the two carvings.

In the second arrangement, when a small brightly-colored enameled plaque is substi-tuted for the painting, an entirely different effect is achieved. Metallic brilliance of the plaque tends to draw more attention to the gleaming enameled bowls. Each object in the arrangement stands out on its own. The composition is more active, less soothing in the second arrangement, although equally as attractive as the first. Try experimenting in this way, with sculpture and accessories, until you achieve the effect you want.

Art Creates a Distinctive Flavor

*use paintings to inspire a mood, whether it's of days gone by,
foreign lands, or contemporary and in swing with the present*

Japanese prints, hung in threes, echo the threesome theme of this modern bedroom, and help to establish a definitely Oriental mood. The characteristically long, slender shape of the three prints, and a fourth in the corner, works well with the tall narrow window shades also hung in threes. Plants and foliage reinstate the restful, Far East look of the room, as does the clean lined furniture and simple bedspread. Remember that antique prints such as these usually mingle well with contemporary furnishings, providing they are not ornately framed.

Examples of Early American art and pieces of Americana, give a final fillip to this charming bed alcove inspired by trends of yesteryear. Closely patterned, Early American style wallpaper is an intriguing background for the paintings and other objects hanging on it. American antique art, as well as excellent reproductions, often mounted on a wood plaque like this sailing ship, are available from a number of sources. Miscellaneous objects such as the big key, the American eagle, the old model ship and sepia miniature portraits can be found by rummaging in antique shops. They prove to be attractive wall decorations combined with paintings, as shown here. The placing of this collection deep in an alcove heightens its attractiveness with a sense of mystery. Sculptured white bedspread with deep fringe is the ideal contrast next to the wallpaper, and in fact reflects extra light into the alcove to highlight the collection of memorabilia and art.

Make Your Own Gallery

The long hall of this attractive modern house has been turned into a private art gallery, and this can be an excellent idea to adopt if you have a long hall or corridor that needs a decorative motif. Here the slightly slanted wooden panels allow paintings to rest on a small edge, without being hung, also angle paintings upwards from their rather low position. Shelf above them is ideally suited for the display of sculpture, and if necessary can accommodate invisible light fixtures. Note the beautiful objects displayed with flair, throughout the rest of the room, in particular the figure and brass plaque on the high ledge next to the brick fireplace close to the ceiling. If you cannot afford such an elaborate "gallery" as this one, but want to give a corridor a lift, you could line the walls with colorful paintings and prints. Photographic blow-ups of paintings also look good lining corridor walls.

The bold, colorful activity in these paintings and the rough, textured quality of the room that contains them are in rare harmony. Large wooden shingles make a perfect background wall for an appropriate painting that enhances the shape and pattern of the shingles. Only one painting was used on this wall, for a striking effect. In fact, since the room is quite dynamic itself, the number of paintings was wisely limited. A second, larger painting was used on the dark fireplace wall, while smaller paintings are propped up in the bookcase. Use of the one smaller painting on the wall of shingles appears to give the wall greater height.

See how a nicely balanced arrangement of art work sparks this seating area. By extending the picture area to the edges of the sofa and no further, the sofa's importance is heightened. Rug helps to balance the composition. As well as paintings, framed butterflies and an old clock are used in this arrangement to give it additional flair.

Here you see how potted plants add both color and life to an all white dining room, which otherwise would have looked cold and uninviting. White brick walls, vinyl floor and lightweight garden furniture give the room its basic "outdoor" theme, reiterated through extensive use of plants on three-tiered shelves and in the center of the candelabra. The wrought-iron half-circle planter with its graduated shelves makes an eye-catching focal point, while trailing ivy plant is a decorative asset above the table, yet takes up no surface space. The red clay pots used for the plants ensure healthy growth, and add a more natural garden look to the outdoor theme of the room. The geraniums, cyclamen and azaleas, banked against the wall in this way, dispense with the need for an extra piece of furniture.

CHAPTER TWENTY-ONE

Indoor Gardens

INDOOR PLANTS have become increasingly popular as decorative assets, particularly in city homes where even outside greenery is scarce. An amazing variety of foliage now blooms in homes—flowering plants, evergreens, shrubs, small trees, even palms and rare species from the Orient and deserts. Almost all of them flourish the year round, so that a feeling of Spring persists even when snow is falling outside.

Their decorating possibilities are enormous. A single house plant will highlight a coffee table, a fireplace mantel or a piano, and a large collection of foliage and flowering plants will bring a bay window into dramatic focus. You can spark up your kitchen with an indoor herb garden, or bring early Spring to your entrance foyer with the fragrance of flowering bulbs. A teacart provides an unusual as well as practical place for a collection of potted plants. And there are literally hundreds of places in your home where plants will serve not only a decorative function but a useful one as well. If you don't have enough room for a full-sized room divider between your living room and dining alcove, let a plant divider create the illusion of separate rooms. Leading decorators and architects, who include plantings of all types as part of their designs, are fostering the new trend towards using plants in more places, more often. Even furniture manufacturers are producing furniture with built-in planter tubs and boxes.

Creating yor own indoor garden is easy, and a fun hobby, particularly as you can start or add to your collection of living potted plants any time, and in any season you choose. Of course selecting living plants properly and using them effectively to enhance indoor beauty is important. But it need not be complicated. You don't need "green thumb" talents. You merely have to exercise the same basic good judgment you would in planning and using any of the materials, furnishings or accessories that add to the beauty of your home.

There are two basic types of pot plants. First, flowering plants that may either flower all at one time or keep flowering over various periods of time. Some of the favorites are geraniums, azaleas, begonias, hydrangeas, lilies, roses, gardenias, chrysanthemums, cineraria, African violets, amaryllis, gloxinias, fuchsias, kalanchoes, cyclamen, tulips, poinsettias, daffodils and hyacinths. Second, foliage or green plants, mostly tropical varieties professionally conditioned to grow in almost any climate. Some of the more popular are philodendrons, ferns, jade plants, Chinese evergreens, dracaena, dieffenbachia, ivy, schefflera, rubber plants, sansevieria, syngonium, peperomia, caladiums, coleus, bromeliads and cacti and other succulent plants.

Quality pot plants are those professionally grown, "climate conditioned" and sold in sturdy, porous, red clay pots. The clay pot is preferred by professional growers and florists, because it is the only container that truly provides plants with the growing conditions of the earth itself. Plants in thin-walled, non-porous substitute containers do not have this essential advantage. You will find the majority of the finest, healthiest looking plants of each variety in red clay pots, which make them easier to care for and easier to repot into larger-sized clay containers as they grow. And the clay potted plant can be stood in a decorative tub or planter for special effect.

SELECT: Foliage plants that have dark green, glossy leaves; flowering plants that have firm healthy stems and well-developed but not yet fully opened buds. AVOID: Yellowed, browned, curled or falling blossoms or leaves and drooping stems, all tell-tale signs that a plant's root structure is not healthy.

Ask your florist or garden store to give you watering instructions for each plant and follow them carefully.

Plants require different quantities of water. Some like it dry. Some like it moist. But few can stand **overwatering.** Hence the porous clay pot, which leaches out excess water on all sides, is your best insurance against "drowning" and killing your plants. Generally, if top soil in the clay pot feels dry to the thumb, your plants need water. Use lukewarm water. Do not allow plants to stand in water. It's best to water all your plants at once, pouring gently until water runs out of the bottom drainage hole of the clay pot.

Do not expose plants to temperatures that are too warm or too cold. Most plants are best kept at temperatures between 60 and 70 degrees. Ask your florist about this. Keep plants away from drafts, heating units, gas or chemical odors. Be sure to ask your florist what amount of light is best for each plant in your collection. Flowering plants generally like more light, but in varying degrees. Foliage plants usually do better with less. Group sun-loving and shade-loving plants together, when possible. Apply a fertilizer that can be dissolved in water about once a month. Don't over-fertilize. For good grooming large-leaved plants can be lightly dusted with a soft camel's hair brush. You can also use commercial substances to spray plants, to make leaves shiny. But be careful not to get it on the undersides of the leaves. Finally, turn a spotlight on your indoor garden for a dramatic effect. This is a good supplement if plants do not get much light, as long as it is not too close to them.

334

Dress Up a Room Divider with Foliage

*Plants and flowering shrubs, grouped together on
or against a room divider, help to give extra
emphasis to the divider. They also add texture,
color and life at little cost*

Through use of foliage, designer John Elmo, A.I.D., effectively breaks monotony of a wood paneled divider, which separates this dining area from rest of living room. Large circle, cut in center of divider, is filled with potted plants. Clever lighting subtly accentuates these. Other plants used in dining area and attractive metal furniture echo garden mood.

Large boxes of plants placed at the edge of this raised living room floor help to re-emphasize the division between entrance hall and living room. They form a "hedge" of greenery which combines with patterned hall floor to separate two areas, yet the plants do not detract from the open-plan, spacious feeling. The ornamental tree in a white tub restates the "green look" of the entrance hall. Other plants and shrubs are used extensively throughout the rest of this penthouse apartment for a true rooftop garden air. Designer Gary Pizzarelli, A.I.D.

A simple wood frame forms a decorative divider and provides a perfect setting for indoor plants in this foyer. Unusually shaped pots and vases are used for the plants for effective silhouettes ... a sea shell, a pottery basket, a low bowl; on the top shelf a handcrafted jar with side attachments. The plants receive plenty of natural daylight for full, abundant growth through the panel of aqua color-in-the-glass block window used in the foyer. The thick, patterned glass also adds a modern touch to the exterior of the house, while its soft aqua shade creates a sea-like feeling behind the plants.

This free-standing, custom-built divider comes with its own plant box, seen here filled with a mixture of greenery. It makes the perfect divider for a small or large room, and also looks well pushed back against a wall. The plants add just the right finishing touch.

Use Plants in Any Room of Your Home

for a fresh, open air feeling, whether it's kitchen, bedroom, or bathroom

This kitchen has a touch of summer the year through, with its profusion of plants growing on top of the wall cabinets. Abundant look was achieved through using a dozen or more potted plants along the shelf above the sink. More greenery rests above electric clock, and is scattered in other parts of the kitchen to repeat the theme. Baskets of fern hanging from ceilings, geraniums, and azaleas also work well in a kitchen. The plants here are all potted, so they can be lifted down for easy watering.

Unusual shaped bath tub and shower has its own miniature garden. Flowering plants line one edge of the marble tub, are repeated on the window sill for a lush look. There is often a spot in the bathroom for a collection of foliage such as this. A row of glass shelves is perfect for a garden grouping.

An indoor window box can be an effective addition to your living room decor. These boxes are fun to plant, if you are blessed with a "green thumb." This teak box is lined with tiny pebbles, and each plant is individually potted for easy care and watering. It is particularly pretty because plants are varied in species, height and size, for a miniature garden look.

A small indoor garden was created in this recessed window of an elegant bedroom. Fine trellis work replaces blinds at window, and does double duty as a frame for crawling ivy. Hanging plants create unusual silhouettes against the window; large and small potted flower plants fill in floor area in window. The same effect can be achieved in a bay window or alcove. Designed by John and Earline Brice, A.I.D.

Let Plants Flower Around
a Window or a Painting

for a fresh, decorative look

This living curtain of spring flowering foliage and plants is made possible by use of new "hanging planters" suspended by chains from curtain rods. Hanging planters, consisting of flower pots, with matching clay saucers, are specially treated to keep water from dripping on floors. They are now available at florists and garden centers throughout the country. Planters can be had ready-made. Holes are pre-drilled in clay saucers, to hold chains for suspending both saucer and clay-potted plants. The plants in this attractive "curtain" include azaleas, philodendron and pothos. The window interest is supplemented by finishing the bare edges with ball fringe.

Wide window sill is filled with a junior jungle of greenery for a greenhouse look in this dining area. Window acts as a reflector, throws additional emphasis onto potted ferns and other plants. Miniature flower paintings are scattered amongst the foliage for a dash of color. Cotton paisley cloth and green glassware seem to echo the jungle-green theme.

Real Indoor Gardens

*a collection of rooms that bloom the
year through, with flowering plants and foliage*

This built-in garden nook provides the focal point in this tasteful seating arrangement. Filled with ferns in pots and miniature rose plants in individual clay pots and saucers, the recessed indoor garden also adds a note of serenity to the conversation area. Tiled wall and front of recess make a smooth background for the plants, with statue and wall plaque emphasizing the garden theme.

Indoor gardening on an elegant scale is catered to in this attractive sitting room. Double-textured vinyl tiles which look and feel like step stones cover the floor, while bands of walnut wood vinyl frame the stone-like squares in the manner of an outdoor terrace. Cabinets for hi-fi, television and recordings are planter-topped and raised, to leave room for a garden of African violets below. These are top-lighted for drama. A tangle of ferns and flowers fills the planter-top of the cabinet. Other plants sprout around the room, and can be watered at will since the new flooring takes splash and splatter, is easy to wipe clean. Garden room designed by John Bachstein, A.I.D.

Brick wall of this novel dining area has been given the garden treatment, to replace a defunct fireplace. Two layers of brick form a floor-level shelf for flowering plants; raised centerpiece holds a jungle of ferns, finishing touch is the decorative fountain on the wall. The area rug adds vitality to the light airy atmosphere created by the garden wall, also repeats and enlarges geometric pattern of walls.

A lush variety of foliage plants in natural red clay pots makes a pleasing miniature forest for the totem, adding colorful interest in this garden corner in a sitting room. Green foliage plants are seen at their best against light, plain backgrounds such as this brick wall. The pots add a splash of color that blends with the totem, are also perfect containers for the plants as they ensure healthy growth.

Designer Edmund Motyka, A.I.D., goes all-out to imbue a small dining area with an eighteenth century, bower-like charm. The exotic palms, one of them almost ceiling-high, plus a lush assortment of other small trees and plants are the main decorative assets in the room. They sit well against the sleek vinyl floor, muted walls and plain window shades. These cleverly scaled window treatments consist of textured white window shades set within a framework of wide molding: they lend an airy brightness to the room and filter sunlight for the room's many plants. Carrying the period garden-house look still further is a round table flanked by Chippendale bamboo chairs. Use of many plants in this way dispenses with the need for lots of furniture, and is a good idea to adopt if you are trying to furnish a dining room on a budget.

A collection of plants and space-saving strategy turn a small, glass-enclosed apartment terrace into a delightful urban sunroom-den. Interior designer Fred Shrallow mixes the new with the antique, in colors taken from nature, to create a cozy and charming room that looks and lives larger than its actual dimensions. Handsome window shades, custom-printed in a three-dimensional design in sky blue and white, dramatize the window walls without circumscribing the small area. They are hung under matching valances, for a clean, contemporary look that enhances the architectural line of the converted terrace. Because the shade cloth is translucent, the potted plants atop the antique dry sink thrive in the filtered sunlight. A pair of hanging plants also benefit from this transmuted light and add a decorative touch without usurping limited floor space. Lightly scaled wicker and wrought iron chairs add comfortable sunroom seating, are in keeping with the mood set by the many plants. Everything here, from the vinyl-impregnated shades to the red tile floor, hides easy upkeep talents beneath a charming country mood, which is completely at home in the city.

CHAPTER TWENTY-TWO

Outdoor Living in the City

⚜

THE APARTMENT TERRACE or backyard has a new dimension today, as an "extra" room in the summer months. Even the smallest, dullest outdoor space can be transformed, can become an extension of your home for entertaining and relaxing in the warm weather.

It's easy to create a colorful patio, and with imagination and ingenuity it need not cost much. The basic ingredients are bright paint, a collection of plants and shrubs, and a fence if you need to screen off the area for privacy. Brick walls look best when painted white or pale pink; and if your fence is made of wood, leave it in its natural state, or simply paint with varnish. Remember also that too much white will create a blinding glare in the sunny months, especially when used in one large area.

Once the shell of the patio is created, you can add garden furniture and other accessories as you can afford them. If your patio is small, don't clutter it up with too much furniture. Your basic needs are a few chairs, a table, and a barbecue, if you intend to have cook-outs. A gay umbrella adds color and a "furnished" look, without taking up too much floor space, and a mobile cart or tea trolley is useful for drinks, ice, glasses and china. If space is at a premium, find a cart that can be used indoors and simply wheel it out when you need it.

If you are not hindered either by lack of space or money, you can really give your patio a glamorous look. Garden furniture is more decorative and luxurious than it has ever been. All of it is lightweight, hard wearing and comfortable, particularly metal furniture which comes in rainbow colors, with comfortable cushions and back pads. You can have anything from the utilitarian table and straight chairs, to a sofa, a chaise, or a lazy-back swing. A canopy and electric lights are other handsome additions to any patio or terrace. But if these are too costly, there are many other accessories now available. For lighting at night you can use candles in heat-proof glass containers, and the old fashioned spirit or oil lamp is romantic as well as practical. Many of the

Oriental novelty stores carry a line of large, multi-colored paper umbrellas, which cost little. They add bright flashes of color to an outdoor setting, and are easy to handle and store away. A stone statue, picked up cheaply at a secondhand shop, a straw basket filled with brilliant paper flowers, a string of Chinese lanterns, and several large plastic cushions in bright colors scattered around the floor are a few other inexpensive ideas that add spark to a patio.

When it comes to cooking outdoors, there is a wide range of barbecues now on sale. They run the gamut of prices, from the do-it-yourself type which you assemble yourself, to the more elaborate electric spits. Any hardware store will supply you with price lists and recommend the kind most practical for your purposes, and it's worthwhile investigating all types before buying.

Terraces

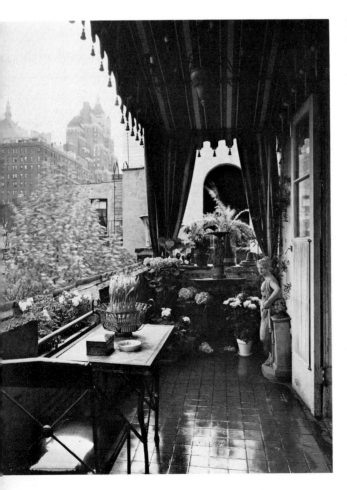

Even a small or narrow terrace can be given a sparkling new look, as illustrated here. Designer Michael Greer, A.I.D., N.S.I.D., covers the whole of this terrace with a striped, fringed awning of rust, grey and white. Antique English lead fountain is surrounded by a collection of flowering plants and ferns, intermingled with statues. An antique bronze Empire table and chairs serve for dining or drinks.

Almost any city terrace or even a backyard can be transformed into an elegant spot for summer living and entertaining, at very little cost. Here, this city terrace takes on a look of sophistication, through its tent-like canopy and profusion of flowering shrubs and plants. Very little furniture was needed for the finishing touches, and so expense was kept to a minimum. Most elaborate construction was the canopy, with its real tent roof and side drapes. It offers protection from sun and rain, is easy to clean and store away in winter. Lots of plants give the terrace a bower-like feeling; the stone statue and water fountain add an old world air in keeping with the canopy. Candles, in an old lantern on table, plus other accessories, enhance the romantic atmosphere. Designer David Barrett, A.I.D., N.S.I.D.

This tranquil setting sits among the rooftops, high above big city bustle, and adds an extra dimension to town living. The spacious terrace is perfect for entertaining guests, as well as for family brunches and dinners the summer through. High wooden fence ensures privacy, while the natural beauty of greenery and shrubs planted in portable, redwood boxes adds a true country atmosphere. Black wrought-iron furniture is durable but easy to move around, and its vivid cushions are comfortable as well as colorful. A yellow and white striped canvas canopy gives the terrace a dash of glamor, also offers shade on hot days. When necessary, furniture can be moved back against fence, to make room for buffet or cocktail party guests. Glass door and windows help to carry the attractive setting indoors, give living room a charming outlook.

This colorful umbrella and a green trellis screen transform a tiny backyard into a bright corner for summer eating. White paint and a floor-level box of flowering plants were less costly additions that bring extra life to the area. Umbrella-table and chairs are of a durable lightweight metal, with chair seats made of resilient vinyl webbing. Furniture is easy to store away in the winter months; in fact chairs can do double-duty in a kitchen or teen-agers' room. Umbrella easily dismantles from table, for compact storage.

That little backyard does not have to gather dust and grime, and go to waste. It dresses up with a coat of paint, a collection of shrubs and some sleek garden furniture, becomes a summer garden nook where you can enjoy the sun and entertain friends. In this city backyard smart flagstones and a wooden trellis were the first steps in a transformation job. Back wall was painted pristine white, and a collection of shrubs and plants were added for color and a country look. When the shell was complete, pieces of good-looking garden furniture were chosen, to complement the lavish atmosphere of an old backyard which had become a sparkling patio. Sofa, chairs and stool are upholstered with comfortable, foam rubber cushions. All furniture is of white wrought metal, easy to wipe clean, lightweight to handle. Tables are glass-topped.

More and more interest is focused on outdoor entertaining today, even in the city. No matter how small the area, an attractive terrace or patio can be created. This patio measures only twelve feet by twenty, yet with a wooden fence and a scattering of foliage a complete garden terrace is created. A rustic atmosphere sets the mood of this particular patio, shown readied for an evening barbecue. Outdoor furniture in black matte-finished wrought iron was chosen for its simple shaker lines and timeless design. Upholstered cushions are in a colorful crewel print that complements the garden's green foliage. They're reversible, zippered for quick cleaning, and easily recoverable for an inexpensive decor change. The charming idea of using an antique lantern for soda and soft drink storage is as decorative as it is practical. Here, just a few patio accessories punctuate the casual setting. Note the handsome jardiniere that is used as a stand for a bowl of fruit. And the green vase has an extra-hefty candle that is guaranteed to burn with a soft glow for several hours, fully protected from wind and weather. Barbecue, glass-topped tables, and colorful pottery plates and dishes complete the picture of casual elegance.

This apartment dweller, for very little money, created a charming private terrace on the garage top of an apartment house. Tile floor, picket fence, greenery and an umbrella-table combine to make a tranquil corner for Sunday brunches or candlelight dinners. Vivid yellow chairs pick up the sunflower pattern of the umbrella; white table matches chair supports and the mobile serving cart in foreground of photograph. This makes the perfect "silent butler." Laden with all types of food and drinks, it helps take the wear and tear out of entertaining, and is big enough to hold a lavish selection of refreshments. Wise choice of furniture kept expense down to the minimum.

PART FOUR

Important Periods in Furniture Design

CHAPTER TWENTY-THREE

18th & 19th Century English Furniture

How to recognize:
Queen Anne; Early Georgian, style of Chippendale;
Late Georgian, styles of Hepplewhite, Adam Brothers, and Sheraton;
Regency

THE 18TH CENTURY was one of the richest periods in English furniture design. Queen Anne marked the beginning of a new era of comfort and grace in furniture, a distinct break away from the more utilitarian styles of the Dutch designers prominent in the preceding William and Mary period.

But Queen Anne was a transitional few years, before the great craftsmen of the elegant Georgian Period took over. These master cabinetmakers and designers were the innovators, the dictators of style and taste, and their influence was far-reaching. European and American furniture makers copied their designs, and today Georgian pieces are still the most popular in antiques, proof of their classicality in design and their great craftsmanship. **Thomas Chippendale** was the first 18th century master craftsman, and his furniture is known as **Early Georgian.** His successors in the latter half of the century were **Sheraton,** the **Adam brothers** and **Hepplewhite.** Their furniture is known as **Late Georgian.**

Regency furniture takes its name from the **Prince Regent,** who later became George IV. This early 19th century furniture, brilliant, bold and reflecting the exotic tastes of the Prince Regent, is in vogue again. **John Nash** was the great arbiter of taste during this period.

18th Century English

The handsome dining room is decorated in Early Georgian. Dining table is from the George I period, while yew wood china cabinet is dated 1770; chairs are late George II, about 1750, and the chandelier is pure Queen Anne. An 18th century needlepoint carpet completes this setting, designed by J. Frederic Lohman, A.I.D. Color scheme is green and red, with a hint of gold in the drapes.

Queen Anne

THE QUEEN ANNE period dates from 1702 to 1714, following the William and Mary era. It had a brief span, lasting only 12 years, before the great master craftsmen of the 18th Century, Early and Late Georgian periods, took over. Walnut was the principal wood used, and for this reason this period is often called the Age of Walnut. Queen Anne furniture is still popular today, and is used extensively.

1. Side chair with cabriole legs, fiddle back. 2. Corner chair showing shell motif on knee. 3. Desk-on-frame with slant top, slender legs. 4. Bed with high posts supporting a tester. 5. Small scale sofa with cabriole legs. 6. Typical highboy with flat top, curved legs. 7. Lowboy with cabriole legs, shell motif. 8. Dining table of the drop-leaf variety. 9. Tilt-top tea table with piecrust edge.

Although some of the Queen Anne furniture shows a lingering influence of the Dutch designers, as did the preceding period, more freedom was given to local craftsmen and essentially English designs developed. Furniture of the Queen Anne era has more grace and comfort than previous styles. The upright, uncomfortable chairs prominent in William and Mary designs, were replaced by upholstered chairs, and the easy chair was introduced. Wide, flaring chair seats came in, to accommodate the huge skirts worn by the ladies of the court. Many chairs did not have arms, while the backs of chairs were shaped to fit the body for additional comfort. The cockleshell ornamental carving was the most popular, on the knees of cabriole legs, on chair backs, in the middle of drawers and aprons. This ornament and the cabriole leg are perhaps the most outstanding features of this period. Other feet used were the claw-and-ball, the paw, and the club which was the most popular.

Furniture surfaces were kept plain, without paneling or molding. Veneering was extensively used, and lacquer work was popular. Dining tables were usually of the drop-leaf variety; chests of drawers, highboys and lowboys, beds with high slender posts supporting testers were also popular. In general, construction was of the *curved line* variety.

One of the main features of the Queen Anne chair was the solid, fiddle-back shaped splat, with uprights in sweeping contours. These backs were generally narrow. Underbracing was not used. Queen Anne construction was used by later designers, who added their own ideas to it. This showed up prominently in the Georgian period.

Early Georgian

Thomas Chippendale (1705-1779)

THE BROAD TERM *Georgian* is usually applied to all furniture made during the reigns of the first three kings of that name, in the 18th century. It was a period of great change and outside influence on English furniture.

Travel abroad was the vogue, particularly to France and Italy; trade with the Orient created interest in styles and all things Chinese; archaeological excavations of ancient Roman cities stimulated a classic revival. *Because of these diverse influences, it is easier to understand the whole Georgian period if it is broken down into Early and Late.*

The great innovator during the Early Georgian Period was Thomas Chippendale, the son of a woodcarver, who was himself a peerless carver and designer, and also a master craftsman. He was the first cabinetmaker ever to have his name associated with a furniture style.

Apart from his designing ability, he was a good businessman and sales-man. In 1754 he wrote and published the first book on furniture, the now cele-brated *The Gentleman and Cabinetmaker's Director*. Through this book he made individual designs identifiable with the maker's name. Publication of the book resulted in a host of imitators — but they also helped to consolidate his style.

Chippendale was particularly clever at drawing on ideas and designs from other periods and other countries. With some validity, critics have charged that he freely picked up other designs without acknowledgement. This may be true, but he always added his own style and distinction to his furniture. Chippendale adapted Oriental motifs, and evolved what is known as Chinese-Chippendale. The Gothic also inspired him, and he revived the pointed Gothic arch and the burgeoning crocket. Yet to each of these he added a grace and charm peculiar to his own age.

The early part of the 18th century saw the introduction of mahogany, around 1725. This rich, easily carved wood was Chippendale's favorite.

His style is richly carved in mahogany, with free use of graceful and beautifully proportioned curves. His work may sometimes be more difficult to recognize *easily,* because of his borrowings, but generally a substantial beauty with marvelous carvings are the signs of a genuine piece of Chippendale.

The claw-and-ball foot is one of the most characteristic motifs. This foot was used with cabriole legs; other feet also used with cabriole legs were the club, web, paw, scroll, leaf, dolphin and slipper. He used the straight leg in his Gothic and Chinese styles, the cabriole in his other designs. The arms of his chairs were curved and flaring at the end, and usually joined the uprights at an angle; while the supports were shaped forward at the side rails of the seat. The backs were inclined to be square in outline, with serpentine-shaped tops.

Chippendale was free in his use of motifs and some of his favorites were scrolls, acanthus leafs, knotted ribbons and interlaced straps. He also used rococo shells and large curves, as well as the C scroll, lion heads and masks. Although mahogany was his favorite wood, he sometimes used walnut.

1. Gothic chair with extensively carved splat, straight front legs. 2. Chair in Chinese Chippendale style with decorative, openwork back. 3. Large cabinet with the typical swelling front, broken pediments. 4. Elaborate highboy with scrolled bonnet top, carving on legs and bottom center drawer, and the typical claw-and-ball foot. 5. Chaise lounge or day-bed is upholstered in leather, has straight carved legs, and looks like an extended armchair. 6. Settee with extensively carved back and legs, and Chippendale's favorite claw-and-ball foot. 7. Heavy pedestal desk with leather top is typical of those used in libraries of great houses during the Chippendale period.

During the Early Georgian Period, Chinese fretted ornament and Chino-iserie bibelots were favored; Oriental porcelains graced the dinner table, Chinese silks and brocades added richness to bedrooms. From France came the elaborate combinations of C and S scrolls, which were often used with great effect in hardware and gilt mirrors.

Chippendale made all kinds of furniture, including bookcases and side-boards. It was always solidly constructed, and much of it is in existence today. Because of Chippendale's love of mahogany, the Early Georgian Period is often called the Age of Mahogany. For quick identification look for: construction — curved and straight; details — cabriole leg, claw-and-ball foot, pierced splat, ladder-back; Chinese fret, carving of the finest type.

Late Georgian

JUST AS CHIPPENDALE borrowed ideas from Chinese and Gothic designs, the great designers of the *Late Georgian Period* also turned to foreign countries and bygone ages for their inspiration.

The master craftsmen of that time, the brothers Adam, Hepplewhite and Sheraton were motivated by classic Pompeii and Herculaneum, and the elegance of the French court. The motifs most typical of this Late Georgian Period are of classic origin, such as the acanthus leaf and honeysuckle, ram's head, winged griffin and lion, laurel garland and urn, all derived from Italian sources.

Following Chippendale's lead, these other designers all published hand-books which made their styles known to other craftsmen in Europe and America.

It was during this period that the English silversmiths designed and made the now celebrated Georgian silver so much in demand today. Inspired by the Adam brothers and their insistence on perfection right down to the last detail, silversmiths turned out beautiful plate and tableware. Josiah Wedgwood also caught the Adam craze and commercialized it, becoming the greatest English potter (1730-95). The cream-colored earthenware, named Queensware, was his first important pottery accomplishment. Other notable wares were his black basalt, jasperware, gold and silver lustreware.

The Adam Brothers

(1765-1790)

THE FOUR ADAM BROTHERS, Scots by birth, were undoubtedly the most force-ful dictators of taste in interior decoration during the Late Georgian Period. And their influence in overall design is still felt today.

1. Chair with upholstered square back, slender legs and flattened, shaped arms supported by extensions of the front legs. 2. Console table, semi-circular in shape, with delicate front molding and leg detail. 3. The classical urn, one of the motifs that constantly reappears in Adam furniture, carving and molding. 4. A typical Adam panel showing daintily carved design. 5. The floral swag, often used with variations of the urn and other classical motifs in Adam designs. 6. Intricately carved molding for ceiling, door frame, wall or panels. 7. Floral swag carving on a typical Adam mantlepiece. 8. Less elaborate carved molding for ceiling or wall panels. 9. Chair with upholstered arms, supported by extensions of front legs. 10. Sofa frame showing human figure design detail typical of Adam work.

In actuality the four brothers were not furniture makers, but architects by profession. They were also decorators and designers, employing others to carry out their designs. A Swiss painter, Angelica Kauffman and her husband, Antonio Zucchi, also Cipiani and Pergolesi filled their wall panels and ceilings with paintings and Italian gesso work. It is more than likely that Chippendale, Hepplewhite and perhaps Sheraton also worked for the Adam brothers, as did Josiah Wedgwood.

The brothers built palaces for the nobility, houses for the middle classes, terraces, bridges, even streets and squares. And in almost every instance their work was classically beautiful. Although they were by no means furniture makers, the Adam brothers always designed furniture to fit their rooms. Many sideboards with urn-shaped knife-boxes and classic brackets, pedestals, clock cases and mirrors were designed by them. They even designed the carriages, the plate and the sedan chair for Queen Charlotte.

The craze for Chinoiserie popular in the Early Georgian Period waned from the inception of the Adam epoch. Their style reflected the spirit of Pompeii and Herculaneum, in a purer type than was expressed in the late Louis XVI adaptations. It left its deepest impressions on ceilings, side walls and mantlepieces produced under the architects' directions. They were usually tinted in jasper or the palest grey colors. Circles and ovals were used as frames for pictures and mirrors. They also favored mythological ornament, such as the hexagon, octagon and lozenge-shaped panel, wreath, fan medallion, draped or with figures; the sphinx, griffin, sea horse, goat, faun, ram's head, the caryatid and other classic motifs found in Roman, Pompeiian and Etruscan work. These were carved in marble and wood, molded in stucco, inlaid, and painted on walls, ceilings and furniture. The Adams' designed walls, ceilings, mantlepieces, door knobs, escutcheons, locks — everything that went into a room including tabletops and furniture panels. In fact the brothers were so earnest in imparting their spirit to the entire room, that they even insisted on the carpets being in unison with the surroundings. The palest tints of color were used on walls and for upholstery, with neutral tinted carpets to match. Even tablecloths corresponded in pattern, and the unity of a scheme was followed through in the silver plate, the tabletops, even the snuff boxes.

The Adam style was a complete departure from the massive and somewhat ponderous compartment ceiling of the Jacobean era. Instead the brothers adopted light moldings, delicate stucco frames and painted ornaments. They advanced the theory that dining rooms should never be hung with tapestry or damask, *"which retain the smell of victuals."* Instead they used stucco, statues and paintings. As a result many of their rooms depended on the work of the painter and sculptor, and often lacked coziness. They were usually circular or semi-circular, or with circular recesses.

The gesso work popular in Italy was adapted, and their ceilings were part in relief and part painted, the plaster put on cameo-like, with great delicacy. At first Italian artisans did this work, until Josiah Wedgwood furnished the plaques and friezes for the later Adam work. Of the four brothers, Robert and James were the creative ones.

The style of the Adam brothers is distinctive and therefore easily recognized. Construction: usually straight, small in scale. Details: legs square and tapered, or round and fluted. Oval and wheel backs, urn finials and other classic motifs, painting, inlay, carving and Italian gesso work. Woods used were mainly mahogany or satinwood.

George Hepplewhite

(1770-1790)

HEPPLEWHITE UNDOUBTEDLY DERIVED most of his classic feeling for furniture from the designs of the Adam brothers. In all probability he made some furniture after their designs, and for the great houses the brothers designed and decorated.

In spite of following the classic lead of the Adams', Hepplewhite did bring

1. Chair with shield back and with the typical unbroken curve along the top. Open back features the Prince of Wales feathers motif. 2. Chair with interlacing shield back and short arms, shows how back is always supported by a rail above the seat which joins curved continuations of the back legs. 3. Close-up showing details of the interlacing heart back, typical in Hepplewhite design. 4. Close-up showing details of a square back chair with vase shaped back splats. 5. Small drop-leaf table, known as the Pembroke table, shows the graceful, refined lines favored by Hepplewhite. 6. Close-up of the slender, fluted legs which appear on chairs, tables, sideboards and sofas. 7. Close-up of the Prince of Wales feathers motif, introduced by Hepplewhite and prominent on much of his furniture. 8. Tall, slender legs and low back on sofa give piece a fragile appearance. Carving is always sparingly used. 9. Hepplewhite desks were lighter, raised on tapering legs, often featuring tambours on the upper part, as in this piece. 10. Hepplewhite did much to develop and improve the sideboard. This is a typical design, with slender legs, spade feet, inlay decoration. 11. Larger Hepplewhite sideboard features six slender legs, serpentine front and his concave corner construction.

his own individual style to furniture. He emphasized lightness, gracefulness and elegance, with a pure line of beauty. Because of this his influence was widespread, particularly with American cabinetmakers, including Duncan Phyfe. Like Chippendale he published a furniture styles book, *The Cabinet-Maker and Upholsterer's Guide,* which helped to identify his name to a style.

Most of Hepplewhite's work was refined and free from bizarre motifs. It showed a great deal of the Louis XIV influence, which he often copied or modified.

Even though his style had slender characteristics, he achieved sturdy English qualities and much of his furniture is in existence today. It is easy to distinguish Hepplewhite by the graceful straight leg forms, the serpentine fronts, and concave, cut-in corners. For ornamentation he used wheat ears, Prince of Wales feathers and bell flower husks. He usually used shield-shaped backs, and unusual, short, curved arms on chairs. Although Hepplewhite employed curves, these were always modified. Chairs were the most famous of his productions, with the shield-shaped back the most distinctive. His other chairs had the hoop back, the interlacing-heart back and the oval back. Most of his chair backs were supported by a rail above the seat, which joined the slender, curved continuations of the back legs.

Some other designs popular with Hepplewhite were the lyre, the honeysuckle, the urn and the "S" curves. The seats were frequently rounded at the back; others were square and tapering. They were usually upholstered, with the upholstery brought down over the frame. Legs were straight, square and tapered, terminating in a spade foot. The tapered, round leg was also used, and sometimes carved with an intertwining spiral band.

Although Hepplewhite favored mahogany, he also used rosewood, satinwood, tulipwood, harewood and other rare selections. Painting was the favorite decoration. To recognize Hepplewhite look for: construction — curved except chair legs; detail — shield and oval chair backs, square tapered legs, spade feet, serpentine fronts, painting, inlay, veneer.

Thomas Sheraton

(1750-1806)

THOMAS SHERATON WAS the last great designer of the 18th century.

He was a master of cabinetmaking and inlay work, but waited until mid-life to move from provincial Stockton-on-Tees to London. At first he was not as successful as Chippendale and Hepplewhite had been, but during the last decade of the 18th century and the early years of the 19th century, the Sheraton influence dominated the style of English and American furniture. Through his book, *The Cabinet-Maker and Upholsterer's Drawing-Book,* he became widely known, and his furniture designs were much appreciated by working cabinet-makers in both countries. His *Drawing-Book* went into three editions — 1791, 1793 and 1802.

Sheraton followed classic lines, and frankly adapted many of the Louis XVI styles. But to these he added his own conception and artistic knowledge. The result was a subtle gracefulness, a remarkable appreciation of form and

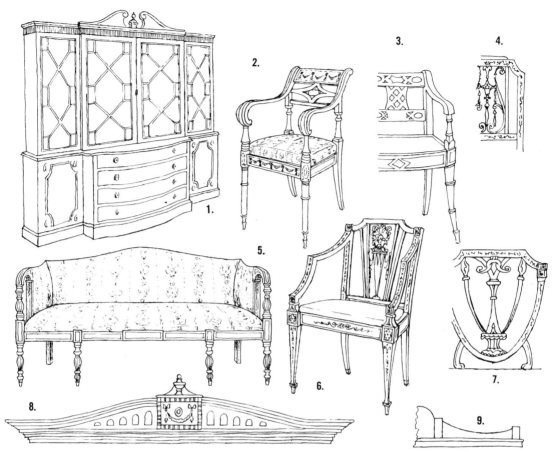

1. Bookcase with a serpentine front and inlaid drawers. 2. Chair with fretwork panel and gracefully curved arms. 3. Typical Sheraton chair. Splats always rest on cross frames never seat frame, and seat frame shows in upholstered chairs. 4. Detail of chair back showing central panel rising above top rail. 5. Sofa with graceful lines and light slender legs. 6. Chair with square back incorporating all the elegant design details favored by Sheraton. 7. Close-up of a beautifully proportioned shield back chair. 8. Detailed, shaped pediment of a bookcase. 9. Less elaborate, shaped pediment of a Sheraton bookcase.

correct geometrical proportions. This is a prominent characteristic of all Sheraton furniture, and his work at all times shows classic dignity, refinement and restraint.

He leaned heavily on perpendicular lines, giving his designs purity and beauty. He never designed short curves, and whenever he used the curve it was a graceful sweep. Sheraton used the oval to a great extent, while the lyre, slender urns and latticework were also characteristic. Reeding and fluting also marked his style. For decoration he used swags, the cockleshell, the star, fan shapes and small ornamental disks. Inlay was his favorite decoration, and he used many rare and beautiful woods. Turning, veneering and painting were also favored by Sheraton, and any carving was delicate and light.

Sheraton knew construction, and although his furniture was light it was structurally sound. The legs were very slender and were often rounded, tapered and reeded. Another type of Sheraton leg was square and tapered; while during the latter part of his career some of the table legs were spiral turned, with the acanthus leaf used as decoration. Sheraton feet were never conspicuous. He favored the spade foot, as did Hepplewhite, the block foot, and sometimes the French foot, which curved outward slightly.

The most typical Sheraton chair back was square, with a central panel rising slightly above the top rail. The lower rail usually kept the back well up from the seat. Arms started high on the uprights of the chair, swept downward in a very extended "S" shape to the supports. These were frequently a continuation of the front legs.

There is a marked similarity between Sheraton and Hepplewhite designs. However, Sheraton used more underbracing and often the X-shaped stretcher; he also permitted a part of the seat frame to show, while Hepplewhite pulled his seat cover well over the apron.

Sheraton was a master at assembling a variety of woods, even though mahogany was favored. For his inlays, he used satinwood, tulipwood, sycamore and rosewood. A Sheraton piece is easily recognizable because of this beautiful inlay work. Other details to look for are: construction — straight line; details — chair backs square or oblong, legs tapered, square or round; turning, fluting, reeding.

Regency

(Early 19th Century)

ENGLISH REGENCY FURNITURE takes its name from the Prince Regent, who later became George IV. The Regency Period, which flourished in the early 1880's, saw the blossoming of a fresh, imaginative exuberance in all fields of design — particularly in clothes and furnishings.

The young men of the time, those dashing Regency Bucks, strutted around in the startlingly different, modish clothes introduced by Beau Brummel; while interiors took on a bold new brilliance that was surprisingly colorful after the lightness of the late 18th century interiors. To say that taste at that time was exotic is an understatement. Everything that was daring, different and fantastic caught the eye and captured the imagination — particularly of the Prince Regent.

For once, considerable influence was exerted by the personal tastes of the monarch. From his early days, when he was Prince of Wales, the Prince Regent had developed a passion for building and decorating houses—a passion unsurpassed by any other English sovereign. Unhappily his palace at Carlton House was destroyed, but much of the furniture has remained in royal possession. Within recent years his Royal Pavilion at Brighton has been restored, and this is a prime example of the succeeding fantasies of this somewhat eccentric monarch. The earliest pieces are comparatively simple, but become increasingly fantastic as romantic and oriental elements became more popular with the 19th century. At the Pavilion, the future George IV indulged to the full a taste for the exotic which embraced everything from Chinese dragons to Egyptian sphinxes. One of the most successful extravaganzas at the Pavilion is the Chinese Music Room, in red lacquer, with red and gold dragons supporting the ceiling, carvings, bells, fretwork and almost every other decorative device incorporated.

John Nash was the great designer during the *Regency Period,* and his interiors in the Royal Pavilion are the most brilliant examples of pure **Regency**. It is his interiors which have stimulated a new interest in this period.

In essence, the mainstream of furniture design around 1800 reflects the severe neo-classicism prevalent throughout Europe. Despite this new silhouette, English cabinetmakers retained many of the motifs of the Renaissance, exaggerating the size and decorative importance of these classical forms, as Napoleon was doing in France. Anthemion and acanthus leaves, lyres and lions' heads, urns and sphinxes were all boldly appliqued in brass, or painted on Regency furniture. Greek curves were retained and emphasized. Egyptian and Chinese motifs were used, and lacquer-and-bamboo furniture was popular. Doors were elaborately painted in rich colors and gold leaf, many of them lavishly decorated with carvings and ornamentation such as bells, dragons, and fantastic overdoors. Curtains were also elaborately and asymmetrically draped, and mirrors were used to cover whole walls.

However, the furniture which accompanied some of these exotic outbursts *was* handsome in line and superbly crafted, with accent on rare woods, inlays and brass mounts. The severe lines of some of the furniture was often offset by the more elaborate drapes and upholstery. If the Regency look was heavy, it was certainly striking and dramatic. Backgrounds of rooms were painted in dark colors, such as browns, reds and fir-green. From this period came two new forms of furniture, the revolving bookcase and the extension table.

1. Breakfront designed to display china or books is massive in scale, features elaborate carved columns flanking doors. 2. Double curves appear in this stool with animal heads and lion paws. Piece reflects Egyptian influence in Regency period. 3. Bookcase on casters is scaled down and classically simple. 4. Chair with straight back, slightly curved legs and upholstered seat features sweeping, curved arms popular in Regency design. 5. Chair showing Chinese influence —cane back and seat, carved dragons supporting arm rests. 6. Classically simple chair with upholstered seat and concave back. 7. Sofa of classic outline is richly upholstered with outward flowing, curved arms and small, carved legs. 8. Scaled down bookcase/cabinet features molding around top, prominent columns with flow into feet. 9. Elegant, high standing writing desk is typical of the more intimate sized Regency pieces, also features molding along the top. 10. Chinese influence is apparent in this elaborate, lacquered sewing table with compartments and lid.

18th & 19th Century Mixed

Here you see how two periods can be mixed together for a beautiful whole. Designer J. Frederic Lohman, A.I.D., used 18th and 19th century antiques to create this tranquil sitting room. Octagonal table holding lamp, in the foreground, was once a wine cooler of 19th century origin. Chair behind it is Italian. On the opposite side of the room the sofa is flanked by a pair of 19th century English Regency spoon chairs. Table left of sofa is English 18th century, has a drop-leaf and is a Hepplewhite, while its companion table on the right side is 19th century, made of rosewood with shaped legs and hoof feet. Up in the front of the picture are two identical tables, with French lacquer work tops and hand-forged bamboo-gilt-iron legs.

For dining off a small entrance foyer, depth is achieved by a mural. The columns and Adam decor help to create a feeling of separateness, which lends comfort and grace to dining. The front door, the frieze around the ceiling and the chairs have the delicacy of the pure Adam period. The design of the rug in the entrance hall is taken from a crest of the Royal Family. Designed by Leona Kahn, A.I.D.

The columns, ceiling frieze and wall paneling help to create a true Adam feeling here. In this classic dining room by T. Miles Gray Associates, A.I.D., N.S.I.D., magnificent 18th century furniture and accessories have been used. The elegant oval dining table is of mahogany inlaid with rosewood, while the four white-and-gold dining room chairs are decorated with trophy panels. Handsome crystal chandelier has matching wall sconces, with silver candelabra finishing the effect on the table. Wall panels and full-length drapes are made of an antique satin of rayon and acetate, copied from a French museum fabric designed in 1874. The delicately patterned pink, white and clover-green print insets are reminiscent of trophy panels and are beautifully framed by the wall moldings. The soft pink fabric lining the draperies is used again for seat pads. The result is a room with a definite Adam flavor, in furniture, architecture and color scheme.

This room is a perfect example of the light English Adam period. It has a garden feeling, and a soft color scheme of beige and gold. The area rug is designed from Gibbings carvings, mirror above the console is Chippendale. Designed by Leona Kahn, A.I.D.

The dining room of Blair House, looking from one of the drawing rooms. Here you see the repetition of the pale yellow and gold color scheme. Sideboard is 18th century American, three-pedestal 18th century dining table is of mahogany, as are the sixteen chairs. These are upholstered in yellow antique satin with an almost invisible stripe of grey-blue. The rug has a gold ground with a floral pattern: a six-fold chinoiserie-decorated leather screen conceals the door to the pantry.

Blair House, Washington, D. C.

18th & 19th century furniture graces three rooms
of the nation's guest house

MRS. FRANCIS HENRY LENYGON, F.A.I.D., Chairman of the American Institute of Interior Designers' National Committee on restoration, with her working committee of Mrs. Ellen McCluskey, F.A.I.D., and Stephen J. Jussel, F.A.I.D., recently completed the refurbishing of the first floor of Blair House, the nation's guest house in Washington.

Eighteenth and 19th century English and American furniture was used, and three of the rooms are illustrated here in color, showing how well this mixture works.

The front and back drawing rooms and the dining room all open into one another suggesting a one-color scheme as they are used simultaneously for large receptions. Because the rooms are dark, with no prolonged daylight, a light yellow wall color with a slight green tint was selected to give a suggestion of sunshine. Cream was chosen for the woodwork. Gold curtains of a fine silk damask with a silk tassel fringe hang at all the windows, which overlook Pennsylvania Avenue and a formal rear garden. Accent colors are provided by the lavish flower arrangements. Eighteenth and early 19th century Empire and Regency antique crystal and ormolu chandeliers illuminate the rooms.

Two *Hepplewhite* sofas covered with honey-yellow flecked antique velvet were placed in front of the windows in the two drawing rooms facing each other. Flanking the sofas are *Hepplewhite* armchairs covered in blue and honey-yellow cut and uncut velvet. Wing chairs used in the rooms are covered with yellow and beige cut and uncut velvet. In front of the two identical black and grey marble fireplaces, are two benches covered in the same tone of honey antique damask, trimmed with handsome fringe. The same colors are repeated in the small chairs, and the Chinese rugs in both rooms are yellow, beige and blue. Two side tables in each room, of inlaid satinwood, are contributions from the White House, as are the mirrors which hang above them. The same color scheme was repeated in the dining room.

Front drawing room of Blair House, showing honey-yellow color scheme and blue patterned Chinese carpet. Hepplewhite sofa and chairs are here upholstered in honey-yellow velvet.

This is the back drawing room of Blair House, almost identical in color scheme and decor to the front drawing Room. Here the two Hepplewhite chairs are upholstered in blue velvet.

CHAPTER TWENTY-FOUR

18th & 19th Century French Furniture

*How to recognize: Louis XIV, Régence, Louis XV,
Louis XVI, Directoire, Empire*

THE WHOLE OF the 18th century and the early part of the 19th century were the two richest periods of furniture design in France, just as they were in England.

During the long reign of Louis XIV, from 1643 to 1715, furniture styles remained steadfast, changing little except to become more lavishly embellished. For 72 years, the King exerted the greatest influence on style. His taste ran towards richness and splendor in furnishings, and an opulent grandeur pervaded interiors. The **Louis XIV period** is known to be the most magnificent in France's history.

After the King's death in the early part of the 18th century, **Régence furniture** came into fashion. But this was a transitional period and lasted only a few years. It was followed by the **Louis XV era.** The new King was greatly influenced by his two mistresses, Du Barry and Pompadour; furniture took on a more delicate, feminine quality, and was also richly embellished.

During the reign of **Louis XVI** furniture styles took a swing towards the more classic lines of Greece and Rome. This was because Queen Marie Antoinette was classically educated, and because ancient ruins were being excavated. The **Directoire period** flourished after the Revolution. But like Régence, this was a transitional few years before **Empire styles** came into vogue. **Napoleon Bonaparte** was the great arbiter of taste and style during this time.

Louis XIV (1643-1715)

THE DISTINCT FURNITURE styles of the Louis XIV period flourished in the last half of 17th century and the beginning of the 18th century. This age was marked by courtly grandeur, and is probably the most magnificent of the French periods.

Louis XIV ruled for many years, and as he was the greatest single influence on style, furniture designs remained steadfast through six decades. Furniture of this period is still used today, but does not have universal popularity.

The Louis XIV style was broad and splendid, with many straight lines and very few curves. It was classically severe and symmetrical, decorated beautifully but not to excess. In many instances it was built for grandeur rather than comfort.

Two opposite views were expressed in the furniture. The structure was formal and rectangular, while the decorative motifs were informal. The ornament was always large in scale and alike on both sides, or bi-symmetrical. The shell was often used. New types of decoration such as carving, painting, gilding, inlaying, lacquer work and metal mounts were developed. Oak, walnut ebony and chestnut were used extensively, with various rare woods for inlays. Marble was frequently used for tabletops, and upholstery was very rich.

Andre Charles Boulle was the most successful furniture designer of the period, and was appointed the King's cabinetmaker. He was renowned for his beautiful ebony furniture, inlaid with tortoise shell, brass and other metals so that it resembled a brilliant mosaic. He also used chiseled mounts of gilt for decorative motifs.

Some of the legs were straight, while others were cabriole in shape. The four legs of a chair were always alike. Feet used were paws, cloven hoofs or carved acanthus leaves. The backs of the chairs were a feature of the Louis XIV style. They were high and straight at the sides, and often straight across the top; X-shaped stretchers were also used.

To recognize Louis XIV styles look for: construction — mainly straight, massive in scale, formal. High backed carved and upholstered chairs, commodes and marble-topped console tables of special interest. Details — metal mounts, carving, painting, gilding, inlay, marquetry, lacquer; straight and curved stretchers, cloven hoofs.

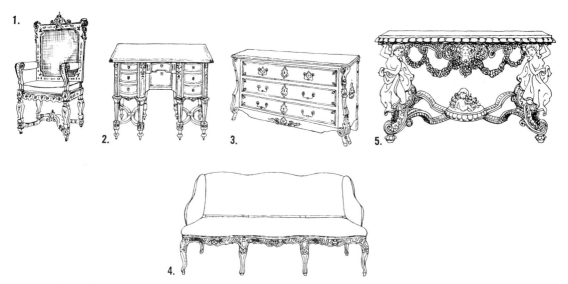

1. Throne-like chair with a high, straight back is massive in scale and shows the formality of Louis XIV pieces. 2. Desk with center recess or kneehole is typical of a French court piece of the period. This one is elaborately decorated in the style of Andre Charles Boulle. 3. Lowboy features decorative metal mounts on drawers and frame, and cloven hoof feet. 4. Classically severe lines of this upholstered sofa are softened by the carved frame and legs. 5. Marble topped console table with elaborately carved base features large scale, symmetrical figures.

Régence (1715-1723)

THE RÉGENCE, OR Regency, period covered a brief span of eight years. During these years, France was ruled by a Regent, hence the appendage of the name Regency to furniture designs which developed during those years. It was really a transitional period in design, marking the change between the two monarchs, Louis XIV (1643-1715) and Louis XV (1715-1774).

During the Regency many new objects appeared, such as commodes and chiffoniers with numerous drawers: secretaries that concealed a variety of things under closing panels: falling flaps on the sides of writing tables. Styles in general were simpler and less embellished than during the preceding Louis XIV period. Some Regency furniture is used today but, generally, popular taste leans towards Louis XV and Louis XVI which succeeded the Régence period.

Régence canape sofa, copied from an original French design, dated around 1717. Curved arms and back are typical of that period.

Régence bergere (chair) copied from the original, signed by 18th century craftsman Michel Cresson. Both these Régence pieces are from the Yale R. Burge Museum Collection, copied from the original French designs signed by master craftsmen of that period.

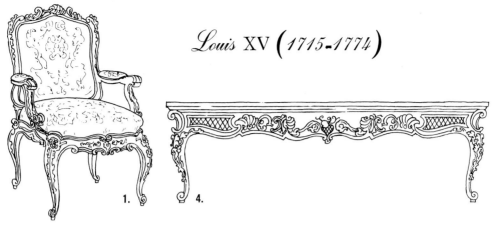

Louis XV (*1715-1774*)

1.   **4.**

THE REIGN OF Louis XV was marked by vice, immorality and licentiousness. But, because these weaknesses were covered by a hypocritical cloak of refinement, art flourished.

The court of the apathetic Louis XV lived in excessive luxury where beauty was the keynote, and millions of francs were spent on entertainment, objects of art, clothes and furniture. Interiors of the time were exquisitely beautiful and richly embellished.

Louis XV was influenced by his two successive mistresses, Madame du Barry and Madame de Pompadour. *Their influence on furniture fashions produced a strong feminine trend, which flourished with the aristocracy.* Today, the extreme ornamentation of the Louis XV is not used, but the lines have been adapted in some furniture.

Under the guidance of the two Royal courtesans, furniture makers produced ladies' writing desks, cabinets, dressing tables, corner commodes and a variety of mirrors. They were all graceful and dainty in construction, decorated with delicately colored silks, tapestry and embroidered covers. The mirrors were ever present and a big feature in decoration, perhaps because of the elaborate toiletry and the vanity which existed at this time.

Structures of sinuous curves and contours developed during this period. There were no straight lines, and the flowing lines became increasingly delicate and refined. No classic motifs were used.

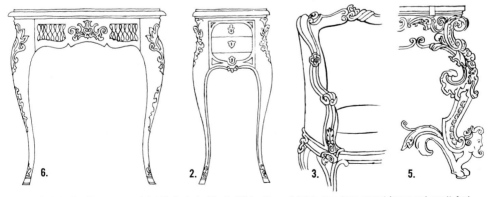

6.   **2.**   **3.**   **5.**

1. Chair featuring the curves and details typical of Louis XV furniture. Cabriole legs have carved knees and scroll feet. Carved arm supports join seat frame on all Louis XV chairs. 2. Side table with curved legs, onyx top and all the dainty, feminine characteristics of this period. 3. Chair with a broad, round seat and back has a carved frame which joins seat frame. This is exposed on all Louis XV chairs. 4. Table with marble top and curved legs features rococo (rock and shell) carving on the apron. 5. The elaborateness of ornamentation in this period can be seen in this close-up of a table leg. 6. Small table with a marble top features metal inlay and carving.

A characteristic of the later style, influenced by Madame de Pompadour, was a combination rock and shell motif, known as rococo. The endive leaf, the shell ornament and twisted forms gave a sumptuous effect to furniture, and were beautiful to the eye. Louis XV furniture invariably has a cabriole leg. The feet were scroll leaf, and the dolphin head was sometimes used. Arms of chairs and sofas were short and flaring, with sharply curved supports: while the backs were broad with the framing ornately carved. They were usually upholstered, as were the seats. Underbracing, which had been X-shaped in the time of Louis XIV was not used. Ornamentations were dominant, plain surfaces were avoided. Moldings were lighter in effect and panels were longer and not square.

The types of decoration used were carving, inlaying, painting, gilding, and elaborate metal mounts. Wreaths, flowers, lozenges, human figures and shells comprised the major motifs. Mahogany, walnut and ebony were the most popular woods, but other exotic woods were used for inlay work. The colors were very light and gay, the most fashionable being white and gold, pearl-grey, silver, rose, light greens and delicate blues.

To recognize Louis XV look for: construction — curved line, elaborately decorated, expressing luxury, grace and sensuous beauty so predominant during the King's reign. Other details are the cabriole leg with French scroll foot, bombé fronts, draped canopies over beds, rococo scroll, carving, inlay, marquetry, painting, gilding, veneering and metal mounts.

Here you see the graceful lines of the Louis XV period. These two chairs are both copied from the original signed by L. Delanois. The side chair is perfectly matched to the fautieul (chair with arms), and both are covered in watered silk taffeta. Also by Yale R. Burge.

Louis XV caned fautieul (chair) with knife-edged cushion. Copied from the original signed by P. Forget, from the Yale R. Burge Museum Collection of French reproductions. Note the curved legs, scroll carving.

Louis XV side chair, copied from the original signed by L. Gourdin. Note the elaborately carved legs which are balanced by the gently curved back.

This Louis XV table is typical of the period. Made of oak, it has upholstered fabric top, studded round the edge. From the original signed by Jean Laurent.

Louis XVI (*1774-1793*)

DURING THE REIGN of the ill-fated Louis XVI and his equally doomed queen, Marie Antoinette, there was a return to the classic furniture designs of Greece and Rome.

This change came about for a variety of reasons. Firstly, Marie Antoinette had been classically educated, and her leanings were towards the simple, straight lines of Ionic and Corinthian designs. Secondly, archaeologists were digging up ancient ruins whch helped to popularize and supplement the Queen's interest in classic design. Thirdly, and most important, was the state of France in 1774.

By the end of Louis XVs reign of extravagances, the government was near bankruptcy, the monarchy weakened, and the population drained and exhausted. The first seeds of the Revolution had been sown when Louis XVI took over the throne of France. In an effort to quell the revolutionary rumblings and the discontent of the populace, Louis XVI tried to minimize Court expenditures. The excesses and luxuries of the preceding reign were banished to some extent. Although the Court still lived in a state of opulence, it was by no means as extravagant as Louis XV's Court.

In trying to placate public opinion, Louis XVI curbed spending enough to influence styles of clothes and furnishings. Everything became less elaborate.

This Louis XVI bergere (chair) is typical of the period, with it[s] upholstered back, straight fluted legs, and carved motifs o[n] chair back, also on top of legs. It is copied from the origina[l] signed by Georg Jacob, and is from the Yale R. Burge Museu[m] Collection of reproductions.

1. The straight lines and restrained decoration of the Louis XVI period can be seen in this chair. It has a square back, padded arm rests and a gently curved seat frame. 2. Small table is classical in concept, with balanced ornamentation on apron, straight, slender legs and curved stretchers. 3. The laurel wreath was one of the classical motifs used to decorate furniture, walls and fabrics in this period. 4. Close-up of the straight, tapered leg which emerged in Louis XVI styles. 5. Classical Greek columns and motifs are featured on the legs and apron of this marble topped table. 6. Marie Antoinette basket of flowers is another typical decorative motif of the period.

Furniture was still beautiful, but much plainer and less embellished than it had been. Following the classical trend, this period's furniture changed from the curved line and the cabriole leg to the straight line; from unbalanced ornamentation to balanced ornamentation. Architectural details, such as the classic Greek column tops of Ionic and Corinthian design returned. The style was more homelike, and the general effect was dainty, graceful and elegant. Curves, when they appeared, were long and slender.

Sofas were longer and were supported by a number of straight fluted legs. Beds no longer had the curved outlines of the previous style and the wood was almost always visible. Posts were usually crowned with a pineapple, a plume of feathers, or other ornament.

Carving in the design of a twisted rope was a common motif. Acanthus leaves, bows and rosettes, staffs entwined with laurel leaves, oval plaques, mahogany veneers were all used, as were flaming torches, fluted columns, lyres and urns. Bound arrows formed the corners of many bureaus and commodes. The woods, when not gilded or enameled, were left natural. Today, bedroom furniture in the Louis XVI style is still widely used. To recognize Louis XVI easily look for: construction—straight line, small in scale, classic in detail. Other details—chair backs upholstered, carved or cane; classic motifs, such as urns, pendants, husks, lyres, oak leaves.

Directoire (1795-1799)

THE DIRECTOIRE WAS France's recovery period after the shock of the bloody, six year revolution. Established in 1795, it took its name from the Directoire government, which came into power after the two-year Reign of Terror. It lasted only four years, until the Directoire government fell in 1799 to a coup led by Napoleon Bonaparte.

Although it lasted only a brief four years, this was long enough for designers to sketch in the outlines of a new style. Directoire then merged into Empire, twenty-five years during which the personality of one man, Napoleon Bonaparte, dominated decoration and furniture.

Directoire furniture was a simplified version of the styles current in the preceding Louis XVI period. The lines were straighter than in Louis XVI pieces, and most of the furniture had a delicate look to it, although it was sturdy and well-constructed. Fruitwoods were used extensively, because of restrictions on foreign trade, and metal furniture was popular, probably for the same reasons. The names of earlier cabinetmakers, Riesener and the Jacob brothers, carried over to the new period, but Percier and Fontaine soon rose alongside them as the prime furniture makers of the era. David was the great innovator of style during the Directoire period. His influence was still felt during the Empire years, as he was the principal interpreter of Napoleon's ideas in furniture and decoration.

Window treatments became more tailored, following the straight line trend, and striped satins and silks were fashionable materials for drapes and upholstery.

The campaign chair was one of the most successful innovations of the Directoire period in the 18th century. It is still popular today, because of its great comfort, lightness and hard wearing qualities. Here you see a reproduction of the Directoire campaign chair, from the Yale R. Burge Museum Collection. It has the metal frame popularized during this period, with leather seat, back and strap arms. The brass feet, arm knobs and other decorative motifs are typical of the Directoire period.

Empire (1799-1814)

As NAPOLEON BONAPARTE gained in power, after his coup of 1799, so his influence on style and taste increased. His ideas, and even whims, were followed in everything from military uniforms, ladies' clothes and hairstyles to furnishings and interior decoration. His personality alone dominated all, for a quarter of a century.

In furniture, the delicate style of Directoire was taken over and developed "for the good of the state." It was aggressively nationalistic, and an impressive series of motifs inspired by the Egyptian Campaign were developed. Sphinxes, pyramids, obelisks and lotuses appeared on everything.

Declared First Consul for life in 1804, Napoleon soon had himself proclaimed Emperor of France and King of Italy. From Italy, around this time, came reminiscences of Imperial Rome, including acanthus leaves, laurel wreaths, winged victories, torches and cornucopias. Even Napoleon's personal motif of bees is supposedly taken from the Barberinis, an Italian family. The plain N, surmounted by a royal wreath, or the imperial eagle which so often led the French legions to victory, appeared as motifs on furniture, even plate and glass.

Throughout the whole period the straight line remained dominant. In effect, Empire was a return to the classic lines of Greece, Rome and Egypt. Chairs of Greek outline and Roman decoration detail are very prominent in this period. Typical Empire ornaments include winged figures in a variety of forms, emblematic of liberty: Greek vases, and decorative motifs such as laurels, lyres, the warrior's helmet and the dove. Mahogany was the chief wood used. This was decorated with heavy bronze and gilt mountings, for a handsome appearance. Stateliness and dignity are the main features of Empire furniture, and perhaps Napoleon preferred the styles of antiquity more than the effeminate furnishings of Louis XVI, which preceded his time of authority.

Most Empire pieces display large surfaces of highly polished wood, with ornamentation either inlaid or appliqued. The gilt, and other metal detail, was used chiefly to animate color schemes that were dark and rich. Round tables were the fashion, usually mounted on a pedestal or tripod base. Marble appeared as tabletops. Beds became classic ceremonial couches, with scrolled ends. They often took the form of day beds, whose raised backs permitted their use as sofas pushed against the wall. The chaise longue appeared, as did love seats. Consoles, often topped with marble or porphyry, had a variety of supports – obelisks, Egyptian motifs, bronze caryatids. Small bronze busts and heads, marble obelisks and sphinxes were used as ornaments on consoles and tables. Fabrics favored precise, overall medallion or wreath designs and stripes. As in the Directoire period, window treatments were on straight, tailored lines.

It is easy to recognize Empire. Look for: construction – the straight line and classical shape, proportions heavy, stately, sometimes ponderous; detail – Classic motifs, Egyptian decorations, such as sphinxes, obelisks, Napoleonic N, laurel wreaths, doves, eagles, warrior's helmets, winged figures; brass, ormolu, bronze mounts on mahogany.

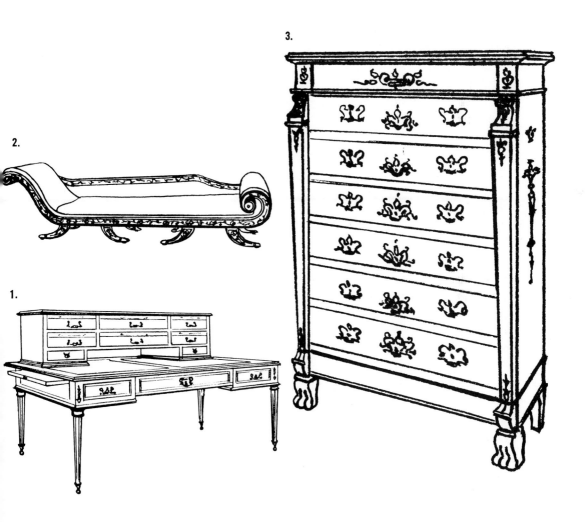

1. Desk with simple rectangular lines has metal mounts, reeded legs. As with most Empire furniture, large areas of polished wood are displayed. 2. Récamier sofa, following classic Greek lines, is long and slender with a low back. High curved arm is balanced by the scrolled end. 3. Heavier lines of the Empire period are reflected in this chest. Design details also typical of the period are paw feet, Egyptian carving and gilding so favored by Napoleon Bonaparte.

Louis XV, *Louis* XVI *and* Régence *Mixed*

This charming sitting room is decorated in Louis XVth country style, and illustrates how well this period fits into a modern apartment. Designed by Maurice Weir, A.I.D., N.S.I.D.

That this is the house of a collector is evidenced by the great pains which have been taken to achieve perfection. The malachite candelabra adds a startling note to a room whose color is otherwise almost Grisaille in feeling. The 18th century lacquered secretary opens to show magnificent wood. **Sofa in front of window is Louis XVI, chairs Louis XV and tripod table Régence.** Designed by Leona Kahn, A.I.D., N.S.I.D.

Louis XV and Louis XVI period antiques shown off against a subtle color scheme of mole-grey and gold and muted orange, in a New York drawing room. Gold and grey damask draperies, an antique Russian chandelier and crystal and ormolu lamps complete the French room. The only contemporary element is the terrazzo carpet in gold and grey. Designed by J. Frederic Lohman, A.I.D.

In this picture you see the formal dining room in the same gracious apartment. The Italian painted Louis XV chairs are upholstered in apricot and gold, the draperies are apricot silk bound in deeper apricot. The chandelier is antique Venetian, small table is Louis XV.

This third view of the apartment shows the foyer. Louis XV and Louis XVI furniture has been mixed by the designer to create an impressive entrance hall. Commode in the foreground is transitional, from the period between Louis XV and XVI. The chairs at each side of it, and another at the far end of the foyer, are Italian Directoire painted chairs. An Italian Louis XV red lacquer chest is flanked by a pair of Louis XV sofas.

This charming room decorated in shades of yellow and white shows a combination of Louis XV and Louis XVI furniture. The pair of chairs flanking the commode are Louis XVI, as are the sofa, table and open-back chair in the foreground. The commode is Louis XV, with a Lowestoft vase lamp on top. The wooden figures in the window wall alcoves are 18th century. Designed by Leona Kahn, A.I.D., N.S.I.D.

Four Views of a Modern Apartment—
Where Antiques Create an Opulent Mood

THE DINING AND living rooms of this apartment have been decorated solely in period furniture, proving the point that antiques can be used in rooms of contemporary architecture, if handled skillfully and combined with accessories that echo the mood of the furniture. **Louis XV and Louis XVI** pieces have mainly been used in this apartment designed by Michael Paul Feldman, N.S.I.D.

1. In this dining room, the antique mirrored wall helps to create a feeling of spaciousness often lacking in most modern apartments. The carpet was specially designed to repeat the turquoise velvet of the chairs and the yellow, silk damask drapes. The dining table is from the **English Regency** period, while the chairs are **Louis XV.** The magnificent crystal chandelier is **Louis XVI. 2.** In this second view, the living room area is featured. The same color scheme of yellow and turquoise used in the dining area is repeated, as are the drapes and the specially designed rug which picks up the yellow and turquoise. **Louis XV** sofa is covered in turquoise silk, drapes are of yellow silk damask. A wallpaper mural and column treatment helps to create personality and interest in a standard L-shaped living-dining room. **3.** View of the living room, looking towards the foyer. A pair of columns (only one visible in photograph) were installed to create a separation between these two areas. Electrified brackets on either side of the **Chinoiserie** cabinet are hung on the decorative ribbons which conceal the wiring. **4.** This view of the main living room wall shows the **Louis XV** sofa against the background of the sepia wallpaper mural. An antique Venetian walnut table seems to echo the browns and gold in the mural. On the table is a collection of objets d'art, snuff boxes, porcelains and bisque. White candles in antique gilt candlesticks complete this decorative arrangement.

1.

3.

2.

4.

Louis XVI Drawing Room in Gold and White

*designed by Mary E. Dunn, F.A.I.D., captures the classic beauty
of this 18th century period of decoration*

This Louis XVI drawing room, off-white glazed in gold, is paneled with wallpaper moldings in tones of gold. The cornice, panel and stile moldings are different designs simulating carved wood moldings, with light and dark tones, giving perspective to each area. The herringbone-pattern parquet floor is a wood vinyl product, the rug is an **antique Koulah**. The **Louis XVI bergere** is covered in gold damask; and the antique canape is covered in orange velvet. An antique black and gold lacquer secretary occupies the center of the south wall, opposite the double window framed in gold silk taffeta. A black lacquer Chinese coffee table completes the canape. **Louis XV and Louis XVI** tables hold the crystal and black tole lamps which light the room. A rock crystal chandelier casts a soft glow over all.

Beyond the walls of this Louis XVI bedroom-sitting room are housed all the "necessaries" of today's living . . . TV, hi-fi, shelves and drawers. The Louis XVI writing table and chair enhance this corner of the room. The French lamp is signed by Thomire. Designer Leona Kahn, A.I.D., N.S.I.D.

The grandeur of yesterday is revived in this pink and gold dining room. The 18th century **Boiserie** (wall paneling) has been cut down from 15½ feet to 8½ feet; gold trophies in narrow panels depict musical instruments. The console was originally an overdoor in the great house where it was discovered. **Boiserie** and chairs are all Louis XVI. Soft pink chair upholstery material, pink brocade drapes and pink area rug all help to cast the rosy glow which seems to permeate the room. Opulent crystal chandelier completes the picture. Designed by Leona Kahn, A.I.D., N.S.I.D.

Louis XV, Louis XVI and Directoire Furniture

Although the elements of this collection are actually in miniature, the correlation of each item, from the transitional secretaire, the bronze busts, the jasper on the inlaid porcelain fireplace to the period glass, helps to achieve the perfection of the **Petit Salon** in the French 18th century manner. The two chairs are **Louis XV,** the bench is **Louis XVI** and the round tables are **Directoire.** The beautiful blue color scheme is taken from the embossed rug, with the two yellow lamps echoing the yellow flowers in the rug pattern. Note the pleated fabric used on the ceiling which combines with the drapes to create a tent-like effect. The total result is a restful and charming retreat where a woman can read, entertain friends or answer mail. Designed by Leona Kahn, A.I.D., N.S.I.D.

French Drawing Room Decorated with
Louis XV, Louis XVI and Directoire Furniture

This drawing room in the French manner features eight of the twelve "Months of the Year" designed by Fragonard fils in 1808 and printed by Dufour of Paris. The figures are brown, grey and turquoise on a bois-de-rose background. These panels are mounted on the "Pingree House" wallpaper on a bois-de-rose background with the design in brown and turquoise. **This is a very rare, old wallpaper and is the only complete set which exists in the world today.** An antique Persian rug is used in the center of a herringbone-patterned floor of Brazilian rosewood vinyl. The furniture is Louis XV, Louis XVI and Directoire. An antique Directoire canape is covered in deep turquoise velvet; a pair of Louis XV grey-painted open armchairs are covered in brocade; and a Louis XVI armchair is covered in grey and turquoise striped silk. A rare, antique Louis XVI mantel of Isabella marble occupies the center of the back wall, over which hangs a painted trummeau with a gold carved wood panel. The andirons and fire tools are antique. Directoire commodes and Louis XV and Louis XVI tables hold crystal and black tole lamps to light the room. A crystal and gilt chandelier adds the finishing touch to a beautiful room. Designed by Mary E. Dunn, F.A.I.D.

This unusual sitting room decorated in French 18th century style has a fresh, garden feeling achieved through use of plants and flowers. The elegant desk and the yellow chair are both Louis XV, while the blue upholstered chairs are Directoire. Walls are covered in fabric matched to chairs for a feeling of coordination. Designed by Yale Burge, A.I.D., N.S.I.D.

Different styles from one century can easily be combined for a beautiful effect, as shown in this elegant room designed by Michael Greer, F.N.S.I.D., A.I.D. It is 18th century in concept, and includes Louis XV and XVI and Directoire furniture, dated from about 1715 to 1799. The chest and stool in front of it are both Louis XV, chair in far left of picture is Louis XV, while the three-leg table, loveseat near screen and chair in foreground are all Directoire. Note the lovely symmetrical window treatment.

Louis XVI and Empire

An octagonal entrance hall in a French country house with four panels of "The Monuments of Paris" antique scenic wallpaper. The furniture is Empire and Louis XVI, and the floor is Versailles parquetry. Note how the beautiful blue walls echo the colors in the wallpaper. Designed by Mary E. Dunn, F.A.I.D.

This handsome roll-top Empire desk with brass inlay and gallery is a perfect example of the fine lines predominant in that period of French furnishing. It blends well with a gracefully carved Louis XVI desk chair, upholstered in brocade. A pair of Louis XVI marble and bronze candlesticks have been electrified and topped with shades as lamps. They flank a porcelain parakeet.

Empire Period

This elegant dining room in a French country house is furnished with Empire furniture. The walls are painted a pale aubergine, with taffeta curtains in the same color trimmed with beige fringe. The dining chairs are covered with gold cut velvet. Designed by Mary E. Dunn, F.A.I.D.

Directoire Period

The living room here is in French Directoire style. Each piece has been carefully placed to show it off to its best advantage; clever grouping of sofa and chairs make for comfortable conversation areas. Beyond the three unusual draped Roman arches is a small dining area. Designer Michael Greer, F.N.S.I.D., A.I.D.

Directoire and Empire Mixed

This Directoire bed has metal side rails and stretchers typical of the period. It has been fitted with a box spring and mattress, round end-bolsters and back cushions to act as a sofa during the day. Painted armchairs are of the Empire period, as is the writing table with its finely shaped legs. Upholstered walls and ceiling create a simulated tent effect, which hints of Napoleonic campaigns. The antique Aubusson carpet is green with fuschia, orange and beige flowers. The tole chandelier has its original shade. Designed by Michael Greer, A.I.D., N.S.I.D.

Louis XV and Louis XVI with Second Empire

Second Empire white marble mantel is a focal point in the living room of New York antiques dealer Michael Bertolini's apartment. Andirons are also Second Empire and the gold leaf mirror is First Empire, circa 1810-20. Objects on the mantel include a Thomire clock, circa 1790, English Battersea boxes and French patch boxes, Louis XVI bronze dore candlesticks made in Paris, circa 1780. The console, which conceals a radiator, was cut down from a Second Empire china cabinet and is of mahogany and ebony with bronze dore captials. White urn is old Vienna porcelain, and the painting above the console is of Lully, court musician to Louis XIV. Chair is covered in celadon velvet, and Italian silk draperies in the Louis XV style are also celadon.

This second photograph of Mr. Bertolini's apartment shows: Louis XVI open armchairs, c. 1790, upholstered in caramel corduroy; Charles X satinwood desk, c. 1830; Charles X satinwood coffee table, c. 1830, with ormolu mountings and black marble top. Bench at desk is Louis XV, c. 1780, of gilded beechwood covered in celadon silk. Aubusson rug is in salmon, caramel, blue and brown, and dates from about 1830. Lamp on desk is a Louis XVI bronze dore bouillotte lamp by Thomire. Lamp at right was made from the leg of a Directoire console, c. 1800. In foreground of photograph you see a close-up of an English coffee urn of silver with a London hallmark, c. 1890. Cups, sugar pot are Old Vienna, c. 1830.

Here you see a close-up of the Charles X satinwood desk, circa 1830, which becomes a showcase for collectibles in Mr. Bertolini's apartment. Louis XVI bronze dore bouillotte lamp and the small clock are by Thomire, late 18th century French artist in bronze. The pink opaline vase is one of a pair of Second Empire cornucopias. Red leather box with ormolu mountings is English Regency, and the small box at right is Second Empire French, of malachite and ormolu.

CHAPTER TWENTY-FIVE

18th & 19th Century Early American Furniture

How to recognize: Provincial, Early Colonial,
18th Century Colonial, Federal

IT IS WRONG to think that the development of the Atlantic seaboard was due entirely to English settlers. Immigrants from all over Europe flocked to America, and the Dutch, Italian, German, Spanish and French all added their ways of life to the American heritage and helped form the national taste.

Although the English influence in furniture finally dominated, isolated pieces of other styles truly belong in the great furniture category known as **Early American.** The colorful pieces of the Pennsylvania Dutch, the hardy burgher products of New York and the Hudson Valley, and the baroque French curves of New Orleans can all be found in Early American rooms. This is why the most typical rooms are actually mixtures of a variety of styles, born in Europe and adapted here to suit the diverse tastes of the early international settlers.

Early American furniture can be broken down into two distinct categories: before the Revolution and after the signing of the Declaration of Independence. **American Provincial** and **Early Colonial** flowered before the Revolution, while **18th Century Colonial** and **Federal** came after.

American Provincial

THE PROVINCIAL FURNITURE made by early American craftsmen is rustic in character. It stems directly from the various peasant styles of European countries, and much of it was made by traveling joiners and cabinetmakers. Although it includes pieces of fine craftsmanship, it is informal in the broadest sense of the word. In effect, it suggests big, congenial families and country life in rambling farmhouses. To its originators it was not really a style at all, but simply the most practical way of making furniture from the most plentiful materials.

Often the construction and detail of these pieces was crude, the styling simple, and the furniture was usually finished with brightly colored painted designs.

The most well-known of **American Provincial** is **Pennsylvania German,** (often miscalled Pennsylvania Dutch, derived from Deutsch), a vividly decorated peasant style which originated in Germany and Switzerland. It is still being made by the descendants of early German settlers.

Persistence of style is evident in other types of Provincial furniture. The Windsor chair, for instance, has enjoyed ensuing popularity since the early 18th century, and is still being made today. Quality of workmanship was part of the religion of the Shakers, who settled in New England in the 19th century. The furniture they produced is unusually delicate and simple, Provincial in character, and their built-in storage gives it affinity with contemporary designs.

During the 17th, 18th and 19th centuries, local styles were developed all over the country by the different settlers. Some styles remained local, others found universal popularity. Although newer immigrants varied the original patterns, the basic lines were always simple. The form was usually straight and clean-cut, with few curves. Popular woods were pine, cherry, maple, oak, ash and hickory. Often they were gaily painted. Some of the pieces which emerged were the pine wagon seat, the Windsor chair, a variety of rocking chairs, the Windsor love seat, corner cupboards and dressers. In the late 17th century the butterfly table appeared; other tables had gate-legs or were drop-leaf. The Pennsylvania Dutch Dower chest, painted chests of drawers, and the tall Shaker chest with abundant storage, are other typical pieces of American Provincial.

To recognize American Provincial furniture look for: rustic characteristics, simple lines; pine, cherry and hickory woods; gaily painted motifs.

Pennsylvania Dutch. 1. Chest-on-chest cupboard is a typical storage piece. 2. Chair with a rush seat has a variation of the fiddle back and simply turned round legs. 3. Small scale dresser built on rustic lines features a raised gallery on top and lower level shelf. 4. Pine corner cupboard built on straight lines is another typical storage piece of the period. 5. Bride's dower chest, or **Kaz** as it was called, is the most famous of all Pennsylvania Dutch pieces. It is highly decorated with bright colors and is used for storing linen. 6. Typical kitchen dresser with high drawers and shelf for displaying pottery plates and dishes. **Windsor Chairs** were named for Windsor Castle but adopted here. Originally made by wheelwrights, hence the use of bentwood back frame, supported by spindles and legs pegged into saddle shaped seats. 7. Windsor chair with a hoop back. 8. Bow back Windsor chair is a variation in shape. 9. Braced back (high) Windsor chair is another common shape. **Shaker.** 10. Shaker craftsmen were clever innovators and made such pieces as this rocker with a high slat back. 11. Another practical Shaker piece was the drop-leaf table.

Early Colonial

EARLY COLONIAL FURNITURE, like American Provincial, was of necessity the very simplest type. Basically it was made for utility, and was generally patterned after models which the colonists remembered from their homelands. As the colonies prospered, architecture became more elaborate and more sophisticated furniture appeared.

The first major influence was a Dutch-English style, then in favor in England. William of Orange had popularized the Dutch style when he came to the English throne, and he and his queen, Mary, lent their name to the style of the period, around 1688-1702. Elaborate stretchers on highboys, lowboys and tables, plus scrolled legs, are the widest known characteristics of this furniture. Scrolls which could be turned on a lathe were the first form of decoration used on American furniture. Later carved feet borrowed from Dutch and Spanish sources began to appear, and the slat backs, typical of early chairs, gave way to a primitive form of slat, which was the forerunner of the carved work on late 18th century chairs.

It was about 1690-1710 that both William and Mary and Queen Anne styles began to be adopted in America. At this time carved and painted Hadley chests, produced in the Massachusetts Colony, also appeared. The Dutch *kas,* highboys with turned legs, press cupboards and bonnet top cabinets were fashionable, as were walnut-framed mirrors in the Queen Anne style, canopy and fourposter beds, pedestal tables and sideboards with cabriole legs.

Even the most expensive furniture was made of solid wood, unfinished except for staining or waxing. Veneering and shellacking was still unexploited. Pine was the most popular wood, particularly for paneling, as were other available woods such as oak, birch, maple and walnut.

To recognize Early Colonial look for: Americanized versions of William and Mary and Queen Anne styles; construction — straight, sturdy, often unsubtle; cabriole and curved legs on some tables and sideboards; the table chair, painted chests, Dutch *kas.* Woods — pine, walnut and maple.

18th Century Colonial

AS THE 18TH century Colonials prospered and became property owners, they began to search for local craftsmen whose production could compete with imported furniture. They owned fine houses, and wanted equally as fine embellishments for the interiors; pieces imported from abroad were necessarily expensive, transportation both difficult and lengthy.

A group of American furniture makers left their mark on this period—in particular John Hancock, Moses Dodge, John Goddard and Gilbert Ash. Their basic models came from England, but the cabinetmakers and designers soon produced typical transformations to suit American tastes.

Lesser craftsmen worked from Chippendale's *Director* and later from Hepplewhite's *Guide*. Up to the Revolution, the Chippendale style was the most dominant. This emerged from a background of Queen Anne and worked towards the refinements of Hepplewhite and Sheraton. It was similar to Queen Anne in overall line, often with rococo embellishments and occasional French, Gothic and even Chinese derivations.

Two kinds of leg are typical of this period: the curved cabriole with a claw-and-ball foot in high relief, and a straight square leg with reeding or fluting on the outer side. Scale was ample in all pieces and broken pediments were common and more elaborate than in the preceding period. Carving included scrolls, the well-formed shell, pierced back splats, strapwork. Toward the end of the century the Hepplewhite influence was predominant, and motifs included Prince of Wales feathers, medallions, heads of wheat and festoons.

New pieces began to appear, to satisfy growing household needs. The chest-on-chest, the linen press, tilt-top tables and the kneehole desk were among them. After 1785 came the two-and-three part dining table, the breakfront secretary, the field bed and the tambour desk. Wing chairs, the Martha Washington chair, highboys, piecrust tables and block front desks are also typical of this period.

Mahogany was the most popular wood, with cherry, gum and curly maple as secondary choices. This period also saw fine craftsmanship in the lesser decorative arts. Baron Stiegel of Pennsylvania and Caspar Wistar of New Jersey made the famous glass which is widely collected today, and Simon and Benjamin Willard were master clockmakers. The manufacture of wallpaper began in 1763, and marble was quarried locally for the first time, after the Revolution. Philadelphia, Boston and Charleston were the leading furniture style centers of this period.

As the century progressed, windows became larger in size, and drapes more elaborate. Fabrics were rich, and Chinoiserie wallpapers, crystal chandeliers and exquisite silver began to appear in the finer homes.

Colonial Williamsburg in the middle of the 18th century was one of the gayest spots in the Western world. The Virginians led a carefree life of courtly balls, suppers and assemblies. Money was abundant for expert craftsmen and their products, and homes glittered with finery. These homes, basically Anglophile in outlook, often outdid English houses in grandeur. In fact, styles were often exaggerated and taste became almost over-refined. The Governor's Palace at Williamsburg is without doubt the finest example of 18th Century Colonial furniture and furnishings, and the overall style of the period.

To recognize 18th Century Colonial look for: derivations of Chippendale, Hepplewhite and Sheraton; carved and gilt mirrors, Wedgwood candelabra, Waterford and crystal chandeliers, Martha Washington chair, wing chairs, consoles, sideboards, breakfronts. Details: cabriole leg, straight leg with fluting, tambour doors, block fronts, extension tables. Wood: mahogany or cherry.

1. Americanized version of a Chippendale chair is of Philadelphia origin, features rich rococo carving, the cabriole leg with claw-and-ball foot in high relief, pierced back splat. 2. Americanized version of a Hepplewhite chair has a shield back and the typical straight, square legs, is of New England origin. 3. Americanized version of a Chinese Chippendale chair is of New York origin, has a ladder back and straight, square legs with reeding on the outer side. 4. Newport chest with a block-front and raised top panels carved with the large shell motif. 5. Chest-on-chest with the characteristic block-front, broken pediments, carved finials. 6. Americanized version of the Chippendale sofa features a taller back and typical claw-and-ball feet. 7. Typical bookcase of this period is heavier in style, with block-front, broken pediments, carved finials and the shell motif. 8. American Hepplewhite chest with a swell front is smaller, less elaborate.

Federal

AFTER THE REVOLUTION, America's new feeling of nationalism had a marked influence on furniture styles and the decorative arts.

In the early part of the 19th century, a new style emerged which is known as Federal. It manifested itself in the use of patriotic and classical motifs. This classic influence was also prevalent in Europe at the time. In France it had a political motive and was influenced by the personality of Napoleon; in England it was of archaeological origin.

But in America the classical influence was a symbol of the young Republic's new ideals; and following the trend, Thomas Jefferson built Monticello and the University of Virginia, and Charles Bullfinch the Boston State House.

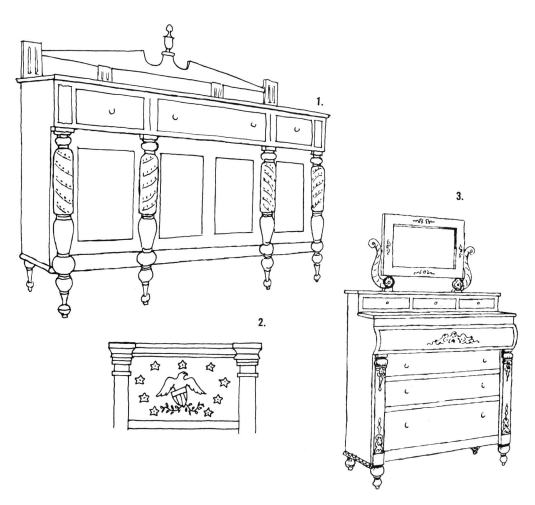

1.

3.

2.

Federal motifs include the patriotic eagle, the thunderbolt, the trumpet, as well as the classic acanthus leaf, the lyre, the saber, the cornucopia leg, lion's mask and paws, rosettes and bowknots.

There is a fine detail on all Federal furniture. Legs were reeded or otherwise framed. Drawers were often finished with a fine raised hairline of wood called cock beading, and the use of color veneer round the edges gave interest to large, plain surfaces. Brass was often used for ornaments such as feet, casters, drawer pulls, and ring handles. About 1825 china and glass drawer pulls began to appear.

A typical Federal piece is the round convex mirror surmounted by an eagle. The eagle also spreads its wings over secretaries and chests, chimney pieces, valances, and was a favorite tavern sign. A variety of patriotic emblems and historic scenes appeared on clocks as decoration. On the other hand, china, glass, silver and plate were all molded in classic forms. Popular fabrics were damask, brocade, satin, taffeta, *toile de Jouy,* printed cotton and silk.

Two outstanding furniture designers put their individual stamp on Federal furniture. Duncan Phyfe was a Scot who catered to New York's more prosperous families and translated the Sheraton and Hepplewhite influence into the American vernacular. Samuel McIntire, an architect from Salem Massachusetts, helped to establish the overall forms.

1. Sideboard with decorated front columns displays the sturdy, heavier lines of a typical Federal piece. 2. Patriotic motifs came into prominence, particularly the eagle. This is a typical carving on a Federal mantlepiece. 3. Chest with the irregular front and attached mirror predominant in Federal pieces of this kind. 4. Chair built on severe lines, is upholstered and has little carving on arm supports and the frame. 5. Clock decorated with the patriotic eagle typifies accessories of the period. 6. Only the simplest turnings were used, as on this bedback.

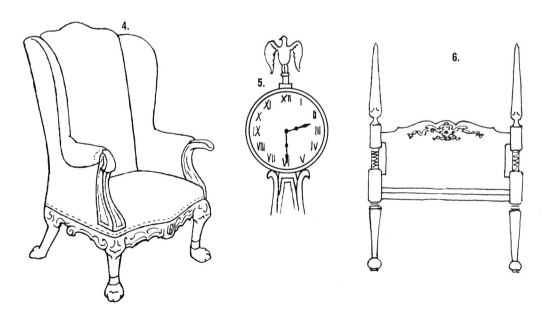

Duncan Phyfe (1795-1854)

DUNCAN PHYFE, WORKING in the United States during the 19th century, was materially influenced by both Hepplewhite and Sheraton. Yet in spite of this, all of his furniture was basically a new creation, with his own indelible stamp on it. So that while it *does* resemble furniture of the English masters, it has characteristics which are easily identified as those of Phyfe.

From the influence of the English master craftsmen, Phyfe turned to the styles of the French Empire, in response to requests from his clients. But his work on these lines is generally considered inferior to his earlier work. In his later work Phyfe designed furniture which he himself described as "butcher furniture" because of its heaviness, and its lack of the grace and beauty of his first pieces.

1. Typical Phyfe sofa built on classical lines with sleigh front arms and ornately carved feet. 2. Dressing table with pedestal and carved S curves supporting the attached mirror. 3. Chair with fluted, curved front legs and splayed back legs. Feet are plain. Back is low and square. 4. Drop-leaf table with column pedestal and curule feet. 5. Small table features the lyre pedestal favored so much by Phyfe. 6. Lyre appears again on the back of this side chair. 7. Detail of a Phyfe pedestal with four feet. 8. Sofa on classic lines with wooden arms carved with lyre motif. 9. Close-up of sofa showing details of sleigh front arms and ornately carved feet.

His legs on tables, chairs, sofas were straight, reeded and fluted; other chairs had concavely curved legs, while some tables were supported at each end with lyre-shaped bases. The backs of chairs had the lyre motif, X-shaped pieces either straight or curved, and shaped bars between uprights. He made several types of dining tables, usually sectional or extension, with the lyre often appearing in the pedestals. This motif sometimes appears on smaller tables, but the most recognizable feature in Phyfe pieces is the lack of straight lines in both tops and legs. His table leaves are nearly always slightly rounded, with a clover leaf pattern at the corners; pedestals are sometimes crossed lyres or finely carved pillars, and he seldom made a table with four vertical legs.

Phyfe relied on decorations such as acanthus leaves, ovals, plumes and the lyre; he also used carving, turning, veneering, reeding and inlay. In his early work he occasionally used brass. This metal is used more liberally in his later periods. Phyfe preferred mahogany and generally worked with this wood.

In this spacious farm kitchen you see a fine **collection of genuine Early American furniture.** Accessories are also Early American, including pewter candlesticks, tray, copper measures, wood bucket and warming pan arranged around fireplace. Soft green walls of wood paneling and beams add to the country atmosphere of the kitchen as does the 20th century vinyl flooring in a Dutch hexagonal design.

Colonial Williamsburg Dining Room

In this beautiful Colonial dining room, the paneling and wallpaper were copied from the dining room in the Governor's Palace; the draperies are made of Williamsburg blue damask, while the furniture copied from the Palace is reproduction, and the rug is antique Ghiordis. The prints, brasses, chandelier and blue and white ware are reproduction. Designed by Mary E. Dunn, F.A.I.D.

In this apartment, **Oriental accessories** are mingled with furniture of **18th Century American** origin. The lowboy, Queen Anne in styling, dates from the late 1700s. Chippendale style chairs flank the lowboy, and above it hangs an American portrait. Lamp shade was made to identically match the Chinese vase that is now a lamp. Birds are a pair of Chinese porcelain cranes, of fine proportion.

View of this living room in a home decorated by antique dealer C. Alan Hudson, Jr. shows a mantel from a house in Philadelphia, circa 1720. Needlework ships are all Early American, the one at upper right being one of the few battle scenes ever done in needlework. Brass fender and andirons are early fireplace equipment from Philadelphia. Lamp bears the label of the maker, Cornelius of Philadelphia, and dates from 1854. Pembroke tables are mahogany. Walls are white with Sutter gold woodwork. Sofa is done in Williamsburg blue homespun, and chair is covered in Sutter gold, blue and white chintz.

Corner setting in this home shows Governor Winthrop serpentine front desk, c. 1720, made of maple and with its original brasses. Chair is a country piece of pine and maple, interesting because of its half-spindle back. Paintings are from a collection of marine oils, and are in their original frames. Lamp is by Cornelius of Philadelphia and dates from 1854. Among objects on the desk are a pink and white Staffordshire pitcher and a New Hall pitcher with shell design. By C. Alan Hudson, Jr.

The chairs in this dining room are by Duncan Phyfe, the great American furniture maker of the 19th century. Small sideboard in foreground is a Hepplewhite piece of Baltimore origin. Large mahogany sideboard is a transitional piece, not strictly Federal nor strictly Empire, but with attributes of each. Mantel is a reproduction of a country piece, but fender actually dates from 1740; of wire and brass, it was made in New York State. The candlesticks on the mantel are Early Victorian, about 1837. Decorated by C. Alan Hudson, Jr.

The Ground Floor Library of the White House

a miniature museum of Americana,
furnished by the American Institute of Interior Designers
with rare 18th & 19th Century American antiques

IN 1962, THE American Institute of Interior Designers completed the redesigning, the rebuilding and the refurnishing of the ground floor Library of the White House. It was presented to Mrs. John F. Kennedy as a gift to the nation in June of that year. Here and on the following pages are four full page photographs of the Library as it was decorated by the A.I.D., and as it looks today.

Mrs. Francis Henry Lenygon, F.A.I.D., of New York, Chairman of the A.I.D., National Committee on Historic Preservation, served as Chairman of a small White House Project Working Committee composed of Mrs. Ellen Lehman McCluskey, A.I.D., and Stephen J. Jussel, F.A.I.D., both of New York.

The Working Committee spent fourteen months redesigning the room, supervising its reconstruction and assembling its furnishings. Many months were spent on research, textile selection and weaving and the acquisition of authentic and suitable furnishings. The rare furnishings make the Library a miniature museum of Americana, described by Mrs. Kennedy at the time as "One of the most beautiful and historic rooms in the White House. . . . a room that is of great interest to the President."

Because of the authenticity of the room's design, its rare 18th & 19th Century American furnishings and its attractive and friendly atmosphere, it will remain for many generations to admire and enjoy.

The structural details of the room are consistent with the late 18th century work of John Hoban, the original designer of "The President's House." The built-in book shelves which cover the walls on four sides rest on cupboards with well-proportioned paneled doors. A simple molded cornice surrounds the room above bookshelves, doors and windows. The paint color varies in different lights from cream to pale yellow. The predominant colors in the floor covering and furniture coverings are yellow, apple-green, henna and brown. Bookbindings add extra color to the room. A distinguishing feature of the room is the wood mantel from a house in Salem, Mass., attributed to the famous American architect Samuel McIntire.

This close-up photograph of the **fireplace wall of the White House Library** shows the fine detail on the wood mantel from a house in Salem, Mass. It is attributed to the noted American architect Samuel McIntire, whose work was prominent in the Federal Period. The two armchairs, with cane sides and backs and green cushions, are Regency, were chosen for comfort as well as grace. The two matching carved footstools covered with Indian embroidery are 18th century. The pair of Sheffield plated Argand lamps, gracing occasional tables at each side of the fireplace, were a gift from General Lafayette to General Knox. The mantle clock is Sheraton, and a card table in the right hand corner, holding a bust and vase of flowers, is by Duncan Phyfe.

A Duncan Phyfe sofa, matching armchair and side chair are grouped together in front of a bookcase along the window wall of the Library. Yellow cushions repeat the various golden shades used throughout the room. The high backed chair in the corner is a Martha Washington style chair covered in dull gold velvet. The other Duncan Phyfe armchair is placed in front of desk. Two beautiful Chinese porcelain vases, mounted as lamps with white shades, were originally in the Morgan Collection and are described as K'ang Hsi period 1662-1722.

The White House Library, showing the full effect of the room as a whole. The octagonal library table with leather top is a perfect match to the other 18th and 19th Century American antiques used throughout the room. It is placed in the center of the beautiful Aubusson rug, directly in front of the Duncan Phyfe sofa and chairs. The other Duncan Phyfe sofa and chairs are not shown in this photograph.

In this corner of the Library the second Duncan Phyfe sofa and two of the side chairs, from a ten piece suite, are grouped together. The six foot long sofa has the same yellow cushions as its sister piece, but the two side chairs have pale apricot cushions echoing the soft pink in the Aubusson rug.

Strictly modern is the theme of this sitting room. In this corner close-up a handsome black leather buttoned sofa on a metal frame is offset by a bright blue wall. Muted green carpet echoes the color of the base around the walls. An architectural screen acts an an "op" art divider, is matched in feeling to the look-at-walk-on "pop" art rug. Potted tree adds to the modern look.

CHAPTER TWENTY-SIX

Modern Furniture and the Contemporary Look

THE SLEEK, OFTEN stark lines of modern furniture evolved with the advent of modern architecture. Both these new concepts in design were born of the revolution against tradition which was started by such famous architects as Frank Lloyd Wright and Le Corbusier.

It was Le Corbusier who called the house "a machine for living" and stripped it clean of ornamentation. His homes were strictly functional and stressed pure, even stark simplicity.

The modern home, built on the basic premise of function, air, light, open planning and a new dimension of spaciousness, demanded furniture that blended with and reiterated the sparse, clean look. Furniture became simple, highly functional and streamlined.

Today, modern furniture has lost that somewhat *cold* look which it had initially. In fact most of it has grace and elegance in line and shape. And use of rich fabrics, leather, metals and woods has given it a new feeling of warmth without loss of its basic, pristine beauty.

Mies van der Rohe, Eero Saarinen, Florence Knoll, Charles Eames, Harry Bertoia, and Danes Poul Kjaerholm and Arne Jacobsen are some of the most notable designers who have left their personal imprint on modern furniture design. Mies van der Rohe's famous Barcelona chair made of leather and stainless steel, Charles Eames' bent plywood chair, and Arne Jacobsen's swan chair are perhaps the best known, and have in fact become modern classics.

Modern furniture is built on the principle of clean cut, sleek lines and lack of ornamentation. But this does not mean that it is *straight* lined or angular. Curves, flares and a flowing feeling are continually incorporated in modern design for that fluid, light-as-air look.

The most popular of the now classical, modern designs are the round occasional table on a pedestal base, contour-shaped chairs molded in one piece, scoop and bucket chairs, square glass tables on low metal legs, low-slung sofas and chairs on pedestal bases. Chairs and sofas without arms and low divans without arms or backs are also prevalent. Woods used are often blond or light such as Danish teak, although rosewood, ebony or ebonised woods and oak are featured. Metals are widely used, for chair, sofa and table frames or legs. Aluminum, stainless steel and brass are the most effective, particularly with the elegant glass and marble-topped tables. Leather, oxhide, rough-textured fabrics and vinyls are the most popular materials for upholstery, because they are rich looking as well as functional and practical. Many of the scoop or bucket chairs are made of see-through or vividly colored plastics, and many other synthetic materials are successfully incorporated in modern furniture designs.

The overall look of the truly modern room is sleek, uncluttered and light. For this reason floors and walls are often bare. Vinyl tiles, teak or parquet wood blocks, marble, tiles and ceramics make ideal floors, with perhaps a lush area rug of fur, skin or wool used occasionally for added warmth. Pictures or mirrors can be used on the walls, but essentially they should be in keeping with the modern concept of the room, and unobtrusively framed. Drapes should be strictly tailored in a fabric that blends with the upholstery. Pale pastel color schemes came into vogue with modern architecture and furniture, perhaps because they best add to the spacious, airy feeling. White, beige, pale blue, and pale yellow are ideal colors for the shell of the modern room, as they make the perfect backdrop for vivid accent colors in cushions, upholstery, picture mounts or an area rug.

These paler shades from the color spectrum also highlight indoor plants and greenery that most designers feature in the modern room today. Lighting fixtures and accessories need to be of current design, if the *pure,* modern room is to succeed.

The Contemporary Look

THE WORD *contemporary* must not be confused with the word *modern,* although this only too often happens. It means—of the present, current, now—and it really expresses an *atmosphere* that is currently popular rather than an actual design trend. Today, for instance, a contemporary room does not mean one that is furnished entirely with strictly modern furniture. In effect, a contemporary room is one that is decorated in the way which is **currently** fashionable.

The vogue at the moment is for a room that is furnished with a mixture of antiques, traditional and a few modern pieces or accessories, in pale colors with perhaps a sleek vinyl or wood floor. There are no basic rules, except that it must be a mixture of old and new . . . this is now the fashionable trend and therefore it is **contemporary.**

Japanese furniture or Chinoiserie, Victoriana or Americana **mixed** with traditional pieces, light gay colors for walls, floors, upholstery all add up to the contemporary look.

The traditional rocking chair with a modern look. Gracefully curving teak frame holds floral upholstered seat which is shaped to fit the body for extra comfort. Club chairs with pedestal base and the updated stove add to the modern mood, which is echoed in the textured drapes, paneled wall and painting. Wall-to-wall carpeting of acrylic fiber is a luxury touch, and easy to upkeep.

The striking pieces in this modern rooftop apartment are by Danish designer Kristian Vedel. The designer, winner of a lengthy list of international awards ranging from a gold medal at the Triennale (1960) to the Lunning Prize in 1962, has used exotic Brazilian rosewood for the framework of the pieces. These are a high-backed chair, low-backed chair, ottoman and glass-topped table. As a foil for the rosewood's rich dark reds and browns which are streaked with black veinings, a black oxhide is used for upholstery. Cushions rest on high-tensile-strength nylon webbing; contour-molded rubber is used for slip-on arms and backs. Even the under-shelf of the table is dramatic—aluminum is used for facing on one side, rosewood veneer on the other.

As the perfect background for his starkly beautiful modern dining room furniture, designer Robsjohn-Gibbings chooses marble flooring, laid in large, smooth blocks. It adds an air of elegance, a sweep of color and richness to the room. Only decoration on the walls is a group of native masks, massed together in an artistic grouping. Folding metal screens act as dividers between dining-living areas, without blocking out light and air. Uncluttered spaciousness is the theme of the setting.

This handsome wall-length storage unit and server proves the point that modern furniture is not necessarily cold and sterile. Here it adds warmth to a small dining area, with its colorful collection of objects, and rattan-covered doors. Dining table and chairs are of matching wood, with yellow upholstery on chairs picking up wall tones. The L-shaped room is cleverly divided into two separate yet coordinated sections by the matching carpeting and area rug in soft melon shade.

Here you see all the elements of modern design: brick textured wall, vinyl floor, sleek-lined furniture. Rich color scheme of yellow, brown, chocolate and coffee plus pristine white is warm and welcoming. The area rug ties together the various colors in the foyer and living room.

Stainless steel furniture has lost that sterile look. Here you see it featured in a colorful and practical family room. The warm, vibrant colors used in the room blend easily with the gleaming, stainless steel furniture. Three walls are painted sunshine-yellow, with the fireplace wall covered in a vivid printed cotton fabric. The upholstered chair in warm orange and the brilliant pink and yellow pillows harmonize with the walls, as do the yellow side chairs. Highly polished tile floor reflects stainless steel log basket and chair frames. Flower bowl and other accessories are also of stainless steel. The result is a strictly modern room with a fresh, warm appeal, and immense practicality because of easy upkeep.

Modern Furniture Sets the Style and Pace of Model Home at Reston, Virginia

Designer J. Frederic Lohman, A.I.D.
Creates six rooms of clarity and pristine beauty

NEW YORK DESIGNER J. Frederic Lohman decorated four of the model homes in the "totally planned" city of Reston Virginia, plus the Country Club's club house, the Bottle Club and the Hospitality Center. All of his interiors are sleekly modern, traditional or contemporary, except for the Hospitality Center. As this is housed in an old southern style mansion, Mr. Lohman used Early English and Early American furniture to blend with the period architecture.

Here and on the following pages we show you six of the rooms in one of the model homes designed by Mr. Lohman. All of them are essentially modern in concept, and are fine examples of the style, livability and comfort that can be achieved with modern furniture and furnishings.

This is a shot of the dining room, directly adjoining the living room. Narrow metal ribbon strips demarcate the two areas without creating a totally divided look. Color scheme of living room is repeated in dining room for a coordinated whole—black and red played against white walls. Carpet and dining chairs are red, chairs have black metal backs and frames; they are offset by teak and black wall unit which has four downward lamps.

Tranquility and serenity pervade this living room—a mood conjured up through masterly decorating. Designer Lohman wanted to create a feeling of an unbroken flow from the terrace outside into the room. Finely textured fabric draped at the huge picture window, a highly polished black vinyl floor and white walls all contribute to this effect. Even the modern chairs with stainless steel pedestals seem to have a light-as-air floating look, as does the marble-topped table.

Master bedroom has a strictly tailored elegance which comes from the simple but effective bedback and fitted spreads. The room is sparsely furnished, but cork floor, chequered drapes and pictures add a feeling of warmth. Color scheme is rich but subdued—grey, yellow, orange and tan. Curving chair in forefront is ochre.

A beautifully designed storage-unit-and-dressing-table is matched to bedback, in this second shot of master bedroom. Ingeniously fitted make-up lights on metal shafts of unit are reinforced by five downward lights.

Soda pop colors are used in this delightfully fresh girl's room. A variety of gay pinks and sunshine yellow are combined with frothy white, while slickly modern furniture adds to the sharp, pristine look. White forms the shell for walls and vinyl floor; pink tailored bedspread echoes the pink sunflower curtains, scoop chairs are bright yellow. Cushions and other accessories repeat the soda fountain colors in a gay melange.

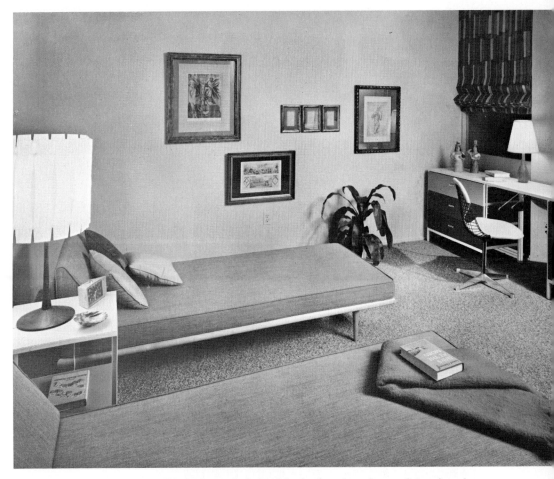

This guest room is designed for day-through-evening use. Color scheme is a mixture of glowing autumnal tones—golds and dull greens. Carpet is golden, bedspreads are green, with these colors repeated in accessories. Dressing table doubles as a desk, and beds are perfect daytime sofas. Unusual grouping of pictures, plant and jazzy shade add warmth to the sleek, tailored furniture.

This boy's room has the "op" art look, created through striped wall paper and drapes, and a combination of blue, green and white repeated. Rug is green, bedspread blue. Straight-lined furniture adds a masculine look.

The contemporary atmosphere of this octagonal-shaped study springs from a combination of old and new. Paneled walls are strictly modern, yet when combined with leather bound books and other accessories they take on a traditional air. The straight-lined desk is definitely a product of this era, but black desk chair and chaise are both antiques, as is marble-topped occasional table. Wall plaque and desk lamp, andirons and brass pot are other echoes of the past. Pulling the whole together are a polished wood floor matched to walls and a bright blue, fringed area rug which follows the octagonal shape of the room.

Pure contemporary design is particularly notable in this living room designed by William Pahlmann, F.A.I.D. Combining comfort and luxury, the sofa is upholstered in soft eggshell and gold and has a walnut sleigh base. The low, round coffee table has a revolving travertine top that locks into position. One end table has a slate-grey top and dark walnut base; the other is a low rectangular table characterized by curved gallery end sections. Paneled wall is offset by marble fireplace wall and colorful Indian print shade. Antique Chinese lamps and unusual pictures complete the truly contemporary look.

Mixing periods for a highly contemporary look can be fun. Here it is done to perfection, and old and new blend happily together for an original effect. This Danish modern teakwood wall unit surrounds the old fashioned grate, while other Early Americana and antiques are scattered around the room. Note the Early American eagle lamp, old paintings and plaques massed in vicinity of wall unit—none of them look out of place. Danish modern often blends easily with the straight lines of American Provincial furniture; witness the high-backed chair and low oak table. Designer Paul Krauss, A.I.D.

Japanese Look is Contemporary

EVER SINCE MARCO POLO'S caravan returned to Venice in the Middle Ages, the Far East has influenced design. In those days, Oriental rugs, richly inlaid teak furniture and exquisite jade were status symbols. In the 18th century, English sea captains rediscovered the Far East and the Orient again provided inspiration. This time it was the simple, straight-line furniture and stylized royal dragons that decorated wealthy homes.

Now the Far East is again reinterpreted and prized for its functional, uncluttered look and open planning — some of the essential ingredients of contemporary design. As an example is this unusual dining room, by Richard Himmel, A.I.D., which highlights the Japanese talent for detailed decoration and their love of brilliant color. Result: a room that is serene and quiet.

The walls are covered in a breathable vinyl fabric reminiscent of grass-cloth, and the floor is vinyl in a marble pattern. Both are white to enlarge the room and accent the sparseness of the furnishings. The dining table and chairs are dramatic and commanding with their unornamental straight lines. Like the shoji screens, the wood is Oriental teak. Panels of the screen are filled with vinyl fabric in cerulean-blue, mint-green and bronze. The texture of the colors gives the lacquered appearance of *japanning*. The same colors are repeated in the handsome rug which is a prized possession in the room. Richard Himmel has placed a small pool at the entrance of the room to project the atmosphere of a tranquil inner court, separated from the rest of the house. The life-size Buddha, world globe and collection of trees and plants add finishing touches.

PART FIVE

The Second Home

Sitting room and outer terrace seem to merge together in this beautiful country residence, through clever use of floor-to-ceiling plate glass window walls. The house is full of other fine features; note unusual domed roof with skylight windows, circular white brick fireplace that sits both inside and out, overhang roof that protects terrace, gives it a **lanai** effect. Polished brick floor also moves out onto terrace, for that flowing feeling; inside walls are all of fir plywood paneling, furniture is strictly contemporary. The uniquely different architecture helps the house blend with the surrounding countryside, also brings the big outdoors inside. Yet the house is totally weatherproof, practical and easy to run.

CHAPTER TWENTY-SEVEN

The Basic Essentials

THE SECOND HOME falls into three categories.

They are (a) a permanent "second" residence, which you mean to maintain throughout the year while still retaining and using your first home; (b) a weekend home which you plan to use the year round; (c) a summer or winter vacation home which you will use only in the appropriate season and close part of the year.

Only you yourself know what kind of second home you want and can afford. However, whichever kind it is, careful planning and thought must be given to the basic essentials before you build, buy or rent.

The most basic essential of all is just how much time you are going to be able to spend in your second home. This obviously determines the amount of money you are going to invest in the home. For instance, it would be foolish to make a big investment in a house you will use only rarely. Once you have answered these two questions, you can then sit down and work out a budget for your second home—in other words how much money from your income you can afford to allocate for the second place. And remember, it is not only the cost of building, buying or renting the actual house, but also the cost of furnishing it, moving the furniture, general maintenance indoors and out, and weekly travelling expenses involved.

The location of your second home and its convenience in terms of travel come next. You don't want a house that makes commuting unbearable; or one that is miles away from shops, public transport and community facilities, if you have children.

The size of your family and family needs naturally determine the size of your second home, and there are no cut and dried rules. One point to bear in mind, when viewing houses, is the size of the lot on which the house stands. Is it big enough for your future requirements? Could you build an extra room, if necessary? What are the outdoor living facilities? For instance, does it have a patio or space enough for one to be built, and of course, is there an area where a swimming pool could be built, if not immediately at a later date? These are vital basic essentials you should remember, and you should also check local zoning laws about building additions on to the house, as well as a swimming pool. Zoning laws differ with locations, so go into all the local rules and regulations before buying. (See Chapter Thirty of this part for basic essentials about building swimming pools.)

When viewing potential second homes, use the guidelines which are given in Chapter One, Part One of this book. They will help you to check the house's basic structure, plumbing, drainage, winterization central heating and air conditioning equipment, and general overall condition. Also check the outside condition of the house, as well as the garden or lot. Is the roof in good condition, are the walls weatherproof? Is the ground already landscaped or is it growing wild? Outside maintenance can be an expensive item on your budget, as can the upkeep of gardens, unless you happen to have a green thumb, of course. Garage facilities are important. If the house does not have one, make sure there is enough space for one to be built.

Insurance

DON'T OVERLOOK OR neglect the insuring of your second home, particularly if it will be left uninhabited part of the year. You have two compelling reasons for insuring your home—the first is that you are liable to the public for damages incurred as a result of negligence involving your property; the second is that you have property subject to loss, through theft, fire, lightning, and floods. Insurance permits you, the insured, to shift the risk of loss to the insurance company in return for a premium.

The best way to go about insuring your second home is to consult a reputable insurance broker. The broker is licensed by the state to transact insurance business, and he represents you (his customer) in locating an insurance company that offers the best policy for your needs.

Mortgages

IF YOU ARE renting your second home, the financing of it is relatively simple. Once you have found the right place, you only have to sign the lease and pay the rent. However, if you want to buy or build, the financing of it can present problems. Today, few families can afford to pay cash for a house — particularly a second or vacation home. A mortgage can solve this problem.

In simple terms, a mortgage is a legal instrument whereby a piece of property is put up as a security against a debt. The buyer of the property makes a given down payment, leaving a balance which is borrowed from a bank, credit union or other source. In turn, the buyer gets a mortgage loan, and promises to reimburse the lender over a period of time. In the meantime, the lender owns the property. There are three basic types of home mortgage loans. These are: (a) mortgages insured by the FHA (Federal Housing Administration); (b) mortgages insured or guaranteed by the Veterans Administration; (c) mortgages without insurance or guarantee, known as conventional mortgages.

These three types of mortgages are financed by commercial banks, savings and loan associations, mutual savings banks, life insurance companies and other sources. Because mortgages and contracts vary, and are extremely technical, it is best to get further details about them either from your bank or a reputable real estate broker. They can best advise you on the right kind of mortgage that suits your needs and your income.

Moving Day

MOVING INTO THE second home can be a major production, and in more cases than not it usually is just that. However, most moves can be made without mishap. It will pay you to sit down and work out what can be done well in advance, to make the final stage less hectic. There are three stages to moving into a second home.

1. SELECTION: Don't take anything to your second or vacation home that is not strictly necessary. This means clothes, children's toys, books, games, basic equipment, and any other items.

2. PREPARATION: If you plan to do your own packing, what can you pack now? Decide on china and glassware; seasonal clothes you will need there, but are not using currently; any other items from your permanent home which you intend to leave in the second home, and which are not in daily use. Any new buys from stores should be delivered directly to your second home, when you are there to receive them. This not only prevents an overflow of packages in your permanent residence but also saves on moving costs later. The same thing applies to furniture which is being reupholstered for your second home. Send it out well in advance so that the pieces will be ready when you make your move, and have them delivered directly to your new home. Do the same with drapes, slipcovers and carpets that are in need of cleaning before they go into your new place. Have them shipped, delivered or mailed to their new abode, straight from the dry cleaners.

3. PACKING: Pack dishes in barrels or drums, wrapping each dish in newspaper, so that there is enough newspaper between it and the next object. Fragile objects can be packed in a container lined with a sheeting of latex foam, available by the yard. Many movers use that method. Plastic dinnerware such as break resistant melamine does not need special packing, and is a good buy for the second home. Pack it in an ordinary box and use it for the first meals in the new house. Linens should be packed in cartons, not in dresser drawers should you be moving a chest or dresser. Most modern dressers are too lightly constructed to carry heavy weights. But it's not a good idea to pack a carton so that it bulges on top — use several, if necessary, to transport linens and blankets. Experienced movers like to use colored tape or tags to mark items that go into special rooms. That way, moving men can put tagged items of one color in the designated room and save confusion later. Mark cartons right side up. Take things you will need the first night with you — nightclothes, toiletries, kitchen equipment and linens, if they have not already been moved. Outdoor furniture, garden equipment and tools can be sent or taken well in advance.

A professional packing service makes the move easier, if you have a lot to be transported. They supply you with special cartons and wardrobes for clothes in advance. But not everyone can afford it. The weekend is a good time to move into the second home, when the man of the house is around to help with special chores.

Everything that can be done in the second home before the actual move itself, will make moving day so much easier. Hanging drapes, arranging pictures on the walls, washing windows, waxing floors and general cleaning is an insurance against total confusion.

And the wise homemaker will pack a picnic basket stocked with a good dinner for the first night. A picnic cooler is ideal for transporting refrigerator foods.

❧

CHAPTER TWENTY-EIGHT

Furnishing Your Second Home

❖

THE BASIC RULES of decorating outlined in the preceding chapters apply to your second home. But there are a few extra points to bear in mind. If you are furnishing a large or small *permanent* residence the furniture needs to be solid and long lasting, because it will be in constant use and taking hard wear.

The *style* of your second home is an important factor in your decorating plans. If you have chosen a colonial or period style house, try to echo the house itself with appropriate furniture such as antiques or at least antique reproductions. Modern architecture demands furniture that is streamlined and modern in design.

The weekend retreat or vacation home needs less elaborate furniture. In fact you can get away with almost any manner of furnishings. Discarded pieces from your attic or items from junk shops can be revamped with bright paint and new upholstery, and if you are a "do-it-yourselfer" you can have a lot of fun doing up these pieces. Metal or wicker furniture also fits well in weekend homes, and is perfect through summer into winter if you use your cottage the year round.

Most importantly, don't make your second home a duplicate of your city dwelling. In fact, try and make it just the opposite, so that you can give expression to your decorating flair and expand your tastes. On the following pages are a collection of ideas for decorating your second home, from dining rooms, kitchens to sitting rooms and bedrooms.

Porches with a Promise

THAT OLD PORCH that seems like a waste of space can become an exciting extra room. Make sure that it is weatherproof, and then give it a dash of vivid paint, some colorful pieces of furniture and you can enjoy it the year round.

PORCH CONVERTS TO PARLOR or a guest room in this country home. It was designed by Paul Krauss, A.I.D., who used a variety of new fabrics made with rayon for a stunning effect. Screening off sliding glass doors with thickly woven fabric laminated to window shades and reverse-mounted to rise up from the floor, Mr. Krauss creates a colorful back wall which admits sunlight above and simultaneously assures privacy below. Fabrics are used throughout the porch and are convincing evidence that textiles can be key components of a room. The rich red-orange-mustard cloth on the shades boasts a hand-loomed look previously unattainable through machine construction, and the upholstery fabrics are as noteworthy for eye appeal as for practical wear assets. Shock-shades of blued and yellowed red predominate, with regal purple for the chair covering adding formal elegance amid rustic surroundings. Wood siding is used for one wall, and an old fashioned stove fitted with gas unit and vent neatly solves heating problems. White shaggy rug, candelabra, brass lamp, brass and glass table add luxury touches.

Here you see how a glass-fronted porch becomes an elegant dining room in a weekend home. Smart black and white tiles create a harlequin effect on the floor, with white wooden walls adding to the pristine look. Glass-topped dining table and matching metal framed chairs are elegant yet hard wearing. Hanging plants, palm and greenery bring the garden look indoors, while antique stove, mirror and unusual candelabra add charm. Designed by David Barrett, A.I.D., N.S.I.D.

A sunny conservatory designed to make the most of daylight hours, becomes a second sitting room in a second home, through clever decorating. With the addition of a few pieces of furniture, the conservatory becomes a comfortable corner for daytime relaxing, and for aperitifs and after-dinner coffee in the evening. The seating pieces and tables are in cast aluminum with an antiqued black finish. Brilliant crimson upholstery contrasts effectively against the white tile floor and white window shades. A collection of flowering plants in an indoor window box adds a summer feeling, and can be maintained through winter. Because furniture is lightweight, hard wearing and easy to handle, it can also be used outdoors.

A tropical island mood, colorful and informal, is interpreted here in easy-care fabrics to transform a converted sun porch into a setting for family fun. Vividly striped casements of polyester fiber filter the sunlight. They are also easy to wash, drip dry and need little ironing—if any. Casements are framed by simple plywood panels, set slightly forward so the casements can be drawn behind them to leave the windows uncovered. The brilliant blue nylon carpeting is soft, sound-deadening, practical and easy to spot-clean. It will also resist signs of wear even under constant use and is ideal for the vacation home. The casual, comfortable furniture echoes the tropical island mood, as do the plants and accessories. Lamps over corner table are inverted wicker wastepaper baskets fitted with bulbs.

Six Sitting Rooms with Relaxation in Mind

THE SITTING ROOM of your second home has one necessary ingredient — it should convey a feeling of relaxation. Whatever style you choose for your decor, comfort and tranquility should be your foremost considerations. Whether you decide to go Early American, traditional or modern, relaxation is the most important factor. Here and on the following pages are six sitting rooms which are diversely different in style and decoration. Yet all have one common denominator — a mood of peace and comfort.

All the traditional ingredients of a country sitting room are incorporated here, from ceiling beams to fireplace, flagged floor and deep, comfortable sofas. Although room is large, with a high ceiling, an intimate atmosphere is created through clever furniture arrangement. Two king-sized sofas, one a four-seater and the other a three-seater, are placed together for an L-shape around fireplace; the two chairs at window side of the room are part of grouping yet do not block traffic lanes. Designed by Erica Lemle, A.I.D., N.S.I.D.

Traditional leather furniture with a contemporary look is combined with a rugged stone fireplace and skin rug to create a country lodge atmosphere in this comfortable sitting room. Wood paneling on one wall and beamed effect on other walls adds a feeling of texture and warmth, also maintains the rugged mood. Upholstered furniture includes a deep restful sofa, a tufted-back recliner (with five reclining positions), and a swivel rocker. The upholstery fabrics complement the mood of the room with their lush, burnished leathergrain design and rich coloring.

Mellow tones of maple furniture and red painted walls are combined to create an Early American mood here. Limited area of this **entrance hallway** is given the effect of a cozy sitting room, with a pleasing arrangement of small furniture pieces, such as secretary, rocker and settle. Settle, which is an adaptation of an Early American Deacon's bench, provides additional seating space as well as hidden storage area beneath the seat. Braided rug and brick tile flooring enhance the homey, Provincial atmosphere of this extra sitting room in a small country retreat. Green painted stairway and soft accents of green in printed wallpaper and other accessories create a warm color harmony gainst the red background.

A collection of Early Americana is the focal point of this cozy sitting room and dining alcove in a country cottage. An antique tavern table, heirloom portraits and a hurricane lamp show the owner's interest in authenticity. Comfort and practicality also predominate. The comfortable club chair and ottoman are upholstered in a washable vinyl fabric that shows Early American scenes in colonial blue and white. The blue walls, which add such a rich look to this rustic retreat, are covered with vinyl while the peppy absinthe-green tablecloth, cushions on the Windsor chair and captain's chairs are also made of easy-upkeep vinyl. Deft use of accessories, such as antique wooden bucket holding centerpiece flowers, owl on step, horse and plant arrangement on mantlepiece, drawers on wall, all create a highly personalized look to a charming weekend home. Decorated by Ving Smith, A.I.D., and Charlotte Smith.

Furnishing a second home need not be expensive. Here a modern effect is created at little cost through use of a wall unit and wicker furniture. The main wall of this summer apartment sitting room features a wall-to-wall arrangement of shelves and cabinets, holding everything from hi-fi and television, to books, accessories and providing miscellaneous storage space. Wicker sofa and chair are light and garden fresh and enhance the summery vacation mood. The bright, printed fabric used for drapes and on chair in foreground contrasts imaginatively with the boldly patterned area rug. The result is a room that is gay, young and easy to clean. Designed by Paul Krauss, A.I.D.

Clean modern look is created here through deft use of color and streamlined furniture. Yet only **two** colors are used in this summer sitting room—vivid burnt-orange and cream. Neutral walls and floor make an ideal backdrop for the orange carpet and upholstery; cream is picked up on the reeded chair, sofa and table frames, orange is picked out on the cabinet doors. A completely uncovered window and extensive use of foliage completes the bright open feeling of this sunny holiday room.

Country Kitchens With a Rustic Air

THE RUSTIC COUNTRY kitchen has a special kind of charm, with its flagged floor, open hearth, beamed ceiling and gleaming copper pots. Your second home is the ideal place to recreate the old fashioned farmhouse kitchen, particularly if you have lots of space. If the kitchen in your second home is large, make it serve as a dining room, too, in the truly Provincial manner. If it is small, you could remove the doors and let its decorating theme flow into the dining room, so that the two are totally integrated. Early American kitchen furniture can often be found in antique shops, while many beautiful reproductions are being made today. And don't forget the wealth of new products which will make your decorating tasks easier and more successful. Don't worry if your second home kitchen does not boast old oak beams and a flagstone floor. For very little you can buy a variety of materials that simulate flagstones, tiles, grained wood, pine paneling and old oak — which all go down on the floor or up onto walls and ceilings. Refrigerators and ovens also come with gaily painted doors, Dutch tiles or louvered effects. Accessories such as old Americana, copper pots and pans, brass and pewter can be picked up cheaply in country antique shops, even city junk shops.

This spacious kitchen in a country home combines 20th century efficiency with truly rustic charm. Flagged floor and wood paneled walls carry through into the intimate little dining room, for an integrated look. But kitchen can be closed off by louvered doors. Echoing the country theme is the refrigerator with its rich brown louvered doors and brass handles. Set into wood paneled wall below painting, it looks like a cupboard and does not detract from the decor of the kitchen. It is designed to give the utilmate in food storage without shouting that it's functional. Blue and white tiled wall, copper pots and old spear are authentic touches.

The charm of Colonial architecture and furnishings need not be compromised in order to incorporate modern flooring materials. Here an embossed linoleum, in a realistic wood plank design, helped modernize a century-old kitchen without detracting from its original Early American charm. Sink, oven and refrigerator units are aligned along window wall, and do not intrude into the room. The farmhouse kitchen serves as a dining room, is furnished with genuine Early American furniture and accessories.

Here you see a contemporary country kitchen that mixes modern appliances with Early American furnishings and really succeeds. The walls and ceiling are wood paneled for the rustic look and a vinyl tile floor with an antique brick effect reiterates this theme. Together the two combine to create the perfect shell for the Early American furniture, such as the Lazy Susan-style dining table, chairs and corner cupboard. Oven and refrigerator have rich brown doors echoing the kitchen's color scheme, and are set into wall cabinets so as not to intrude. Cafe curtains, and other accessories, such as old lamp, add finishing touches.

Decorative Themes for Country Dining

rooms in the relaxed mood

THE DINING ROOM in your second home has one basic requirement — easy up-keep. No one wants a lot of household chores in a weekend retreat or vacation home. Even the dining room in a *permanent* second residence should be practical, to ease the work load.

Clean-cut elegance is the keynote here. Parquet wood floor in this country home was left bare—to show off the beautiful graining and for easy cleaning. Glass table top rests on a gracefully curved, fine cast aluminum double-pedestal base. Matching chairs are sculptured with complementary grape motifs on backs, legs are simple. Chair cushions are easy to wipe clean, long wearing. Other furniture in room is a side serving table (not shown in picture). Plants and crystal chandelier add decorative interest. This furniture can be used on a terrace during the summer.

1. The owners of this country cottage wanted to decorate the dining room in American Provincial style. To restate the theme set by the antique furniture, they covered floor, door and wainscotting with wood vinyl, ridged like dressed lumber. Not only is it authentically Provincial but it is practical. Fingerprints and spills are relinquished at the whisk of a soapy sponge. Early American-type wallpaper and candelabra, plus other authentic accessories, add finishing touches.

2. This modern house demanded sleek-lined furniture to echo the open, airy feeling of the rooms. Here you see a shot of the amply sized dining room. Full length, gauzy drapes are easy to wash and dry, and polished wood floor needs little upkeep. Refectory style extension table is surrounded by chairs with contoured backs and gently angled walnut frames, combined for effectiveness and comfort. Particularly outstanding is the cane, used as an upholstery fabric, stretched up and over the back of the chair to provide a double layer thickness.

3. Old beams and the expansive fireplace in this dining room set the style for the decorating theme. To reiterate the mood of days gone by, Early American furniture was chosen. Because genuine antiques were not available, fine reproductions were used. The drop-leaf extension table and oxbow chairs are so authentically styled they look like the real thing. And of course they are hard wearing. This dining room proves the point that good reproduction furniture can be used successfully with Early American architecture.

2.

3.

Sleek look in the dining room of a beach home is created through its pristine shell—wood paneled walls and apple-green vinyl flooring. Both are easy to clean and make an attractive setting for the lightweight but durable alumaloy furniture. Boat-shaped, glass-topped table and the chairs are adorned with a graceful Greek key motif. Beige vinyl upholstery is easy to wipe clean, is long lasting. Furniture is dual purpose as it can be used outdoors if desired.

Country-Style Bedrooms

*A collection of ideas to inspire the decorative mood
of your "second home" bedrooms —
whether French-chateau-grand or cottage-simple*

The master bedroom of this large country home is decorated with Queen Anne furniture in the manner of Colonial Williamsburg. It is more than a bedroom, as it can be a second sitting room for the woman of the house. Pale, greenish-blue walls contrast beautifully with the dark parquet floor and mahogany furniture. Williamsburg design bedspread has matching drapes for headboard.

The guest room of this weekend cottage is a mixture of old and new, with a rural look pervading. Gone are the days when one dared to use only one pattern in a room, surrounded by solids. Now you can freely mix stripes, plaids and prints, as shown in this charming country bedroom. The stripes in the wallpaper (mustard and white) coordinate with the floral bedspread and tier curtains in mustard, olive and black against antique white. The olive-toned petticoat matches the upholstery of the comfortable barrel chair, and the area rug picks up the print colors in light-to-dark blocks. Lamp repeats the olive tone in a glossy ceramic and the curtain rod is olive, too, with a flat finish. The wood floor has been painted in the Provincial manner in pale olive.

Old country houses often have awkwardly shaped rooms, particularly bedrooms set high in the eaves. Here an odd, sloping wall was turned to advantage and becomes the decorative focal point in this country bedroom. As the ceiling of the room is high, sloping wall seemed even more prominent. The decorator decided to accentuate this rather than try camouflage. Red and white toile wallpaper was used, and was picked up again in fabric for chair. Mulberry-red was used on back wall to echo the red patterned toile; the vivid color also makes an excellent backdrop for the white Williamsburg design bedspread and ruffled canopy over bed. Arched window alcove was painted a matching mulberry.

A fourposter seems appropriate in a country bedroom. Here the antique bed is a Spanish import, as are the commode, secretary and chair. They have been cleverly combined with some modern pieces for a charming effect. Upholstered headboard was added for extra comfort, is matched in color to boudoir chair. The quilted, scalloped-edged coverlet with diminutive floral pattern has a solid colored, ruffled petticoat attached. The colors are blue, pink, lime. Draperies and ruffle on fourposter are of the same fabric, while cafe curtains match headboard. Accessories are a mixture of old and new—modern lamp, painting, and artificial flowers; antique candlestick and wall cupids.

Emily Malino, well-known interior designer, makes the most of this tiny bed-sitting-guest room in a country home, by adapting Japanese Tokonoma-alcoves to an entire window wall facing the garden. By using handsome laminated window shades alternately with the shallow shelves in this simple wall-to-wall construction, she creates an even greater three-dimensional quality. The easy-to-duplicate built-in minimizes the imbalance of the wall, creates desk and dressing table space that are lighted by fluorescence above, and provides a simple framework for the window shades, hung reverse roll, in Japanese scroll fashion. The shades are called upon to perform several decorative and functional roles at one and the same time. They conceal air conditioner at the right and minimize old-fashioned radiator. The tangerine and yellow design on white is an unusual abstract pattern that aids and abets the three-dimensional deception. The "door-shade" joins the others in providing privacy or blackout talents at will. The entire room is developed with a masterly combination of dual-purpose pieces and color follow-through.

Rocky Mountain Ski Lodge is Built for Fun

with a no-chores, easy-care emphasis

Every part of the country has its own idea about what makes a perfect vacation house. To Colorado designers J. Marshall Morin, F.A.I.D., and H. Albert Phibbs, A.I.D., there's no argument at all—the snowy mountains and sunshine of their native state make a ski lodge in the Rockies the ideal leisure home. Shown here is the ski lodge designed by them. It is full of brilliant ideas which could be adapted in your winter vacation home, wherever it is.

Both designers are enthusiastic skiers and they have built into the lodge all their convictions about what belongs in the perfect ski cabin: **warmth, comfort, and the absolute minimum of upkeep.**

The designers chose carpeting and fabrics all of nylon fibers for good looks, rugged wear and easy maintenance.

The whole living area is carpeted wall-to-wall with glowing gold tweed made of nylon. It provides a cheerful, sound-deadening background for the many activities that center in this room, and takes casual treatment in stride, thanks to sturdy nylon. The carpeting also covers steps cantilevered from a massive stone chimney, and flows over a low bench along the back wall of the room. **Cushions on the bench make it a sofa by day. At night, cushions are removed and warm sleeping bags filled with soft, resilient polyester fiberfill are spread out on it for the inevitable overflow guests. The carpeting helps discourage drafts around the bench, and adds one more layer of comfort under the sleeping bags.** The furniture was chosen for day-long duty. The round table and modern captain's chairs serve for dining, cards or games. Two comfortable tub chairs pull up to the fire or over to the table; their cushions are covered in gay striped upholstery with a handwoven look. All the upholstery fabrics are made with nylon for long wear. The sunny yellow draperies are of acrylic fiber, are not affected by the elements.

The design of the lodge is simple, sturdy and big in scale. Walls of Western red cedar decking are stained soft sage-green, a cheerful contrast to the orange and gold of carpet and fabrics. Walls, too, were planned for easy care: they won't need repainting. The giant chimney is of rough native Colorado stone. Logs for the open fire are stored under the hearth, which also serves as the first step of the staircase. Hearth and steps can also double as extra seats if necessary.

Beside the front door is an ingenious storage idea—a large pile of flat stones in several levels on which are stacked sleek Head skis and poles, wet parkas and icy boots, to drip dry. Accessories are simple, in the mood of the lodge. Dramatic and economical is the gallery of ski photographs, matted in white, from the pages of a ski magazine—an easy decorating idea for do-it-yourselfers.

One-Room Ski Lodge for Three Has Luxury Highlights

Compact living at its best is featured in this charming one-room ski lodge, and many of the bright ideas illustrated can easily be adapted in any type of vacation home. The combination living-dining area converts at night to sleep three comfortably. Two on the velvet-covered couches, a third in the wall-bunk set in the paneled wall above the couch at right. Occupant of the wall-bunk has a gay floral curtain to pull for privacy—a smart trick for this kind of vacation home or even in a children's room. Ample storage cupboards are provided in far corner, which includes a wine shelf; other storage space is available under couches. Pegboard wall above dining leaf holds kitchen utensils, while barbecue acts as support for dining leaf, is also handy for cooking and serving. Ceiling hung centerpiece above barbecue is wood paneled and set with Dutch tiles, a perfect backdrop for the yellow and copper pots. It also acts as an air vent "chimney" for cooking fumes. Luxury highlights are the wormy chestnut paneled walls, velvet upholstery and wall-to-wall carpeting. Concealed lighting set in the ceiling and in one wall, plus antique chandelier with candles, add to the warm glow created by the muted gold color scheme, and to the luxury look. Enlarged mountain photograph is a clever and attractive wall mural, echoes the ski atmosphere. Detailed planning made this room a success, rich accessories give it the plush look. Exterior glimpsed at right features Early American cedar siding. Small kitchen and bathroom areas not shown in this illustration. Designed by Vladimir Kagan, A.I.D.

Old Barn Converts into Charming Country Home

wood and stone set the design theme

AN OLD BARN has great possibilities as a second home, and is fun to convert and design, especially for do-it-yourselfers. The old barn shown here, in its reconverted state, was turned into a charming weekend retreat through thoughtful planning.

It had two levels — a large ground floor area and a wide gallery running along two walls as the upper floor. The gallery was reached by an old staircase which was removed and replaced with a wider, sturdier set of stairs. Before the new staircase was put in, the ground floor area was divided into two halves by the addition of a "second" raised floor. The step-up area was covered with wall-to-wall carpeting for a luxury look, and repeated on the stair steps. An antique brick fireplace was built as a focal point; it is ceiling-high with a long hearth.

The rough-hewn wood of the barn was left bare to contribute its own design interest to the setting, and combined with the stone fireplace it creates a rustic look. The bright orange carpeting used in the step-up living area sets the color scheme, while similar autumnal tones of upholstery fabrics echo the mellow feeling. A mixture of antique and traditional pieces of furniture were used.

Remember to thoroughly check floorboards of upper levels and staircases, if you are reconverting an old barn. Wood is often rotten and dangerous; it should be replaced with sturdy new planks that can always be stained to match original wood.

1. Here you see the living room of the old barn with the focus on the step-up area and staircase. The raised floor is covered with bright orange acrylic fiber carpet that is luxurious, long wearing and easy to clean. Same carpet is used on the staircase leading to the upper gallery. Sofa and chairs are covered in a muted orange tweed. Antique wooden tables repeat the look of the plank walls; long wooden table along back wall is actually attached to wall with brackets, acts as an attractive catch-all for magazines, lamp, greenery, or can be used for dining. Black piano and leather stool pick up the tone of the leather armchair in foreground of picture.

2. Focal point of the living room is the antique brick fireplace which rises to ceiling; it has long hearth. In this second area of the living room floorboards were left bare and highly polished for a rich look. Floor is highlighted by a yellow area rug patterned with green and gold. In the far corner is a glimpse of the bar, also the upper-level study which leads to the master bedroom. Red chair and ottoman, two black leather chairs add contrast colors to this area.

1.

2.

CHAPTER TWENTY-NINE

Outdoor Living Areas that Have Everything

*ideas for creating fresh air settings
that add to family enjoyment and relaxation*

YOUR SECOND HOME is the ideal place to create an outdoor living area. Whether it's a terrace, patio, *lanai,* enclosed garden or sunroom you and your family will get countless hours of enjoyment out of it the year round. In summer it's the perfect place for entertaining and relaxing; in winter it can be a decorative asset filled with seasonal plants.

A *carefully planned* outdoor living area increases your leisure time by decreasing the amount of time required for maintenance of the area. For instance,

decks and paved floors are easier to upkeep than grass: they withstand heavy traffic better and you are saved the inconvenience of starting new patches of turf. Furniture legs stay cleaner, look better when used on hard surfaces, and area can be quickly hosed down for cleaning. Flat, stone paving, tiles and wood are the ideal floors to put down, although there are other materials you can use such as vinyl tiles and vinyl carpeting.

Privacy is the next consideration. Fencing, brick walls, high-growing shrubs are all ideal, and can be attractively designed to add to the decorative effect of the yard.

When planning your outdoor living area remember to include lighting facilities for nighttime entertaining, and electrical outlets for portable appliances such as barbecues, or music equipment like a hi-fi; you might also want to include step savers such as an intercom system or extension telephones.

If you are putting down a paved or tiled floor, remember you can create an unusual effect by leaving planter spaces to be filled with shrubs, greenery and flowering plants. Small rock gardens, a fish pool or fountain add to the overall appearance, and if you have a green thumb you might try your hand at a miniature Japanese garden.

Outdoor furniture should be durable, lightweight, and easy to store in the winter months. White is the most popular color for furniture frames, and you can introduce lots of accent colors in cushions, umbrellas, tablecloths and accessories.

A *lanai* is often the most efficient answer to the outdoor living problem. Its roof gives protection from rain or too much sun, but open sides preserve all the advantages of outdoor living and entertaining. The basic structure need not be expensive to erect, and you can use wood for the roof with metal or wood supports. When the *lanai* is furnished, hung with a few poster prints, and accessorized, it can be a "second" living room which all the family can enjoy.

Any small yard, terrace, patio or porch can be transformed, at little cost and with the minimum of work. All you need is imagination and some willing hands.

The small terrace adjoining this living room in a country home needed very little refurbishing. The magnificent, garden-and-sea view was decoration in itself. Red bricks were put down for color interest and to define the small dining area; black-painted iron railings were added along the edge of the terrace for decorative reasons and as a safety measure for children. The elegant **lanai** furniture is made of durable alumaloy, painted white. Table has textured glass top, cushions are in bright turquoise, matching hostess wagon provides serving surface and it handily wheels wherever needed.

In contrast this huge terrace is designed for family relaxation of all kinds and for big summer parties. Whole terrace area is covered with ceramic tiles, which are durable and easy to hose clean. Careful planning made this big terrace work well. Its total area is broken by steps leading to lawn, and by sections left open for fish pools and plants. Furniture can be moved around, and under overhanging roof of house which creates a **lanai** effect. Tiles used on this terrace are identical in color and design to those used on the floors of the adjoining house, for an effect of complete integration.

Small Terraces that Work Well

even the smallest yard can be rejuvenated
with planning, clever use of furniture and materials.
The three areas here are all totally different in concept,
yet each one serves a multitude of purposes for outdoor living

The narrow terrace beyond the sliding glass doors of this bedroom was covered with white tweed vinyl carpet, and becomes an ideal spot for breakfasts or Sunday brunch. The vinyl carpet is easy to cut and lay, comes in a variety of colors. It is water-repellent, withstands all spills and stains, is easy to clean. This type of carpeting is ideal for outdoor use, on larger patios, **lanais,** and around the edge of swimming pools, as it has a non-slip surface. Cushions on garden chairs and on lacquered straw chair in bedroom are covered with wipe-clean vinyl fabric.

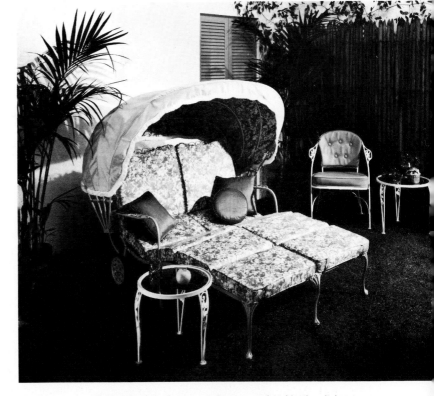

At first this back terrace seemed too small to be of any real use. The addition of sleekly tailored sectional furniture made it function as a cozy corner for relaxing, even for snack meals or cocktails. Four chair sections can be used as one long seating arrangement, or as a sofa to seat three with a spare chair. Here they are arranged in twos, with matching table in between. Round table completes the setting. Furniture is of rust proof alumaloy, painted white. Cushions are covered in white vinyl, are easy to sponge clean. Matching tables have textured glass tops, and can easily be used indoors. Plants and greenery add a cheery note of color.

Garden furniture is gayer and more comfortable than it has ever been. Here you see a small back garden livened with a luxurious two-seater chaise, complete with its own umbrella. Small round glass tables are just big enough to hold a snack or cold drink, are easy to move around, like the straight chair. Chaise is on wheels, is also easy to move. Redwood fence ensures privacy, yet adds to the rustic look of the garden. Tubs of plants complete the garden, which costs little to redo.

Outdoor Rooms Geared for Entertaining

THE FRESH AIR rooms illustrated on the following pages are sleekly luxurious, yet practical at the same time.

Each one is highly different in concept, style and decor. All have one thing in common — perfect planning. All are geared to successful living and entertaining, either strictly family style or on a super scale.

The rooms incorporate a wealth of new ideas that are easy to copy, that also take the backache out of summer living. Whether your taste runs to an

Lanai... Hawaiian Style

The Hawaiian Islands inspired this beautiful **lanai**, which is part of the outdoor living area of a California home. Because of its permanent structural shell, the **lanai** works the year through. Roof is covered, and although walls and doors have an open-work effect they give some protection on cooler or rainy days. Doors which open outwards, and matching walls, bring the garden inside, while the garden effect is repeated in the **lanai** with plants and flowers. Vinyl floor has a pebbled look, is cool, durable and easy to maintain. Furniture is simply styled, in a South Sea Island mood; bamboo seats are painted vivid turquoise to match walls, clean-lined table is bright yellow for a splash of color in the all-green room. Connecting doors in the **lanai** are of open-work wood or glass for a see-through effect; pieces of native carved wood line the small indoor rock garden at left of picture.

Furniture was kept to a minimum for a cool, open-air feeling. Ideas worth noting: vinyl floor, open-work walls, vividly painted furniture, indoor rock garden. Dining table is a quick and easy project for the smart do-it-yourselfer, is simply a large slab of wood attached to two straight pieces for legs.

Hawaiian *lanai,* a family sunroom, a Texas style barbecue patio or an English garden room, you will find a crop of up-to-the-minute innovations that can be adapted to your own outdoor living area, your particular way of life.

The three basic ingredients that make these outdoor rooms work are: sleek, hardwearing, easy-clean floors; a sound structural shell on three or four sides; lightweight, durable furniture. Colorful accessories, plants and flowers give the settings added garden freshness and beauty.

Family Sunroom that Works the Year Round

This weatherproof sunroom was designed by Ving Smith, A.I.D., and Charlotte Smith, and is especially commendable because it can be used in winter as well as the summer months. It has lots of clever innovations which would bring a touch of flair to any sunroom or outdoor living area. Wall which fronts onto the garden is totally practical. It is made entirely of plate glass, from floor to ceiling, and brings the feeling of the outdoors **inside.** Sliding glass doors (not shown in picture) open up fully for an open-fronted **lanai** effect. In winter the doors remain closed, and concealed central heating makes the room work as a family-entertainment center. The sectional glass wall shown in picture runs down into the fish pool, splits it in half so that the pool can be enjoyed both inside and out. Small birdcage for parakeets adjoining pool has mesh screen

walls inside, a glass front looking onto garden. Surrounded and filled with greenery, this also helps to bring the outdoor feeling inside the sunroom. Rough stones used on the exterior walls of the house are cleverly incorporated into the room's decor, used for wall behind birdcage and round the edge of the fish pool. Sleek rubber floor of deep blue-green is flecked and striped with white for a tailored look, is hard wearing, soundproof and simple to keep fresh. Chairs are upholstered in a softer turquoise, echo the floor Other furniture in the room (not shown here) includes a bar, comfortable sofa, hi-fi and games table.

Barbecue Patio is Texas Inspired

Although this barbecue patio is supremely elegant it is also immensely practical. It is not an "add-on" but was planned in the blueprint stage and built at the same time as the house. It also has a **lanai** look about it, with its beamed, weatherproof roof and side walls and open front. The same materials used inside the house, mainly ceramic tiles and blond wood paneling, are repeated on the patio for that truly integrated look. These materials are also super-practical: both tiles and wood are hard wearing, long lasting, easy to keep clean and fresh. Small brown ceramic tiles are used on the deck-like floor of the patio, while larger white tiles line the area behind the barbecue. The barbecue itself is covered with green, blue and white ceramic tiles. Blue hood adds an extra fillip of color, but is practical, as it also takes away food and smoke fumes. These pale colors surrounding and used on the barbecue are not as impractical as they look—all are easy to sponge clean. The sleek, pristine look of the patio shell demanded matching furniture, so ultra-modern scoop chairs and a pedestal table were chosen. Shrubs and plants not only add to the decor, but repeat the mood of the surrounding garden (not shown here). Although this patio is an integral part of the ranch house, it could easily be adopted as an "add-on," particularly if you have an overhanging roof. Designed by Emily Malino Associates.

Garden Room with an English Look

The English countryside inspired this charming garden room, styled on the lines of a **lanai**. It has a covered "weatherwise" roof and, although the three sides are open and framed with drapes, these drapes can be taken down in the winter months. The vinyl floor has a pebbled look, is equally weatherproof, also hard wearing and quick to hose down. A beautiful, wrought-iron valance runs along the ceiling on three sides of the room, is repeated in the arch behind the statue, also on a screen door—foreground right of picture. The elegant high-backed metal chairs echo the mood set by the wrought-iron work, are highly practical. Flowering shrubs, the statue and small fountain are the only decorative accessories used, are attractive without being expensive additions. Dining table is an easy do-it-yourself project; it's a kitchen table skirted in pink cotton and topped with an organdy tablecloth. To adopt this garden room all that is needed is a sound roof and a hard-wearing floor for the basic shell. The drapes are simple to make, need not be costly, and the wrought-iron valance can be replaced by one made of wood and painted to tone with the drapes. Here the overall color scheme is pale green and pink, echoing the garden feeling. To create a true "garden" look stick to metal furniture, plenty of flowering shrubs; a stone statue also adds to the overall effect.

The Picnic Upgraded:
Meals Outdoors Take on a New Elegance

*table settings and notions for eating out in the open
. . . whether for fun brunches or candlelight dinners*

As TERRACES, PATIOS and *lanais* have become more streamlined and luxurious, so have meals eaten outdoors. The old-fashioned picnic has been upgraded, has in fact developed a grand manner. Gone is the tablecloth stretched out on the grass, with paper cups and plates. In its place are tables and chairs that have a feeling of permanence and the formality of a dining room. Table settings are as beautiful as they would be at a candlelight dinner—in fact the only difference is that the setting is out in the open, instead of indoors.

This is due not only to the new luxury of outdoor living areas, but also to the wealth of attractive, low-cost garden furniture and accessories now on the market. Tableware made of *unbreakable* plastics or melamine is as beautiful as real china. Cooking facilities are designed for easy handling, such as charcoal barbecues, electric spits and rotisseries. Outdoor electric outlets bring lights and music outdoors. In fact your outdoor living area can be as comfortable, as elegant and as practical as you want to make it—whether you have a small garden or a lush *lanai*.

The garage at the end of this paved drive was unattractive and decrepit. White paint on the doors, windows and under the roof, was used to give it a pristine look. Edging of doors and hinges were painted black for tailored contrast. With the addition of a hanging bird feeder, the old garage became a sparkling backdrop for dining area of an adjoining terrace. Old metal wheelbarrow was also painted white, and filled with plants. Simple wooden garden table and two benches were planed and waxed for a smooth look; tablecloth and beautiful tableware were added for a touch of elegance in the charming rustic setting. Designed by Erica Lemle, A.I.D., N.S.I.D.

Table setting here echoes the mood of this Hawaiian-style **lanai,** furnished with bamboo and rattan furniture. Large round table is set buffet style, with white melamine dinnerware. This has an appropriate bamboo pattern of bamboo reeds and leaves in avocado and turquoise, with two-tone accessory pieces in avocado and white. For the centerpiece, an assortment of luscious fruits on a miniature surfboard which rides a wave-tossed sea made of blue-sprayed crushed paper; exotic flowers and leaves complete the inviting picture. Linen napkins in a deep bronze shade accent the tones of the pineapple tops in the centerpiece and the real bamboo handles of the knives repeat the dinnerware motif and add to the Polynesian theme. The setting is not only carefree in spirit but also in upkeep; dinnerware is unbreakable, furniture easy to move around and long wearing.

Unusual color schemes move outdoors with ease. Here the pale aqua wall on a small patio inspired the delicate table setting, while white trellis arch entwined with greenery makes a pretty backdrop. This dressy, out-of-doors table setting is easier on the homemaker than it looks. The dinnerware is break-resistant, in a pattern of pale blue, aqua and violet flowers; the cloth is drip-dry nylon eyelet over an aqua liner. An unusual centerpiece, of artificial pastel fruits, flowers and a butterfly, repeats the dinnerware colors, as does the graceful floral streamer. Result: a beautiful table that costs little to achieve, resists breakages and spills.

Much of today's terrace furniture has a new-found elegance and comfort. Here this set of table and chairs does double-duty, as it is perfectly at home indoors or out. High-backed chairs have upholstered backs and cushions, frames with a reeded effect, in metal that simulates wood. Rounded glass-topped table on a pedestal base is large enough for a sit-down meal or buffets. In winter weather the complete set moves indoors, serves as an extra dining table or card table.

This garden furniture is not only elegant and comfortable, but supremely practical. Made of white enameled steel mesh, all of the pieces are **folding**, including cart and table, for easy carrying, winter storage. The furniture can even be used indoors in winter, either in a recreation family room or a child's room. The set comes in pristine white or green, but can be easily sprayed any bright color to add verve to a terrace. Detachable foam rubber cushions covered in green fabric provide extra comfort, can be removed on rainy days. Furniture is rustproof. Other bright ideas on this terrace are the hanging plants, the red tiled flooring.

CHAPTER THIRTY

Three Elements Bring Added Luxury to Outdoor Living

Swimming Pools, Landscaping, Lighting

❧

THE GARDEN AREA of your second home need not go to waste. With planning, imagination and a small outlay of money you can turn it into a luxury spot the whole family can enjoy. Three basic ingredients go into the luxury look outdoors—a swimming pool, landscaping, lighting.

You may not have the space, or, more importantly, the money to have both a pool and a landscaped garden. But certainly the lighting is a **must,** because it gives your garden area day-into-night life. Furthermore, outdoor electrical outlets and fitments are easy to install and cost very little today, so they won't make a big hole in your budget. And they add effective beauty to pool, terrace or landscaped area after dark.

Pools, too, no longer cost a fortune to install. They come in all sizes, shapes, materials, and there are even do-it-yourself pools for the husband who likes such projects. Landscaping essentially should be done by an expert, and prices vary according to your needs and the size of your lot. If you happen to have a green thumb, much of your landscaping can be another do-it-yourself project—but this is not recommended unless you really know what you are doing.

The three basic ingredients for outdoor luxury are incorporated here—pool, landscaping and lighting. All have been carefully and cleverly planned for beauty, easy maintenance, day-into-night life. Unusually shaped, free form pool is set in the middle of grass lawn, with a wide, flagged surround for traffic and to preserve beauty of lawn from wet feet, scuffing, wear and tear from furniture. Landscaping was designed to enhance beauty of outdoor setting. also to maintain privacy from neighboring homes. Small trees and shrubs border raised deck, larger trees and bushes follow the edge of the property to act as a substantial screen instead of fencing or low wall. Small circular patio adjoining kitchen is flagged in smaller tiles for additional pattern interest; also it withstands heavy traffic and food spills and it's easy cleaning. Raised deck area up steps is an extra "sun" spot, can be used at night for cocktails, dancing. **Note** clever use of lighting in this setting. Spotlights hide under overhanging roof, while larger spotlight on roof corner can be directed towards pool or flagged patio; swivel spotlight attached to railing of raised deck can be trained on any part of garden. Pool and patio furniture is lightweight, easy to move around, hard wearing of rust-proof metal; chaises on deck are wood, with back wheels for pushing into any direction. Cushions are all of waterproof, sponge-clean fabrics, perfect for outdoor use. Designed by Erica Lemle, N.S.I.D., A.I.D.

Swimming Pools

*today you can make a big splash in your own backyard
or garden for less than the cost of a new car*

A SWIMMING POOL of your own is no longer a high priced luxury and beyond your reach, as it once was. In fact you can own a pool for less than the price of a new car. Not only does a pool give you that extra summer pleasure for the entire family, but it is a home improvement investment that adds to the value of your home and property.

Many families in relatively low income brackets are beginning to build their own pools. This is because of the new low costs, installment plans and bank loans. *Today most banks are prepared to give loans for pools, because of the pool's investment value.*

Perhaps the most important factor in the swimming pool boom is the new, relatively low cost of building, which has evolved through new methods of construction. In the past, pools were expensive because they were of poured concrete. The introduction of Gunite pools made by spraying concrete through a hose started the price drop. However, it is the prefabricated pool made of aluminum, steel and fiberglass, and the plastic liner, that has put a swimming pool within everyone's reach.

Pool scene here is elegance personified—but is also full of practical ideas. Wooded forest area at end of garden offered a natural screen for privacy, so only fencing at one side was required. This was built of wooden slats, like louvered doors, and graduated in height. Pool is surrounded by practical wooden deck, hard-wearing, easy-to-clean and slip-proof. Sun couches are also of wood with comfortable mattresses, and wheels for quick and easy moving. Raised platform at far end is reserved for entertaining—snacks, cocktails, dining. Three-sided tent-like canopy or marquee is effectively different, offers protection against too much sun, summer breezes. Banquettes with upholstered cushions line the three sides of the marquee, and back section of fabric rolls up like a window shade for a view of the forest behind. Accessories such as Chinese statue, Japanese wind mobile on fence, flowering shrubs add finishing touches. Concealed lights in marquee area make the pool a perfect spot for evening entertaining. **Note:** practical basket in far corner on step is the ideal solution for wet towels, damp swim suits. Designed by David Barrett, N.S.I.D., A.I.D.

Pool Facts

SWIMMING POOLS CAN be of poured concrete, sprayed concrete, fiberglass, galvanized steel or aluminum. Poured concrete pools are economical in the warmest states, such as Florida, California and Hawaii, where the ground never freezes. Elsewhere, the concrete must be thicker, making the pool more expensive—above $3,000. Sprayed concrete is more flexible than poured, but costs the same in all but the warmest states. It is good however, for getting free-form effects and unusually shaped pools.

The most inexpensive way to build a pool is to use the plastic liner—a huge, one-piece plastic (usually vinyl) bag, fabricated to the size and shape of your desired pool. The plastic liner may be supported by several types of

Garden, terraces and pool area of this country house were all carefully planned to integrate with each other, and as an extension of the home for total enjoyment. **Pool was strategically placed:** it is close to house for convenience, framework of house acts as a screen; foliage of surrounding landscape ensures privacy on other three sides of pool; positioning of pool catches noon and afternoon sun. For complete coordination, the same flat flagstones were used around pool, in paved garden, on steps, on sun ledge adjoining house. Rock gardens and plants add to the general landscaped look of the total area; small terrace at far end of pool, with umbrella, table, chairs, is reserved for snacks and drinks. Pool itself is of galvanized structural steel with aqua-green vinyl interior.

material, even those that would not necessarily hold water, such as wood or concrete blocks. However, steel, aluminum and fiberglass can also be used, but remember they are usually more expensive than wood or concrete blocks. This prefabricated type of pool can be built for well under $2,000—and it is the type that the homeowner can partly build himself, saving on costs even more. Upkeep of the pool with a plastic liner is less, since the liner never needs repainting (they are color-impregnated), and no scrubbing is necessary as dirt is easily brushed off the smooth finish of the liner.

Of course all pools need a certain amount of upkeep, and accessories such as water filter, underwater vacuum cleaner, pool cover and steps are usually essential. Extras such as underwater lights, diving board, heating system can always be added later. Most pools need between two to four hours care every week, sweeping, vacuuming, adding chemicals. However, the water does not necessarily have to be changed often, as filtering and chemicals keep the water pure indefinitely—in fact, for well over a year. In winter, it is advisable to leave the water in the pool, as the water or *ice* counterbalances the frozen earth pressing in on the pool's sides.

There are legal complications to owning a pool, as it is a hazard to children and pets. *A locking gate is a must, as is liability insurance.* Local zoning laws should be carefully checked before you start building a pool, as some zoning laws forbid them or have their ownership depend on the neighbors' approval.

There is also the added expense of terracing around the pool—although most homeowners can do this themselves. Wood decking is perhaps the most economical, although tiles, vinyl, vinyl carpet and flat stones or bricks can also be used.

Position Your Pool for Convenience and Enjoyment

SUNLIGHT, WIND, PRIVACY and convenience are vital factors in the positioning of your pool.

SUNLIGHT:
Plenty of sun on a pool adds to the enjoyment; also, the water stays warmer longer so that evening dips are a pleasure. Place the pool where it gets most of the noon and afternoon sunshine. The diving board should be positioned so that the diver has his back to the sun and is not blinded by it. For very hot days, it is important to have shade near the poolside. Umbrellas or an extension canopy attached to the wall of the house are ideal; make sure trees and shrubs do not overhang the pool or shade it.

WIND:

Protection against breezes is important, for comfort in and out of the water, and to prevent wind-blown leaves and debris from falling into the pool. The skimmer on your pool should be installed so that it works with the wind and draws dust and debris from the surface.

PRIVACY:

Pool should be placed to give maximum privacy for relaxation and pleasure. Fencing or various landscaping arrangements are best.

CONVENIENCE:

It is important that your pool is positioned in a convenient place. It should be thought of as an extension of your home, and placed close to the house, if possible. Preferably it should be close to a door that's handy to the kitchen for food and beverages.

A cabana is a practical addition to any pool, and if it is gay and colorful it enhances the beauty of the poolside setting. The one shown here is not costly to build. It has a raised, wood-plank deck area and wooden walls. Back wall is painted bright blue, with louvered type side screens painted white. A white canvas canopy offers shade, also adds a decorative touch. Changing rooms leading off deck area have wooden walls in a shingle design, straw matting floors. Furniture reiterates blue and white color scheme, is made of durable alumaloy, with resilient vinyl webbing in bright two-tone colorings. The chaise has adjustable back for easy sunning, and the stacked tables are handy for snacks. Colorful floor cushions, bird cage and plants add the finishing touches.

This beautiful pool in its charming rustic setting has rugged galvanized structural steel side walls and vinyl interior. The galvanized layer guards the steel from rusting or corroding. Even if scratched, its electrolytic action keeps the exposed steel from the rusting or corroding effects of chemicals, water or weather. There is no chipping, cracking or disintegration. You never see or touch the steel of this pool—its strength is silent and unseen. The surface you do see and touch is the tile-smooth, but tough, 20-gauge vinyl aqua-green interior which is electronically fabricated for permanent service. It is totally impervious to chemicals, water and ordinary abuse, and so flexible it won't crack in "deep-freeze" below-zero weather. It stays firmly in place held by tons of pool water. Vinyl interior stays permanently fresh, and dispenses with the need for constant repainting some pool interiors require. Vinyl interior is also easy to clean, and the pool never needs emptying, in or out of season.

All the ingredients in this pool setting are practical as well as decorative. Whole garden area is fenced with white wood and lined with firs and other greenery for extra privacy, as well as beauty. Higher fence behind deck area is of darker, unpainted wood for an unusual play of color and texture against blond polished wood decking. The deck is L-shaped, turns the corner and moves down one side of the pool. The marvelous marquee on wheels is vividly gay, and provides shade wherever you need it. The three seating pieces arranged as a couch can be separated into individual chairs, are upholstered in bright orange vinyl, cannot be damaged by wet swim suits. Two arm chairs are upholstered in a contemporary print that echoes the lining of the marquee. Matching tables with glass tops, and set of stacked tables can be moved around at will for snacks, drinks, or poolside necessities. **Note:** wood decking, which is non-slip, easy to maintain, low cost to install; mobile marquee which can "wander" into any part of outdoor area, folds easily for winter storage; vinyl-upholstered furniture, quick-drying, sponge-clean, perfect for indoor use in cold months, as are glass tables.

Indoor pool that's the epitome of luxury has a host of ideas you can adapt for yourself—whether your pool is inside or out. Total floor area, interior of pool are tiled in varying shades of blue ceramic tiles for a sea-like effect. Stone pillars between windows add to the open-air look, support lowered, valance-like soffits which contain diffused lights; use of lattice work on back wall and lush collection of tropical plants repeat outdoor feeling. Lattice work is painted blue to match seascape color scheme of pool room. **Note:** ceramic tiles, as they are hard wearing, don't chip, weather outdoor elements well; use of underwater lights, not only pretty but practical for nighttime swims; use of foliage and tropical plants for a South Seas feeling. To create this same tropical garden you need to build a half wall at one end of pool as a backdrop for greenery. (Here it is in white stone but you could use wood covered in vinyl or simply painted white.) Plants need to be set in a small trench or well, so plant pots don't show. **Add:** two large planter pots at each end holding palms or flowering shrubs; lattice screen which could be attached to white wall and act as a "privacy screen" outdoors.

Outdoor Lighting

LIGHTING IS THE most effective "accessory" for outdoor living at night. Firstly, it is easy to install and relatively inexpensive. Secondly, it gives your patio, garden, swimming pool, even tennis court a "round-the-clock" extension, so that you get added benefit from them all.

Apart from all the practical aspects of nighttime outdoor lighting, it also throws a whole new light on the natural beauty of trees, flowers, swimming pools and fish ponds—a fairyland look in fact.

Every type of light is available for outdoor use—in any number of sizes, shapes and designs. There are swivel spotlights that can be hidden under overhang roofs and used to floodlight an area. Underwater lights bring a new luminous look to swimming pools, lily ponds, fish pools and fountains. Carriage-type lamps and lanterns can be attached to walls for an old world look, while smaller hanging lanterns can be strung between trees. Colored fairy lights (the kind used on Christmas trees) effectively light up a dark shrub or small tree; other small pin-spotlights can be hidden high in a tree, behind shrubs, in a clump of flowers for a magical glow. Apart from their decorative uses, outdoor lights are also a safety measure along dark garden paths, wooded areas on your property, on garden steps and other possible danger spots.

The second swimming pool is all set for nighttime entertaining, with the lights turned on in full. Pool and umbrellas are lit in the same way as the pool in the picture **below** as are tree trunks. However, small pin-spotlights (not shown in photograph) are ranged along lawn edge and trained onto flagged terrace surrounding pool, for an almost daylight look.

awn, wooded area and pool are enhanced at night by electric lights used cleverly for this magical effect. Underwater fixtures in pool reflect upwards and cast a glow on the water, while other small spotlights hidden n clumps of plants are trained on tree trunks. Additional lighting is used under umbrella rim and in tree branches. Small standing lamps are used at corner of lawn (in forefront of photograph) and at opposite side f pool near chair and table grouping. Direct lighting under umbrella is bright enough to read or sew by, nd the whole garden area can be used just as it is in the daytime. Apart from the practical aspects, the iew of the garden from inside the house is an effective panorama.

All manner of outdoor sports can be enjoyed at night, through use of cleverly placed lights. Here spotlights atop tall metal posts are strategically placed so that tennis players can have an evening game. Other lamps are hidden in the wooded areas for extra light and to bring foliage into focus.

477

The beauty of this lily pond would be lost after dark, without the clever placement of underwater lights. These are attached with small clamps to side of pool walls, others float under imitation lily leaves, are inexpensive, easy to install.

Here small standing lanterns, ranged at the side of the steps and throughout the garden, create a fairyland effect. They also ensure safety and prevention of falls. Spotlights are attached to tree trunks, half way up, and trained upwards to play on branches. Umbrella has light attachment under the rim, for comfortable dining outdoors after dark.

A light outside your door is a friendly welcome to arriving guests. It also enhances the beauty of your entry, is a safety precaution on dark nights. Here you see how effective a combination of glass window and old fashioned lantern can be. The random clear glass block, set in an attractive panel, lends an air of charming distinction to the entrance of this home. Similar to the bulls-eye glass of Colonial days, glass block brings softly diffused light to the entryway when the interior is illuminated to create an eye-catching after dark "picture." In addition to its decorative value, the panel helps cut fuel costs because the glass block has the insulating value of an eight-inch brick wall.

In this entryway the light is fixed in the center of the porch ceiling, so that it illuminates the whole area with almost "daylight" light. It is a two-fold precaution—against accidents and to enable the houseowner to see, from inside, who is at the door. Another practical idea shown here is the illuminated house number—a boon to visitors in winter, or on dark summer nights.

Landscaping

how does your garden grow?

THE LANDSCAPING OF the exterior areas around your house should be as personal in taste and design as your interior decoration.

A driveway and garden are usually the first impressions a visitor has of your home. They should be as trim and well cared for as your house itself.

Naturally, landscaping, like most things, depends on individual taste. Some people prefer a wild, natural look in gardens and outdoor areas: others, the clipped hedges, planned walks, plantings and ordered flower borders of the stylized English garden.

Before planning your landscaping, check the zoning regulations of your community. This must be the first step, as many zoning laws determine the limitations on the height of trees, shrubs and other foliage, and their placement. Interior and corner property lots often differ in these respects.

The cost of landscaping varies with each house, as does the planning. The location of the house on the property, the size, shape and elaborateness of areas planned for trees, shrubs, lawns and flowers are of course the controlling factors. The larger, more intricate garden naturally costs more than a smaller area. Here are some good, basic pointers to remember when planning your landscaping:

PRIVACY:

Shrubs, bushes, a cluster of trees can serve as screens from adjoining properties, walks, roads and create a park-like effect at the same time. Clever landscaping of a patio, terrace or swimming pool adds to their usability and attractiveness, also provides perfect privacy.

INTEGRATION:

A driveway should be fully blended with the foliage to create an attractive first impression of your property. The proportion of trees, grass, shrubs, bushes and flowers should be carefully balanced with concrete, graveled, asphalt or flagstone driveways to dispense with a paved, sidewalk effect.

SHADE:

A single, large tree may be a joy to look at, but make sure it does not obscure the house or shade it too much; plant a tree or cluster of trees at the edge of a lawn, so that you can get the most benefit from the shade on hot days. Make sure the trees do not overhang swimming pools or sun patios, and obscure the sun. Also bear in mind that trees near a pool mean falling leaves and debris to clean out of the water constantly.

LEVELS:

A garden on flat land can be planned with little regard to change in grade (level). Some land is not totally flat, so do not overlook grading problems in your plans. However, a garden that has more than one level is more interesting and much more effective designs can be achieved. But, naturally, the costs are higher.

DRAINAGE:

If you are designing your own garden before calling in a landscaper, remember to settle the drainage problems first, or discuss it with the expert. You don't want puddles, ruined turf and plants, so settle the drainage system in the beginning.

BASIC PLANTING:

Once your design is completed, you have two courses you can follow in the planting plans. If your budget allows you to do the whole planting job at once, the sequence should be as follows: plant shrubs and trees first, then sod or seed your lawn. Should it be necessary to carry your landscaping over a period of years, plant lawn first, add trees, shrubs and flowers later when you can afford it.

PLANS:

Your garden requires landscape plans, just as the interior of your home. If you have definite ideas about what you want, and the effect you wish to achieve, draw up some rough plans on graph paper. Then you can discuss the project fully with the landscaper. If you are an amateur gardener and wish to do your landscaping yourself, you will still need a set of plans to determine each area of your property.

EQUIPMENT:

Once your landscaping has been planned and executed, start thinking about purchasing some of the newest garden tools. Today you can buy *power mowers* that do almost everything a hand mower can do; *vacuum sweepers* which help make beautiful carpets of your turf; *motorized trimmers* that make marginal manicures of lawn edges quick and easy; *a small power cultivator* which takes the monotony out of weed-chopping and row-hoeing; *a good sprinkler* that makes watering easier (but remember it can never take the place of a top quality applicator that provides slow, steady, deep soaking); *a small power tractor* which is a boon where you have real work to be done on your property. All these motorized or power tools take much of the backache out of gardening. Smaller tools such as shears, clippers, hoes and spades are sufficient on small lots, or if you intend to do the minimal of gardening yourself. And remember, when planning your outdoor area provide a small shed for motorized power tools, and small gardening equipment.

Landscaping starts at the open end of this patio, turns the corner near the trellis wall and circles the house. Its border effect helps to define the house boundaries, without actually cutting it off from the surrounding, **natural** countryside. The cultivated area was cleverly planned so that it blends with the wild, wooded area. The patio itself was carefully landscaped, following this theme. Small square patches were left open in the pale blue ceramic tiling that lines the terrace. These were then planted with turf, plants, bushes and a small tree. Planter pots of flowers are used along back wall (behind trellis in left hand corner) for a dash of color.

Rocks and Waterfalls Give Distinctive Look to Gardens, Terraces and Patios

A ROCK GARDEN, surrounded by flowers and plants, and with a running waterfall or pool, is an effective addition to any garden. Such an arrangement can even be used successfully on a small patio, a terrace or in a *lanai*. In the past, creating such a rock garden has posed many problems, particularly for the amateur gardener. Finding the right shape and size rocks, transporting them, arranging them cleverly and building them, has been difficult. That is why the new lightweight fiberglass rocks now being manufactured in all shapes and sizes are such a wonderful boon in landscaping.

Each rock formation is hand crafted in molds that have been painstakingly prepared from real rocks. The natural coloring is obtained through the use of powdered rock applied to the fiberglass. The rocks are made to last a lifetime. Neither soil, moisture, heat or cold will have any effect on the fiberglass structure. The large variety of rock shapes and sizes makes for greater ease in choosing rocks for almost every purpose — even for an indoor setting. By combining the rocks with a waterfall many new concepts are possible, and when surrounded by shrubs, small trees and flowers, the results can be quite breathtaking.

Running water provides an amazing effect of peace and serenity, and the waterfall or pool combined with the rock formation can be used as a focal point in your garden. It can dress up a small backyard or terrace, and as mentioned above, go indoors in the winter months.

You can make a rock garden from the fiberglass structures in any size you wish. It can be six feet tall or small enough to fit on a coffee table.

If you are a clever gardener, you can make your own rock garden. If not, the suppliers of the fiberglass rock structures will design and build it for you, complete with garden and foliage arrangements to your own design.

Here you can see the special effects created with the artificial rocks, both with and without waterfalls and pools.

This photograph shows the **larger** terrace of the house. Again blue ceramic tile was used for the entire terrace area, which was landscaped in the same manner. Small patches of grass and plants break up the long terrace walk, for added interest. Small tree overhangs fish pond at far end of terrace in patio area. Note how clever drainage system works: water from pond runs down two steps into second pond set on lawn and is drained away from there. As the house is on a small hill, the problem of different grades in the garden was solved by clever use of tiled steps which graduate down to lawn. The whole slope was turfed for a rolling lawn effect, shrubs, trees and bushes planted at bottom of rise for beauty, shade and as a natural screen from neighboring house.

This large-sized rock garden creates a beautiful corner in a garden. The fiberglass rocks, of different sizes, are grouped together, with the waterfall running in the middle and falling into a small pool surrounded by lesser sized rocks. Apple blossom tree, flowering shrubs, mossy ground plants and flowers surround the rock garden for a truly natural look. The result is an intriguing focal point in a garden that might otherwise have been dull.

This rock garden and waterfall is smaller and less elaborate than the one illustrated above. But it is just as effective and gives added interest to a grouping of foliage in the background. The miniature fall is set in its own bowl, and is undecorated, relying on the greenery behind and the pot plants for effect. However, foliage can be added or imbedded for interest, if required. The fall is portable, is 36 inches high can be used indoors.

Here you see how the fiberglass rocks, with a pool and surrounded by small plants, can be used on a stand to dress up the dullest corner of a patio or terrace. It comes in its own bowl 40 inches wide and stands 36 inches high.

These fiberglass rocks are grouped together and imbedded with plants for a softening effect. A grouping such as this can be used at the base of a tree, at the corner of a lawn; several similar groupings can be aligned together to define the rise or fall in the level of your garden, or along both sides of a garden path.

Real and Artificial Rocks and Plants Can Be Combined for Effective Landscaping

TRULY UNUSUAL LANDSCAPING can be achieved today through a mixture of real and artificial plants, real and fiberglass rocks. These arrangements, combined with waterfalls and pools are striking groupings for garden, terrace or patio — and they can be used indoors or on city terraces.

New techniques which have been developed give the artificial foliage a true-to-nature look, and all are resilient enough to be left outdoors in winter. In fact, changing weather conditions actually enhance the plastic foliage — whether it's sun, wind, rain or snow. Exposure to the varied elements takes the new, bright shine off the plastic, helps to make leaves and blooms look even more natural.

New York landscape artist Harold Dyson is one of the foremost experts on these new combinations, and he creates highly individual effects through the use of live, preservations of live and artificial plants, shrubs and small trees. He mingles them with real and fiberglass rocks, adds pools and waterfalls for the finishing effect. Three of his landscape arrangements are illustrated here, to show you what can be achieved with the combinations.

1. Harold Dyson transformed this dull backyard into a cheerful garden through careful planning and expert handling of the landscaping. Flat stones were laid down for a crazy paving effect, with small niches left for small ground plants and flowers to peep through. To break the monotony of the high brick wall he built a fence, which also acts as a backdrop for the foliage. This is a combination of real and artificial plants, shrubs and small trees, planted in boxes and tubs.

2. Here you see a close-up of the rock garden, shown at the bottom of the steps in the first picture. In this instance, Mr. Dyson used real rocks, but plants are a combination of live and artificial.

3. This is one of Harold Dyson's more elaborate landscapings, designed for a big garden or patio. The large rockery, graduated in size, is made of fiberglass and real rocks, intermingled together for a truly natural look. The rockery is set against three panels, built mainly for an effective backdrop and to show off the foliage. But the panels are also a good screening device for added privacy. A variety of plants and flowering shrubs range over the rockery, and these are also a mixture of live and imitation. Finishing touches are the waterfall which trickles down from the top of the rockery into the pool, and the plants floating on the surface of the pool.

Fences

A FENCE CAN make or break your garden. It needs as much thought and *planning* as your landscaping. The most important aspect of building a fence can be done while you're seated at a desk or sipping coffee in the patio. This is the job of planning. First step is to list the things you want your fence to do. For example, a fence can admit sunlight and allow air to circulate or it can block them out. It can furnish varying degrees of privacy. A fence can protect your garden from the neighborhood wildlife and childlife, or it can keep your children and pets in the yard so you know where they are. You can use a fence as a space divider, to define an outdoor living area, or to screen a service yard. A fence can be a handsome backdrop for plantings, and help set just the right mood for the entire garden. Architecturally, a fence can be a picture frame for the home setting, or it can complement the house and make it look larger. Make sure the design fits your pocketbook — and your carpentering abilities if you are going to build it yourself.

This handsome fence adds character to a garden, makes an ideal backdrop for the foliage and flowers used as a border. Four-by-four redwood posts are flanked by translucent plastic inserts and topped with pyramidal caps of redwood. The one-inch roughsawn redwood vertical elements in the solid panels can be varied in treatment.

...and Flowers

NO GARDEN OR patio is complete without flowers—whether they are integrated into a landscaping, used in borders, planted in beds or simply potted and ranged around a paved area. They add color, beauty, and richness. Choice of flowers and the planning of their integration is just as important as the blueprinting of your total outdoor area. For a truly beautiful flower arrangement, make sure the various species you use blend well together and that their colors do not clash. Before buying seeds, cuttings or plants decide the total effect you want to achieve. You may prefer the ordered, stylized borders of an English country garden, or a "growing free," wild look; you may want to mingle flowers with small bushes, flowering shrubs; or perhaps mass a variety of species together for a sea of color and eye-catching interest.

The growing-wild look of the foliage on the far side of this paved patio is balanced by the elegant, ordered border of topper snapdragons, all colors mixed for a rich effect. They are new rust-resistant Fl. Hybrids that are vigorous growing and defy the heat. But it's the shapely spikes and wonderful color range that makes them the outstanding beauties of the snapdragon world. Three shades new to snapdragons are shown here—flaming orange-scarlet, clear lavender and a unique rose-pink. Large, closely placed flowers form gracefully tapered, towering spikes in bloom from midsummer on. A wealth of sturdy laterals, hugging the main stem at the base of the plant, create a bush-like effect, pleasing in backgrounds and borders. Toppers have long strong stems that are ideal for cutting. The dark green plants grow 3 feet tall.

A line-up of small shrubs and bushes, clustered together, form the border in front of the wall at the far end of the lawn. Other shrubs and flowers are mingled together around the edge of the terrace area, with a variety of large and small potted plants scattered about the terrace. This is a good idea to copy, as it carries the garden theme onto a paved area. On table in foreground is a potted Blue Wonder, the biggest of all early asters. Up to 4 in. across it resembles incurved chrysanthemums in form. The glistening petals make up flowers of an unusual bright blue. Vigorous 15 in. plants produce a wealth of bloom, have long stems for cutting.

The three elements that bring added luxury to outdoor living all come together here. Kidney shaped pool is the focal point of the landscaped area at back of this house. Lamps at edge of lawn and concealed in shrubs and trees effectively light the area at night.

Look of the 60s: Arches, an ancient structural form, are being revived by so many architects and decorators that they typify **the look** of the 1960s. Marvin Culbreth, A.I.D., uses the arch form here in cherry paneling to unify an irregular-shaped room and underscore the elegance of high ceiling and fireplace wall. The unusual wall treatment looks more complicated than it really is. **Any woodworker, skilled or amateur, can build a wall like this.** Basic construction is simple, finishing is unnecessary because wood is prefinished paneling with a factory-applied fine-furniture finish.

PART SIX

Do-it-Yourself Projects

CHAPTER THIRTY-ONE

Projects for Experts and Beginners

❧

THESE DO-IT-YOURSELF projects are not too difficult for amateurs and all of them are easy for the experts in this area.

Each one of the projects is dollar-and-sense wise. Apart from this, there is a great deal of satisfaction in creating something new for your home, yourself. And you can have lots of fun when the rest of the family joins in and makes them joint efforts.

The do-it-yourself ideas, here, cover a wide range. *We show you how to make a sewing corner, create a studio room, how to make valances and unlined drapes, how to re-upholster with foam rubber and how to decorate window shades. There is a six page step-by-step guide with instructions and photographs showing you how to hang wallpaper. Pegboard projects showing you how to save space, and ingenious storage units are also featured, plus a guide to building your own sauna bath.*

On the lighter side, the nine pages of fun do-it-yourself ideas cover decorating with beads, using towels and sheets for clever effects, and making your own fourposter bed through brilliant use of fabrics.

And for the handy husband we show you how to stretch your house with add-on rooms.

If you have never tried any do-it-yourself projects before, start with the simplest ideas. As you become more proficient you can graduate to the more ambitious schemes.

First...A Compact Sewing Corner

Both functional and eye-catching—a real contribution to any home where space is at a premium. Panels of wood-grained paneling are attached over old walls, with a framed section of white pegboard to mount spools and sewing supplies. The portable sewing machine is on a table which doubles as a desk. Tabletop space is supplemented by a wall-hung work shelf and a wicker basket for yarns and trimming supplies.

Make a Studio Room

SLIPCOVERING a couch or daybed makes a room attractive as well as useful. Achieve this custom look with the following diagrams and instructions.

TO SLIPCOVER A DAYBED

Cover the mattress as you would a cushion, making it reversible. Measure the length and width of the mattress and add 2 inches for all seams. Cut two sections, a top and a bottom. Then measure the depth of the mattress, adding 2 inches for seams, measure the two sides and ends, adding 1 inch for each seam. Finish all seam edges with welting. Sew welting to edges of the top and bottom sections,

493

then join boxing, leaving an opening across one end and along a quarter of one side. Insert two heavy zippers, one on the end and the other on the side with zipper end latches meeting at the corner.

Finish the base of the daybed, as seen in Diagram A, with a floor-length skirt, placing inverted pleats at center and corners. Join skirt to a strip of the same fabric about 6 inches wide along each side and across ends. Cut a length of muslin to cover top center portion, allowing 1 inch for seams. Pin to strips and sew.

Stitch lengths of tape to inside corner seams and tie to legs of daybed to hold cover in place. Several types of bolsters may be used, such as box, wedge, round or square. The bolsters may be covered in contrasting or matching fabric as directed in Diagram C.

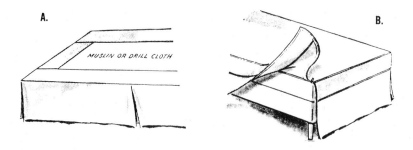

A.

MUSLIN OR DRILL CLOTH

B.

TO MAKE A DAYBED COVERALL

As seen in Diagram B, cut one piece of fabric the length and width of the mattress, adding 1 inch for seams. Cut fabric for back section the length of the mattress, and wide enough to reach 1 inch from floor when hemmed. Cut strip for boxing the length of the mattress plus the length across each end, adding 1 inch for seams. Add a pleated or gathered skirt across the front and both ends. Finish all seams with welting or piping, using zipper closing at each side of back section.

TO MAKE ROUND BOLSTERS

A round soft bolster stuffed with kapok or other soft filling is first made with a muslin tube-like covering. It is then slipcovered with the selected fabric.

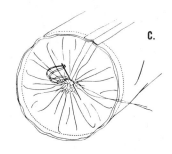

C.

Cut the fabric for the tube on the true lengthwise and crosswise grains. The diameter of a bolster may be 6 to 10 inches for a studio or daybed, and the length should be the same as the width of the mattress or, the two bolsters should measure the length of mattress. This is a matter of taste.

Cut two complete circles allowing 1 inch for ½ inch seam. That is, cut 9 inch circles if finished bolster is to measure 8 inches. Then cut one piece the length of the bolster (crosswise grain) and the width (lengthwise grain) the circumference of the end pieces. Add 1 inch for seams.

Bring crosswise edges of the center section together, right side to inside. Pin and stitch taking ½ inch seam leaving 6 to 8 inch opening near one end for turning and filling. Press seam open. Pin end pieces to tube, right sides to inside. Baste and stitch. Turn right side out and fill with kapok or other filling. Pack firmly to round out tube. Turn edges of opening inside, pin, then whip opening by hand.

Cut outer fabric on same grain and measurements. If a zipper closing is used allow extra 1½ inches on center section for ¾ seam. Leave opening 1 inch longer than zipper. Finish end seams with same edge finish of welting, etc., used on daybed cover.

Designer Zita Zech, A.I.D., turns a small room into a charming studio. It will also double as a guest room when needed. Gingham check wallpaper on walls matches fabric on daybed. Matching walls and daybed not only give the illusion of more space, but add spark and taste. A clever arrangement of prints adds a personal touch to the room.

STRAIGHT OR SHAPED VALANCES

BOTH STRAIGHT OR shaped valances should be made over foundations of stiff material such as buckram, and should be lined and interlined. When a quilted material is used, interlining is not required.

Cut buckram the exact measurement of finished valance, using paper or muslin pattern as a guide, particularly if valance is to be shaped. Then, cut cotton flannel interlining and selected fabric 1 inch wider on all edges. Next, cut lining ¼ inch wider on all edges.

Place fabric wrong side up. On this, place interlining. Pin and baste or stitch along all the edges and press. Next, place buckram against interlining. Turn edges back over buckram 1 inch. Clip turned back edges at inside curves and notch edges on outside curves. With needle and strong thread, catch-stitch edges to buckram. Turn under edges of lining ½ inch. Pin to back of valance and slip-stitch as shown in Figure 1.

BOX VALANCES

An open top wooden box or base, as shown in Figure 2 is required.

Cover front of board with cotton flannel. Cut strip of flannel 1½ inch wider on all edges for turn-under. Using heavy-duty thread, catch edges of flannel, working diagonally from edge to edge as shown in Figure 4, Step A.

Cut material on the crosswise grain the length of the board plus end sections, matching the pattern, if necessary. Add 1 inch to the width for seams.

For an attractive finish, use cording or a welted edge.

CUTTING BIAS FOR CORDING

To cover cord, see Figure 5. Cut material on true bias. When several yards of bias are needed, first cut a square the full width of fabric. Fold fabric on the true bias; bring the lengthwise edge to the crosswise edge. Press fabric and cut on the fold. Stitch lengthwise edges together, taking a ¼ inch seam and press seam open. Then bring crosswise edges together, extending the bias edge the width of the strips required. Stitch and press. One yard of fabric 36 inches wide will cut approximately 24 yards of 1½ inch wide bias strips.

Another method of cutting bias is to bring the lengthwise thread evenly along the crosswise thread. The fold resulting is the true bias grain. Press the fold lightly. Mark the width for bias strips, measuring from the fold. A bias gauge is helpful in cutting bias without measuring. First, cut on the fold. Set the gauge for desired width and place on point of scissors. Join bias strips on the lengthwise grain. Maintain evenness of strips by extending points beyond the edges the width of the seam ¼ inch.

For box valance cut bias 2½ inches wide. Turn edges to underside ¾ inch and place cord in fold. Stitch, using a zipper foot. Stitch cording as in Figure 5, Step C to edges of valance, taking a ½ inch seam.

Place material over the board, drawing cording to the very edge. Turn back wide edge of bias and tack cording to the edge of the board through seam allowance as shown in Figure 3. Then turn wide edge under and tack to wooden base. Tack across ends.

If valance is to be lined, cut lining material on crosswise grain the same width and length as board plus the measurement of end sections. Turn edges under ½ inch and pin in place as shown in Figure 4, Step B.

Using a curved needle, slip-stitch lining in place. Use L-shaped brackets to mount the valance over the window.

A valance can create an exciting window with pleated, gathered, ruffled, circular, straight or shaped styles to choose from. It can be in contrast with or match your drapery fabric. It can also combine and be an all-in-one valance and drapery.

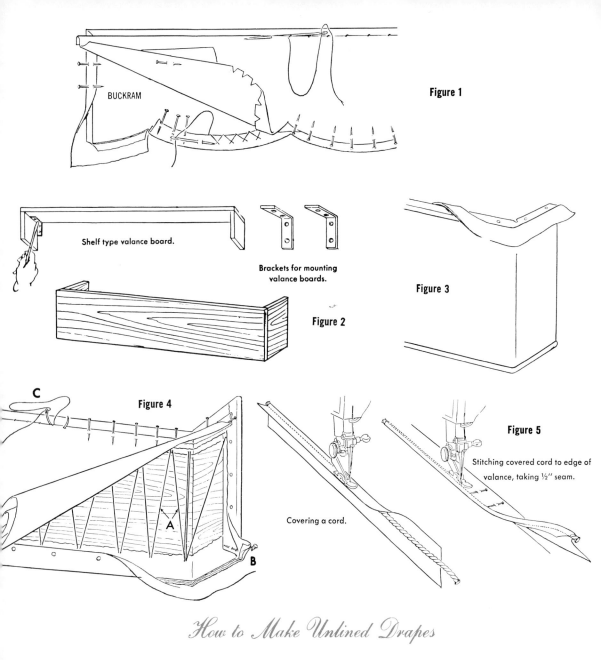

BUCKRAM

Figure 1

Shelf type valance board.

Brackets for mounting
valance boards.

Figure 3

Figure 2

C

Figure 4

A

B

Covering a cord.

Figure 5

Stitching covered cord to edge of
valance, taking ½" seam.

How to Make Unlined Drapes

DRAPERIES ARE USUALLY made of medium weight or heavy fabrics. They may be unlined, lined or interlined, depending on the fabric and its treatment — whether formal or informal in style.

There are several accepted lengths for draperies—window sill, bottom of the window apron, or floor length. Floor length is the type most commonly used, and for traditional or formal treatment may extend slightly onto the floor. In a country or provincial-styled room, draperies are often window sill length for informality, while a cafe curtain, sill length, lends lightness and air. Draperies hang straight from a rod or track to the length you have chosen. They may act as a frame for a window, or may meet at top center—if so, may be draped to either side and held back with ornamental tiebacks or those made of the same fabric.

When the style of drapery has been selected and coordinated with the proper rod or track, measurements can then be taken. *For Length*—Measure from top of rod or track to length desired. Add to that length measurement the allowances for top and bottom hems. Add 1 inch for the heading, 4½ inches for top hem and seam, and 3½ inches for lower hem. If a double hem is used at the bottom, add 6 inches instead of 3½ inches. *For Width*—Measure from edge to edge of window frame. To this measurement add distance from curve of rod to wall, adding 1 inch on each end for seams. Fullness of drapery averages twice the width of space covered.

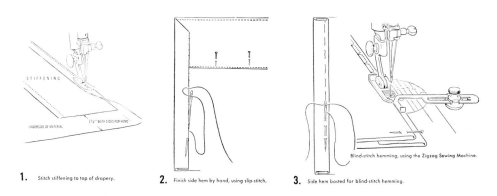

STIFFENING

UNDERSIDE OF MATERIAL   1½" BOTH SIDES FOR HEMS

Blind-stitch hemming, using the Zigzag Sewing Machine.

1. Stitch stiffening to top of drapery.   **2.** Finish side hem by hand, using slip-stitch.   **3.** Side hem basted for blind-stitch hemming.

UNLINED DRAPERIES are informal in treatment and usually made of medium weight material. Most any type of top finish, shirring or pleats is suitable. In addition, a plain valance or cornice board may be used. For a *pleated heading,* allow 5½ inches at top and 5½ inches at bottom for a 2½ inch double hem. Cut strips of crinoline for stiffening 4 inches wide and 3 inches shorter than the width of each drapery. Pin strip to underside of heading ½ inch from the top, starting 1½ inches from the edge. Stitch along lower edge of strip, then turn top edge of fabric over stiffening ½ inch and stitch, as seen in Step 1. Turn top hem to underside along edge of stiffening. Press and pin in place.

Side hems, as shown in Step 2, may be put in by hand, machine or blind stitched. For hand stitching or straight machine stitching, turn edge ½ inch to underside, then turn 1 inch for hem. Pin hem in place for stitching.

To blind stitch hem, as seen in Step 3, using a zigzag attachment, pin hem in place; then run a row of hand basting ¼ inch from turned edge. With wrong side of drapery up, turn hem under to right side, exposing the ¼ inch edge. Turn 2½ inch double hem at bottom and finish by hand or machine.

If 1 inch double side hems are used, cut stiffening 4 inches shorter than the width of each drapery length as shown in Step 4. When using a heading with slot pockets (Step 6) for pleater pins (Step 5) allow 2 inches at top for heading and seam. Pin right side of heading to right side of drapery fabric 5/16 of an inch below the edge across top. Consider the "return" of the drapery at each

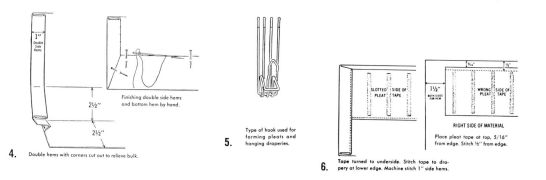

4. Double hems with corners cut out to relieve bulk.

1"
Double
Side
Hems

2½"

2½"

Finishing double side hems and bottom hem by hand.

5. Type of hook used for forming pleats and hanging draperies.

SLOTTED SIDE OF PLEAT TAPE

1½"
BOTH SIDES
FOR HEM

RIGHT SIDE OF MATERIAL

5/16" ½"

WRONG SIDE OF PLEAT TAPE

RIGHT SIDE OF MATERIAL

Place pleat tape at top, 5/16" from edge. Stitch ½" from edge.

6. Tape turned to underside. Stitch tape to drapery at lower edge. Machine stitch 1" side hems.

side, and position slot pockets so that pleat comes at the turn of the rod. Stitch, taking ½ inch seam; then turn heading to underside. Press and stitch ¼ inch from lower edge of the heading.

Draperies Add to the Style of a Room

This floral print is from a collection inspired by historical fabrics from France. Window treatment is part of a Colonial American interior created by Shaw and Draper, N.S.I.D., to harmoniously integrate fabrics with period settings. The valance and floor length draperies in a finely slubbed formal satin are an interesting textural contrast for pine floors and exposed ceiling beams. Furniture, paintings and accessories are from the collection of the Museum of the City of New York.

How to Re-Upholster With Foam Rubber

The tricky and, up to now, strictly professional job of re-upholstering has been made remarkably easy for the amateur with a new technique using latex foam rubber. This material is easy to handle and can be cut to shape. Because of its resiliency it makes very durable and attractive seat cushioning. The tools for this project are readily available: scissors, glue, staple gun and a webbing stretcher are the basic needs. The above room features furniture with handsome latex foam rubber cushioning. Notice how cushions can be shaped to give style to simple furniture, as with this rocking chair.

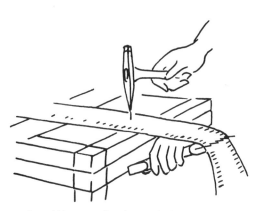

A webbing stretcher is a valuable tool that lets you put leverage on webbing to draw it tight. Buy a stretcher in a hardware store or else make one yourself from scrap wood.

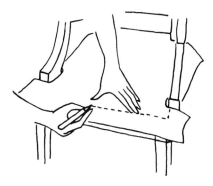

A paper pattern of the chair seat is very handy, especially when the seat curves and cannot be measured accurately with a ruler. Use brown wrapping paper and a marking pen.

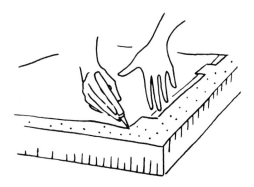

Allow an extra half an inch all around when marking the pattern on the latex foam rubber. The extra rubber is compressed by the fabric and keeps the material trim and neat.

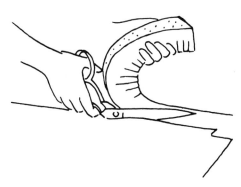

Stout scissors will cut two-inch latex foam rubber cushions easily. Thicker cushions should be cut on a bandsaw. Many upholstery shops cut cushions to size from a pattern.

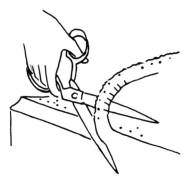

Undercut the cushion slightly if you want to make a rounded edge. The foam rubber is pulled down and tucked underneath to create a rounded edge that is solidly cushioned.

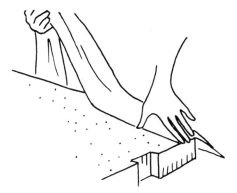

Plain muslin strips rubber cemented to the top of the cushion are tacked to the chair frame to hold the cushion in place and help shape it. Pulling down makes a rounded edge.

Apply two coats of rubber cement to both the foam rubber and muslin, allowing the first coat to dry completely. When the second coat is tacky, join the two surfaces.

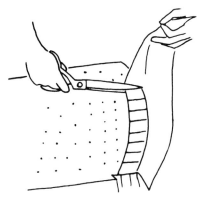

Cut V-shaped notches in the muslin if the cushion is curved so that the cloth will lie flat on the cushion. The width of each notch depends on the sharpness of the curve.

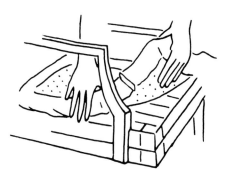

When the rubber cement is completely dry, place the cushion on the chair and tack or staple it to the frame. A staple gun is handy here because you use it with one hand.

Pull down on the muslin strip to give the cushion edge the degree of curve you want. Tuck extra cloth underneath and staple to the frame. Trim extra cloth with shears.

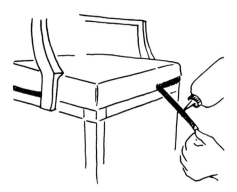

The finishing touch is the addition of a piece of upholstery braid or gimp to cover the staples. Run a bead of glue on the back of the braid, then press it in place.

Making corners is not really hard. Pull the material around the corner, lift up the excess, and staple. Then pull the remaining cloth straight down and trim it to size.

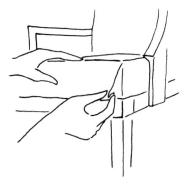

Fold the remaining edge underneath and tack or staple it in place. It may be necessary to sew the vertical slit shut. Use thread that matches the fabric and will not show.

Window Shades:

care and decoration

ALWAYS CHECK TO see if your window shades are washable when you buy them, as this type of easy care will extend their wearability. All better shades are treated so they can be wiped clean with mild soap and water. Those that are not washable can be refreshed with a good wallpaper cleaner.

Soap-and-water-care is not necessary often if window shades are dusted or vacuumed at regular intervals — how often depends on whether one lives in the city, suburbs or country. Washable window shades may be spot-cleaned with a damp cloth on occasion, but for a complete cleaning job, there are a few simple rules that will make the chore easier and more efficient:

1. Place the shade on a flat surface and wash it section by section, working on the area in front of you. Use a sudsy cloth or sponge and as little water as possible. Avoid letting water run onto other sections of the shade since this may cause marks that are difficult to remove. "Damp rinse" each section separately and wipe dry before going onto the next. 2. Reverse the shade and repeat the process on the other side. 3. Hang at the window, pulled down to full length, until dry. Overnight is advisable for thorough drying. 4. Here is a finishing touch that insures best results. After the shade is thoroughly dry, roll it up to the top of the window and leave it rolled up for ten or twelve hours. This simple "roll-up" trick leaves your shade pristine and fresh for the season ahead — and as perfectly flat and "ironed looking" as a brand new window shade.

HOW TO APPLIQUE WINDOW SHADES

This Early American window treatment designed by Rebecca Petrikin, A.I.D., uses cutouts of a companion fabric to trim a window shade and coordinate with drapery material. Here are some easy instructions to follow, for you to use cutouts on your window shades.

Motifs cut from closely-woven fabrics, such as polished cotton, chintz and percale are best for applique. To keep raw edges from ravelling, paint the cutting line on the back with colorless nail polish before cutting. If large areas are to be done, spray the back of the fabric. Test nail polish or spray first since some fibers such as acetate will dissolve. Cut out carefully with small, sharp scissors

and arrange pieces as a complete design on the shade. Then apply glue to the reverse side one cut-out at a time, making sure the entire surface is covered before pressing on the shade. Smooth out carefully, checking that all edges are secure with no air bubbles. If fabric is sheer, spread glue on shade cloth. After pasting is completed and dried, protect face of fabric with a coating of spray.

STENCILING ON WINDOW SHADES

A popular 18th century art form, stenciling, is revived on window shades by designers Bishop and Lord for these shades in a tiny entrance hall-dining area. The pattern along wall and framing window repeats shade pattern. Materials needed: stencil paper, stencil knife, stencil brushes, Prang Textile colors (available in art supply shops), masking tape, old plate for mixing colors, rags, cleaner and extender.

1. Trace design on stencil paper, leaving at least a two-inch margin all around. Make separate stencil for each color. Cut out design with sharp stencil knife.
2. Place stencil in position on window shade and hold down with masking tape.
3. Mix colors on old plate to create desired shade, add an equal amount of extender and re-mix.
4. Gently dip stencil brush in color and drag off most of paint on piece of paper (brush must not be too wet for this technique). Hold brush in vertical position and work color onto surface with a circular motion, starting at edge of opening and moving slowly to the center. Carefully lift off stencil and wait for first color to dry before placing second color over it or next to it. Clean brush thoroughly in cleaner before reusing for different color.
5. Leave stencils to dry for one hour. Then wet clean rag with textile cleaner. Gently wipe off paint from edge toward center of cut-out shapes.
6. Allow finished print to dry for 24 hours, then "set" with a warm iron for permanency. Set iron on low temperature and go over each section of design for six minutes, using dry pressing cloth between iron and shade.

How to Care for Marble

JUST THROUGH USE in your home, marble may become a little dull in appearance; it may lose a little of its brightness and lustre, but this situation can easily be remedied. Wash your marble with clean cloths and fresh lukewarm water. Twice a year wash it with a mild detergent as an additional safeguard, for this will remove any residue dirt which might become ingrained.

Marble surfaces should be treated like any other valuable piece of furniture, and it is therefore recommended that coasters be used under glasses, spilled liquids or foods be immediately wiped up and the area washed.

Foods and beverages that will mar the finish of fine wood also may mar marble. Moisture rings may result from sweating glasses; beverages containing

acid fruit juices or carbonation may etch the finish. With care this will not happen.

Marble will also, just through use, very likely lose some of its beautiful polish and acquire an occasional scratch. Fine scratches may be buffed away and the entire surface repolished whenever necessary with putty powder applied on a damp cloth. This polishing may be done by hand or with an electric polisher. It does take persistent effort, however; so if you lack the time, the energy or the patience, your local marble dealer will be glad to do it for you for a modest fee.

Waxing is never necessary for marble, but if you prefer to wax yours, use a colorless, light paste wax. Waxing of white marble is not considered advisable as it may in time give a yellowish tone to the marble.

POULTICING STAINS

Most stains will require the application of a poultice, and this poultice can be made of white blotting paper, white paper napkins, white cleansing tissue, or commercial whiting. The poultice should be soaked in the required solution and kept from drying out while it is on the marble. It can be covered with a piece of glass or a sheet of plastic (a vegetable bag would do) which will keep the moisture from evaporating while the stain is being drawn out of the marble, a process which may take from one hour to forty-eight, depending upon how old the stain is.

Once the stain has been removed, the area may require polishing with putty powder applied to a damp cloth. Keep the putty powder damp as you polish and rub the area persistently rather than vigorously for about a minute. Remove the putty powder with a dampened cloth, polishing as you go, folding and refolding your cloth to fresh damp areas until the marble is clean and the surface shines.

CHAPTER THIRTY-TWO

Stretch Your House With An Add-On Room

ADDING ON ROOMS is a tradition in America. Just look at those Cape Cod houses that grew in all directions as the family and its needs increased. Today, though, additions are a little more orderly and a lot easier to obtain.

Pre-fab units, plans and pre-cut lumber, windows and doors are available, and can be integrated into your present home and—presto, "instant room."

In some cases where extra land is at hand, you may prefer to build a separate unit in the manner of a guest house or family leisure room. This can relieve other parts of your home from much wear and tear, and serve as a clever outlet for teen-age parties, clutter of hobby materials and the sound of hi-fi music.

If extra land isn't available, often useable living space can be salvaged from part of the garage. This is in the tradition of the old turn-of-the-century "coach house."

When you think of salvageable space don't overlook another American institution—the attic—if you're lucky enough to have one. On these pages you'll see how that extra space can be made sophisticated and charming for better living.

Before the construction of the new room, this split level house wasted space and allowed no privacy in the back for outdoor living. Architect Wallace Kaminsky designed an arched roof system of translucent fiberglass panels that admit natural light to interior and give an upward dimension. Ribbed pattern of plywood adds design interest. Perforated aluminum louvers shield occupants from total view and at the same time permit additional natural light. The frame of the room is of fir and California redwood with staved lumber core doors painted bright blue. The frame is painted black. Measuring 20 x 20 feet, the room is large enough for family leisure activities and dining. A slate floor in a natural charcoal color blends with the black frame, white roof structure. Inside wrought-iron furniture picks up the blue color of the two exterior doors.

This tired, unused basement room with patched, uneven walls was remodeled and made into a useful living space by facing the walls with pre-finished walnut paneling. No maintenance or refinishing is required to keep the warm wood texture in good condition. Doors into the room were faced with the same panel treatment to give an unbroken appearance to the walls. In one corner, a bar arrangement was constructed to become the refreshment center. A sink and refrigerator unit with adequate counter-top space and wall shelves holds supplies and serving items. Recessed lighting in the ceiling provides extra light and acoustical tile soundproofs the room. A four-color floor lends practicality for wear and care purposes.

Designed by Robert Houseman

A Peter Pan Playhouse or kitchen is set high amid leafy boughs where real birds sing and wooden counterparts serve as shade pulls and cupboard handles. Cabinets in smoked walnut, raspberry and grape plastic laminate repeat the colors of nature. Openwork arches with sailcloth blinds shade open areas.

An old barn moved from a neighboring farm was renovated, at little expense and family labor, into a storage area and family summer room. Shown to the left, the barn was just a shell. New furring strips were added, and 4 x 8 foot panels of spring cherry paneling nailed to this foundation. The paneling is a printed hardboard

costing little more than paint. It gives some insulation, is pre-finished and easily installed. Matching molding was used around the door, windows and along baseboard. A white-painted colonial style door with traditional iron hardware is in keeping with the weathered grey of the barn siding. Furnishings from the main house were arranged for a quiet retreat.

Weathered California redwood in an add-on outdoor patio dining area is accented by planters of greenery in red terra-cotta colored clay pots. Vines are trained over the wall sections to give color and design in a natural manner. Provincial-styled chairs carry out the casual country theme.

514

Here is a fun do-it-yourself project that is easy to copy. This attractive, colorful room was once an unused attic. The addition of a large skylight window set in the sloping wall, plus colorful blue and white wallpaper used on all wall areas gave it a new dressed-up look. Matching fabric was used to upholster chair and for bedspread. Tasseled blue area rug on squared-off white vinyl floor repeats the blue color scheme.

A carport becomes a party place for teenagers when one wall is striped with brilliantly colored plastic-laminate-covered doors. The central panel folds down to form a table. Barbecue gear, games, furniture and tableware are stored in compartments behind. Designed by Edmund Motyka, A.I.D., the area uses potted garden greenery inside the entertainment section and an open fence displays shrubs and trees of the garden. Floor is flagstone.

CHAPTER THIRTY-THREE

How to Hang Wallpaper

WALLPAPER IS EASY to hang yourself, if you know how to go about it. On the following pages are a set of step-by-step instructions and pictures showing you how to do it. When buying your wallpaper it's always a wise idea to check the paper's qualifications; for instance, is it already factory trimmed and pasted or untrimmed and unpasted? Is it washable? Once you have this information you will know just how to handle the paper when you get it home. Obviously, paper that comes already prepared is the simplest to use. All you have to do is wet and hang it, once you have done all your measuring and cutting.

Before the step-by-step instructions and photographs, here are some useful tips which will help you in your wallpaper hanging.

Helpful Hints

PASTE: When mixing wallpaper paste, follow package directions carefully and stir until entirely free of lumps. Paste should be about the consistency of cream —thin enough to brush smoothly, thick enough to permit sliding the paper on the wall. Tie a string across the paste bucket as a rest for the pastebrush.

WATER RESISTANCE: Practically all wallpapers are water-resistant some are truly washable. To make certain, test a scrap piece by rubbing with wet sponge. If color is affected, be especially careful to avoid paste on the pattern side.

CEILINGS: Papering a ceiling goes much faster when two people do it...a "hanger" to position and smooth out the strips, and a "helper" to unfold the pasted strips ahead of the "hanger." Two stepladders supporting a walking plank are also very helpful.

WHERE TO START: Although papering is usually begun next to a door or window casing—or in a corner—there is one notable exception. If you are hanging a large-scale pattern and the room has a fireplace, center the first strip over the fireplace and hang to the right until you reach a corner or doorway where you wish to end. Then go back to the strip over the fireplace and hang to the *left* to finish the room.

BORDERS: These should always be hung last. Cut about 6 feet of border from the roll, paste and fold as with wall strips. Start in the least prominent corner of the room, hanging about 1″ of border on the wall at the ceiling line, turning the corner and continuing around the room. Your last border strip should go flush into your starting corner, covering the 1″ overlap.

THE "TOP" OF THE PATTERN: Some patterns, such as a geometric design, appear to be the same whether held "upside down" or "right side up," but they're not. The "top" of the pattern is usually the free end of a fresh roll, but if you have any doubts, see how the design is displayed in your dealer's sample book.

MIS-MATCHING: A certain amount of mis-matching is inevitable—particularly in corners, which are seldom true. There will be one other location in every room where the pattern will not match, but you can control it. For example, if you start beside the entrance door to the room and paper clear around the room, you'll end up with the last—and mis-matching—strip above the same door. On the other hand, you can start at the door and paper around to any desired corner, then go back and paper from the door—in the *opposite* direction—until you reach the corner selected for the mis-match. Survey the room before you start and select the least noticeable location for the mis-match.

"DROP-MATCH" PATTERNS: It is suggested that beginners select "straight across match" patterns, which require less care in tearing strips than "drop match" patterns in which the design is intentionally staggered so that only every other strip is identical at the matching level. Check this with your dealer when selecting paper.

follow these instructions carefully and you'll be proud of the result

Read everything before you begin

HOW TO ESTIMATE ROLLS NEEDED

Regardless of the varying widths of wallpaper patterns (18″, 20½″, 24″, 28″, etc., after trimming), each single roll contains 35 square feet. Figure 30 square feet of usable paper per roll because of possible loss in matching. The chart below will tell you how many single rolls you'll need for the room. You'll actually buy your paper in 2 or 3 roll "bolts" (depending on the width) in order to give you 5 or 6 full floor-to-ceiling strips from a "bolt."

ROOM ESTIMATING CHART

Distance Around Room in Feet	Single Rolls for Wall Areas Height of Ceiling			Number Yards for Borders	Single Rolls for Ceilings
	8 Feet	9 Feet	10 Feet		
28	8	8	10	11	2
30	8	8	10	11	2
32	8	10	10	12	2
34	10	10	12	13	4
36	10	10	12	13	4
38	10	12	12	14	4
40	10	12	12	15	4
42	12	12	14	15	4
44	12	12	14	16	4
46	12	14	14	17	6
48	14	14	16	17	6
50	14	14	16	18	6
52	14	14	16	19	6
54	14	16	18	19	6
56	14	16	18	20	8
58	16	16	18	21	8
60	16	18	20	21	8
62	16	18	20	22	8
64	16	18	20	23	8
66	18	20	20	23	10
68	18	20	22	24	10
70	18	20	22	25	10
72	18	20	22	25	12
74	20	22	22	26	12
76	20	22	24	27	12
78	20	22	24	27	14
80	20	22	26	28	14
82	22	24	26	29	14
84	22	24	26	30	16
86	22	24	26	30	16
88	24	26	28	31	16
90	24	26	28	32	18

This table is based on a single roll covering 30 square feet of wall area. Deduct 1 single roll for every 2 doors or windows of average size.

ABOUT THE SELVAGE

Wallpaper is originally made with an undecorated edge, or selvage—about ½"
wide—along each side of the roll, to prevent damage to the pattern in shipping
and handling. Depending on the pattern you select at your dealer's the rolls
will either be:

A untrimmed (selvage still on)

B trimmed or perforated on one edge only

C trimmed on both edges

D trimmed on both edges, with dry paste on the back

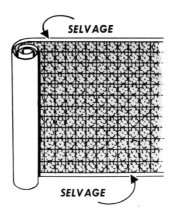

LEFT-OVER PAPER

If you have paper left over, keep it for repairs when necessary. You can also
use it to cover wastebaskets, folding screens, books, etc.

Wallpaper with a Dutch tile pattern is used on walls and window shutters for an integrated look. A room with an extra high ceiling seems cozier when papered—here textured paper is used and is repeated as a trim on the shutters.

THERE ARE THREE methods of joining the seams in hanging wallpaper.

One is the "butt" method, in which you fit the edges tightly together, with no overlap, like this:

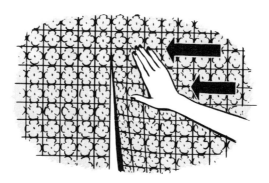

The second is the "lap" method, in which one strip is lapped over the selvage of another, like this:

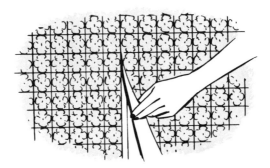

The third is to "wire edge" the strips — a variation of the butt method — in which one strip is lapped over the other — and into the pattern — very slightly ... about $^1/_{16}$".

All three techniques are satisfactory, but butting produces a more "finished" wall and avoids a double thickness of paper at the seams. It is the method explained in this chapter. If your walls are rough or uneven, you'll get a better job by lapping or wire-edging the seams.

In butting or wire edging, the selvage is trimmed off *both* edges of the roll. In lapping, only the *left* selvage is trimmed off when hanging from left to right, or the *right* selvage when hanging from right to left. (Wallpaper is usually hung from left to right across the wall, but some room layouts lend themselves to the opposite direction.)

Most wallpaper stores will trim your paper for you, but you should tell the dealer which hanging method you will use so he can trim the selvage properly. (If you plan to *lap* the seams, also tell him whether you will hang the paper from left to right or right to left.)

These Simple Tools and Materials Will Speed Up the Job

You probably have some of this equipment already, and can buy (and often rent or borrow) any missing items at your local paint-wallpaper or hardware store.

1. SMOOTHING BRUSH
for smoothing the paper on the wall.

2. PLUMB LINE AND CHALK
(A length of string with some kind of weight on one end is fine. Use colored chalk to coat string.)

3. SHEARS
for cutting and trimming.

4. SEAM ROLLER
(or chair caster) for pressing seams.

5. SPONGE & BOWL
for wiping down strips.

6. WHEEL KNIFE OR RAZOR BLADE CUTTER
for trimming at baseboards, casings, etc.

7. WALLPAPER PASTE
(Get a good quality paste.)

8. WALL SIZE
for preparing walls before papering.

9. PASTE BUCKET AND BRUSH
for applying wall size and wallpaper paste.

10. YARDSTICK
for measuring strips.

11. PATCHING PLASTER AND WALL SCRAPER
for repairing plaster cracks.

12. SANDPAPER
for sanding patched wall areas.

13. STRAIGHT EDGE
as guide if trimming the selvage yourself.

14. STEPLADDER

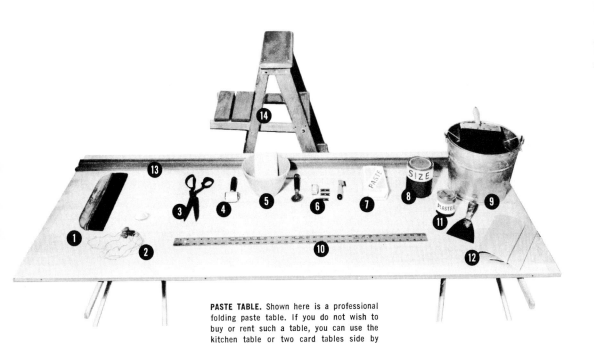

PASTE TABLE. Shown here is a professional folding paste table. If you do not wish to buy or rent such a table, you can use the kitchen table or two card tables side by side. Cover with brown paper — don't use newspapers.

FIRST...PREPARE THE WALLS

You can paper over old wallpaper, **providing it still adheres tightly.** If it is loose here and there, remove the loose paper and feather the edges with sandpaper. If the paper has been on the walls for many years and is generally loose, you'll save time and trouble later by taking it off. Use a wallpaper steamer, which you can rent at most paint and wallpaper stores, or soak the paper off with a mixture of water and a special wallpaper remover — also available from your dealer.

If the walls are painted or unpainted plaster, they should be prepared as follows:

PATCHING: Inspect for gouges, cracks and rough spots. Use wall scraper to remove loose crumbling plaster, and fill holes and cracks with patching plaster. When dry, sandpaper smooth. Wash off any calcimine (whitewash) with a strong soap solution and rinse well.

SIZING: Mix size according to directions on the package or can, and brush on a thin coat. The size, which is actually a glue, will dry very quickly. If the size turns pink in any area it indicates a "hot spot," which should be neutralized by applying a solution of two pounds of zinc sulphate in a gallon of water. Let dry and re-size.

The joints of "dry walls" (plasterboard) should be taped and the entire wall given a coat of primer-sealer before hanging wallpaper.

PASTED PAPERS: Detailed instructions for hanging trimmed-and-pasted wallpaper are customarily furnished by the manufacturer, and wrapped with the roll when you buy it. While the actual hanging procedures are as described herein, the paper is soaked in water and applied to the wall while still wet.

NOW...PREPARE THE PAPER

1. UNCURLING: Wallpaper is rolled quite tightly and will curl when unrolled. To eliminate the curl, unroll two to three feet of the paper, pattern side up, and drag it firmly between one hand and the edge of the table. Do this several times and you will find the paper will lie flat. It is not necessary to uncurl the entire roll.

2. MEASURING FOR LENGTH: Hold the partially unrolled roll against the wall at the ceiling joint and decide where you want the pattern to "break" at the ceiling line or molding. Mark this point lightly with pencil and put the roll on the table. Starting with your pencil mark, measure off the full distance from the ceiling to the baseboard.

1.

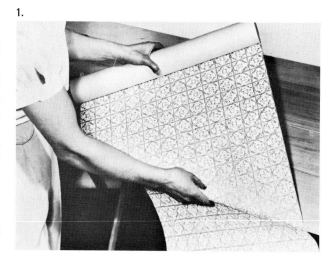

2.

3.

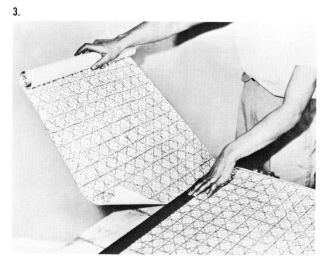

4.

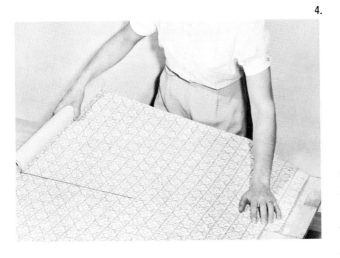

5.

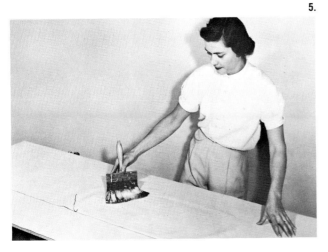

3. TEARING OR CUTTING: Add about 4 inches above your "ceiling" mark, add another 4 inches to the ceiling-to-baseboard distance, and tear off the strip, using a yardstick as a guide. (After you have hung a few strips and become familiar with the pattern match, you can reduce the excess length. Meanwhile, too much is much better than too little.)

4. MATCHING: (Straight-across match.) Lay the roll beside the first strip, unroll and match a second strip to the first. With trimmed paper, move the roll until pattern matches. (With untrimmed paper, match "Join Here" marks on the selvage.) Tear the second strip even with the first and place on top of first, pattern side up.

5. PASTING: After tearing 3 or 4 strips, turn the pile over, pattern side down, and push to back of table. Pull the first strip off the pile, and line it up with table edge nearest you. (This allows excess paste to fall to floor, or on back of second strip where it does no harm.) Apply paste to about two-thirds of the top of the strip, leaving an inch or so unpasted at the very end.

6.

6. FOLDING: When two thirds of the strip is pasted, fold the section in on itself—paste to paste. (If you are doing your own trimming, align the edges of the strip carefully but do **not** crease the fold.) Now repeat the pasting and folding operation on the remaining one third of the strip, as shown. This makes the strip easy to handle in the hanging operation.

7.

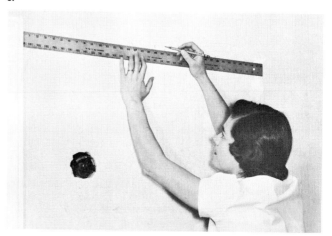

7. TRIMMING: If the selvage has not already been removed, now is the time to do it. Be sure strip edges are accurately aligned. Using a straightedge as a guide and a very sharp knife or razor blade trimmer, cut about $\frac{1}{16}$" **inside** the selvage line to insure its complete removal. (Refer to "Methods of Hanging" for proper selvage to trim.)

8.

8. WHERE TO START: It is usually best to start next to a door or window casing—or in a corner—and it is necessary that the first strip be hung perfectly vertical. To insure this, measure off from the casing or corner a distance about 1" less than the width of the pasted strip and place a tack in the wall just below the ceiling line.

9.

9. PLUMBING THE WALL: Take a length of string which will reach from the tack to the baseboard, chalk it and tie one end to the tack. Attach a weight to the other end and let the weighted string hang free. When the string stops moving, draw it tight against the wall at the baseboard and snap it. This will produce a vertical guide for your first strip.

HANGING THE FIRST
WALL STRIP IS IMPORTANT

10. LINE UP ON PLUMB LINE: Take the first strip you cut originally and open up the longer folded section by grasping the unpasted area at the end. Position strip at ceiling or molding at the desired point and align the right hand edge with your chalk guide line. Give the upper area of strip a few strokes with the smoothing brush to hold it on the wall.

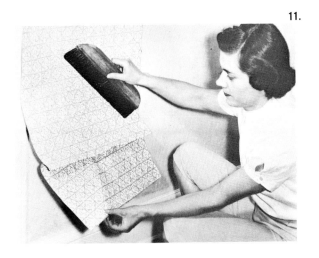

11. OPEN LOWER FOLD: Reach behind the strip, unfold the shorter folded section and guide it gently into place, watching your chalk guide line at the right. When lower section is in proper position, go over the entire strip with the smoother. Brush from the center to the edges in sweeping strokes to remove any air bubbles.

12. TRIM TOP & BOTTOM: Using a wall scraper as a guide and a razor blade cutter (or a wheel trimmer), trim off excess paper at baseboard and ceiling. You can also do this by scoring the paper lightly with the back of a knife or scissors. Pull it away from the wall slightly, cut with scissors on scoring line and brush paper back in place.

13.

14.

13. TRIM AT CASING: Brush the paper firmly into the casing joint and trim off the excess just as you did at the baseboard and the ceiling. If you started to hang your paper from a corner of the room, simply brush the inch or so overlap into the corner and onto the adjoining wall, where it will be covered by the final strip you hang.

14. HANGING SUCCEEDING STRIPS: Follow the same procedure with succeeding strips, hanging them in the same order they were cut. To butt the seams with no overlap (shown here), slide the edge of one strip against the edge of the other, matching the pattern as you position the new strip down the wall. This is the way professionals do it.

15.

16.

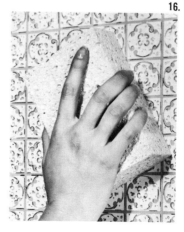

15. ROLL THE SEAMS: After strips have been hung for 10 to 15 minutes, press the seams **lightly** with a seam roller—except in the case of embossed papers where seams are not rolled.

16. SPONGE OFF PASTE: Remove any excess paste **promptly** from pattern, woodwork, etc. If paper is water-resistant, wipe down the entire strip with a wet sponge; use a clean dry cloth on nonwashable paper.

CHAPTER THIRTY-FOUR

Fun Projects for Beginners

MANY WOMEN SHY away from do-it-yourself projects because they feel the schemes are too difficult to carry out successfully. Even the woman who is quick and nimble with a needle is often afraid of more elaborate, constructional projects, mainly because no one wants to waste time, effort and money and end up with a useless object that is destined for the trash can.

On the following pages are a series of fun do-it-yourself ideas—all of them quick and easy to carry through successfully, with little fear of mistakes. In fact all of them have been specially designed for the novice and with an eye on budgets. Any one of them might appeal to you—whether it's the study corner, the beadangle bathroom, novelty storage closets or one of the two fourposter beds. There's even a couple of sewing ideas for the woman who prefers to stay with the needle.

All of them are tried and tested, almost all of them can be started and finished in one day, two at the most. And certainly each adds a touch of color, gaiety and individuality to your home. You might even make them family projects and get everyone involved in an evening of joint effort and the creation of something new for your home.

Beads Sway Again as Decorative Fashion in the Home

OLD IDEA FAST becoming a new thing around the modern home is the use of beads. Strings of beads, permanently threaded on nylon cord, are easy to install and available in all colors to use in living room, bedroom, kitchen, den or bathroom. Their built-in colors stay bright and fresh in the strongest sunlight and stay clean with a light dusting and an occasional dip in the tub.

They can be bought by the yard, so that you have a chance to create personal color combinations for an arrangement that is truly individual, in full-length draperies, kitchen cafes or room dividers. They glamorize plain shower curtains, make exotic vanity skirts, disguise storage areas, or create instant art for plain walls. Their use is limited only by the extent of your imagination.

There is a variety of ways in which they can be mounted. For fixed installations such as room dividers or valances, there is a vinyl tape with pre-punched holes, or a hollow aluminum rod which can be fastened to ceilings or on brackets, both of which hold the top bead of each strand. With pin-on hooks, the tape can also be used on a traverse rod. A small metal hook with a clasp on the top bead, allows the beads to be hung on shower curtain rings, traverse rods or any other installations where a hook can be used. Because they are threaded permanently on nylon cord, the strands can be cut anywhere at all for the correct length. They can be bought in continuous strands in curtain departments and drapery stores from 12 cents a foot, and are easy to handle.

A bathroom in vibrant colors is easy to achieve through the clever use of beads. Here these unbreakable strands are slipped into a special rod and just snipped to fit any area or trim the mirror as shown here. To make the most glamorous shower curtain ever, the rod is attached to the ceiling to make an entire bath enclosure and the red, pink and white beads are backed by a transparent shower liner. The vanity is created without construction just by hanging the rod beneath the counter to hide storage and plumbing. The colorful rainbow beads set the color scheme, which is repeated in rug, towels and accessories. Setting designed by Rebecca Petrikin, A.I.D.

Here you see how the do-it-yourself beads are used to make unusual tie-back drapes in a sophisticated sitting room. Colors of the beads, red, pink and white, match the braid trimming on the room-darkening shades in embossed boucle. The hollow rod which holds the beads was attached to wall under window molding near ceiling, then beads snipped off to correct length for the shimmering curtains which diffuse light without losing the view. This is a quick, easy project that's inexpensive too. Beads cost 12 cents per strand. Special rod is $1.00 per ft.

A little flair and do-it-yourself know-how turns an unused corner into a colorful study area, which works in a kitchen, hall or family room. The same idea could also be copied for a teen-age room or bedroom. An old table was spray-painted bright red, and the top covered with a striped fabric that identically matches the window shade. Fabric was simply stretched across top of table and tacked down underneath. For wipe-clean practical purposes you could use a vinyl or coated fabric. Orange chair was chosen for comfort and to match overall color scheme. A wall light and five distinctive wall plaques added finishing touches. The result is a bright little corner for telephoning and paperwork.

Fresh window dressing and fine table manners are related subjects in this dining area created by clever use of textiles by Paul Krauss, A.I.D. Draping a square border-print table cloth over a circular table skirt, Mr. Krauss converts oblong companion pieces into cafe curtains of diverse lengths, with tops reversed to obtain colorful frames of butterflies and daffodils. Each window holds one of the moderately priced cloths, cut and seamed without fabric waste. Further skirting the matter of expense, the solid color coverlet might well conceal a less than elegant table, or even a plywood-covered barrel storing rarely needed household goods. Curtains are easy to make, also to wash and dry as they are made of rayon and cotton.

Here a sparsely furnished bathroom is given a touch of color and an integrated look through use of bright floral towels that match. In step with the floral theme is the stool upholstered with one of the matching towels. To copy, simply cut large towel to shape of stool, make sure to leave enough material to cover edges and turn underneath stool. Hem all four edges of towel and thread with elastic. When finished you should have a square cover that looks like a bath cap. Slip over stool, simply remove to wash. If you prefer, thread hem with soft white cord that can be drawn tight and tied underneath stool. Do not tack down, as cover would be difficult to remove for laundering.

"Polly Para" stands guard over your best sweaters and woolen blouses — and your fur hats too — and lends a breezy touch of whimsy to your closet as well. She's nothing more complicated than a stack of five hat boxes, fitted with see-through "window" eyes and buttons made of plastic coffee can lids. Two lids taped together hold enough para crystals for sure-fire moth and mildew protection for each box. As the crystals vaporize through the holes in the inside lid and into the box contents, they disappear from view. When "windows" are getting empty, it's time to refill. "Polly's" all dressed up in a design-it-yourself outfit made of cling-on adhesive backed plastic you can find in a riot of colors and patterns at department and five-and-dime stores everywhere. Her coiffure is a pair of bright yellow dry mops, one placed crosswise the other for bangs. If there isn't space for her inside your closet, station her in a corner of your bedroom. Wherever she is, she'll do a splendid job of keeping out moths and mildew, because there's a real magic ingredient built right into each unit. It's "paradichlorobenzene," familiar to everybody as simply "para"— a safe sure chemical that kills moths and moth larvae and even prevents mildew in damp areas. Para is available under dozens of different brand names and at very small cost in department, houseware and hardware stores. You'll see it packaged in the form of small crystals, nuggets, and solid blocks in various shapes from hearts to circles.

Whatever its shape, para releases sure-fire moth protection in the form of vapors that drift downward through clothes placed in airtight closets or containers. Major producers of para advise that from one to two pounds will keep moths and mildew out of 100 cubic feet of confined space (about the size of an average closet.) To avoid wasting the vapors and to get the maximum values from para, it is recommended that all storage areas or boxes should be kept as air tight as possible and sealed wherever practical.

To make "Polly Para," you'll need five round hat boxes, a dozen plastic lids from coffee cans, a couple of dry mops for her hair, and enough self-adhesive vinyl plastic material to cover and trim boxes.

First cut and apply the plastic smoothly to each box; use the dress design shown here, or one of your own invention in a color to contrast with the other covered surfaces of the boxes. Now cut a round hole the exact size of the coffee-can lid in the side of each of the four boxes making up the body, as shown in diagram. Cut two holes for eyes in the top of the fifth box. Using a loose-leaf paper punch, make small holes as sketched, in six of the plastic lids. Match these up with the other six lids to make window containers for the para moth-proofing crystals. The two lids are held together with a strip of ¾-inch gold metallic tape, made into a ring with the adhesive side out and placed against the inside edges of each pair of lids. Before sealing, the space between the lids is filled with para crystals; then a second strip of the gold tape, trimmed to ⅜-inch wide, is added around the outside of the paired lids to hold them snugly together. These are then inserted in the appropriate holes, with the pierced side of each "window" facing inward. Eyes are completed by applying small cut-outs of the self-adhesive vinyl material as shown in sketch. Hairdo is made by placing one dry mop across the head and the other on top of that, front to back, to form bangs. For final touches add ribbon bow, earrings made of gold shower curtain rings taped at either side of head. The finished head is set in place between two plastic-covered lengths of either half-round wood molding or halved cardboard tubing from the roll of vinyl material. These braces are glued into position so that the head will not roll off. All boxes are simply stacked, not fastened together, for easy removal when necessary. The level of the para crystals in each of the see-through lid containers can be checked in a jiffy so you can add a new supply whenever required to keep stored articles properly moth-proofed.

Coveted storage space which conceals its functional assets behind richly covered fabrics is devised by Paul Krauss, A.I.D., with imaginative application of beautiful textiles. This is a project you can easily adopt for yourself, if you need extra storage space. Cutting off just 30 inches from the back wall, he brings forward black-painted wood frames filled with diamond-weave cloth in the brightest reds; the outside panels are Roman shades which can be raised to provide access to the newly created closet space, while the two center sections remain stapled in place to wood frames and complete the backdrop design for the bedroom setting. Headboard, spread and dust ruffle repeat the blue-and-orange-tinged reds from the panel fabric in solid versions.

Here's a charming, budget bedtime story with a do-it-yourself twist for waking hours. This candy stripe window shade is hung reverse roll, finished with a pert blue bow and white moss fringe trimming. It stands alone as a complete window treatment—and sets the theme for the room.

The shade is an exact match to a gay, striped set of sheets, and it was that happy coincidence that inspired designer Paul Krauss, A.I.D., to create a sophisticated, French country bedroom that can easily be duplicated with a few striped sheets by handy, do-it-yourselfers with a flair for sewing.

To coordinate with the shade, two sheets were used to cover the window wall. A matching pillow case was cut and measured to fit the lower part of the window, and turned into a cafe curtain. The bed topper received a special beauty treatment too. A new quilting accessory for the sewing machine was called into play, to make another striped sheet look rich and fluffy as an old fashioned, eiderdown quilt. It is edged with the same fringe as the shade, and white pompons on twisted cords add final flourishes at the corners. A dust ruffle was created from another sheet, in French blue to match the window frame and woodwork.

Create your Own Fourposter

THERE'S A SPECIAL kind of charm about a fourposter bed, even more so when you can create it yourself for little cost and with almost no effort. These two colorful bedrooms might have been dull and ordinary without the unusual "fourposter" effects created with a little wood and some vividly patterned fabrics. In both instances the fabric sets the color scheme of the rooms. Why not adapt this idea and give your bedroom a lift—or that of your teen-age daughter?

A flourish of fabrics enriches a sparsely furnished bedroom and lends an aura of luxury to a low-budget decorating scheme, with a fourposter as the focal point. The design strategy, devised by designer Paul Krauss, is executed with eye-catching print cloth and plotted for individual adaptation by the average home-maker. Starting with an old iron headboard, retrieved perhaps from an attic or second-hand furniture shop, the do-it-yourselfer can restore the pseudo-antique with black paint. The same paint treatment is then applied to four wooden poles joined at each corner to create a square canopy frame. Finials are next attached to each corner of the wooden square; these are fool-the-eye fakes that look truly authentic, are actually rubber balls and dime-store cookie cups, painted black, and threaded together with thin chain. Once the finials have been added, the square frame is hung from the ceiling. Next step is to make full-length drapes, or swags if you like, of brightly colored fabric. These are hung from the corners of the ceiling frame to simulate four posts. To complete the scheme, spread and window curtains are made of the same floral material; walls are painted white, floor enamelled red for the finishing touch—both easy projects you can also do yourself.

In this second bedroom designed by Paul Krauss, A.I.D., the fourposter effect is created on the same prin-ciple as in the first picture. However, in this instance four straight pieces of wood are joined together to form a square frame, painted white and affixed **directly** onto ceiling, instead of hanging from finials and hooks. The frame accommodates simple rods which hold the swags of cloth. This is easier than attaching the swags directly onto wooden frame, as they can be removed from rods quickly and simply for laundering. The four floral swags set the blue-green scheme of the room.

Pegboard Projects

PEGBOARD IS PRACTICAL and functional. It can also be fun if you use it in novel, new ways. Today it is not only made in plain white, but in a variety of different wood finishes, often with paneling to match. So now it can be used in sitting rooms, dens, family rooms, as well as in more utilitarian areas of the home. Pegboard is relatively quick, simple and inexpensive to mount on walls, and with a little ingenuity you can achieve some imaginative effects. Here are five smart do-it-yourself pegboard projects which are easy to copy, and are an asset in any home.

This basement was turned into an attractive workroom-den for the man of the house, through clever planning and a little do-it-yourself expertise. To make his surroundings as pleasant as possible, the owner of this home lined the lower half of the walls with woodgrained hardboard in a handsome cherry. Above the cherry hardboard he used pegboard, framed with molding along top and bottom. The bare, overhead pipes were concealed with soffits faced with a companion woodgrain in a lighter color. Fixture in soffit area gives effective over-desk lighting; other soffit contains small cupboard with sliding door for books, storage. Textured vinyl flooring completed the basic shell. The owner then dressed up the pegboard with framed photographs and mementos, painted an old mahogany desk a light shade to match pegboard, added a comfortable chair and drafting table. A pull-down lamp illuminates this, and installation of a telephone and dictating machine completes the efficient setting for an office in the home.

A two-panel entertainment center is the bright spot in this recreation room. Taking minimum space because the prefinished pegboard holds table tennis paddles, a portable TV set and other leisure-time articles, the wall can be put up for less than $30 by the efficient do-it-yourselfer. The wood-grained pegboard panels are attractive in themselves, besides being functional. Matching panels without perforations are available to give a furnished look to any room in the house. This type of wall is a perfect catch-all in teen-age rooms, nurseries and family rooms.

The placement of a workshop in the home is often a problem, especially when tools are in constant use. Here the best possible use of small space is effected, and floor-to-ceiling pegboard acts as both "catch-all" and sound cushioner to complement the sound-absorbing qualities of the floor covering. This is a vinyl carpet, a better sound deadener than any other smooth-surfaced flooring, and easy to sponge-wipe clean. Pegboard covers all wall areas, while a framed piece of pegboard is added on the right for tools; other equipment is hook-hung above bench cupboard. This has pegboard doors both inside as well as out, so that extra tools can be hung behind the closed doors. The result is a compact, efficient workshop for the man of the house, who can work in peace without worry of noise penetrating the rest of the home. It's also easy to copy; pegboard is simply attached to walls, carpet cut to shape and laid.

You can gain extra space in any small work area through use of pegboard panels on one, or all walls. Here a laundry area gets added efficiency through use of such a panel, plus pegboard fixtures that hold detergents, with hooks for brooms and brushes. This particular pegboard is factory finished in a neutral beige color with a textured print which reproduces the look of monk's cloth. Because of the factory finish, the panels require no painting and are easily maintained by occasional damp-wiping. The panels can be installed over furring strips or wall studs.

Any kitchen wall can be put to work beautifully by adding two elements—handsome new pegboard plastic fixtures used with pegboard panel. The attractive white plastic fixtures fit solidly in the perforations; they are strong and their edges are smooth. Use of this combination makes any kitchen more efficient, as shelves can be used for spice bottles, flavorings, other cooking ingredients and equipment. They also perform well in utility rooms, storage closets, sewing areas and home workshops. Lumber yards and hardware stores are now selling the new fixtures.

Build Your Own Sauna Bath

THE SAUNA BATH, a tradition in the Scandinavian countries has rapidly increased in popularity here. Today you can have your own sauna bath for a moderate outlay of dollars. And if husband is a handy do-it-yourselfer the pre-built sauna can be installed in under an hour. The pre-built sauna arrives as a complete package in easy-to-handle cardboard containers. The room includes walls, ceiling, floor, heating unit and all electrical controls. All that is necessary is to bring electrical service to the room, turn on the switch and in a matter of minutes the sauna is ready for use. No hammers, saws or nails are required as the sauna comes with a special patented locking device that locks the pre-fabricated panels together far more securely than by regular nails or screws. The sauna room can be installed in a spare room, basement, attic, large closet, garage or storeroom. The exterior of the sauna room is mahogany paneled and can be either stained, painted or wallpapered to fit any decor. Although it was designed for inside use, by adding a weatherproof siding and roof to the exterior of the pre-built many exciting ideas can be created for an outside sauna. On the following pages are the step-by-step instructions for assembling the pre-built sauna bath.

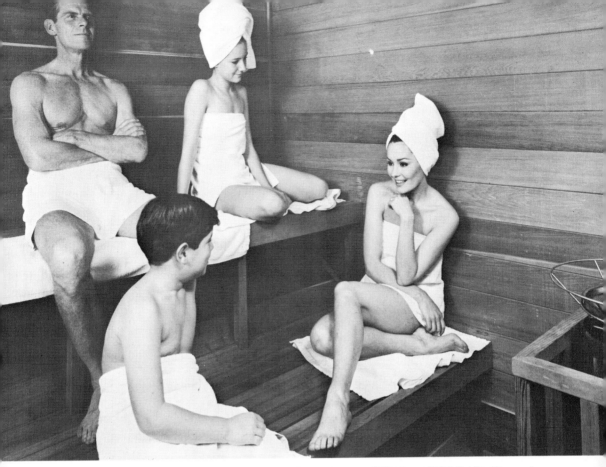

Here you see a whole family enjoying a sauna bath, in the new pre-built sauna which takes less than an hour to assemble.

This is a close up shot of the sauna heater which comes with the pre-built. This is an authentic sauna heater imported from Sweden and built to Underwriters Laboratories standards. It can be used with or without rocks as a dry or wet sauna.

Easy-to-build Sauna Bath

(Step A): The sauna pre-fab room is delivered in two packages. The BTH-6 unit weighs 40 pounds (box size 20" x 20" x 30"). The pre-fab sauna room weighs approximately 1000 pounds crated (box size 3' wide, 3' high and 7' long). The panels are packed in the same order that they will be assembled with the exception of the benches.

(Step C): Place panels #1 and #2 in position creating the first corner. Make sure that the tops of the panels are flush with each other; close both locking devices with special key provided. Note: Always close lower locking device first. (See picture in upper right hand corner.) Panel #1 contains the electrical components and recess space for the upper bench.

(Step B): Place floor panel on level surface making sure door opening is placed in direction desired. (Note: Markings in the border of the floor panel designate correct panel placement.)

(Step D): Place panel #3 in position and lock with panel #2. Panel #3 contains recess space for lower bench.

(Step E): Place end of upper bench in panel #1; insert panel #4 in position without locking to panel #3. Insert upper bench in panel #4 and lock panel #4 to panel #3.

(Step F): Place panel #5 in position and lock to panel #4.

(Step G): Place lower bench in recess in panel #3—rest other end of bench on floor.

(Step J): Lower ceiling panels in place so they drop into position.

(Step K): Place sauna heater on wall of panel #2 and plug into 220V outlet on inside of panel #1. Bring outside 220V wiring 30 amp. to junction box in outside panel #1.

(Step H): Install door panel #8 and lock to panel #1. All that should be remaining now is one wall which is represented by panels #6 and #7.

(Step I): This part is not pictured. Lock panels #6 and #7 together before placing in position. Tilt up panels #6 and #7 and simultaneously slide end of lower bench in recess panel #6. Lock panel #6 to panel #5 and panel #7 to panel #8.

(Step L): Sauna room is now complete and ready for use.

Painting Made Easy

TODAY'S NEWEST PAINTING equipment and paints have certainly taken the backache out of painting or repainting your interiors, refurbishing your old furniture and dressing up new, unpainted woods.

Paint manufacturers are continually introducing revolutionary new products that make painting quick, easy and simple enough for a woman to do herself. Now you can buy paints that are **ultra-hard wearing, scrubbable, quick-drying, odorless, fire retardant, moisture resistant, bubble free, and some that can be successfully applied without removing old finishes.**

The newest painting equipment is relatively inexpensive and very easy to handle. Small rollers and pans, long-handled rollers, aerosol spray cans and a variety of different spray guns make it possible to cover any area, whether large or small, quicker and more efficiently than ever before.

Painting is even easier if you plan ahead. Everything goes quicker if you have all your supplies at hand and follow your plan step by step. Whether you're a novice or an old hand, a chat with your paint dealer is sure to be helpful. He can advise you as to the best product for the surface you want to paint, how much paint to buy, the supplies you'll need and how to make the job as easy as possible. And remember, always read container label directions and cautions carefully before using paint products.

HERE ARE TEN TIPS FOR INDOOR PAINTING

1. Select the paint product best suited for the job.
2. Follow directions on the can.
3. Don't skimp on equipment. Use good quality brushes, rollers and sprays.
4. Protect floors and furniture.
5. Prepare the surface properly.
6. Paint at comfortable temperatures in a dry, well-ventilated room.
7. Wipe up spatters and spills immediately before they harden.
8. Clean brushes, rollers and other tools as soon as you finish using them.
9. Wear rubber gloves while painting and cleaning brushes or tools, to protect your hands and hasten clean-up time.
10. Check that you have the following things handy before beginning: ladder, paint paddle and bucket; water bucket and sponge; sandpaper or steel wool; turpentine or mineral spirits; spackle, patching plaster or wood putty; mixing pails, putty knife, paint can opener, screwdriver; brushes, rollers and roller pan or spray gun; abrasive cleaner; newspapers or drop cloths for protecting floors and furniture; clean cloths or absorbent paper for wiping up spatters and spills.

If you have a small area or small piece to paint or enamel, you can use the handy aerosol spray cans. Spraying is good to use for hard-to-reach places, for mesh or woven surfaces such as rattan or wicker, for small or oddly shaped objects, for quick and easy touch-up work.

When varnishing a wood floor make sure you get one of the newest varnishes that are wear and water resistant, easily applied by brush or preferably by a long-handled roller which you can use standing up. These new varnishes come in true or dull colors, in all wood shades from mahogany to light oak and walnut. They are quick drying, safe and non-slippery and never require waxing.

Other new products to look for are:

> Multipurpose tinting colors that come in tubes and cans, are convenient and dependable for tinting and shading oil base and alkyd paints and enamels. All you do is add tinting color to a small portion of the paint, mix well, then blend thoroughly into the remainder.
>
> Antique spray kit that comes with a base color, and a gold paint which is sprayed on afterwards for an antique finish. Base colors include white, black, red, green, blue and silver. You simply spray with the base color coat, as much as you want. Then immediately apply final coat of gold or texturing for the finish. You can vary the finished effect by holding the can at different distances from the piece you are spraying. There is no waiting — for example you can antique a chair in seven minutes.

This old wicker basket was given a new lease on life through a touch of paint—and in a few minutes it was transformed into an attractive bedroom chest. Base of basket was sprayed dark blue, lid dark red. When paint was dry, unusual brass lock was added for an elegant touch. Dress up old pieces in this way, whether it's a chair, an old chest, a trunk or a kitchen table.

Antique Them...Reclaim Marred, Scratched, Stained Furniture

HANDSOME PAINTED FURNITURE accents are no longer out of the financial reach of the homemaker. A new kit of materials makes it possible for you to create your own at little cost. The materials, called Provincial color glaze, have been developed by the manufacturer for do-it-yourselfers to achieve their own "master craftsman" effects. Old, as well as new, unfinished furniture can be done at home in an antique finish.

The kit is complete with undercoat, color glaze, brush, sandpaper, steel wool, and cheesecloth — all the materials needed to antique one chest or two chairs. There is a complete book of instructions.

Homemakers, busy with varied activities, don't have to worry about spending time removing old finishes. The Provincial color glaze process makes it unnecessary to take off varnish, old paint, or stain. You paint the undercoat right over marred, scarred, checked, or fogged finishes. In fact, they help to create the shaded, grainy antiqued effect.

You simply remove knobs and handles, wash dust and grime off with soap and water, if necessary, or clean away oil or wax with turpentine or mineral spirits, and lightly sand for better paint adhesion.

Provincial color glaze application is basically 1-2-3 steps. First a piece of furniture is painted with an undercoat and then allowed to dry for 24 hours. Then the glaze is brushed on. In the third step, the glaze is wiped. The kit comes in 18 colors, six wood tones, six delicate pale tints and six vibrant deep tones.

Wood Tones Transform Second-hand-me-downs to Elegant Mellowness

One of the new wood tone finishes was used at home to transform the old bedroom piece, shown in the first photograph, into the handsome wood-patterned desk shown in the second shot. The dressing table and chair were picked up at a secondhand store and reclaimed with fruitwood, one of the six colors of wood tones. These paints can also be used on new, unfinished furniture, and on old or new trim and paneling to create subtle shadings and subdued wood patterns.

PART SEVEN

Housekeeping Routine and Household Information

❧

A well-planned kitchen, however large or small, takes the backache out of kitchen routine. This small, gay kitchen was expertly designed for maximum efficiency. Wall over sink, work tops, refrigerator and cooking elements were all aligned to save time and wasted effort. Drawers and storage cupboards underneath L-shaped work tops are handy and roomy; black painted hood is decorative as well as practical for instant removal of fumes and cooking odors. Antique cooking utensils are effective on brick wall, blue painted wood-work adds color. Final touch of luxury is the carpeted floor, an idea that certainly makes life easier for the woman of the house. The carpet is made of wear-resistant, easy-to-clean filament nylon, so it's practical as well.

CHAPTER THIRTY-FIVE

Housekeeping Management

SOME WOMEN ARE lucky enough to be born housekeepers, with efficiency at their fingertips. Nothing phases them and they breeze through their household chores without a care in the world, and in next to no time. Others find the whole household routine baffling, a stumbling block, and fight a constant battle against disorder and the clock. This is not a sin by any means, for we all have varying talents. A bad housekeeper might be a gourmet cook and a talented decorator, or vice versa.

However, the household routine can be simplified and chaos avoided through a little planning — which takes the minimum of effort. Here are some quick pointers which will help you get that household routine under control and, what's more, running smoothly. Once you have put them into operation, you'll find that you have more leisure hours during the day, as well as a contented husband and family.

Household Bookkeeping

IT IS QUITE simple to keep track of how much you are spending on food and other household necessities, if you set up a kitchen bookkeeping system and stick to it. There is nothing more harrowing for a housewife than those constant family battles about where the money disappears and on what. Such battles can be eliminated with your own do-it-yourself bookkeeping system. And it doesn't have to be very involved.

All you need is a large hook and a notebook. Screw the hook into the inside of the door of a handy storage cupboard, preferably above a work top where you unpack groceries and other goods. Before you even unpack supplies, simply put the bill which arrives with the goods onto the hook. At the end of the week, take down all the bills, add them up and enter the total into your notebook. At the end of the month you can check the store's final bill with your own figures, and be sure they match up. You will also have your household expenditures at your finger tips, as a quick and easy reference.

If you do not have charge accounts for supplies of this kind, still make use of the bookkeeping system. It will help you to know just how much you are spending monthly, whether or not you are keeping within your budget, as well as give you an accounting of what you are buying.

The same system can be adopted for other household spending, on such things as cleaning materials, brushes, brooms, mops and general kitchen utensils. Either use a hook behind the door of the storage closet where you keep your cleaning materials, or put the bills into a folder which can be left in a handy drawer. Whichever system you use, the effort involved is minimal and you'll be surprised how much time and temper it saves at the end of the month.

Kitchen Filing System

Do you know what you have in your kitchen cupboards, and more importantly exactly where it is all stored? Or do you waste hours a week looking for supplies you *know* you once bought, but can't find? This means canned foods, cleaning materials, extra utensils and linens.

If you *do* have haphazard cupboards and drawers, spend a day reorganizing them, using a kitchen-goods filing system. Again this is not as complicated as it might sound.

If you have enough room, start by taking everything out of the food cupboards. Now sort out the canned goods from those which are in constant use, such as spices, flavorings, flour, sugar, coffee, vinegar, sauces and ketchups. After you have relined all the shelves with shelf paper, put all the items you use for cooking every day in the cupboard nearest your oven or work top. Place canned foods in top cupboards, particularly goods you use rarely.

Treat your drawers in the same way. Buy several plastic cutlery trays from the five-and-dime, use one for cooking utensils such as mixing spoons, can openers, bottle openers, cooking knives and forks; separate table flatware and keep it in a tray in another drawer. Select a drawer for all kitchen linens, such as towels, dishcloths, and glasscloths; another for insulated mittens and cloths you use for removing hot pans from the oven. Make sure these are in handy reach of the oven or open cooking elements.

If you don't have wall rollers for kitchen paper towels, cooking foil or other food wrapping paper, keep them altogether in a low-placed cupboard, along with new paper garbage bags, food bags and foil.

In other words, make your kitchen cupboards work as efficiently as an office filing cabinet. It's also a good idea to make a list of canned goods and pin it onto the inside door of the cupboard. In this way you can tell at a quick glance what you have in stock. As you use items, simply check them off your cupboard listing.

The Deep Freeze

FREEZERS, LIKE HOUSEHOLD routines and family budgets, must be managed if you are to get the most out of your freezer space. Like everything else, good freezer management starts with a plan. No one can really tell you what your plan should be, as every family's needs differ. However, here are a few good pointers on freezer management.

a. Number in the family, children, their ages and dietary needs.
b. Any other special diet requirements of the family.
c. Family likes and dislikes in food.
d. Amount and kind, if any, of homegrown food available.
e. Amount and kind of home entertaining done.
f. Your own work schedule.
g. Capacity of freezer, comparative savings to be had by freezing various foods.
h. Only freeze foods you need and use often.
i. Keep freezer full or nearly full all the time. A freezer is a large investment, and the more you use the space, the lower your cost per unit.
j. Use freezer every day. Quick turnover of all foods except seasonal ones means an economical operation.
k. Keep an inventory. Knowing what you have helps you plan more interesting meals, also insures foods are used within maximum storage limits.

Good packaging techniques are important when you prepare food for freezing. These techniques protect food against moisture loss and transfer of flavors.

Your collection of freezer packaging equipment should include the following items. Sheet wrapping; plastic, metal or waxed paperboard containers in a variety of sizes; plastic bags; freezer tape and freezer marking crayon. Containers should preferably be reusable and not too expensive. The flat-sided type make for better use of storage space, and ovenware casserole dishes and loaf pans are also convenient for many prepared dishes which need reheating in the oven.

"Saran wrap" is a good sheet wrapping to use. It is pliable and can be molded closely to the object you're wrapping for maximum exclusion of air. It is air-and-moisture-vapor resistant, holds moisture inside the package, keeps air out and gives no odor or flavor to the product wrapped. Because it is transparent, foods can be identified at a glance. However, after sealing the package with freezer tape, it is a good idea to mark on the tape the name of the product and the date it was put down. As you put down food, copy the product and date of freezing into your inventory book, so you know its maximum storage limits. The quickest, easiest way to make a freezer food inventory is with a loose-leaf notebook, broken up into sections marked or headlined for meats, fish, poultry, vegetables, pies, bread and other baked goods, total meals, soups, stews and ice cream. Under each heading jot down the date and description of product, so you know quickly and easily what you have and when it should be used.

How much stockpiling of food you do in general depends on many things. Storage space available, whether or not you have a freezer, budget and family needs. Your stockpiling food plan therefore has to be worked out to individual family requirements. But by using the bookkeeping system, kitchen filing plan and freezer or pantry inventory you can at least do it with the maximum efficiency.

Household Chores

YOUR CLEANING CHORES fall into four categories: daily, weekly, monthly and seasonal. The easiest way to conquer chores is to work out your own plan and stay with it systematically. Once again, individual factors, such as the size of your family and your home, determine your cleaning chores and the way they should be planned. A system which applies to one housewife will be useless to another.

However, by breaking up the chores into four categories you will be able to arrive at your own successful routine. Here are some quick pointers.

1. DAILY: Most homes, large or small, require daily surface cleaning, such as bed making, dusting, vacuuming, dish washing and minimum laundry. Keep surface dirt, dust, grime and simple chores in check, so they don't get out of hand.
2. WEEKLY: Keep a day for the laundry and ironing. By doing it in one fell swoop it gets out of the way much quicker than stretching it over several days. Once a week, sponge-wipe finger marks off woodwork, in as many rooms as you can, so that they are kept in check.

3. MONTHLY: Once a month give one or two rooms a thorough cleaning. Look for small repair jobs that need doing, covers that need cleaning. Go through cupboards, closets and drawers, discard old magazines, newspapers, other items you have been hoarding.
4. SEASONAL: If you have kept to your daily, weekly and monthly system you will find that your seasonal cleaning is almost non-existent. In the spring all you have to do is send drapes and slipcovers that *really* need it to the dry cleaners, have rugs or carpets shampooed, do touch-up jobs on paintwork, replace winter drapes and slipcovers with summer ones, if you have two sets.

In other words, spring cleaning, as our mothers knew it, is a thing of the past if the work load is spread out over the year. The same applies to winter cleaning. In the fall, all you will have to do is change drapes and slipcovers, store garden or patio furniture and rearrange the linen closet.

CHAPTER THIRTY-SIX

Accident Prevention in the Home

ALMOST AS MANY accidents occur in the home as they do on the outside. And most of them are caused through carelessness or lack of knowledge, and of course need never have happened at all.

The home is full of accident hazards, which can easily be removed through a little thought and planning. Use this spot-check to see just how safe a place your home is, and if necessary make changes at once.

1. Are area and scatter rugs firmly anchored to the floor with non-skid devices?
2. Are hard floor surfaces polished with non-skid wax?
3. Are stair treads firmly anchored in position at all times?
4. Is staircase carpet well laid so that it does not work loose?
5. Do all your staircases have solid handrails?
6. Is lighting adequate in all dark spots, such as top of stairs, dark corridors, landings and on steps and paths outside?
7. Is all your electrical equipment in tip-top shape?
8. Are all unused electrical outlets covered?
9. Do you have a sturdy handrail next to shower or bath and a corrugated rubber mat inside bath to prevent slips and falls?
10. Do you have insulated mittens, safety tongs and strainers for handling pots of hot food and liquids in the kitchen?
11. Do you always turn pot handles toward the back of the range out of the way of curious children?

12. Are all walls within 3 ft. of range insulated with fire-resistant material?
13. Do you keep matches in a fire-resistant container out of the reach of children?
14. Do you always make sure cigarette stubs and matches are out before disposing of them?
15. Do you have fireplace screens to prevent flying sparks and embers?
16. Do you have a sturdy stepladder or stepstool for reaching up into high cupboards?
17. Do you keep all stairs and steps free of toys or other items to prevent falls?
18. Do you have a fire extinguisher?
19. Do you keep it in a handy place?
20. Do you make sure razor blades and broken glass or china are all unexposed when thrown out?

Children, even more than adults, are prone to accidents in the home. Check the following lists, prepared by The Children's Hospital Medical Center of Boston, to make sure *your* home is a safe place.

Safety List for Mothers

1. Do you put all medicines (particularly "candy aspirin" and tranquilizers) safely away after you have used them?
2. Do you read the label on medicine bottles each time you give your child a dose?
3. Are all glasses used by your children made of unbreakable material?
4. Are all poisons (any non-food, lye, cleaning agents, ammonia which can be eaten or drunk) stored out of reach of children? Not on floor, in low cabinets, or under sink?
5. Do you turn your pot handles toward the back of the stove? If possible, do you remove your burner knobs when not using the stove?
6. Are the electric cords of your moveable appliances (electric coffee pots, frying pans, toaster, etc.) out of reach of toddlers, so no one can trip on them? And the baby can't chew the cord?
7. Are all baby toys free of splinters and too big to be swallowed?
8. Do you keep the baby and his toys off the kitchen floor when the kitchen is being used?
9. Are your pins, tacks, needles, nuts and popcorn out of reach of pre-school children?
10. Is the high chair or playpen at least two feet away from your working counters in the kitchen?
11. Are your matches and table lighters out of reach of pre-school children?
12. Are your knives and pointed scissors out of reach of your children?

13. Do you stay with your pre-school child when he is in the bathtub?
14. Do you always keep your fireplace screen in place?
15. Do you slow down and take extra care in the 4-7 p.m. hours, when everyone is tired and hungry?
16. Do you slow down and take extra precautions when you are ill, pregnant or menstruating?

Safety List for Fathers

1. Are all poisons (any non-food, kerosene, insecticides, fertilizer which can be eaten or drunk) stored out of reach of children? Not on floor, in low cabinets, or under sink?
2. Do you have a gate at the head and foot of stairs to prevent your child from falling down or climbing up?
3. Are your furniture and lamps heavy enough so that they can't be pulled over easily?
4. Are your hot radiators and pipes covered or insulated?
5. Are your electric cords in good condition? Neither frayed nor damaged?
6. Are your unused electric outlets fitted with dummy plugs?
7. Do you keep electrical devices (radios, electric light pulls, etc.) away from your bathtub?
8. Are your second floor windows properly screened or barred to keep your children from falling out?
9. Are your scatter rugs firmly lined so that they won't slip?
10. Are the stairs well-lighted and fitted with firm handrails and treads?
11. Are your attic and basement free of oily rags and litter?
12. Are any firearms in the home unloaded and locked up?
13. Are porch railings secure?
14. Are garden sprays non-poisonous?
15. Are clotheslines strung out of reach of the children?
16. Are swings and play equipment made of strong but safe materials?

If you have answered "no" to any of the questions on the two lists, make some changes. Your house may have other dangers. Think carefully about these too.

Poison Hazards: How to Avoid Poisoning

**Recognize that a lot of little troubles add up to big ones. Try to take extra precautions when everything begins to go wrong. If you're sick, emotionally upset, menstruating or pregnant, keep a watchful eye.

**If you have pre-school children, remember they love to put everything in their mouths (mouthing is part of their normal growth and a way of learning about things). Toddlers will eat or drink anything. They have been known to drink a whole tin of kerosene without minding the taste.

**If your child sucks or chews "on everything" provide him with safe chewable objects like celery sticks.

**Beware of the dangers of baby or "candy flavored" aspirin. A bottle of 50 can kill a child. Unlike other poisons such as ammonia or floor polishes, "candy" aspirin tastes good and a child will not only eat it if it's lying around, but will search it out on high shelves or in the medicine chest. When urging a feverish child to take baby aspirin, don't tell him it's "just like candy." Say it's a "medicine."

**If you have pre-school children, be sure to store all potential poisons out of reach. Put your medicines away after using them. Most children get poisons from these four places: (1) under the sink or on kitchen shelves (polishes, cleaning agents); (2) bedside or living room table tops (medicines, lighter fluid); (3) the bathroom (lotions, medicines); (4) the basement, back porch or garage (insecticides, paint thinners).

**Be particularly careful when you are moving or going on vacation. Medicines and other poisons are apt to be out of their normal places.

**Young children love to explore pocketbooks. If you carry pills in your pocketbook, be careful where you leave it.

Now check the following list, for poison hazards.

General Safety List

1. Do you store your drugs and household chemicals out of reach of children?
2. Do you put all medicine (particularly candy aspirin and tranquilizers) safely away after using them?
3. Do you read the label on medicine before you give any to your child?
4. Do you keep all drugs, household chemicals and detergents on shelves where no food is stored?
5. Do you throw away old containers that once held poison without re-using them?
6. If you transfer drugs, pills or poisonous substances, do you label the new container?
7. Do you flush old medicines down the toilet instead of throwing them in the trash can?
8. Do you tell children that aspirin is "medicine" not "candy"?
9. Do you always give or take medicines with the lights on, never in the dark?

10. Have you checked your jewelry to be sure you have no jequirity beads?
11. Do you take extra precautions with poisons in times of illness or stress?

If you have answered "no" to any of these questions, make some changes at once. And check the safety lists regularly to make sure poisons cannot get into the hands of children.

Poisons and Antidotes

WHAT IS POISONOUS? You will be surprised at the number of seemingly innocent substances in your home which are deadly in the hands of the young.

Today there are over 250,000 potential poisons which you can buy in your neighborhood stores. And many poisonous substances are in your home which are not labeled "poison."

They are particularly poisonous to children because their small bodies can't absorb as much as those of adults.

Poisoning really depends on the amount swallowed and the size of the person who swallows it, which is why children are so vulnerable.

Aspirin is by far the most common poison — the next nine most common are insecticides, bleach, detergents and cleaning agents, furniture polish, kerosene, vitamin and iron pills and syrups, disinfectants strong acids and alkalies (lye), and laxatives.

If your child has swallowed any of the following substances *DO NOT MAKE HIM VOMIT*. (They may rupture the esophagus or pass into the lungs and damage them.) *TAKE HIM TO THE NEAREST DOCTOR OR HOSPITAL AT ONCE*. And also remember, in all instances of poisoning, to take with you the bottle or box that contained the poison.

HOUSEHOLD ITEMS:

ammonia	metal cleaner
bleach	typewriter cleaner
drain cleaner	gun cleaner
oven cleaner	grease remover
toilet bowl cleaner	carbolic acid disinfectants
corn and wart remover	strychnine rat poison
furniture polish	strong acids

PAINT THINNERS AND FUEL OIL:

washing soda	gasoline
turpentine	lighter fluid
paint thinner	wood preservatives
kerosene	brush cleaner

SPECIAL POISONS:

LEAD PAINT — tastes like candy and is poisonous if swallowed in small doses over a long period. Poisoning occurs because children chew on window sills or other painted areas. If your child "chews on everything," check with your doctor because lead poisoning must be treated before any symptoms appear.

BORIC ACID — is not valuable for treating diaper rash or any common ailment. Poisoning occurs because it is mistaken for a baby's formula mix, or used to treat diaper rash. *Do not keep boric acid in the house.*

OTHER POISONS:

These substances are poisonous to children, but may be vomited. If he swallows any of these, call your doctor or hospital for advice. *You will probably be told to make your child vomit.*

HOUSEHOLD ITEMS:

antifreeze	denatured alcohol	hair dye
camphor	after-shave lotion	perfume
arsenic rat poison	permanent wave solution	liquor
D.D.T. insect poisons	nail polish	beer

MEDICINES:

aspirin	sleeping drugs
"pep" drugs	paregoric
iron pills and syrup	laxatives
reducing medicine	iodine
some douche preparations	eye medicine (atrophine)
vitamins	heart medicines

VOMITING METHODS:

1. Give him Syrup of Ipecac. Dose: 1 tablespoon. Follow this with a glass of milk.
2. Give him a glass of milk, then put a blunt spoon handle down his throat while you hold him face down across your lap.

   After he has vomited, have him drink milk and take him to the nearest doctor or hospital. *If he doesn't vomit within 15 minutes* give him milk and take him to the hospital.

SUSPECTED POISONING:

If you don't know whether the substance your child swallowed is poisonous, call your Poison Center or doctor immediately. They can tell you at once.

CHAPTER THIRTY-SEVEN

Children's First Aid Directory

WHAT DO YOU do if your child *does* have an accident in his home surroundings? The Children's Hospital Medical Center in Boston gave us some of their golden rules for First Aid.

If an accident does occur, don't underestimate the injury. The Children's Hospital Medical Center accident study shows that fewer than fifty percent of the parents were even "very concerned" about the injury at the time it was discovered, regardless of its severity. On the other hand observe the situation carefully before doing anything. Then follow these rules. To grab up a child with fractures, hemorrhage or internal injuries and rush to the hospital may compound his injuries.

THINGS TO KEEP ON HAND IN A FIRST AID BOX

FOR BITES: Calamine Lotion.

FOR BURNS: A roll of thin clear plastic wrapping (ordinarily used to cover food). Plastic-covered gauze squares (1½ in. x 2 ins., 2 ins. x 3 ins., 3 ins. x 4 ins.).
Vaseline.

FOR CUTS: Sterile gauze squares (2 ins. x 2 ins. and 4 ins. x 4 ins.) individually wrapped.
Roll of gauze bandage (2 ins. wide).
Roll of adhesive tape.
Adhesive bandages (various sizes).

TO PRODUCE VOMITING: Ipecac: Syrup form only:
Dose: 1 tablespoon for 1-4 year old.

FOR FRACTURES: Splints (various lengths).

Bites

Insect Bites: Apply cold compresses to help limit the swelling of a bite. Apply calamine lotion to control itching. Your doctor should be consulted if you want to use other medications.

If the swelling, regardless of size, is confined to the area of the sting, it is not a serious matter. Watch the child for other symptoms. If the child develops symptoms elsewhere in the body such as hives and itching, difficulty in breathing or swallowing, or abdominal pain, call your doctor to take your child into the hospital immediately.

Tick and Leech Bites: Do not remove ticks or leeches with bare fingers. Apply the lighted end of a cigarette to the tick or leech or cover them with oil or petroleum jelly. This cuts off their air supply and makes them drop off.

Snake Bites: If the snake is non-poisonous, no treatment is necessary. If the snake is poisonous, work fast. Apply a restricting band above the bite (not too tight) and put something cold on the bite. Take the child to a doctor as soon as possible. Keep him as quiet as possible. If you live in a snake area, consult your local authorities for preventive advice.

Animal Bites: Any bite by an animal (dog, cat, bat, etc.) should be reported to your doctor at once.

Make every effort to locate the animal. DO NOT KILL the animal. He may not show signs of rabies immediately, and should be kept under observation.

Dogs in the U.S.A. seldom carry rabies. Bats, rats and foxes are more common carriers of this disease.

Human Bites: Human bites may often result in severe infection and should be treated by a doctor, if the skin is broken.

Burns

IF A CHILD's clothing catches fire, smother the flames by wrapping the child in a rug or blanket.

For Minor Burns Involving Small Areas: Apply no butter, ointment or salves to burns, except petroleum jelly. Wash the skin surrounding the burn (the burn itself is sterile) and cover with a thin layer of petroleum jelly and a sterile gauze square.

For Burns Involving Large Areas of the Body: Cover the child's burned areas with a thin plastic wrapping (it doesn't stick to the wound) or a clean sheet. Cover him with blankets, and take him to the nearest hospital. Because shock may occur fairly quickly, the child should be in the hospital as soon as possible. A child in shock becomes very pale, breathes rapidly and may lose consciousness. Prompt medical attention is essential.

Electrical Burns: Pull the child away from the source of the current with a board, wooden chair or other non-conductive material.

DO NOT USE BARE HANDS.

If a child is not breathing, apply mouth to mouth respiration as described under Drowning. Electrical burns may be much worse than they appear. Always consult your doctor. Electrical burns can be terribly serious, resulting in permanent deformity to face, mouth or hands. Extension cords (with pronged plugs at both ends) cause many of these deforming burns. If you have children, remove all double-plugged extension cords from your home. Safety cap all unused outlets.

Cuts

If Cut Is Slight: Wash it well with soap and warm water and apply a sterile dressing such as a gauze square or adhesive bandage. Don't apply sulfa, penicillin or antiseptic to cuts unless your doctor recommends it. Antiseptics are seldom as effective as a thorough washing with soap and water.

If Cut Is Extensive or Deep: Apply no medicine; cover the area with a clean bandage and call your doctor.

If A Cut Bleeds: Cover with a clean cloth or gauze bandage and apply pressure over the area with your hand. Many cuts, although not large or serious, will heal better and leave less scarring if stitched. They should be seen by your doctor.

In Cases of Heavy Bleeding: Apply direct pressure to the wound with your hand. In almost all cases, direct pressure is preferable and as effective as using a tourniquet. A tourniquet, improperly used, is dangerous.

When Wounds Occur Out of Doors: Tetanus (lockjaw) may be a severe or fatal complication, unless your child has been previously immunized against tetanus or has had a recent booster shot. All babies should receive a series of tetanus inoculations before they are a year old.

Drownings

REMOVE THE CHILD from the water. Don't leave the child to get help. Immediate and continuous artificial respiration is all important. Place him face down on the ground or floor to allow as much water as possible to drain out. If he is breathing and coughing, he will clear the water out of his lungs himself. No further treatment is necessary. If he has stopped breathing, allow water to drain out for a moment and then start artificial respiration.

Mouth to Mouth Respiration

1. Place the child on his back.
2. Quickly wipe any fluid, vomit, mucus or foreign matter from his mouth with your fingers.
3. Tilt the head back so the chin is pointing upwards. Pull lower jaw forward to keep tongue out of airway.
4. Open your mouth wide and place it tightly over the child's open mouth. At the same time pinch his nose shut. (If the victim is a baby or small child, place your mouth over the child's mouth AND nose, making a relatively leakproof seal.) Blow into child's mouth.
5. Remove your mouth, turn your head to one side and listen for the return rush of air.
6. Keep blowing and listening alternately. For an adult or older child, blow vigorously at the rate of about 12 breaths per minute. For a baby or small child, blow relatively shallow puffs at the rate of about 20 per minute.
7. If after a few minutes the child does not return air, recheck the head and jaw position. If you still do not get air exchange, turn the child on his side and give several sharp blows between the shoulder blades to jar foreign matter loose.
8. Continue the artificial respiration until the child is definitely breathing for himself.

   While administering mouth to mouth respiration, get someone else to call the fire department, police or Coast Guard for a respirator.

Foreign Objects

In Eye: Particles of soot, dirt, dust. Lay the child on his back; hold his eye open with your fingers and pour large amounts of warm water into it. In most cases, flooding the eye with warm water is more effective than attempting to remove particles with the corner of a handkerchief. If a single large particle is present, this may be removed more easily with the corner of a dry clean handkerchief. Be careful not to scrape or rub the eyeball.

If a foreign object (pencil, splinters, etc.) *penetrates* the eyeball, cover the eye loosely with a clean cloth or sterile gauze, and call your doctor immediately, or take the child to the nearest hospital.

In Ear or Nose: Call your doctor. Don't attempt to remove any foreign object from the ear or nose. You may do more harm than good.

In Throat: (swallowing a foreign object.) If the child is not choking, he is in no immediate danger. Most foreign objects that are swallowed pass through the intestine without difficulty.

If the child is *choking and gasping for breath,* turn him upside down, holding him by the legs or ankles, and slap his back vigorously. If this is not effective, take him to the nearest hospital as quickly as possible. Do not push your finger down his throat blindly since this may force it farther down.

In Skin: Remove a small splinter by cleansing the area with soap and water and alcohol and extracting it INTACT with a small pair of tweezers. If the splinter is deeply embedded, don't try to remove it yourself. Take your child to the doctor.

Fractures

IF YOUR CHILD has fallen and has pain, do not move him until you have some idea of the location and degree of the injury. Remember that a child with broken bones may have other injuries.

If the injury is obviously severe, *do not move the child.* Keep him warm and call for expert help.

If it is necessary to move a child with an obvious *fracture of the leg,* give the leg constant support. Strap the injured leg to the other leg at several levels above and below the injury or apply a splint.

If a *fracture of the arm* is suspected, apply a sling before you move the child.

If the *neck or back* is injured, keep the child flat and *make no attempt to move him* until medical help arrives.

If the skin over a fracture is broken *(compound fracture)* place sterile gauze over the wound and get medical assistance immediately. If it is necessary to control bleeding, apply pressure with your hand over the dressing.

Give the child nothing to eat or drink if he has a possible fracture. He may require an anesthetic and recent eating would complicate this.

Internal Injury: If a child has had a bad fall or has been hit by a car, baseball bat or other hard instrument, there is always the danger of internal injury. Internal injury can be very serious and is not always apparent. If the child complains of persistent *pain* or if he turns *pale,* he may have an internal injury. Call your doctor.

Head Injuries

IF A CHILD has a bad head injury or is unconscious, take him to a doctor or hospital *immediately.*

Even if a head blow seems minor, watch the child to see if any of these symptoms develop: drowsiness, paleness, vomiting, or bleeding from the nose, mouth or ears.

Ask him if he has a headache. See if he has any difficulty moving an arm and leg on one side or the other.

If any of the above factors are present, call your doctor right away.

Don't give your child anything to eat or drink until you have talked with the doctor.

Unconsciousness may seem like deep sleep. If he is sleeping very heavily, wake him to make certain he is not unconscious.

Small scalp cuts, while not necessarily serious, may bleed a lot. Control bleeding by applying direct pressure over the wound and take the child to the doctor. Even small cuts may require stitches.

CONVULSIONS:

If a child has a convulsion (as a result of a head injury or for other reasons), quickly place a wooden pencil or some other firm object between his back teeth so he won't bite his tongue. Be sure this is placed well to one side to keep the airway open. Then turn the child on his side, so that saliva or vomit will run out of his mouth, not into his lungs.

If the child's breathing is very noisy, make sure his tongue is not blocking his airway. Pull the tongue out and to one side with your fingers.

Protect the child with pillows or other soft objects to keep him from hurting himself. Make sure he can't fall off the bed or car seat.

Observe the child carefully so that you can describe the convulsion to the doctor. If possible, notice where the convulsion starts (one side of the face or in one arm or leg; may begin with one eye blinking or with stomach pain.) Your description will help the doctor diagnose the trouble.

A convulsion can be frightening, but try to stay calm. The limbs stiffen and then jerk, the lips and face may turn blue, and the eyes roll up. The convulsion will probably end by itself in a few minutes.

NOSEBLEEDS:

In a sitting position, the child should blow his nose to remove all clots and blood. Now insert into the bleeding nostril a wedge of cotton moistened with water or any of the common nose drops. With the finger against the outside of the nostril, apply firm pressure for five minutes. If bleeding stops, leave packing in place. If it persists, call your doctor.

CHAPTER THIRTY-EIGHT

Removing Stains From Fabrics

LEARN THE SIMPLE methods for removing stains at home. Then act promptly when a fabric is stained. Many stains that can be removed easily when they are fresh are difficult or impossible to remove later, particularly after they are set by heat.

Selecting the Method of Removal

Successful stain removal starts with the selection of a method of stain removal that is suited to both stain and fabric.

Kind of Stain: Identify the stain, if possible. The treatment for one kind of stain may set another. If you can't determine what caused the stain it will help if you can tell whether it is a greasy stain, a nongreasy stain, or a combination of the two.

Directions for removing these three main types of stains and for removing individual stains are given here.

Kind of Fabric: Before using any stain remover be sure it will not harm the fabric.

In general, the stain removers recommended will not damage the fibers in fabrics or most special fabric finishes. There are exceptions, however, which should be noted. Exceptions are listed in the description of the various kinds of stain removers and, where necessary, in the directions for removing individual stains.

Some stain removers that do not damage fibers may change the appearance of the treated area so that it looks as bad as or worse than the original stain. They may, for example, cause fading or bleeding of dyes, loss of luster, shrinkage or stretching of the fabric. They may remove nonpermanent finishes or designs. It is often difficult to use any stain remover on such fabrics as satins, crepes, taffetas, silk and rayon moires, gabardines, and velvets without causing some change in appearance.

To determine whether a stain remover will change the appearance of the fabric to be treated, test it first. Test on a sample of the material, if possible, or on a hidden part of the article—a seam allowance, hem, inside of pocket, or tail of a blouse or shirt.

If the substance needed to remove the stain will damage the fiber or change the appearance of the fabric, send the stained article to a professional dry cleaner. He has the skill, the special equipment, and the reagents that enable him to handle many of the more difficult stains and fabrics.

Treating the Stain

Find the specific directions for removing a stain. If you need more detailed information about the remover recommended, including complete directions for applying it, you will find this on the following pages.

Follow directions accurately. Use solutions only in the strengths recommended and for the length of time given.

Work carefully and patiently. Often results depend as much on the way the job is done as on the remover used.

Observe all precautions given for the use of removers that are flammable, that give off poisonous vapors, or that are poisonous if swallowed.

Stain Removers and How To Use Them

To be prepared to remove all the different kinds of stains, you will need to keep four types of removers on hand—absorbent materials, detergents, solvents, and chemical stain removers, such as bleaches.

Although some stains can be removed with only one type of remover, more often removers of two or more types are needed.

You will also need miscellaneous supplies, such as bowls, medicine droppers, and a small syringe.

Keep stain-removal supplies in a place that is convenient but out of the reach of children. Label clearly poisonous and flammable removers.

Absorbent Materials

USEFUL ABSORBENT MATERIALS are absorbent powders, absorbent cotton, sponges, and white or fast-color paper towels, facial tissues, and soft cloths.

How to Use Absorbent Powders

Cornstarch, cornmeal, talc, or powdered chalk will remove some fresh stains, such as grease spatters. They are also used with solvents.

Spread absorbent powder over the stain before it dries. Remove powder as it absorbs the stain by shaking or brushing it off; or use the upholstery attachment of a vacuum cleaner.

After surface stain has been removed, work fresh powder into the stain, then remove as before. Repeat with fresh powder until as much stain as possible has been absorbed.

It may be difficult to use this method successfully on some dark colored articles that cannot be washed. If the white powder cannot be completely removed it may be more conspicuous on dark material than the original stain.

How to Use Other Absorbent Materials

Absorbent cloths, absorbent cotton, absorbent paper, blotters, and sponges can be used to soak up staining liquids before they soak into a fabric. If much of the liquid can be absorbed quickly, the stain will be smaller and easier to remove than it would be otherwise. This technique will work only on fabrics that absorb the staining liquid slowly. It is often useful on such articles as rugs, upholstered furniture, and heavy coats.

To use these absorbents, hold the material so that the liquid is absorbed rather than forced into the fabric. If the stain is not greasy you may be able to remove some of the liquid that has soaked into the fabric by adding a little water to the stain and absorbing this immediately with the absorbent material. Repeat as long as any stain is absorbed.

These materials are also used to absorb stains as they are loosened from fabrics by liquid stain removers.

Detergents

DETERGENTS—SOAPS AND synthetic detergents (syndets)—will remove many nongreasy stains and some greasy stains. They act as lubricants, coating insoluble particles of staining material (such as carbon and colored pigments) with a smooth, slippery film. The particles can then be rinsed out of the fabric.

Liquid detergents are especially useful. They are in the concentrated form needed to remove stains, and can be easily worked into the fabric and rinsed out of it.

How to Use Detergents on Washable Articles

For surface stains, rub a detergent lightly into the dampened spot or rub in liquid detergent. Rinse the stained area or wash the article as usual.

If a stain is deeply imbedded, work the detergent thoroughly into the fabric. One way to do this is to rub detergent lightly into the stained area, then, holding the fabric with both hands, work the stained area back and forth between your thumbs. Bend the yarns sharply so that the individual fibers in the yarn rub against one another. It is this bending of yarns, rather than rubbing the surface of the fabric, that is effective in removing the stain. Go over the entire stained area in this way. Then rinse thoroughly.

On articles such as rugs, on heavy fabrics that cannot be bent easily, or on woolen fabrics that might be felted by too much bending of the yarn, work the detergent into the fabric with the edge of the bowl of a spoon.

How to Use Detergents on Nonwashable Articles

Work detergent into the stained area in the same way for washable articles. Dilute liquid detergents with an equal volume of water. Use as little detergent as possible because it is difficult to remove excess detergent without wetting a large area of the fabric. Rinse thoroughly by sponging spot with cool water or by forcing water through the stain with a syringe. If alcohol is safe for the fabric, use it to rinse out the detergent. It is easier to rinse out the detergent with alcohol, and the fabric will dry more quickly.

Solvents

MANY COMMON STAINS can be removed with the right solvent. Different kinds of solvents are needed for nongreasy and for greasy stains. Water is the most useful solvent for many common nongreasy stains, and it is the only solvent that is neither flammable nor poisonous. When using other solvents, follow carefully the safety precautions listed.

With the exceptions of acetone and trichloroethylene, the solvents recommended will not dissolve or seriously damage the fibers in fabrics. They may, however, change the appearance of the fabric so much that the article is no longer usable. Solvents may dissolve dyes and finishes or cause other changes, such as dulling of the luster and shrinking or stretching of the treated area. Test to be sure the solvent will not change the appearance of the treated area.

To test, use a solvent on a swatch of similar material or on a hidden part of the article exactly as you would to remove a stain.

Solvents for Nongreasy Stains

Water or water with a detergent will remove many nongreasy stains.

Acetone or amyl acetate, alcohol, and turpentine are needed for other nongreasy stains. All are available at drug and hardware stores.

Acetone is used for removing such stains as fingernail polish and ballpoint ink. It should not be used on acetate, Arnel, Dynel, or Verel. Flammable. Poison.

Alcohol (rubbing) is used for a number of stains if it is safe for the dye in the fabric. It should be diluted with two parts of water for use on acetate. Flammable. Poison.

Amyl acetate (chemically pure) is used for the same stains as acetone; it can be used on fabrics that are damaged by acetone. However, impure (technical grade) amyl acetate may damage the same fabrics as acetone. Flammable. Poison.

Turpentine is used on paint stains. Flammable. Poison.

Grease Solvents

Special solvents, such as those used by dry cleaners, are needed for greasy stains. These are available at drug, grocery, and auto-supply stores.

No solvents are available that will effectively remove greasy spots without hazard to the user. Some are flammable. All of those commonly used are poisonous. Serious illness or death can result from swallowing the liquids or from breathing too large an amount of the vapors. Information concerning the degree of toxicity of the different types of grease solvents is given in the discussion below.

Because of the hazards of toxicity and flammability the use of large amounts of these solvents in the home is not recommended. *Use only in small amounts and take the precautions listed.*

Nonflammable: Carbon tetrachloride, methyl chloroform, perchloroethylene and trichloroethylene are nonflammable grease solvents. They may be sold under these names or under various trade names. Trichloroethylene should not be used on Arnel or Kodel.

Carbon tetrachloride is the most hazardous to use because it takes less vapor from this solvent than from the others to poison the user and because the poisoning from it is cumulative. However, exposure to a high concentration of vapors from any of the nonflammable solvents is dangerous; vapors of all of them are more toxic to persons whose blood contains even a small amount of alcohol.

Because carbon tetrachloride is the most hazardous, use one of the other nonflammable solvents whenever possible. They are not, however, as readily available in small quantities as carbon tetrachloride.

Flammable: Petroleum naphthas are the most used of the flammable grease solvents. They are sold under this name or under various trade names. Use only a naphtha with a high flashpoint (the higher the flashpoint, the less easily the naphtha can be ignited).

Do not use naphthas near an open flame or where there is a chance that sparks from electrical equipment or from static electricity may ignite the solvent or vapors. Never use naphthas in a washing machine or put articles that have been cleaned with naphtha in a dryer.

Although the vapors from these solvents are not as poisonous as those of the nonflammable solvents, breathing large amounts of them is dangerous.

Mixtures: Many of the stain removers sold at grocery and drug stores under various brand names are mixtures of two or more grease solvents. They may contain both flammable and nonflammable kinds. The solvents used in these products can be changed without a change in the brand name.

Read the label carefully and observe all precautions listed by the manufacturer. If the label does not tell what solvents are in the product it is safer to assume that it may contain carbon tetrachloride and to observe all precautions for the use of that solvent.

How to Use Solvents

Place the stained area on a pad of soft cloth or other absorbent material. Place stained side down, if possible, so that the stain can be washed out of the fabric, not through it.

Dampen a pad of cotton or soft cloth with the solvent. Sponge the back of the stain with the pad. Repeated applications of only a small amount of solvent are better than a few applications of larger amounts.

Work from the center of the stain toward its outside edge, using light brushing or tamping motions. Professional dry cleaners have found that a fabric is less likely to ring if worked in this direction rather than from the outside edge toward the center. Avoid hard rubbing that might roughen the surface of the fabric. Sponge the stain irregularly around the edges so that there will be no definite line when the fabric dries.

Change the absorbent pad under the fabric and the pad used for sponging as soon as they are soiled to avoid transferring the stain back to the fabric.

For hardened stains (such as old paint or tar stains) place an absorbent pad or blotter dampened with the solvent on the stain. Allow time for the solvent to soften the stain; replace the pad as needed. Finish by sponging the stain.

For stains on delicate fabrics that cannot be sponged without chafing the surface or displacing the yarns, place an absorbent pad or blotter dampened with the solvent on the stain. Replace pad as needed. Do not sponge.

Dry fabrics as rapidly as possible.

On Fabrics That Tend to Form Rings: If a fabric tends to form rings when sponged with a solvent use either of the following methods.

(1) Use method previously described with these variations. Barely dampen the sponging pad with solvent. Apply only enough solvent to dampen fabric—not so much that solvent spreads out beyond point of application. Take extra care in sponging stain around edges, to make sure there will be no definite line when the fabric dries. Dry fabric as rapidly as possible. On some fabrics the formation of rings can be prevented by placing the treated area on a dry absorbent pad and rubbing it lightly with the palm of the hand; be sure the fabric is flat and free from wrinkles before you rub it. Or place it on the palm of one hand and rub it with the other. Rub with crosswise or lengthwise thread of the material.

(2) Or use a solvent-absorbent powder mixture. Add just enough solvent to cornstarch, talc, or other absorbent powder to make a thick crumbly mixture. To make sure the mixture is dry enough, test it first on a scrap of similar material. The solvent should not spread out on the cloth beyond the edge of the mixture.

Apply mixture over the stained area and work it into the fabric with gentle tamping or rubbing motions. Allow mixture to dry on the stain. Brush off and repeat if necessary.

It may be difficult to use this mixture successfully on some dark-colored articles that cannot be washed. If the white powder cannot be completely removed it may be more conspicuous on dark materials than the original stain. **To Remove Rings:** Once rings have formed on a fabric they may be difficult to remove.

If the article is washable, work a detergent thoroughly into the dampened ring as described. Then rinse thoroughly.

If the article is not washable you may be able to remove the ring by rubbing the fabric between your thumbs, or scratching it lightly with a fingernail. A solvent-absorbent powder mixture, used as described above, may also remove rings.

Precautions

When Using Any Solvent Except Water —
• Work out of doors or in a well-ventilated room (open several doors and windows).
• Do not breathe solvent vapors. Arrange work so that fumes are blown away from you, by a fan or breeze from an open door or window. Do not lean close to your work. Solvent vapors are heavier than air and tend to settle unless there is forced ventilation. Do not allow small children to play on the floor in a room where solvents are being used.
• Use only a small quantity of solvent at a time; keep bottle stoppered when

not in use. Unless you are working outdoors, do not pour solvents into an open bowl.

- If you spill solvent on your skin wash it off immediately.
- Observe any additional warnings given on labels of solvent containers.

In Addition, When Using Flammable Solvents —

- Do not use near open flames, including pilot lights on gas equipment.
- Do not use where there is a chance that sparks from electrical equipment or from static electricity may ignite the solvent or vapors. Never use flammable solvents in a washing machine. Never put articles that have been dampened with a flammable solvent in a dryer.

Store Solvents in a Safe Place

When solvents are not in use, keep them tightly stoppered in a place out of the reach of children. In addition to giving off poisonous fumes, solvents are also poisonous if swallowed.

Store flammable solvents where they cannot be ignited by flames or electric sparks.

Bleaches and Other Chemical Stain Removers

CHEMICAL STAIN REMOVERS will take out many stains that cannot be removed by absorbents, detergents, or solvents. The chemical removers react with such stains to form new compounds that are colorless or soluble, or both.

Because some may react with the fiber as well as with the stain, chemical removers are more likely to damage fabrics than the other types of removers. Test before using and follow carefully all directions for their use.

Kinds of Chemical Stain Removers

Chemical stain removers include bleaches, acetic acid, ammonia, iodine, oxalic acid, and sodium thiosulfate.

Bleaches: Bleaches are the most widely used of the chemical stain removers and the ones most likely to damage fibers and fade dyes if directions are not carefully followed. Bleaches should not be used in metal containers because metals may hasten the action of the bleach and thus increase the chance of fabric damage.

Four kinds of bleaches are recommended for home use — chlorine bleaches, sodium perborate, hydrogen peroxide, and color removers.

The first three kinds of bleaches generally remove the same types of stains and, if safe for the fabric, can be used interchangeably. If one bleach is more effective than the others for a particular stain it is recommended in the directions for removing that stain.

Color removers are generally used for types of stains for which the first three are not effective.

Chlorine bleaches are sold at grocery stores under various brand names. They may be in liquid or in granular form. The liquid bleaches act on stains more quickly but are more likely to damage fabrics if improperly used.

Sodium perborate is available as pure sodium perborate powder at drug stores. Also, bleaches that contain 30 to 50 percent of sodium perborate are sold under various brand names at grocery stores; these are in powder form.

The 3-percent **hydrogen peroxide** used for bleaching is sold in drug stores.

Color removers are sold under various brand names in drug and grocery stores.

Other chemical stain removers. Acetic acid or **vinegar** is used for neutralizing alkalies and for restoring colors changed by the action of alkalies. Use 10-percent acetic acid available from drug stores. Or substitute white vinegar, which contains 5 per cent of acetic acid.

Ammonia is used for neutralizing acids and restoring colors changed by action of acids. Use 10-percent ammonia solution, or substitute household ammonia. Avoid breathing ammonia fumes. Poison if swallowed.

Iodine is used only for silver nitrate stains. Use tincture of iodine available at drug stores. Poison if swallowed.

Oxalic acid is used for rust and other metallic stains. Sold in crystalline form at drug stores. Poison if swallowed.

Sodium thiosulfate is used for removing iodine and chlorine stains. Sold in crystalline form at drug stores and, as "hypo" at photographer's supply stores.

How to Use Chemical Stain Removers

Try a mild treatment first. Dampen stain with cool water and stretch stained area over a bowl or place on an absorbent pad. Apply liquid removers with a medicine dropper. Or sprinkle dry removers over the dampened spot. Or, if the article is washable, the stained area or the whole article can be soaked in a solution of the remover.

Do not let the remover dry on the fabric. If it is necessary to keep the remover on the stain for more than a few minutes, keep the area wet by placing a pad of cotton wet with the remover—or with water if a dry remover is used—on the stain. Keep cotton damp until the stain is removed.

Rinse remover from washable articles by sponging area repeatedly with a cloth dampened with water or by rinsing area or whole garment in clear water.

To rinse remover from nonwashable articles, sponge repeatedly with a cloth dampened with water. Or place treated area while still damp on a clean sponge or stretch it over a bowl, then force water through the spot. The sponge is preferable because it absorbs water and so helps to keep it from spreading to surrounding dry areas. Use a syringe to force water through the spot.

If stains cannot be removed by a mild treatment, a stronger treatment may be successful. The treatment may be strengthened by lengthening the time of treatment, using a more concentrated solution of the remover, or raising the temperature of the reaction. All of these ways of strengthening the treatment increase the danger of damage to the fabric.

Additional directions for using each of the chemical stain removers are given on the following pages.

Directions for Bleaches

Chlorine Bleaches

Do not use chlorine bleaches on fabrics that contain silk or wool or on a fabric with a special finish (such as those used to improve such properties as wrinkle resistance, shrinkage resistance, crispness, or sheen, or to produce durable embossed and sculptured designs) *unless the manufacturer states on the label that chlorine bleach is safe.* The resin in some of these finishes absorbs and retains chlorine, which weakens, and sometimes yellows, the fabric. Some fabrics are not weakened or yellowed until they are ironed; then damage may be severe. See directions for removing retained chlorine from such fabrics. Test all dryed fabrics for colorfastness. Do not use in metal containers.

WASHABLE ARTICLES

Mild treatment

Mix 2 tablespoons liquid bleach or ¼ cup granular bleach with 1 quart cool water. Apply to small stains with a medicine dropper; soak large stains in the solution. Leave on stain for 5 to 15 minutes. Rinse well with water. Repeat if necessary.

Strong treatment

Mix equal parts liquid bleach and water. Apply solution with medicine dropper to small stains. If stain is large, dip stained area in solution. Rinse immediately with water. Repeat if necessary. Be sure all bleach is rinsed out of fabric.

NONWASHABLE ARTICLES

Mild treatment

Mix 1 teaspoon liquid bleach or 1 tablespoon granular bleach with 1 cup cool water. Apply to stain with medicine dropper. Leave on stain for 5 to 15 minutes. Rinse well with water. Repeat if necessary.

Strong treatment

Not recommended. However, if stain cannot be removed in any other way, strong treatment given above for washable articles may be used.

Sodium Perborate Bleaches

Do not use strong treatments on fabrics that contain wool, silk, or Dynel because these treatments call for hot water. Hot water shrinks Dynel; hot sodium perborate solutions are not safe for silk and wool. Test all dyed fabrics for colorfastness. Do not use in metal containers.

WASHABLE ARTICLES

Mild treatment

Mix 1 to 2 tablespoons sodium perborate with 1 pint lukewarm water (for wool, silk, and Dynel) or 1 pint hot water (for other fabrics). Mix just before using; the solution loses strength on standing.

Cover stained area with solution or soak entire article. Soak until stain is removed. This may take several hours, or overnight. Rinse well.

If wool or silk is yellowed by sodium perborate, sponge with 10-percent acetic acid or vinegar to remove yellowing, then rinse with water.

Strong treatment

Sprinkle sodium perborate on stain. Dip stain into very hot or boiling water. Stains should be removed in a few minutes. Rinse well. Repeat if necessary.

NONWASHABLE ARTICLES

Mild treatment

Sprinkle sodium perborate on stain. Cover with a pad of cotton dampened with water. Use lukewarm water for wool, silk, and Dynel—hot water for other fabrics. Keep damp until stain is removed. This may take several hours or more. Rinse well.

Or mix 1 to 2 tablespoons sodium perborate with 1 pint lukewarm water (for wool, silk, and Dynel) or 1 pint hot water (for other fabrics). Mix just before using; the solution loses strength on standing. Apply to stain with medicine dropper. Keep damp until stain is

removed. Rinse well.

If wool or silk is yellowed by sodium perborate, sponge with 10-percent acetic acid or vinegar to remove yellowing, then rinse with water.

Strong treatment

Dampen stain with cool water. Sprinkle sodium perborate on stain. With spoon or medicine dropper, pour a small amount of boiling water on stain. Use a sponge or absorbent pad under the stain to absorb the water. Rinse well. Repeat if necessary.

Hydrogen Peroxide

A 3-percent solution of hydrogen peroxide is safe for all fibers; it acts slowly on stains. This solution loses strength on storage. Test all dyed fabrics for colorfastness. Do not use in metal containers.

Mild treatment

Moisten stain with a few drops of a 3-percent solution of hydrogen peroxide. Expose stain to direct sunlight. Add hydrogen peroxide as needed to keep stained area moist until stain is removed.

If above treatment does not remove stain, add a few drops of household ammonia to about 1 tablespoon of hydrogen peroxide. Moisten stain immediately with this mixture, and cover with a pad of cotton dampened with the same mixture. Keep damp until stain is removed; it may take several hours or more. Rinse well.

Strong treatment

Cover stain with a cloth dampened with a 3-percent solution of hydrogen peroxide.

Cover with a dry cloth and press with an iron as hot as is safe for the fiber. Rinse well.

Color Removers

Color removers are safe for all fibers, but fade or remove many dyes. If test of color remover on fabric shows that the remover causes a distinct color change rather than fading, you may be able to restore the original color by rinsing immediately, then drying article in air. If color remover fades the color, original color cannot be restored. Do not use in metal containers.

WASHABLE AND NONWASHABLE ARTICLES

Mild treatment

Dissolve ¼ teaspoon of color remover in ½ cup of cool water. Wet stain with a few drops of the solution. Cover stain for 1 to 15 minutes with a pad of cotton dampened with the solution.

Rinse well. Repeat if necessary.

Strong treatment

For large stains on white or color-fast fabrics, follow directions on the package. For all other stains, dissolve ¼ teaspoon of color remover in ½ cup of boiling water. Drop hot solution on stain with a medicine dropper.

Rinse immediately. Repeat if necessary.

TREATMENTS ARE THE same for washable and nonwashable articles. Unless otherwise indicated, treatment is strengthened by increasing the time the remover is left on fabric.

Acetic Acid, Vinegar

Moisten stain with 10-percent acetic acid or vinegar. Keep fabric wet until stain is removed. Rinse with water. Safe for all fibers, but may change color of some dyes. If dye changes color, rinse stain with water. Then try to restore color by moistening stain with ammonia (see below).

Ammonia

All fabrics except those that contain wool or silk: Moisten stain with 10 percent ammonia or household ammonia. Keep stain wet until it is removed. Rinse with water. If the color of a dye is changed by ammonia, try to restore color after rinsing by moistening with acetic acid or vinegar. Rinse with water.

Wool or silk: Dilute ammonia with an equal volume of water. Moisten stain with this solution and keep it moist until stain is removed. Rinse with water. Add a small amount of vinegar to the last rinse. If the color of a dye is changed by ammonia, try to restore color after rinsing by moistening with acetic acid or vinegar. Rinse with water.

Iodine

Directions given under silver nitrate, the only kind of stain for which it is used.

Oxalic Acid

Safe for all fibers, but may change color of some dyes. If dye changes color after treatment, rinse stain with water. Then try to restore color by moistening stain with ammonia.

Mild treatment: Dissolve 1 tablespoon of oxalic acid crystals in 1 cup of warm water. Keep stain wet with this solution until it is removed. Rinse thoroughly with water.

Strong Treatment: Dissolve 1 tablespoon of oxalic acid in 1 cup of water as hot as is safe for fabric. Use as for mild treatment.

Or, for all fabrics except nylon, sprinkle crystals on dampened stain and dip in pan of very hot water.

Sodium Thiosulfate

Directions are given under chlorine and iodine, the only stains for which it is used.

Directions for Removing Stains

MANY COMMON STAINS can be removed by following one of the three general methods given next. These methods are for removing greasy and nongreasy stains and stains that are a combination of the two.

Also given here are individual directions for removing all common stains. These are listed alphabetically. The individual directions tell whether to treat a stain as a greasy, nongreasy, or combination stain or give additional directions for stains that cannot be removed by one of the three general methods.

Whenever necessary, separate directions are given for washable and nonwashable articles. Directions for nonwashables are for articles made of fabrics that are not damaged by the application of small amounts of water. If water cannot be used on a fabric, only those stains that can be removed by absorbents or by solvents that do not contain water (acetone, amyl acetate, or grease solvents) can be removed satisfactorily by home methods.

General Stain-removal Directions

GREASY STAINS

Washable Articles

Regular washing, either by hand or by machine, removes some greasy stains.

Some can be removed by rubbing detergent into the stain, then rinsing with hot water.

Often, however, you will need to use a grease solvent; this is effective even after an article has been washed.

Sponge stain thoroughly with grease solvent. Dry. Repeat if necessary. It often takes extra time and patience to remove greasy stains from a fabric with a special finish.

A yellow stain may remain after solvent treatment if stain has been set by age or heat. To remove yellow stain use a chlorine or sodium perborate bleach or hydrogen peroxide. If safe for the fabric, the strong sodium perborate treatment is usually the most effective for these stains.

Nonwashable Articles

Sponge stain well with grease solvent. Dry. Repeat if necessary. It often takes extra time and patience to remove greasy stains from fabrics with a special finish.

A yellow stain may remain after solvent treatment if stain has been set by age or heat. To remove yellow stain use a chlorine or sodium perborate bleach or hydrogen peroxide. If safe for the fabric, the strong sodium perborate treatment is usually the most effective for these stains.

NONGREASY STAINS

Many fresh stains can be removed by simple treatments. Stains set by heat or age may be difficult or impossible to remove.

Washable Articles

Some nongreasy stains are removed by regular laundry methods; others are set by them.

Sponge stain with cool water. Or soak stain in cool water for 30 minutes or longer; some stains require an overnight soak.

If stain remains after sponging or soaking, work a detergent into it, then rinse.

If a colored stain remains after the fabric dries, use a chlorine or sodium perborate bleach or hydrogen peroxide.

Nonwashable Articles

Sponge stain with cool water. Or force cool water through stain with a small syringe, using a sponge under the stain to absorb the water.

If stain remains, rub detergent on stain and work it into fabric. Rinse.

A final sponging with alcohol helps to remove the detergent and to dry the fabric more quickly. Test alcohol on fabric first to be sure it does not affect the dye. Dilute alcohol with 2 parts of water before using it on acetate.

If stain remains after detergent is rinsed out, use a chlorine or sodium perborate bleach or hydrogen peroxide.

COMBINATION STAINS

Combination stains are caused by materials that contain both greasy and nongreasy substances.

Washable Articles

Sponge stain with cool water. Or soak in cool water for 30 minutes or longer.

If stain remains, work detergent into the stain, then rinse thoroughly. Allow article to dry.

If a greasy stain remains, sponge with grease solvent. Allow to dry. Repeat if necessary.

If colored stain remains after fabric dries, use a chlorine or sodium perborate bleach or hydrogen peroxide.

Nonwashable Articles

Sponge stain with cool water. Or force cool water through the stain with a small syringe, using a sponge under stain to absorb the water.

If a stain remains, rub detergent on the stain and work it into the fabric. Rinse spot well with water. Allow article to dry.

If a greasy stain remains, sponge with grease solvent. Allow article to dry. Repeat if necessary.

If a colored stain remains after the fabric dries, use a chlorine or sodium perborate bleach or hydrogen peroxide.

NOTE:

Grease solvents: For information on kinds of grease solvents, technique for using them, and precautions to observe when using them see earlier pages. Fumes from all grease solvents are poisonous. Use these solvents only with adequate ventilation. Keep flammable solvents away from flames and sparks.
Bleaches: For information on using bleaches see beginning of this chapter.

Directions for Removing Individual Stains

Acids

If an acid is spilled on a fabric, rinse the area with water immediately. Then apply ammonia to the stain. Rinse again with water.

Strong acids, such as sulfuric (used in batteries) and hydrochloric (used for cleaning brick), may damage or destroy some fibers before the acid can be rinsed out. The amount of damage depends on the kind of fiber and acid and on the concentration and temperature of the acid solution. Often, however, thorough rinsing before the acid dries on the fabric will prevent serious damage. Diluted solutions of weak acids such as acetic (vinegar) will not damage fibers.

Both weak and strong acids may change the color of some dyes. The use of ammonia after rinsing with water neutralizes any acid left in the fabric and sometimes restores colors that have changed.

Adhesive Tape

Scrape gummy matter from stain carefully with a dull table knife; avoid damaging fabric. Sponge with grease solvent.

Alcoholic Beverages

Follow directions for nongreasy stains.

An alternate method if alchohol does not affect the color of the fabric is to sponge the stain with alcohol. Dilute alcohol with 2 parts of water before using on acetate. If a stain remains, use a chlorine or sodium perborate bleach or hydrogen peroxide.

The alcohol in these beverages will cause bleeding of some dyes, which results in loss of color or formation of a dye ring around the edge of the stain. When either change occurs, the original appearance of the fabric cannot be restored.

Alkalies

If an alkali is spilled on a fabric, rinse the area with water immediately. Then apply vinegar to the stain. Rinse again with water.

Strong alkalies, such as lye, may damage or destroy some fibers before they can be rinsed out. The amount of damage depends on the kind of fiber and alkali and on the concentration and temperature of the alkali solution. In many cases, however, prompt rinsing will prevent serious damage. Silk and wool are the fibers most easily damaged by alkalies. Diluted solutions of such weak alkalies as ammonia will not damage fibers. Both strong and weak alkalies may change the color of some dyes. The use of vinegar after rinsing with water neutralizes any acid left in the fabric and sometimes restores colors that have changed.

Antiperspirants, Deodorants

Wash or sponge stain thoroughly with detergent and warm water. Rinse. If stain is not removed, use a chlorine or sodium perborate bleach or hydrogen peroxide.

Antiperspirants that contain such substances as aluminum chloride are acidic and may cause fabric damage and change the color of some dyes. You may be able to restore the color of the fabric by sponging it with ammonia. Dilute ammonia with an equal volume of water for use on wool or silk. Rinse.

Argyrol

Wash stain with detergent and water; this will remove most fresh stains.

If stain is not removed, follow directions for silver nitrate.

Blood

Follow directions for nongreasy stains with one variation. If stain is not removed by detergent put a few drops of ammonia on the stain and repeat treatment with detergent. Rinse. Follow with bleach treatment if necessary.

Blood stains that have been set by heat will be difficult to remove.

Bluing

Follow directions for nongreasy stains.

Butter, Margarine

Follow directions for greasy stains.

Candle Wax, Paraffin

To remove as much wax as possible, place the stain between clean white blotters or several layers of facial tissues and press with warm iron. To remove remaining stain, sponge with a grease solvent.

Or, if safe for fabric, pour boiling water through the spot. Remove any remaining stain with grease solvent.

Candy, Sirup

For chocolate candy and sirup follow directions for combination stains. For other candy and sirup follow directions for nongreasy stains.

Carbon Paper

Regular: Work detergent into stain; rinse well. If stain is not removed put a few drops of ammonia on the stain and repeat treatment with detergent; rinse well. Repeat if necessary.

Duplicating: Sponge stain with alcohol. Dilute alcohol with 2 parts of water for use on acetate. If stain remains rub detergent into stain; wash and rinse well. Repeat if necessary.

If needed, follow treatment above with a chlorine or sodium perborate bleach or hydrogen peroxide.

Catsup, Chili Sauce

Follow directions for nongreasy stains.

Chewing Gum

Scrape gum off without damaging fabric. The gum can be scraped off more easily if it is first hardened by rubbing it with ice.

If a stain remains, sponge thoroughly with a grease solvent.

Chlorine

Use one of the treatments given below to remove yellow stains caused by the use of chlorine bleaches on fabrics with some types of resin finishes, or to prevent such stains from appearing. Use the treatment before the fabric is ironed.

On some fabrics the yellow stains form before ironing; on others, after ironing. In either case, ironing before the chlorine is removed weakens the fibers.

Yellow stains caused by the use of chlorine bleach on wool and silk cannot be removed.

White or faded spots caused by use of chlorine bleach on colored fabrics cannot be restored to the original color.

Treatment for any fabric. Rinse fabric thoroughly with water. Then soak for one-half hour or longer in a solution containing 1 teaspoon of sodium thiosulfate to each quart of warm water. Rinse thoroughly.

To strengthen treatment make sodium thiosulfate solution with water as hot as is safe for fabric.

Treatment for white or fast-color fabrics. A more effective treatment for fabrics that color removers will not fade is to rinse the fabric thoroughly with water, then use a color remover. Follow directions given on the package for removing stains from these fabrics.

Chocolate

Follow directions for combination stains.

Cocoa

Follow directions for nongreasy stains.

Coffee, Tea

With cream: Follow directions for combination stains.

Without cream: Follow directions for nongreasy stains.

Or, if safe for fabric, pour boiling water through the spot from a height of 1 to 3 feet.

Correction Fluid (mimeograph)

Sponge stain with acetone or amyl acetate. Use amyl acetate on acetate, Arnel, Dynel, and Verel—acetone on other fabrics.

Cosmetics—Eye Shadow, Lipstick, Liquid Make-up, Mascara, Pancake Make-up, Powder, Rouge

Washable articles: Apply undiluted liquid detergent to stain. Or dampen stain and rub in soap or synthetic detergent until a thick suds is formed. Work in until outline of stain is gone, then rinse well. Repeat if necessary. It may help to dry fabric between treatments.

Nonwashable articles: Sponge with a grease solvent as long as any color is removed. If stain is not removed, use method given for washable articles.

Crayon

Follow directions for cosmetics.

Cream

Follow directions for combinations stains.

Dyes

Follow directions for nongreasy stains; if bleach is needed use chlorine

bleach or color remover. A long soak in sudsy water is often effective on fresh dye stains.

Egg

Follow directions for nongreasy stains.

Fingernail Polish

Follow directions for correction fluid.

Nail polish removers can also be used to remove stains. Some types are more effective than others. Do not use on acetate, Arnel, Dynel, or Verel without first testing on a scrap of material to be sure it will not damage the fabric.

Fish Slime, Mucus, Vomit

Follow directions for nongreasy stain.

Or, if safe for fabric, pour boiling water through spot from a height of each quart of water. Sponge stain with solution or soak stain in it. Rinse well.

Food Coloring

Follow directions for nongreasy stains.

Fruit

Follow directions for nongreasy stains.

Or, if safe for fabric, pour boiling water through spot from a height of 1 to 3 feet.

When any fruit juice is spilled on a fabric it's a good idea to sponge the spot immediately with cool water. Some fruit juices, citrus among them, are invisible on the fabric after they dry, but turn yellow on aging or heating. This yellow stain may be difficult to remove.

Furniture Polish

Follow directions for greasy stains.

Or, if polish contains wood stain, follow directions given for paint.

Glue, Mucilage, Adhesives

Airplane glue, household cement: Follow directions for correction fluid.

Caesin glue: Follow directions for nongreasy stains.

Plastic glue: Wash stain with detergent and water before glue hardens; some types cannot be removed after they have hardened.

The following treatment will remove some dried plastic glue stains. Immerse stain in hot 10-percent acetic acid or vinegar. Keep acid or vinegar at or near the boiling point until stain is removed. This may take 15 minutes or longer. Rinse with water.

Rubber cement: Scrape gummy matter from stain carefully; avoid damaging fabric. Sponge thoroughly with grease solvent.

Other types of glue and mucilage: Follow directions for nongreasy stains, except soak stain in hot water instead of cool.

Grass, Flower, Foliage

Washable articles: Work detergent into stain, then rinse. Or, if safe for dye, sponge stain with alcohol. Dilute alcohol with 2 parts of water for use on acetate.

If stain remains use a chlorine or sodium perborate bleach or hydrogen peroxide.

Nonwashable articles: Use same methods as for washable articles, but try alcohol first if it is safe for dye.

Gravy, Meat Juice

Follow directions for combination stains.

Grease—Car Grease, Lard

Follow directions for greasy stains.

Ice Cream

Follow directions for combination stains.

Ink, Ballpoint

Sponge stain repeatedly with acetone or amyl acetate. Use amyl acetate on acetate, Arnel, Dynel, and Verel—acetone on other fabrics. This will remove fresh stains. Old stains may also require bleaching.

Washing removes some types of ballpoint ink stains but sets other types. To see if the stain will wash out, mark a scrap of similar material with the ink and wash it.

Ink, Drawing

Black (India ink): Treat stain as soon as possible. These stains are very hard to remove if allowed to dry.

Washable articles: Force water through stain until all loose pigment is removed. Unless loose pigment is removed the stain will spread when you try to remove it.

Wash with detergent, several times if necessary. Then soak stain in warm suds containing 1 to 4 tablespoons of ammonia to a quart of water. Dried stains may need to be soaked overnight.

An alternate method that will remove some stains: Force water through stain until all loose pigment is removed, wet the spot with ammonia, then work detergent into the stain. Rinse. Repeat if necessary.

Nonwashable articles: Force water through stain until all loose pigment is removed. Unless loose pigment is removed the stain will spread when you try to remove it.

Next, sponge stain with a solution of water and ammonia (1 tablespoon of ammonia per cup water). Rinse with water. If stain remains, moisten it with ammonia, then work detergent into it. Rinse. Repeat if necessary.

If ammonia changes the color of the fabric, sponge first with water, then

moisten with vinegar. Rinse well.

Colors other than black. Follow directions for nongreasy stains. If bleach is needed, use a color remover if safe for dye. If color remover is not safe for dye, try other bleaches.

Ink, Mimeograph and Printing
Fresh stains. Follow directions for greasy stains, or sponge with turpentine.
Stubborn stains. Follow directions for paint stains.

Ink, Writing
Washable articles: Follow directions for nongreasy stains. Because writing inks vary greatly in composition it may be necessary to try more than one kind of bleach.

Try a chlorine bleach on all fabrics for which it is safe. For other fabrics, try sodium perborate or hydrogen peroxide. A few types of ink require treatment with color removers.

The strong treatment of any of these bleaches may be needed. It will not be possible to remove stains that require strong bleaches from some colored fabrics without leaving a faded spot.

If a yellow stain remains after bleaching, treat as a rust stain.
Nonwashable articles: If possible, use a blotter (for small stains) or absorbent powder to remove excess ink before it soaks into the fabric. Then follow directions for washable articles.

Iodine
Washable articles: Three methods for removing iodine stains are given below. If the method you try first does not remove the stain, try another.

Water: Soak in cool water until stain is removed; some stains require soaking overnight.

If stain remains, rub it with detergent and wash in warm suds. If stain is not removed, soak fabric in a solution containing 1 tablespoon of sodium thiosulfate to each pint of warm water, or sprinkle the crystals on the dampened stain. Rinse well as soon as stain is removed.

Steam: Moisten stain with water then hold it in the steam from a boiling teakettle.

Alcohol: If alcohol is safe for dye, cover stain with a pad of cotton soaked in alcohol. If necessary keep pad wet for several hours. Dilute with 2 parts of water for use on acetate.
Nonwashable articles: Try the steam or alcohol methods given above first.

If these methods are not safe for fiber or dye or if the stain remains after using them, cover stain with a pad of cotton dampened in a solution of sodium thiosulfate (1 tablespoon sodium thiosulfate to each pint of water) for about 15 minutes. Rinse well. Repeat treatment if necessary.

Lacquer
Follow directions for correction fluid.

Mayonnaise, Salad Dressing

Follow directions for combination stains.

Medicines. (See also Argyrol, Iodine, Mercurochrome, Silver Nitrate.)

Because so many different substances are used in medicines it is not possible to give methods for removing all such stains.

Medicines with an oily base, gummy and tarry medicines. Follow directions for greasy stains.

Medicines in sugar sirup or in water. Wash stain out with water.

Medicines dissolved in alcohol (tinctures). Sponge stain with alcohol. Dilute with 2 parts of water for use on acetate.

Medicines that contain iron. Follow directions for rust.

Medicines that contain dyes. Follow directions for dyes.

Mercurochrome, Merthiolate, Metaphen

Washable articles: Soak overnight in a warm detergent solution that contains 4 tablespoons of ammonia to each quart of water.

Nonwashable articles: If alcohol is safe for the dye, sponge with alcohol as long as any of the stain is removed. Dilute alcohol with 2 parts of water for use on acetate.

If a stain remains, place a pad of cotton saturated with alcohol on the stain. Keep pad wet until stain is removed; this may take an hour or more.

If alcohol is not safe for the dye, wet stain with liquid detergent. Add a drop of ammonia with a medicine dropper. Rinse with water. Repeat if necessary.

Metal

To remove stains caused by tarnished brass, copper, tin, and other metals use vinegar, lemon juice, acetic acid, or oxalic acid. (See directions for using these removers; use lemon juice according to the directions given for vinegar.) The two acids, because they are stronger, will remove stains that cannot be removed by vinegar or lemon juice.

As soon as the stain is removed, rinse well with water.

Do not use chlorine or sodium perborate bleaches or hydrogen peroxide. These bleaches may cause damage because the metal in the stain hastens their action.

Mildew

Washable articles: Treat mildew spots while they are fresh, before the mold growth has a chance to weaken the fabric.

Wash mildewed article thoroughly. Dry in the sun. If stain remains treat with a chlorine or sodium perborate bleach or hydrogen peroxide.

Nonwashable articles: Send article to dry cleaner while stain is fresh.

Milk

Follow directions for nongreasy stains.

Mud

Let stain dry, then brush well. If stain remains, follow directions for nongreasy stains.

Mustard

Washable articles: Rub detergent into the dampened stain; rinse.

If stain is not removed, soak article in hot detergent solution for several hours, or overnight if necessary.

If stain remains, use a bleach. Strong sodium perborate treatment, if safe for the fabric, is often the most effective bleach.

Nonwashable articles: If safe for dye, sponge stain with alcohol. Dilute alcohol with 2 parts of water for use on acetate.

If alcohol cannot be used, or if it does not remove stain completely, follow treatment for washable articles, omitting the soaking.

Oil—Fish-Liver Oil, Linseed Oil, Machine Oil, Mineral Oil, Vegetable Oil

Follow directions for greasy stains.

Paint, Varnish

Treat stains promptly. They are much harder, sometimes impossible, to remove after they have dried on the fabric. Because there are so many different kinds of paints and varnishes it is impossible to give one method that will remove all stains. Read the label on the container; if a certain solvent is recommended as a thinner it may be more effective in removing stains than the solvents recommended below.

Washable articles: To remove fresh stains rub detergent into stain and wash.

If stain has dried or is only partially removed by washing, sponge with turpentine until no more paint or varnish is removed; for aluminum paint stains, trichloroethylene may be more effective than turpentine; do not use this solvent on Arnel or Kodel.

While the stain is still wet with the solvent, work detergent into it, put the article in hot water, and soak it overnight. Thorough washing will then remove most types of paint stains.

If stain remains, repeat the treatment.

Nonwashable articles: Sponge fresh stains with turpentine, until no more paint is removed; for aluminum paint stains, trichloroethylene may be more effective than turpentine. Do not use trichloroethylene on Arnel or Kodel.

If necessary, loosen more of the paint by covering the stain for 30 minutes or longer with a pad of cotton dampened with the solvent. Repeat sponging.

If stain remains, put a drop of liquid detergent on the stain and work it into the fabric with the edge of the bowl of a spoon.

Alternate sponging with turpentine and treatment with detergent as many times as necessary.

If alcohol is safe for dye, sponge stain with alcohol to remove turpentine and detergent. Dilute alcohol with two parts of water for use on acetate. If alcohol is not safe for dye, sponge stain first with warm detergent solution, then with water.

Pencil Marks

Lead pencil, colored pencil: A soft eraser will remove these marks from some fabrics. If mark cannot be erased follow directions for regular carbon paper.
Indelible pencil: Follow directions for duplicating carbon paper.

Perfume

Follow directions for alcoholic beverages.

Perspiration

Wash or sponge stain thoroughly with detergent and warm water. Work carefully because some fabrics are weakened by perspiration; silk is the fiber most easily damaged.

If perspiration has changed the color of fabric, try to restore it by treating with ammonia or vinegar. Apply ammonia to fresh stains; rinse with water. Apply vinegar to old stains; rinse with water.

If an oily stain remains, follow directions for greasy stains.

Remove any yellow discoloration with a chlorine or sodium perborate bleach or hydrogen peroxide. If safe for fabric, the strong sodium perborate treatment is often the most effective for these stains.

Plastic

To remove stains caused by plastic hangers or buttons that have softened and adhered to the fabric, use amyl acetate or trichloroethylene. Test colored fabrics to be sure dye does not bleed. Do not use trichloroethylene on Arnel or Kodel.

Sponge stain with a pad of absorbent cloth or cotton moistened with the solvent. In using these solvents, observe precautions listed earlier.

If the plastic has been absorbed in the fabric it may be necessary to place a pad wet with the solvent on the spot and let it remain until the plastic has softened. Sponge with a fresh pad moistened with the solvent. Repeat until all plastic has been removed.

Rust

Oxalic acid method: Moisten stain with oxalic acid solution (1 tablespoon of oxalic acid crystals in 1 cup warm water). If stain is not removed, heat the solution and repeat.

If stain is stubborn, place oxalic acid crystals directly on the stain. Moisten with water as hot as is safe for fabric and allow to stand a few minutes, or dip in hot water. Repeat if necessary. Do not use this method on nylon.

Rinse article thoroughly. If allowed to dry in fabric, oxalic acid will cause damage.

Precaution: Oxalic acid is poison if swallowed.

Cream-of-tartar method: If safe for fabric, boil stained article in a solution containing 4 teaspoons of cream of tartar to each pint of water. Boil until stain is removed. Rinse thoroughly.

Lemon-juice method: Spread the stained portion over a pan of boiling water and squeeze lemon juice on it.

Or sprinkle salt on the stain, squeeze lemon juice on it, and spread in the sun to dry. Rinse thoroughly. Repeat if necessary.

Sauces, Soups

Follow directions for combination stains.

Scorch

If article is washable follow directions for nongreasy stains.

To remove light scorch on nonwashable articles use hydrogen peroxide. The strong treatment may be needed. Repeat if necessary.

For surface scorch on heavy fabrics you may be able to remove damaged part of the fibers with very fine sandpaper.

Severe scorch cannot be removed; it damages the fabric.

Shellac

Sponge stain with alcohol, or soak the stain in alcohol. Dilute alcohol with 2 parts water for use on acetate. If alcohol bleeds the dye, try turpentine.

Shoe Polish

Because there are many different kinds of shoe polish no one method will remove all stains. It may be necessary to try more than one of the methods given below.

1. Follow directions for cosmetics.
2. Sponge stain with alcohol if safe for dye in the fabric. Dilute alcohol with 2 parts of water for use on acetate.
3. Sponge stain with grease solvent or turpentine. If turpentine is used, remove turpentine by sponging with a warm detergent solution or with alcohol.

If stain is not removed by any of these methods use a chlorine or sodium perborate bleach or hydrogen peroxide. The strong sodium perborate treatment, if safe for the fabric, is often the most effective bleach.

Silver Nitrate

Dampen stain with water. Then put a few drops of tincture of iodine on the stain. Let stand for a few minutes. Then treat as an iodine stain.

Unless stain on silk or wool is treated when fresh a yellow or brown discoloration will remain.

Soft Drinks

Follow directions for nongreasy stains.

When any soft drink is spilled on a fabric it's a good idea to sponge the spot immediately with cool water. Some soft drinks are invisible after they dry, but turn yellow on aging or heating. The yellow stain may be difficult to remove.

Soot, Smoke

Follow directions for cosmetics.

Tar

Follow directions for greasy stains.

If stain is not removed by this method, sponge with turpentine.

Tea (See Coffee.)

Tobacco

Follow directions for grass.

Transfer Patterns

Follow directions for greasy stains.

Typewriter Ribbon

Follow directions for regular carbon paper.

Unknown Stains

If stain appears greasy, treat it as a greasy stain. Otherwise, treat it as a nongreasy stain.

See also yellowing.

Urine

To remove stains caused by normal urine follow directions for nongreasy stains.

If color of fabric has been changed, sponge stain with ammonia. If this treatment does not restore the color, sponging with acetic acid or vinegar may help.

If stain is not removed by method given above, see directions for medicines and yellowing.

Vegetable

Follow directions for nongreasy stains.

Walnut, Black

These stains are very difficult to remove.

Washable articles: If safe for fabric, boil washable articles in soapy water. This will remove fresh stains.

If stain is not removed, use a strong chlorine or sodium perborate bleach treatment.

If stain remains, treat as a rust stain.

Nonwashable articles: These stains cannot be removed by home methods. Send the article to a dry cleaner.

Wax—Floor, Furniture, Car

Follow directions for greasy stains.

Yellowing, Brown Stains

To remove yellow or brown stains that appear in some fabrics during storage or unknown yellow or yellow-brown stains, use as many of the following treatments that are safe for the fabric as necessary, in the order given.

1. Wash
2. Use a mild treatment of a chlorine or sodium perborate bleach or hydrogen peroxide.
3. Use the oxalic acid method for treating rust stains.
4. Use a strong treatment of a chlorine or sodium perborate bleach.

For removal or prevention of yellow stains caused by use of chlorine bleach on resin-treated fabrics.

CHAPTER THIRTY-NINE

Pest Control
Clothes Moths
and Carpet Beetles

How to combat them

CLOTHES MOTHS ARE well recognized as fabric pests. Housewives throughout the country are on guard against them. The fact that they cause widespread damage is due more to weaknesses in control measures than to lack of awareness of the need for control.

Not so well known as clothes moths, but just as destructive to fabrics, are carpet beetles, or "buffalo moths." Carpet beetles are more abundant than clothes moths in some localities, and damage that they do is often blamed on clothes moths.

The larvae of clothes moths and carpet beetles damage fabrics by feeding on them. They feed on anything that contains wool or other animal fibers.

The adult moths and beetles do no damage.

Estimates of the damage caused each year by clothes moths and carpet beetles in the United States range from $200 million to $500 million.

Description of the Insects

TWO SPECIES OF clothes moths and four species of carpet beetles commonly infest homes.

The webbing clothes moth and the casemaking clothes moth look much alike. The full-grown larvae are about ½ inch long, and are practically hairless; they are white, except for the dark heads. The adult moths are yellowish or buff, and have a wingspread of about ½ inch.

The larvae of the carpet beetle, the furniture carpet beetle, and the varied carpet beetle are elongate-oval in shape, are never more than ¼ inch long, and have brownish or black bristles that give them a fuzzy appearance. The full-grown larvae change into small beetles mottled with white, yellow, brown, or black.

The black carpet beetle is easily distinguished from the other three species. The larvae are yellowish, golden, or dark brown, they may get to be ½ inch long; the slender bodies are tapered from the head to the end of the body, where there is a tuft of long brown hairs. The adult beetles have solid black bodies and brownish legs.

Stages of Development

CLOTHES MOTHS AND carpet beetles pass through four stages of development—egg, larva, pupa, and adult.

The female moths and beetles lay soft, white eggs in clothing, in the pile of upholstering, in cracks, and in other concealed places. A moth lays from 100 to 300 eggs, which hatch in 4 to 8 days in summer. A beetle lays about 100 eggs, which hatch in 8 to 15 days in summer. Hatching takes longer in cool weather.

Under conditions normally existing in homes, the black carpet beetle has one generation a year; the other carpet beetles and the clothes moths have two, three, or four generations a year.

As the carpet beetle larvae grow, they shed their skins, or molt, several times.

Food and Habits

AS SOON AS THEY are hatched, the larvae begin eating. They feed on wool, mohair, hair, bristles, fur, feathers, and down. Thus they attack clothing and a wide range of household furnishings, including blankets, comforters, rugs, carpets, drapes, pillows, hair mattresses, brushes, upholstery, and hair padding in upholstered furniture.

They also feed on organic matter—hair that falls from pets, lint, and dead insects—that collects in places infrequently cleaned.

Besides feeding on all these materials, black carpet beetle larvae feed on grain products.

Clothes moth larvae usually stay on their food material. A webbing clothes moth larva spins a silken webbing to form a feeding tube, which is attached to the food material. A casemaking clothes moth larva spins a protective case, which it drags about.

Carpet beetle larvae, which do not spin webbing, are more active, crawling from place to place. You may find them on cotton goods or other things on which they do not feed. They often live behind baseboards and moldings, in cracks in the floor, in corners, behind radiators, in the air ducts of heating systems, on closet shelves, or in dresser drawers.

Adult clothes moths prefer darkness, and do not flit about lights; but they may be seen flying lazily in darkened corners, or at the edge of a circle of illumination. When clothing or other objects on which they are resting are suddenly moved, the moths run or fly to conceal themselves.

Adult carpet beetles fly readily, are attracted to daylight, and are sometimes found on window sills. They like sunlight, and in the spring large numbers are outdoors feeding on the pollen of flowers.

How Infestations Begin

IN URBAN AREAS some infestations are started by adult carpet beetles or clothes moths that fly from house to house. An infestation is more likely to be started in this way by beetles than by moths.

The insects are sometimes carried into homes on articles containing wool or other animal fibers. Most commonly these articles are secondhand clothing, upholstered furniture, and house furnishings.

Carpet beetles breed and feed not only in homes but also outdoors, in such places as bird and rodent nests, and the adults sometimes enter homes from these places.

Carpet beetle larvae may crawl from one room to another. If a hall carpet in an apartment house becomes infested, it is almost certain that some of the larvae will crawl from the hall into rooms that open onto it.

The practice of exchanging woolen scraps for use in making rugs accounts for some infestations. When such scraps have lain unprotected for long periods, they may become infested.

Prevention and Control

To PREVENT CLOTHES moths and carpet beetles from damaging fabrics—
1. Practice good housekeeping constantly.
2. Apply protective treatments to susceptible items.
3. Spray premises with insecticides which effectively kill fabric insects.

If your home is now free of infestation, you can keep it that way by closely following the first two of these lines of effort; but to eliminate an infestation, you must follow all three.

If you must cope with a heavy or widespread infestation, you will do well to obtain the services of a reputable pest-control firm. Such a firm has the equipment, materials, and experience necessary to handle a difficult control job.

Good Housekeeping

CERTAIN ELEMENTS OF good housekeeping have a specific bearing on control of fabric pests in the home.

In cleaning, do a thorough job of removing organic matter on which larvae feed. Besides depriving larvae of some of their food supply, you may, at the same time, remove insects and their eggs.

Clean often enough to prevent lint and hair from accumulating. Give close attention to—

Rugs and carpets;

Drapes and upholstered furniture;

Closets, especially those in which woolens and furs are kept;

Radiators, and the surfaces behind them;

Corners, cracks, baseboards, moldings, and other hard-to-reach places.

Vacuum-cleaning is the best way to remove lint and hair from hard-to-reach places. Use the radiator-cleaning attachment of the cleaner.

To clean rugs, carpets, drapes, and upholstered furniture, use the vacuum cleaner or a brush.

Clean rugs and carpets thoroughly and frequently, and rotate them occasionally. Rotation is important because insects usually feed under heavy pieces of furniture, where cleaning is inconvenient, rather than in the open, where regular cleaning, light, and movement of people keep down infestation.

After vacuum-cleaning, dispose of the sweepings promptly. They may contain larvae, eggs, or adult insects. If you leave sweepings in the cleaner, you may transfer an infestation from one place in the home to another.

Woolen scraps or garments that lie for long periods on shelves, or in corners, boxes, or drawers, are often a source of infestation. Store these things properly or, if you do not want them, get rid of them.

Protective Treatments

There are a number of things you can do to protect fabrics and furs against insect-feeding damage. Some measures, such as dry cleaning and the use of crystals and flakes, kill the insects. Others do not; they keep the insects away or cause fabrics to be resistant to insect feeding.

Clothing and Blankets

Insecticide Oil Solutions

Spray woolens with DDT, dieldrin, methoxychlor, chlordane, lindane, Strobane, or Perthane to protect them from feeding damage by clothes moths and carpet beetles. These insecticides are sold as liquid oil solutions to be applied with a sprayer or in pressurized spray containers ready to use. Follow the directions and observe the cautions given on the container label.

A simple way to prepare woolens for spraying is to hang them on a clothesline. Spray lightly and uniformly until the surface is moist. Do not soak or saturate the woolens. Excessive spray may cause a white deposit after the fabric dries. A slight excess deposit can be removed by light brushing. A heavier deposit may require dry cleaning; the protection is lost when the insecticide is thus removed.

Allow treated woolens to dry before storing them.

Fluoride Solutions

Spraying woolens with a commercial fabric-treatment solution containing fluoride is another way to protect them against the feeding of the larvae of clothes moths.

Before spraying, be sure the woolen articles are clean and free from stains. Apply the spray freely until the surface is uniformly moist. When the articles are dry they are ready for use or for storage.

Fluoride solutions are for treating woolens, not for spraying on walls or floors. Their purpose is to protect the woolens against feeding damage, not to kill insects.

Treated woolens in storage will be protected a year or more; those in use a year, unless washed. The fluorides are removed from the fabric by washing but will withstand several dry cleanings before they are reduced to an ineffective level.

EQ-53 For Washable Woolens

Washable woolens are protected from insect damage when washed or rinsed in water containing a few spoonfuls of EQ-53, a product developed at the Savannah, Ga., laboratory of the U.S. Department of Agriculture.

EQ-53, which is sold under different trade names, is an emulsifiable concentrate in which the active ingredient is the insecticide DDT. There are two other ingredients—a solvent and an emulsifying agent. Wool immersed in water containing EQ-53 picks up DDT, which remains after the wool dries and gives protection against insect feeding.

With this product the housewife can pestproof washable woolens, such as blankets, sweaters, scarves, or socks, at the same time that she washes them. The procedure is especially convenient in the spring, when woolens are being prepared for summer storage, but it can be used any time.

Stored washable woolens treated the EQ-53 way are protected against the feeding of the larvae of clothes moths and carpet beetles for a year or more. Where woolens are put in use after a treatment, rather than stored, they are protected for a season unless they are washed or dry cleaned. Washing may reduce the insecticide below an effective level, and dry cleaning removes it.

The unique advantage of EQ-53 is that it permits pestproofing to be combined with washing, but it can also be used to pestproof clean woolens, if they are washable. To apply it to soiled woolens, follow these directions:

If you wash woolens by hand—
1. Weigh dry woolens or estimate weight.
2. Wash woolens in the usual way.
3. Pour EQ-53 into the first rinse water at the rate of 1 tablespoonful for each pound of dry woolens.
4. Soak woolens a few minutes, then stir 3 to 5 minutes with a paddle.
5. Follow with the normal rinsing and drying.

If you use a washing machine—
1. Weigh dry woolens or estimate weight.
2. Put woolens, water, and soap in the tub, as if preparing for washing in the usual way.
3. Pour in EQ-53 at the rate of 1 tablespoonful for each pound of dry woolens.
4. Wash, rinse, and dry in the usual way.

To apply EQ-53 to clean woolens, follow the same directions but, instead of washing the woolens, merely rinse them; do not use soap.

Your woolens will be free of any odor of EQ-53 after they are dried.

Woolens shrink and become matted if improperly washed. When treating woolens with EQ-53, follow proper washing procedures. Use lukewarm water and a mild soap or detergent. EQ-53 itself does not affect shrinking or matting.

Paradichlorobenzene and Naphthalene

You can protect stored woolens by putting paradichlorobenzene crystals, or napthalene flakes or balls, in the container or closet in which they are stored.

As these chemicals evaporate, they produce a vapor. To be effective, the vapor must be in a concentration sufficient to kill insects. The proper concentration kills both clothes moths and carpet beetles. The mere odor of paradichlorobenzene or naphthalene does not repel insects and is no indication that there is enough vapor to kill them.

Much depends on whether the container or closet will hold the vapor. The container, which may be a trunk, chest, box, or garment bag, should be airtight. If you store the woolens in a closet without first placing them in individual containers, see that the closet is tightly closed. If there are cracks around the door, seal them with tape or fit the door with gaskets; if there are cracks in the interior walls, floor, or ceiling, close them with putty or plastic wood. Protection is lost if the closet door is opened frequently. Even in a tight closet that is kept closed, it takes several days for the vapor to build up to an effective level. Effectiveness is greatly increased if a closet is used for storage only.

In a trunk-size container use 1 pound of crystals, flakes, or balls. Scatter them between layers of garments or blankets.

In a closet use 1 pound to each 100 cubic feet of space. The vapors are heavier than air. The crystals, flakes, or balls should therefore be placed in a shallow container on a shelf, or suspended from a clothes rod or hook in a thin cloth bag or perforated container.

Clothes moths or carpet beetles in a closet can be quickly killed by vaporizing paradichlorobenzene crystals with a vacuum cleaner. A special attachment is provided for this purpose.

Cedar Chests

Cedar chests make good pestproof containers primarily because of their tight construction. They should be made of red cedar (*Juniperus virginiana*). At least 70 percent of the chest proper should be made with ¾-inch heartwood. They may be veneered on the outside with hardwoods, such as walnut or mahogany, without affecting the pestproofing value. The cedar-oil vapor kills small larvae but is not effective against larger ones. Therefore make sure that woolens are free of larvae when stored.

Treat cedar chests that are several years old as you would any other container in which you store articles susceptible to insect damage. Scatter crystals, flakes, or balls between layers of the stored articles.

Other Practices

Woolens can be protected from feeding damage by wrapping them in paper or sealing them in a cardboard box. Before wrapping or sealing, be sure the woolens are not infested. In making a paper bundle, carefully fold back and seal the edges of the paper.

Dry cleaning kills all stages of clothes moths and carpet beetles but gives no protection against reinfestation. Protective treatments are applied by many cleaning establishments and pest-control firms.

You can rid woolen articles of insects, and their eggs and larvae, by brushing and sunning them. Brush thoroughly, especially in seams, folds, and pockets. If they cannot find protection from the light, larvae missed in the brushing will fall to the ground from clothing left hanging in the sun.

Rugs and Carpets

Spray a 5-percent DDT oil solution on rugs and carpets every 12 to 18 months. Use 1½ to 2 quarts of spray on a 9-by-12 rug of average weight, if you spray the entire rug.

Fluoride solutions are also satisfactory for protecting rugs and carpets. Follow the manufacturer's directions for applying.

Give special attention to parts of the rug that will be under a piano, sofa, bookcase, or other heavy furniture, and to parts that will be under radiators or around heat registers. If there is a rug pad containing animal hair or wool, and it has not been treated by the manufacturer, spray it on both sides.

In spraying wall-to-wall carpeting, give special attention to the edges, all the way around.

If you have expensive broadlooms or oriental rugs, and fear that lack of experience in spraying may cause you to mar their appearance or otherwise injure them, it is advisable to call on a pest-control or carpet-cleaning firm that is experienced in treating rugs and carpets.

Commercial rug cleaning destroys larvae, eggs, and adult insects in rugs and carpets but prevents reinfestation only if a special treatment is given for this purpose.

Rugs and carpets are protected against insect feeding when placed in commercial storage. In home storage they may be protected by spraying with DDT oil solution or fluoride solutions or by using paradichlorobenzene crystals or naphthalene flakes.

Household Furnishings

To protect furniture upholstering and drapes containing wool or mohair, spray them with any of the solutions discussed earlier except do not use dieldrin, lindane, or chlordane on furniture.

These sprays applied to the outside of furniture, mattresses, or pillows help prevent infestation of the down or hair inside, but do not control an existing infestation.

Felts and hammers in pianos often become infested and so badly damaged by clothes moths and carpet beetles that the tone and action of the instrument are seriously affected. The solutions discussed before will protect the felts and hammers, but the treatment may damage other parts of the piano if applied incorrectly. To avoid this, you may wish to call a piano technician to do the job.

Furs

If you store furs at home through the summer, protect them with crystals, flakes, or balls in a tight container.

We do not recommend applying protective sprays on furs.

Furs in commercial storage receive professional care and can be insured against damage.

Surface Sprays

Surface spraying is the chief means by which insects living in the structure of the home are eliminated. It also has protective value.

The insecticide is applied to surfaces where larvae and adult insects are likely to crawl. When the spray dries, a thin deposit of insecticide remains. For several weeks or months the deposit kills insects that crawl over it. Thus it may kill insects before they have a chance to damage fabrics, and may prevent them from becoming established in your home. For continuous control and prevention, spray surfaces once or twice a year.

Contact spraying, the purpose of which is to kill insects by direct application, does not always give full control. Moths and beetles hit by the spray are killed, but they may be only a small part of the total infestation. Many may be in proctected places where you cannot reach them with a spray.

Selecting an Insecticide

Select an insecticide that is effective in killing fabric insects.

A 3- to 6-percent DDT oil solution kills both clothes moths and carpet beetles when it hits them directly, but the dry deposit is effective against moths only.

A spray containing 2 percent of chlordane, 3 to 5 percent of premium grade malathion or ronnel, or ½ percent of lindane, heptachlor, dieldrin, or Diazinon is effective against both clothes moths and carpet beetles, whether it hits the insects directly or whether they come in contact with the treated surface. These should be applied only in accordance with the precautions listed earlier.

Hence, use DDT only if you are sure your problem is the control of clothes moths alone. If you have an infestation of carpet beetles, or are not sure which insect it is that requires control, use chlordane, malathion, lindane, dieldrin, heptachlor, ronnel, or Diazinon.

Applying the Spray

Apply the insecticide with a household sprayer that produces a continuous coarse mist.

Satisfactory surface treatments can be applied with pressure sprayers that look like aerosol dispensers but produce a coarse spray. These liquefied-gas surface sprayers are distinguished from aerosol dispensers by their labels, which show that they are for use in spraying surfaces.

Places to spray: Along the edge of wall-to-wall carpets; closets; behind radiators; and corners, cracks, baseboards, moldings, and other hard-to-clean places. These are places where insects may be living. If you cannot reach some of them, apply the insecticide as close to them as possible, so that carpet beetles (larvae or adults) will crawl over it as they emerge from hiding.

Take clothing out of closets and apply the insecticide to corners, to cracks in the floor and walls, along baseboards, around shelves, and at ends of clothes rods.

Aerosols

An aerosol is a spray in the form of a fine mist that floats in the air for a time. It is applied by releasing it from the metal dispenser in which it is purchased.

An aerosol in a clothes closet kills flying clothes moths; it also kills clothes moth larvae that happen to be exposed to the mist. It does not moisten surfaces as coarse mist sprays do; hence it does not give lasting protection.

Few aerosols are strong enough to be effective against carpet beetles.

Aerosol dispensers should not be confused with the liquefied-gas sprayers mentioned in the discussion of surface spraying.

Insecticidal Dusts

You may find carpet beetle larvae in floor cracks, especially under rugs. The blocks of parquet floors tend to separate slightly, leaving a checkerboard of cracks. Black carpet beetle larvae can thrive in the lint, dust, and bits of hair that accumulate in these cracks.

Getting spray into numerous floor cracks is a tedious task. You may prefer to use a 10-percent DDT dust. If there is a rug, take it up; then sprinkle the dust on the floor, brush or sweep it into the cracks, and put the rug back in place.

You may use a dust gun to blow DDT dust into cracks behind moldings or baseboards and into other places that are difficult or impossible to reach with a surface spray.

You may use a 5-percent chlordane or 1-percent lindane or dieldrin dust, but apply it only to cracks around the edge of a room, behind baseboards, or under rugs. There are indications that chlordane, dieldrin, and lindane are more effective against carpet beetle larvae than is DDT, but they should not be applied throughout a room (see Precautions).

Applying a dust is an easy way to treat attics or basements where there are numerous cracks in which carpet beetle larvae can live.

Fumigation

Before present control methods were developed, fumigation of an entire house was a common method of controlling carpet beetles. Clothing and furnishings were left in the house during the fumigation. This method, which is expensive and requires vacating the house, is seldom used today to meet ordinary control problems. Moreover fumigation is dangerous. In some localities it is subject to legal restrictions. Only professional pest-control operators should fumigate.

Fumigation gives quick and satisfactory control, but there is no assurance that it will kill all the beetles in a house, and it does not prevent reinfestation.

Although fumigation of an entire house is seldom necessary, the best action to take against clothes moths or carpet beetles living in the down in pillows, or in the hair padding of furniture or mattresses, is to have the infested article treated with hydrocyanic acid gas in a fumigation vault. This fumigation service is provided by many pest-control and storage firms. The treatment kills the insects, but it does not prevent reinfestation.

Precautions

In General

Most insecticides are poisonous to people and to animals. . . . Keep insecticides where children and pets cannot reach them. . . . When applying them, do not contaminate food, dishes, or kitchen utensils. Do not store them with food. . . . Do not breathe too much of the spray mist or the dust. . . . If insecticide is spilled on the skin, wash it off promptly. . . . Change your clothes if you spill insecticide on them. . . . Keep children and pets off sprayed surfaces that have not dried. . . . When you have finished applying an insecticide, empty unused material into the original container, clean the sprayer or duster, and wash all exposed surfaces of the body with soap and water.

Infants' Apparel

Apply insecticides to infants' sweaters, blankets, or other woolen articles only if they are to be stored. Launder or dry clean them before returning to use.

Diazinon, Dieldrin, Chlordane, Heptachlor, Lindane, Malathion, and Ronnel

Do not use on furniture; on rugs and carpets, use only for spot treatments. Dry clean clothing and bedding treated with dieldrin, lindane, or chlordane before using them. Do not use any of these insecticides in the concentrations recommended in this chapter for overall spraying or dusting of the interior of rooms.

Oil-base Insecticides

Do not spray oil-base insecticides near open flames, sparks, or electrical circuits. . . . Do not spray them on silk, rayon, or other fabrics that stain easily. . . . Do not spray them on asphalt-tile floors, because they will dissolve the asphalt. . . . They will also soften and discolor some linoleums and certain plastic materials; if in doubt about spraying such a surface, test the spray on a small inconspicuous place. . . . If you apply one of these insecticides to the cracks in a parquet floor, apply it lightly; an excessive amount will dissolve the underlying black cement, and the dissolved cement will stain the floor.

Weight on Damp Furnishings

Do not put any weight or pressure on sprayed rugs, carpets, or upholstered furniture (as by walking, sitting, or pressing with the hand) until the spray has dried. Doing so gives the damp pile a mashed-down appearance, which persists for several days.

PICTURE CREDITS

614

INDEX

YOUR OWN DECORATOR NOTES